Reformation Spirituality

Reformation Spirituality

The Religion of George Herbert

Gene Edward Veith, Jr.

Lewisburg
Bucknell University Press
London and Toronto: Associated University Presses

Associated University Presses
440 Forsgate Drive
Cranbury, NJ 08512

Associated University Presses
25 Sicilian Avenue
London WC1A 2QH, England

Associated University Presses
2133 Royal Windsor Drive
Unit 1
Mississauga, Ontario
Canada L5J 1K5

Library of Congress Cataloging in Publication Data

Veith, Gene Edward, 1951–
    Reformation spirituality.

    Bibliography: p.
    Includes index.
    1. Herbert, George, 1593–1633—Religion and ethics.
2. Reformation in literature.   3. Reformation—England.
4. Spiritual life—History of doctrines—17th century.
I. Title.
PR3508.V39   1985   821'.3   83-46176
ISBN 0-8387-5071-0

Printed in the United States of America

Contents

To Jacquelyn Veith

Acknowledgments

This study began as a doctoral dissertation at the University of Kansas. Since then, it has been expanded and contracted, rethought and rewritten, "tortur'd in the space / Betwixt this world and that of grace" ("Affliction [4]," 5–6). In fact, studying Reformation theology has made me especially aware of the "unmerited gifts" that have made this study possible. I am grateful to the Graduate School of the University of Kansas for a Summer Dissertation Fellowship, which greatly facilitated my research. I owe a great deal to my dissertation adviser, Richard Hardin, for his expert guidance, for his generous attention to my manuscript, and for giving me so much "free rein." The other members of my committee also deserve special thanks. Max Sutton, both informally and in a seminar he organized on Christianity and Literature, has helped me greatly in many ways, and I credit him with introducing me to Herbert. John Macauley, a church historian, in giving me the perspective of another discipline, helped me penetrate the religious stereotypes that have become enshrined in literary history and with which I had always been content. I am also indebted to another member of the Department of Religious Studies at the University of Kansas, Robert Minor, for his explanations of Calvinism and Arminianism, stressing the importance of the doctrine of "eternal security." The Reverend Donald Kirchhoff, pastor of Mt. Olive Lutheran Church in Miami, Oklahoma, has been very helpful in introducing me to Lutheranism. Much of the research was done at the libraries of the University of Kansas, with the Spencer Research Library giving me access to invaluable resources and expertise. The librarians of Northeastern Oklahoma A & M College have given valuable assistance in this project. The library of the University of Oklahoma has also proved useful and accessible. Thanks also goes to the various people who read the manuscript and who made many helpful suggestions. I especially want to thank my wife, Jackquelyn—for the typing, for her unfailing support, and for much more. To these and to many others, I am grateful.

Gift upon gift, much would have more,
And comes.

("Gratefulness," 15–16)

I would also like to express my appreciation to the publishers who granted me permission to quote from the following copyrighted material:

Calvin: Institutes of the Christian Religion, edited by John T. McNeill; translated by Ford Lewis Battles (Volumes XX and XXI: The Library of Christian Classics). Copyright © MCMLX W. L. Jenkins. Used by permission of The Westminster Press, Philadelphia, PA.

English Literature in the Sixteenth Century Excluding Drama by C. S. Lewis. Copyright © 1954 by Oxford University Press. Used by permission.

The Latin Poetry of George Herbert: A Bilingual Edition, translated by Mark McCloskey and Paul R. Murphy. Copyright © 1965 by Ohio University Press. Used by permission.

The Literary Temper of the English Puritans by Lawrence Sasek. Copyright © 1961 by Louisiana State University Press. Used by permission.

Luther: An Introduction to His Thought by Gerhard Ebeling, translated by R. A. Wilson. Published in Great Britain in 1970 by William Collins Sons. Copyright © 1972 by Fortress Press. Used by permission.

Luther's Works. Volume 4 © 1964. Volume 5 © 1968. Volume 8 © 1966. Volume 10 © 1974. Volume 14 © 1958. Volume 26 © 1963. Concordia Publishing House. Used by permission.

The Protestant Mind of the English Reformation 1570–1640 by Charles H. and Katherine George. Copyright © 1961 by Princeton University Press. Excerpts, pp. 56, 66, 70–71, 126, 132, 134, 170–71, 318, 327–28.

The Theology of Calvin by Wilhelm Niesel; translated by Harold Knight. First published in Great Britain in 1956 by Lutterworth Press. Published in the U.S.A. in 1956 by the Westminster Press. Used by permission.

The Works of George Herbert, edited by F. E. Hutchinson. Copyright © 1941 by Oxford University Press. Used by permission.

Introduction

The Protestant Reformation has not been fully assimilated by literary critics. The aesthetic richness of medieval Catholicism, with its vision of cosmic "order" both mystical and rational, has been far more appealing and intelligible to modern critics. With the Reformation, though, according to most literary historians, the medieval sense of community gave way to individualism, the guilds were replaced by capitalists, the art of the Middle Ages was destroyed by the iconoclasts. The "Puritan" is often presented as the image of the Reformation, dressed in black with compressed lips, an enemy of all pleasure and beauty, legalistic and authoritarian, despoiler of the liturgy and the theaters, self-righteous and hypocritical. Opposed to the Puritans in England, on the other hand, were the Anglo-Catholics who, although opposed to the papacy, maintained the best of the medieval Catholic practices and traditions as exemplified in the *Book of Common Prayer* and kept alive a spirit of "Christian humanism" against the narrow-minded extremes of the Calvinists.

Serious studies of sixteenth- and seventeenth-century English history, however, have been revealing that these kinds of generalizations do not really apply. Sir Philip Sidney, we are told, was of the "Puritan" party; it is easy to imagine his opponent who denounced poetry as a "Puritan," but it is more difficult to imagine the defender of poesy, who is not usually thought of as wearing black, as part of the Reformed movement. King James, enemy of presbyterianism, turns out to have been a convener, along with many of his "high church" bishops, of the Synod of Dort, which fixed and defined Calvinist dogma against the new theology of the Arminians. If the religion of Calvin is assumed to have been too strict in its morals, at the time, we discover, it was condemned as being too lax. If it seems oppressive today, at the time it was hailed as liberating.

There are several reasons why the religion of sixteenth- and seventeenth-century England has been difficult to understand. Above all, theologies change. Luther and Calvin did dominate the Church of England during this period, as modern church historians have shown, but the distinct spirituality of the Reformation was fairly short-lived within mainline

Protestantism (although it did and does survive). Whereas at first epis-
copalians, presbyterians, and congregationalists agreed in their understanding of salvation, the essential Reformation doctrine, the different
ecclesiastical parties eventually drifted apart in their theologies. With the
Restoration, Arminianism succeeded Calvinism as the established theology. Calvinism, left to the "dissenting" sects, itself changed from its
earlier versions. As theologies change, they tend to be read back into
history. Thus nineteenth-century Anglo-Catholicism is responsible for the
"Anglo-Catholic versus Puritan" model as a way of interpreting the religion
of the seventeenth century. Stereotypes, nonhistorical assumptions, and
polemics, as well as theological complexities, stand in the way of our fully
comprehending the religious milieu of Renaissance England, the age of
Spenser, Sidney, Shakespeare, Donne, and Milton.

   This work is an attempt to penetrate behind some of these obstacles, to
present Reformation spirituality phenomenologically, that is, from the inside, as it was understood and experienced. It is primarily, though, a
critical study of George Herbert, who seems to me one of the greatest of all
religious poets. In studying the religious beliefs and experiences reflected
in his writings, I found that Calvinism not only helps to explain Herbert's
poetry, but also Herbert's poetry helps to explain Calvinism. One cannot
simply explain Herbert's religious poetry in his own terms without also
reconstructing the religious background of his age. It became necessary to
map out the spiritual landscape that Herbert and his contemporaries took
for granted. In effect, then, in this study I am trying to do two things at
once: to illustrate the major elements of Reformation theology by means of
Herbert's poetry, and to explain Herbert's poetry with the aid of Reformation theologians. My thesis throughout is simply that Reformation spirituality and the poetry of George Herbert mutually illumine one another.

   Literary scholarship, like theology, involves change and controversy.
Modern interest in seventeenth-century religious poetry began with the
"metaphysical revival" fostered, among others, by T. S. Eliot, who found
the techniques and mind-set of poets like Donne and Herbert extremely
valuable to his own needs as a poet.[1] The "metaphysical poem," with its
convoluted imagery, multilevel language, and intellectual difficulty,
proved especially fascinating to the "New Critics," whose concerns were to
explicate the complex workings of individual, self-contained poems. Seventeenth-century scholarship entered a new phase, however, perhaps best
exemplified when Rosemond Tuve challenged some of the conclusions of
the brilliant modernist poet and "New Critic" William Empson. In his *Seven
Types of Ambiguity*, he discussed certain "ambiguities" in Herbert's depiction of Christ in "The Sacrifice." To Empson, the imagery of the vine, an
obvious sacramental symbol, called to mind "the Dionysiac revellers (and
their descendants the tragedians)." Christ climbing the cross reminded

him of a boy climbing a tree to steal apples, which, in turn, is a Freudian symbol of incest.[2] To these and other ahistorical misreadings, Rosemond Tuve responded with the first full-length critical book on Herbert, *A Reading of George Herbert* (1952). Tuve's magisterial discussion of typology, patristic allusions, and medieval conventions proved that metaphysical poetry was not so "innovative" as the New Critics had thought, but that it was part of a rich literary and intellectual tradition apart from which it cannot be accurately understood.

This historical, "contextualist" approach, which seeks to understand a literary work by means of exploring its "tradition," has dominated seventeenth-century criticism. Tuve's *Elizabethan and Metaphysical Imagery* (1947) was a seminal study for the whole period. Rosemary Freeman's *English Emblem Books* (1948) showed how the popular illustrated devotional manuals of the time could help explicate the symbolism of the poems and also the very imagination of the age. Ruth Wallerstein's *Studies in Seventeenth-Century Poetic* (1950) studied medieval and Renaissance rhetoric, as it was taught in the schools of the day, and showed how it related to the very composition of the poems.

Such scholarship was different from the sort of historicism that the New Critics were reacting against. These scholars were not assembling biographical or historical minutiae for their own sake. They were giving "readings" of the poems, explaining imagery, and unfolding allusions and techniques in illuminating, although historically disciplined, ways. Like the New Critics, their attention was on the poem itself, and their concern as critics was to analyze its complexities and interpret its meanings. This marriage of historicism and formalism is exemplified in two books published in 1954. Joseph Summer's *George Herbert: His Religion and Art* balanced historical and biographical research with impeccable "new critical" readings of the poetry. More influential in the period as a whole was *The Poetry of Meditation* by Louis Martz. This book provided both a source and a methodology for subsequent critics. Martz drew attention to the techniques of religious meditation as promoted by the Counter-Reformation and developed by such figures as Ignatius Loyola and Francis de Sales. Ignatian meditation systematically engaged the imagination, the intellect, and the will in a way that is analogous to the "meditation" inherent in a religious poem. Not only did Martz provide a great many sources to mine, as subsequent scholars found more and more varieties of meditation and poems that reflect them, but he also established a method of approach. A scholar first presents a historical concept that seems applicable to poetry in some way; that concept is used then as a lens through which the poems are "read." Recent seventeenth-century scholarship thus usually has at least one foot solidly planted in history, however far-ranging its speculations may be. Even radical critics such as Stanley Fish tend to ground their readings in a preliminary consideration of a historical model, whether it is Augustinian rhetoric _(Self-consuming Artifacts)_ or techniques of catechizing _(The Living Temple)_.

This historical impulse, though, has often until recently been conditioned by an explicit or implicit medievalism, which looks to writers and theologians of the Middle Ages or of the Counter-Reformation as ways of understanding the literature of Renaissance England. One reason is probably the general blurring of the earlier, overstrict categories between the Middle Ages and the Renaissance, so that the great critic C. S. Lewis could remark to Nevill Coghill, "I _believe_ I have proved that the Renaissance never happened in England. _Alternatively_ . . . that if it did, _it had no importance._"³ To be sure, the Renaissance represents a development of medieval culture, as Renaissance humanism grew out of medieval classicism and the Protestant Reformation grew out of the experience and learning of an Augustinian monk. Yet _something_ happened—the social structures, the intellectual establishment, the Church, and the very lives of the people were very different in sixteenth- and seventeenth-century England from what they were in the High Middle Ages. Medievalists tend to stress the continuity, certainly treating the "new" features, but seeing them as not belonging to the essence of the time. They are interruptions of the "tradition," precursors of the "modern" way of looking at things. Medievalism, though, is not simply an emphasis of scholarship. It is also, paradoxically, an important strain of "modern" thought. The Roman Catholic revival of the 1940s and 1950s and the Anglo-Catholicism of T. S. Eliot, W. H. Auden, and many other intellectuals represent not a reaction but a response to modernism, so that medievalism itself grew out of the modernist movement. When someone like Eliot, certainly a "modernist," discerns the chaos of modern experience, the medieval world view, with its rituals and immediate sense of the Holy, seems compelling and strong, giving a sense of order by which the modern world can be seen more clearly.

Barbara Lewalski has recently challenged this medieval approach to Renaissance literature in her monumental study _Protestant Poetics and the Seventeenth-Century Religious Lyric_ (1979). Supported by exhaustive scholarship, Lewalski argues that seventeenth-century English poets owed more to Protestant influences than to Counter-Reformation and medieval Catholic resources. As one reviewer remarked, it should not seem to be such an audacious claim that "Protestant poets writing in a Protestant country by and large turned out religious lyrics of a Protestant character."⁴ Indeed, there does not seem anything radical about her thesis or about her methods. Like the earlier literary historians, she deals primarily with typology, biblical symbolism, meditation techniques, and emblem books. Yet, by showing how the Protestant versions differ from their medieval and

Counter-Reformation counterparts, Lewalski has challenged the hegemony of the medievalist reading of seventeenth-century literature.

This "Protestant" approach is not confined to Lewalski, who has urged a "revisionist" treatment of the entire period. Other historical critics, of course, including Joseph Summers, have pointed to the relevance of Luther, Calvin, and other Protestant thinkers to the literature of the time. Interestingly, some of the more radical critics, such as Stanley Fish, have been making what are essentially "Protestant" readings of these texts. One reviewer of Lewalski associates her work with "Stanley Fish's neo-Calvinist faction and its artistic nihilism."[5] Actually, much of her book is an attack on Fish, especially with his idea that Protestantism tended to minimize art and language. Still, it may be that Lewalski is to Fish as Tuve was to Empson, both of them correcting and disciplining the ahistorical tendencies of a brilliant but exasperating critic. Just as Tuve's medievalism was eventually made to support the explications of the New Critics, Lewalski's scholarship may well indirectly serve the needs of contemporary critical theory.

There is a major misconception, though, about Lewalski's work and that of other critics who stress the importance of Reformation thought for English literature of the Renaissance. For example, Heather Asals, in an introduction to her excellent book on Herbert, cites Lewalski, but insists on the specifically *Anglican* character of Herbert's verse. "What bothers me," she says, "is the growing tendency to turn *The Temple* into a 'Protestant' poem, a tendency which neglects Herbert's own personal commitment to Anglicanism. . . . My purpose here is partly to restore Herbert as a specifically Anglican poet."[6] Now, Lewalski never says that Herbert is not a staunch Anglican—he certainly had little sympathy for any of the dissenting sects and was fully committed to the Bishops, to the Book of Common Prayer, and to the Church of England in all of its articles, customs, and beliefs. No one should question that. What Lewalski is saying, though, is that Anglicanism itself, especially in the seventeenth century, was part of the Reformation movement. What that implies is widely misunderstood, both by medievalists and by "Protestant" critics. For example, Asals makes central to her discussion of Herbert the doctrine of the Real Presence of Christ in the Sacrament. That "Anglican" doctrine, whereby the Eucharist is both ordinary bread and the Body of Christ at the same time, derives not from "Catholic" theologians but from Martin Luther. The "both and" formula, which Asals goes on to relate in precisely the Reformation manner to the function of language, was anathematized by Rome (in Transubstantiation the bread ceases to be bread and becomes the Body of Christ only), but it was central to Luther's whole concept of salvation and it has remained so throughout the Lutheran tradition. "Protestant critics", in turn, having in mind various post-Reformation varieties of Protestantism, would tend to make the mistake of minimizing Herbert's sacramental theology. Both "medievalists" and "Protestant" critics often lack a precise understanding of what Reformation spirituality involved.

One point especially needs to be stressed. For this period it is not necessary, and in fact it is highly misleading, to contrast "Anglican" and "Protestant" as if they were two separate categories. No member of the Church of England of this time—not even Laud—would see himself as being "Catholic" in the sense stressed by the Tractarian movement of the nineteenth-century. The Bishops, the liturgy, the *via media*, High Church, Low Church, Nicholas Ferrar—all of seventeenth-century Anglicanism understood itself as being in conscious reaction against the medieval and Counter-Reformation Church, and it was permeated by Reformation ideals and assumptions. It is certainly true that there were many controversies and contentions, issuing finally in civil war. Yet these were Protestant controversies, between Luther's understanding of the sacraments and Zwingli's, between Calvin's understanding of the will and Arminius's. The issue of church government was especially important. When the papacy was rejected, that left the local Bishops to rule the church, but many of the Reformed Churches were urging government by elected elders (*presbyters*), or even insisting on a congregational system, whereby the local church ruled itself. Such systems, audacious and politically unsettling in their democracy, were matters of virulent controversy not only in England but throughout Protestant Europe. Nor was England the only country to insist on episcopalian rule; Lutheran Scandinavia did the same in the face of similar controversies. For all of the debates and factions, though, everyone, even Laud, would accept the general view of Scripture and the Christian life documented by Lewalski. Their understanding of salvation and the relationship to God would agree more with Luther than with Rome.

The biggest hindrance to a correct understanding of this period probably has to do with terminology. The word *Puritan* is no doubt most to blame. The word is so vague in its meaning, so difficult in its application, as my first chapter shows, that many Church historians no longer find it useful. There were those who wanted to "purify" the Anglican liturgy even more than had been done already. Yet many of those were ardent believers in the episcopacy. Many who objected strenuously to one practice would defend the others. To extend the word *Puritan* to mean repressive moralism and straitlaced conservatism is to make nonsense of the term. If anything, Puritans were the liberals of the day in their openness to change and to democratic ideals. The term *Calvinist* conjures up pictures of Puritans with their black costumes, compressed lips, and angry God. This too is misleading. The Church of England was saturated with Calvin's theological contributions, which were not limited to Double Predestination and Genevan church government. This was true of High Church as well as Low Church factions. When Barbara Lewalski cites the broad influence of Calvin on the imagination of the time, one should not think immediately of the May-flower Pilgrims. Consider, for example, Bishop Joseph Hall. A hyper-Calvinist who was an official envoy from the Church of England to the Synod of Dort, which hypostatized Calvinist dogma, he also insisted on the principle of "No bishop, no church." Considered a "low churchman," he became an important functionary of Archbishop Laud and, when the Civil War broke out, he defended the King. An accomplished writer and man of letters, this Calvinist defended the episcopacy and was the target of Milton's *Animadversions*. Joseph Hall's refusal to fit any of the conventional categories is no fluke, but is the rule. Similar blurrings of "Anglican," "Puritan," "Calvinist," and "Episcopalian" occur for nearly every figure of the period, as a survey of biographies will demonstrate. Even "Protestant" interpretations often accept these distinctions, so that a discovery of a Calvinist reference in Herbert is made to imply that he is some sort of dissenter, as if he is somehow less than a staunch High Church Anglican. If Lewalski "tends to obliterate theological distinctions which have long seemed useful," as one reviewer complains,[7] it is because those distinctions are artificial and anachronistic, and often obscure the facts.

It is apparent, then, that it is not simply seventeenth-century poetry but the religion and spirituality of the age that need to be explicated. This study is an attempt to do that—to explore George Herbert's religion and his poetry and, in so doing, to uncover the structures of Reformation spirituality in a way that should be useful for other students of the English Renaissance.

This study owes a great deal to Barbara Lewalski, although it differs from hers in many ways. This work was substantially finished when her book was published. Had her book come out earlier, the present volume would no doubt reflect her work much more than it does now. As it is, her exhaustive scholarship has at many points corrected and added credibility to my own. Despite some overlap, however, our emphases and methods are not the same. Lewalski focuses on "biblical genre theory, biblical tropes, Protestant ways with emblem, metaphor, and typology, and Protestant theory regarding the uses of art in religious subjects."[8] This study focuses on the theology of the lyrics themselves; that is, it attempts to recover their assumptions and to explain the kind of religious experiences that they record. Lewalski explores the Protestant understanding of the Bible as a basis for the aesthetic of the time. Her concern is to explore the imagination of the people of the age, to explain their modes of thinking, showing how they reacted to symbols and expressed themselves through language and through art. This study seeks to uncover what lies behind this aesthetic and this imagination. Its focus is on the Reformation concept of salvation and the relationship to God.

Since Lewalski is dealing with the Protestant imagination as a whole, she is able to minimize some of the differences between the writers of the period. One reviewer observes that, "between Herbert with his fascination for Anglican practices and Edward Taylor, the New England Puritan, there would seem to be more significant differences than her treatment of the two figures suggests."[9] Again, Lewalski is not dealing with the many differences and controversies but with the shared *imaginative* assumptions that transcended specific doctrinal or ecclesiastical disputes. My study, though, does try to account for some of the differences evident in seventeenth-century religious verse. It does so by stressing the major conceptual shift within Protestantism signaled by the Synod of Dort, in which the emphasis on the action and the will of God, codified by Calvin, was challenged by a new emphasis on the action and will of human beings, codified by Jacobus Arminius. Arminianism offered a different understanding of salvation which, like Calvinism, was present in both "High Church" and "Low Church," so that both Laud and Milton were Arminians. This theological controversy is important in understanding the very marked differences in the religious poetry of the time, between that of Herbert and Donne, for instance. The similarities between the poets of the age are important, but so are the differences, and I have tried to account for both.

Besides these different areas of emphasis, our methods are also different. The great effect of Lewalski's book is due partially to the fact that she is following the same methods and the same materials that the medievalists had been using—in her scholarly study of typology, emblem books, meditative forms, and other shared popular "traditions" she makes herself the heir of Rosemund Tuve even while she reinterprets her findings. My study, on the other hand, is historical in its appropriation of the theologians of the day, giving pride of place to Luther and Calvin but also drawing on the contemporary English preachers and theologians. It is also phenomenological in its method. That is, it seeks to reconstruct structures of experience and patterns of belief, presenting them from the inside, with conscious and rigorous sympathy. Questions about the objective truth or validity of these doctrines are *bracketed*, to use Husserl's term, on the grounds that intrusive criticism is always distancing. Thus, in the discussion of the very difficult doctrine of predestination, I am not here concerned either to attack that doctrine or to defend it. Rather, my concern is to describe that doctrine from the point of view of the people who held it and to reconstruct the sense in which it was, in the words of the *Book of Common Prayer,* a doctrine of "unspeakable comfort." Although I may use a passage from Luther to explain one of Herbert's poems, I will often use one of Herbert's poems to explain a passage from Luther. The phenomenological method is not concerned simply with explicating individual poems, although I hope that this study does cast light on individual lyrics and is thoroughly grounded in the literary texts. Rather, it is concerned also with larger patterns of meanings and experiences, to which, in fact, poetry can provide a unique access.

Terminology is very important and often misleading in this field, so I should define my terms. By *Reformation* I mean the religious movement initiated by Luther. *Reformed* refers to the distinctly Calvinist and Zwinglian branches of the movement, so that the term *Reformation* embraces both the Lutheran and the Reformed traditions. It is true that I sometimes associate "Luther and Calvin" more than either theologian (especially Luther) would like. The differences between them are very important. Luther, like many Anglicans, integrated his understanding of salvation into a sacramental theology, whereby the Gospel is conveyed and received in the sacraments, in the regenerative waters of Baptism and in the Real Presence of Christ in Holy Communion. Luther also rejected Calvin's Double Predestination and his rationalistic, sometimes reductive method that is in contrast to Luther's strict biblicism. (It has been observed that Calvin's major work is a systematic theology; Luther's major theological works are commentaries on the Bible.) Luther and Calvin have in common, however, the principle of "divine monergism,"[10] that God initiates and accomplishes everything in the work of salvation, which I take as the distinguishing mark of Reformation spirituality. The term *Calvinism* may be so loaded with misleading associations that I would do better to avoid it, as I do *Puritan*. By *Calvinist* I do not mean any particular position on Church government or the liturgy; rather, I intend by the term the theological positions developed in *The Institutes* and formulated in the Synod of Dort. Similarly, *Arminianism* does not refer to Laud or any ecclesiastical faction, but simply to the alternative soteriology addressed by that Synod. *Anglican* I use simply as an adjective to describe the beliefs and practices of the Church of England at that time. *Spirituality* I take to mean the religious and mystical life, as distinct from the intellectual and doctrinal formulations of *theology*. These two are closely related, especially with Reformation theologians, but the distinction needs to be kept in mind. The emphasis of this study is on *Reformation spirituality*, that is, the experiential rather than the theoretical, the poetry rather than the philosophy of the movement.

It should also be stressed that *Reformation spirituality* is not confined to, nor is it always present in Protestantism generally. Other kinds of spirituality can be termed *Protestant*, which simply means a Christian apart from the Roman Catholic and Eastern Orthodox traditions. Even in the seventeenth century, Arminianism and "enthusiasm" were offering competing views of the relationship between human beings and God. *Protestantism* went in many directions, while Reformation *spirituality*, as distinct from ecclesiastical positions, can be found even within Roman Catholicism. In many ways, Reformation thought is closer to medievalism than it is to many brands of Protestantism today. Luther and Calvin denied that they were innovators, and elements of their thought exist in the Middle Ages and in the Church Fathers. St. Augustine especially was their forebear in his understanding of salvation, as was, of course, St. Paul. This

Augustinian and Pauline tradition has always been present in the Roman Catholic Church. Thus the poetry of Francis Thompson and the fiction of Flannery O'Connor, both Roman Catholics, offer especially good examples of the clash between sin and grace as articulated by Luther and Calvin.

In offering a comprehensive account of Herbert's religious beliefs as expressed in his prose and poetry, both individual poems and larger issues in Herbert scholarship should be clarified. Discussion of his terminology and citation of specific parallels to theological texts should, of course, illuminate particular poems. More broadly, the Reformation paradigm of law, justification, and sanctification as the sequence of the Christian life helps to explain the sequencing of poems in *The Temple*. The Calvinist concept of "the perseverance of the saints" helps to explain the difference of tone and content that exists between the religious verse of Herbert and that of Donne. Although my purpose is not simply to explicate various poems but also to recover for literary historians a specific spiritual tradition, I have tried to ground my discussions as far as possible in Herbert's works. George Herbert, measured by any standard—his craftsmanship, his mastery of language, his poetic and religious subtlety, the profoundness of his spiritual experience—may well be the greatest of all religious poets. As such, he deserves to be studied in his own terms.

Reformation Spirituality

1

Seventeenth-Century Anglicanism: The Reformation and George Herbert

> Blessed be God! and the Father of all mercy! who con-
> tinueth to pour his benefits upon us. Thou hast elected us,
> thou hast called us, thou hast justified us, sanctified, and
> glorified us.
> —George Herbert, "A Prayer after Sermon"

Serious studies of George Herbert invariably come upon his Calvinism. Rather than its being seen as a solution, though, it has been treated as something of a problem. How is it that a theology associated with determinism, austerity, the impoverishment of the liturgy, and "puritanism," with all of its negative connotations, can produce such winsome religious verse? Herbert, the High Church Anglican with his poems filled with sacramental and liturgical imagery, is no Puritan—yet the elements of Calvinism are very evident, as recent scholars have shown, although most prefer to view him in terms of medieval and "Anglo-Catholic" models. The problem is not so much a misunderstanding of Herbert, it seems, as it is a misunderstanding of seventeenth-century English Calvinism.

This misunderstanding has been stressed by no less a critic, poet, and theologian than Coleridge, who pointed to Calvinism as a psychologically and spiritually liberating system of spirituality, suited to poetry and to joy. Coleridge not only saw the positive side of Calvinism, but explained why it is so difficult to penetrate and why it is so generally misunderstood. Its own terminology, according to Coleridge, obscures its essence. Calvinism, says Coleridge, is a lamb in a wolf's skin—"horrible for the race, but full of consolation to the suffering individual." Calvinism, according to Coleridge, is "cruel in the phrases," but not in its doctrine.[1]

In order to understand the religion of Renaissance England and that of

George Herbert, one of the greatest religious lyricists, it is necessary there-fore to understand the theology of Calvin from the inside. Not only can Calvin help interpret Herbert, but Herbert can help interpret Calvin, be-cause through poetry the inner spiritual core, what Coleridge called the "lamb" of Calvinism, which made it so compelling for his age, is presented unveiled.

This is a historical study, in which I try to place Herbert in the religious milieu of his time; a critical study, in which I interpret Herbert's poetry and the structure of *The Temple* with the help of Reformation theologians; and something of a phenomenological study, in which I see in Herbert the subjective correlative, as it were, to objective Protestant doctrine, and in which I try to explore the relationship between theology and poetic form.

First, it will be helpful to establish the historical context of Herbert's poetry, defining terms and clearing away misconceptions.

i. The Protestant Reformation and the Church of England

The theological impetus of the Protestant Reformation, and its differ-ences with traditional Roman Catholic thought, can perhaps best be sug-gested by the four intimately related slogans that became rallying points of the Reformation cause: Grace alone *(sola gratia)*; Faith alone *(sola fide)*; Christ alone *(solō Christo)*; Scripture alone *(sola scriptura)*.[2]

The initiative for human salvation or for any kind of religious action, according to the Reformers, belongs to God. Whereas traditional Catholic doctrine and that of modern theology emphasize human freedom and human action, Luther and Calvin emphasize the freedom and action of God. A human being is incapable through sin and an essentially fallen nature of being reconciled with God or even of desiring to be reconciled with God. However, God Himself is supremely active, seeking out human souls, overriding their corrupt wills, saving them through His Incarnation in Christ, wherein God fulfilled His own commandments to humanity and took upon Himself their penalty for breaking them. Salvation, then, for the Reformers, is by "grace alone" and in "Christ alone."

Although any Christian would agree that salvation is by grace and through Christ, the Reformers understood grace, not as with Roman Catholic orthodoxy, as the means by which God makes human actions meritable in His sight, so that the sacraments can communicate "infused grace" that sanctifies a person's incomplete "good works," but rather as forgiveness of sin.[3] God, according to the Reformers, forgives sin—original and actual, venial and mortal—once for all in Christ. There is no question for Luther or Calvin of "dying in a state of mortal sin" and going to Hell, a whole lifetime of holiness erased, or of atoning for one's own sins in Purgatory, or of struggling with an inventory of good deeds and bad in terms of which one's eternal destiny is determined. Rather, salvation, which is not based on human merit at all, or on human activity, moral or ceremonial, is assured for Lutherans and Calvinists insofar as it is based not on the work of sinful human beings, but on the work of a gracious, never-failing God.

One's response to God's grace, as revealed in Christ, is faith, the sole means of accepting what God has done. Despite later tendencies in some Protestant thought, faith is never in Reformation spirituality mere assent to doctrinal formulations, but is a vital trust and a consciously realized dependency on Christ.[4] The ground of faith and the means by which God's grace is communicated is the Holy Scripture. Once again, a fallen human being can, by his own powers, know nothing of God (the scholastic confidence in human reason was universally attacked by the Reformers). One can know of God only what God actively reveals of Himself through His Word. Human traditions, philosophy, theology, and mystical experience can have no religious validity except insofar as they agree with what God has said in Scripture, which testifies to God's saving purpose in Christ.

Thus, for the Reformers, the concepts of Grace, Faith, Christ, and the Scriptures are inextricably linked. They have in common the notion that *God* is the active partner in the divine-human relationship. The conventional paradigms of the soul seeking God, the soul ascending to Heaven, the sinner striving to come to God, are all exactly reversed: God is the one who seeks, strives, and descends. God incarnates Himself in Christ; God reveals Himself in Scripture; God seeks out the sinner; God, for the early Reformers, gives faith.

It is important to notice that the Protestant Reformation was not simply a movement for ecclesiastical or liturgical reform. Indeed, it existed along with a very traditional liturgical system in the Lutheran churches, as well as in the Church of England. Rather, at its essence was the issue of salvation and a distinct understanding of the relationship between the human being and God. It is also important to realize that, for the Reformers, this understanding was not new, but is detailed in the Scriptures, especially the writings of St. Paul, and was held by many of the Church Fathers, especially Augustine, whose soteriology, if not his ecclesiology, was followed in detail. This Pauline and Augustinian view of salvation was by no means eradicated in the medieval church, as witness Bernard of Clairvaux, although it was officially highly qualified by the scholastics in favor of a more human-centered spirituality based on "works" and "merits." It remained for Luther to recover and to reemphasize this "God-centered" view of salvation, which he found in Scripture and in his own experience. Calvin's role was that of a systematic theologian, who rationalized and put into intellectual terms (thereby changing and distorting, Luther would say) the central concepts of the Reformation.

This, then, was the tradition that dominated the Church of England

during the lifetime of George Herbert. Henry VIII broke with the Roman
Catholic Church in 1534, not so much because of theology (Henry having
just refuted Martin Luther, winning for himself the title "defender of the
faith" from the Pope), but for essentially political reasons. On the other
hand, his adviser and archbishop, Thomas Cranmer, who would put together the *Book of Common Prayer,* became very much involved in the new
movement. Under Edward VI, Reformed spirituality flourished in England. Queen Mary, in turn, reacted strongly against Protestantism,
martyring the most noted leaders of the Reformation in England and driv-
ing away scores of exiles to Geneva, Calvin's great testing ground for the
new religious thought. With Elizabeth's accession to the throne, the exiles
returned in prominence, bringing the Genevan experience to the universities and to the court. Universities such as Cambridge, Herbert's alma ma-
ter, with faculty drawn from the Genevan exiles, turned out a generation of
"reformed" clergymen into the English parishes. The popular anti-Catholic
backlash, triggered by the Spanish Armada and various plots against the
Queen, solidified the "Protestant" character of the English Church under
Elizabeth.[5] Despite virulent controversies over ecclesastical government,
the liturgy, the nature of the sacrament, and so on, most Protestants in
England and on the Continent were agreed on the fundamentals of the
Reformation faith, especially on the crucial understanding of salvation.

This agreement, though, would not last long. The reformers believed
that God accomplishes everything necessry to salvation; to make salvation
contingent in any way upon the efforts of the individual human being was
to nullify grace, to reintroduce the bondage of legalism, and to render
salvation insecure. Yet the doctrine of *sola gratia* created problems if logically pursued. What of human freedom? Does God choose *not* to save some
people? What is the rationale for morality? To solve these dilemmas, some
theologians began to put some of the burden of salvation back upon the
human being. Among the Lutherans, Melanchthon proposed the concept
of synergism—that the human being cooperates with God in the process of
salvation. Synergism was firmly rejected in the Lutheran *Formula of Concord*
(1577), but in the Reformed churches—those identified with Zwingli and
Calvin, rather than Luther, including the Church of England—a more systematic challenge was presented by the Dutch cleric Jacobus Arminius
(d. 1609), who, in effect, offered an alternative Protestant theology built
around the freedom of the human will.

To combat Arminianism, the Reformed Churches, including the Church
of England with the active support of King James, convened the Synod of
Dort. The five points of the Arminians were answered with what were to
become known as the five points of Calvinism:

1. Total depravity. The soul, of itself, is incapable of doing good; the natural state of the will is rebellion against God. Arminians insist that some
   degree of free will is present even in a fallen soul.

2. Unconditional Election. God chooses sinners to whom He will give salvation as a free gift, contingent upon no conditions whatsoever. Arminians, on the other hand, teach conditional election, in which salvation is contingent upon the free choice of the soul to accept Christ and follow God.
3. Limited Atonement. Christ's death saves only the elect. His sacrifice is particular rather than universal. Arminians, though, insist on universal atonement. Only believers can be saved, but potentially anyone can become a believer and be saved by Christ's sacrifice.
4. Irresistible Grace. God overmasters the sinful will so that His saving mercy cannot be rejected. Arminians insist that the free gift of salvation can be spurned and rejected by the human will.
5. Perseverance of the Saints. Since the work of salvation is completely and unconditionally accomplished by God, it is impossible to fall from Grace or to lose one's salvation. Arminians, with their emphasis on the will, insist that one who has experienced salvation can nevertheless fall away from God and be condemned to Hell.

For Calvinists, salvation is a function of God's will—as such, it is secure. For Arminians, salvation is a function of the human will—God's compliance is assumed, so that salvation or damnation depends upon continual human choice.

The Synod of Dort, in answering the Arminians, did, perhaps, systematize too strictly the all-important doctrine of salvation by grace. The Lutherans, who characteristically insist upon upholding both terms of a scriptural paradox even at the expense of a logical system, responded to the synergists in a very different way. Thus the *Formula of Concord* teaches that salvation is completely the work of God; at the same time, corollaries such as the Limited Atonement are rejected as unscriptural. Classical Lutheranism teaches election to eternal life, but not election to damnation; salvation is a gift, but grace is universal and potentially anyone may be saved.[6] Calvin, though, wove a tight system, which Arminius threatened to unravel, replacing it, as a Reformed theologian, with a tight system of his own. Although Lutherans would disagree with the harder edges of the Calvinist Five Points, their understanding of grace is essentially anti-Arminian. The Synod of Dort, especially for England, remains a major watershed for Protestant theology, with the Calvinist position representing the older elements of Reformation spirituality, and the Arminian position representing the wave of the future.

Eventually, Arminianism would displace Calvinism in the Church of England, finding expression not only in the ceremonialism of Laud, but more deeply in the revivalism of John Wesley. During Herbert's lifetime, however, Calvinism was the norm, both for episcopalian factions and for presbyterian ones. There was a native English reaction to Calvinism along Arminian lines,[7] but Arminianism, founded by a Dutch radical, was at first mainly confined to the separatists, a point that is very important to keep in mind when talking about "Puritans" and Milton.[8] (Bunyan, for example, was a "General Baptist" as opposed to the "Particular Baptists." The latter group held to Calvin's doctrine of "particular," or Limited Atonement. Bunyan's Church emphasized the Arminian doctrine of "general" or Universal Atonement.) At the same time, its emphasis on the will was much closer to that of traditional Catholicism, so that it also eventually attracted liturgical conservatives and traditionalists, such as Lancelot Andrewes and, most significantly, William Laud. Like Calvinism, Arminianism was flexible liturgically. When Laud became Archbishop of Canterbury in 1633, at issue were not only liturgy and church government, but a major theological shift away from what had been traditional Anglican Protestantism. Herbert died the same year Laud became Archbishop, before the battle lines were clearly drawn. In general, Herbert followed the older Anglican tradition of Calvinist spirituality, which, in his time, was nearly always combined with a deep reverence for the ceremonial rites of the church.

The term *Calvinism*—associated with determinism, liturgical iconoclasm, moralism, and asceticism—is seldom used with precision. The five points of Calvinism do imply predestination, though not necessarily determinism, but this is not the focus of Calvin's thought. The five points say nothing about liturgy, church government, or the nature of the sacraments. Far from being moralistic, the problem of Calvinism is that it can drift toward antinomianism and immorality, since salvation can be neither won nor lost by one's "works." Calvinism, attacked now for its strictness, was originally attacked for its permissiveness. Far from being ascetic, Calvinism was in conscious reaction to monastic asceticism, which rejected marriage and sexuality and insisted upon fasts and mortification of the flesh.[9] Far from being "a theology of fear," Calvinism offered to believers who had been taught to continually be terrified of Hell the assurance that salvation is free and that it can never be lost.

One reason Calvinism is so generally misunderstood is later developments within the Calvinist tradition. The "supralapsarian" controversies, which argued over the exact time before the creation of the universe when God was choosing whom to save and whom to damn, the elaborate schemes of introspection and good works designed to reveal whether one is of the elect—such concerns of the later Calvinists were explicitly forbidden by Calvin himself. As the Established Church became more and more Arminian, the only remaining Calvinists became those of the nonconforming and presbyterian factions, with whom Calvinism is now practically synonomous. Calvin's followers have thus obscured the specific influences of Calvin's theology in the religious life of the Renaissance.[10]

The impact of Reformed theology is further obscured by the categories of *Anglican* and *Puritan,* in terms of which literary historians usually study the period. It is true that there were ecclesiastical controversies, especially toward the beginning of Elizabeth's reign, when the organization and liturgy of the church were still more or less open questions, and the issues

flared again with the accession of Laud.[11] Some Anglicans favored an episcopalian church government, others a presbyterian. Some believed that
various traditional ceremonies should be retained; others, that the *Book of
Common Prayer* did not go far enough in eliminating "superstitious" rites.
There was another group, the separatists, which for various reasons rejected the Established Church altogether, opposing both the episcopacy
and the presbytery in favor of congregational government. The term *Puritan* in this period is reserved by church historians for those of the Established Church who wished to "purify" the church from within toward a
more presbyterian government and liturgy.[12] One problem is that literary
historians tend to classify both presbyterians and separatists together as
"Puritans." While presbyterians do tend to be Calvinist, insisting upon the
Genevan model of church government as well as the Genevan theology,
the separatists encompassed a variety of beliefs, including that of the
anabaptists, and were often Arminian in soteriology. Milton, to take an
important example, is regularly classified as a "Puritan," but he is not a
Calvinist. A separatist, Milton takes the Arminian position on each of the
disputed five points (*De Doctrina Christiana* 1. 3, 4, 16, 17, 25). That the term
is also used for the New England colonists in America, who were separatists (albeit Calvinists), adds to the confusion. John Robinson, the pastor of
the Mayflower congregation, makes distinctions that are often overlooked,
disassociating his belief from that of the Puritans: "The papists place the
ruling power of Christ in the Pope, the Protestants in the bishop, the
Puritans in the Presbytery, we in the body of the congregation of the
multitude called the Church."[13] Despite the obvious ecclesiastical and cul-
tural differences between the English conforming presbyterians and the
American separatists, studies of seventeenth-century New England are
regularly cited by critics to distinguish British "Puritans" from "Anglicans."
    Even when such categories are more closely defined, they are still very
difficult to apply. Charles and Katherine George, in their study of the
tracts, pamphlets, and sermons of the time, found that a clergyman who
opposed one liturgical practice, such as the sign of the cross or wedding
rings, would be very likely to defend the rest of them. In fact, they observe
that most so-called Puritans actually turn out to be supporters of episcopacy.[14] The term, originally pejorative, is also confusing in the usage of the
time. Lewis Bayly complains that a stumbling block to religion is "adorning
vices with the names of Vertues" ("as to call . . . spilling innocent blood,
valor; Gluttony, Hospitality; Covetousness, Thriftinesse; Whoredom, loving a
Mistresse," etc.), and vice versa, so that "zeale in Religion" is derided as
"Puritanisme" (*Practice of Piety* [1619], pp. 199–200). Although the term was
usually one of derision—the "Puritan" Martin Marprelate promises to be
even with the Puritans, as well as the Bishops[15]—the title, with its connotations of scrupulous morality, is grandly claimed by the episcopalian, Arminian, ex-libertine John Donne.[16]
    The term *Anglican*, by the same token, can only refer to conformity with

the Church of England, which, in the period between 1570 and 1640, "has shown itself to be indubitably Protestant and, except for some tendency to retreat from the extremes of predestinarian ideology, essentially Calvinist in viewpoint."[17] *Anglo-Catholicism* had not yet been developed and there was, as the Georges document, agreement on the fundamentals of the Protestant faith, despite the ecclesiastical controversies. John Whitgift, Archbishop of Canterbury (1583–1604), was the implacable enemy of "Puritan" views of the liturgy and church government. Whitgift persecuted presbyterians, enforced full use of the liturgy, insisted upon clerical vestments, forbade private religious meetings, and suppressed "Puritan" writings and their authors. But Whitgift, the major target of the Martin Marprelate tracts, was also a zealous Calvinist who initiated the Calvinistic Lambeth articles in response to nascent Arminianism,[18] and established the writings of Heinrich Bullinger, Zwingli's successor in Zurich, as a means of educating the Elizabethan clergy.[19] Charles and Katherine George illustrate the weakness of the modern distinction between *Anglican* and *Puritan* by citing a controversy in which the "Anglican" Archbishop Whitgift condemns his "Puritan" opponent for not believing sufficiently in predestination and for believing that "the doctrine of free-will is not repugnant to salvation."[20] King James also bitterly opposed the presbyterians ("no Bishops, no King"), but he was one of the conveners of the Synod of Dort.

One of the most popular books of devotion was *The Practice of Piety* by Lewis Bayly, a bishop and courtier under King James. Bayly dedicated his book to Prince Charles, to whom Bayly was a chaplain and who would later as King Charles I be executed by "Puritans." *The Practice of Piety, Directing a Christian how to walk that he may please God* was first printed in 1612, went through eleven editions in only seven years, and remained in print until 1842. As with the mainstream of the Anglican Church, the book emphasizes church order and the sacraments and is thoroughly Calvinistic in theology. Enormously popular during the Renaissance, *The Practice of Piety*, although written by a bishop and a courtier, became the property of the "Puritans" after the Restoration. Its most obvious impact on English literature is that it was one of the two books that made up the famous dowry given to John Bunyan.[21]

The point is, the Anglican Church of Herbert's day, in its main stream, was both ceremonial in its liturgy and Calvinist in its theology. The *via media* of the Church of England was largely then a liturgical goal (Herbert's "The British Church" is about the adornment of the different churches). Theologically, with the Jesuits on one extreme and the anabaptist "enthusiasts" on the other, Calvin is currently said to have "held in check the extreme right and the extreme left in modern Christendom and prevented the triumph of either."[22] Originally, Calvin himself occupied the *via media*. After the Restoration, Calvinism and main line Anglicanism would go in different directions, but Herbert's own religious milieu resists the later categories.

Lawrence Sasek summarizes the inconsistencies of terms such as *Puritan* and *Anglican* as used by literary historians:

A "Puritan" opponent of the stage may be an orthodox Anglican who fought the puritans and, conversely, an active puritan opponent of the established Church can, in literary history, turn out to be quite unpuritanical. For instance, George Herbert, the loyal Anglican, was more "Puritan" in literary temper, than Andrew Marvell, the civil servant of the puritan government.[23]

As for the "Puritan" opposition to the theater, Sasek shows that the attack against the stage was not especially characteristic of the "Puritans," but that it was often stated in identical terms by "Anglicans" such as Nicholas Ferrar. "In fact," according to Sasek, "few churchmen of any persuasion can be found to defend playhouses."[24] Because the terms *Puritan* and *Anglican* are so equivocal and potentially so misleading, it seems better to avoid them in favor of separate terms for ecclesiastical position and for theological doctrine (Whitgift might be described as a Calvinist episcopalian; William Perkins, as a Calvinist presbyterian; Laud, as an Arminian episcopalian; Milton, as an Arminian separatist, etc.).[25]

Herbert is a Calvinist, but he is emphatically episcopalian; as such, he is opposed to presbyterianism. In fact, Herbert took part in the liturgical controversies in his youthful "Musae Responsoriae," an attack on the Scottish presbyterian Andrew Melville for his criticism of the liturgy of the Church of England. Herbert himself, in describing the three sections of Melville's tract, narrows his point of disagreement to questions of ritual rather than of doctrine:

> Ritibus una Sacris opponitur; altera Sanctos
>   Praedicat autores; tertia plena Deo est.
> Postremis ambabus idem sentimus uterque;
>   Ipse pios laudo; Numen & ipse colo.
> Non nisi prima suas patiuntur praelia lites.
>
> (4. 3–7)[26]

> [One part opposes sacred ritual;
> The second praises sacred authors;
> The third is full of God. About the latter two
> Our minds are in accord: I also praise
> Holy men; I, too, worship God.
> The first contentions only lend themselves
> To disagreement.
>
> (trans. McCloskey, pp. 10–11).]

Significantly, Herbert chides Melville for invoking Calvin and other Reformers, claiming that their positions are not against those of the Church of England.

Quò magis inuidiam nobis & crimina confles,
   Pertrahis in partes nomina magna tuas;
Martyra, Calvinum, Bezam, doctúmque *Bucerum,*
   Qui tamen in nostros fortiter ire negant.

                                                        (33. 1–4)

[To instigate adverse opinions and incriminations
Against us, you highhandedly incorporate
Famous names to your side: Martyr, Calvin,
Beza, learned Bucer. But still they won't go
Against our cause.

                              (trans. McCloskey, pp. 46–47).]

Herbert is correct. Calvin never denounced episcopacy as a means of church government.[27] Calvin urged order and decorum in worship. He also opposed the tendency to make minor ceremonies a matter of contention. Ceremonies, says Calvin, "ought to be variously accommodated to the customs of each nation and age." Traditional practices may be changed but "I admit that we ought not to charge into innovation rashly, suddenly, for insufficient cause. But love will best judge what may hurt or edify; and if we let love be our guide, all will be safe" (*Institutes* 4.10.30).[28] Herbert says as much in regard to controversies over whether one should kneel or sit at Holy Communion: "contentiousnesse in a feast of charity is more scandall than any posture" ("The Country Parson," 22:259).[29]

That Reformation spirituality could coexist with the traditional liturgy and a high view of the sacraments is abundantly illustrated by Lutheranism, with its conservative ritual and its insistence on the Real Presence of Christ in the Eucharist. Luther was not so influential in the Anglican church of the seventeenth-century as Calvin, but liturgical conservatism, such as Herbert's, looked more to Lutheran ideology than to that of Rome.

Calvin was no villain to sixteenth- and seventeenth-century Englishmen. John Donne, who was no Calvinist, cites Calvin more than any other Protestant commentator, according to his editors. Donne considered Calvin "worthy to be compared to the *Ancients,* for the exposition of Scriptures" (3:177), elsewhere ranking him as equal to Augustine.[30] Even when he disagrees with Calvin, Donne does so with deference to his "religious wisdom" (7:432). In fact, the modern image of Calvin as a narrow-minded dogmatist is exactly reversed by Donne, who warmly appreciates what he sees as Calvin's tentativeness:

It hath been observed amongst Philosophers, that *Plato* speaks probably, and *Aristotle* positively; *Platoes* way is, It may be thus, and *Aristotle,* It must be thus. The like hath been noted amongst Divines, between *Calvin,* and *Melanchthon; Calvin* will say, *Videtua,* It seems to to be thus, *Melanchthon,* It can be no otherwise but thus. But the best men are but Problematicall, onely the Holy Ghost is Dogmaticall.

Donne's respect for Calvin is especially noteworthy in that in most of the theological controversies he would oppose Calvin (and in an age when the *ad hominem* argument was the norm). Hooker is similarly respectful and complimentary to Calvin, showing the necessity of his church order to the Genevan situation, while arguing, as Calvin would agree, that presbyterianism is not binding on all nations. Moreover, although Hooker modified Calvin's tendency to minimize reason and otherwise qualified his thinking, in the understanding of justification and especially on the crucial question of whether salvation can be lost, Hooker followed Calvin.[31]

Nor was Calvin's popularity confined to the divines. Thomas Norton, author of *Gorboduc*, the first English tragedy, was also the major translator of the *Institutes* into English (so that it could be said that Calvinists not only closed the theaters, but opened them as well). Arthur Golding, the great translator of Ovid, was also the important translator of Calvin's commentaries. C. S. Lewis is hardly sympathetic, but his characterization of Calvinism in the fashionable sixteenth-century intellectual circles and at the court, is especially useful:

Modern parallels are always to some extent misleading. Yet, for a moment only, and to guard against worse misconceptions, it may be useful to compare the influence of Calvin on that age with the influence of Marx on our own; or even of Marx and Lenin in one, for Calvin had both expounded the new system in theory and set it going in practice. This will at least serve to eliminate the absurd idea that Elizabethan Calvinists were somehow grotesque, elderly people, standing outside the main forward current of life. In their own day they were, of course, the very latest thing. Unless we can imagine the freshness, the audacity, and (soon) the fashionableness of Calvinism, we shall get our whole picture wrong. It was the creed of progressives, even of revolutionaries. It appealed strongly to those tempers that would have been Marxist in the nineteen-thirties. The fierce young don, the learned lady, the courtier with intellectual leanings, were likely to be Calvinists. When hard rocks of Predestination outcrop in the flowery soil of the *Arcadia* or the *Fairie Queene,* we are apt to think them anomalous, but we are wrong. The Calvinism is as modish as the shepherds and goddesses. . . . [*The Institutes*] is, however, a masterpiece of literary form; and we may suspect that those who read it with most approval were troubled by the fate of predestined vessels of wrath just about as much as young Marxists in our own age are troubled by the approaching liquidation of the *bourgeoisie.*[32]

The ecclesiastical and social implications of Calvinism were attractive even to the secular-minded. For the intensely religious person, such as Herbert, its impact was more specific and profound.

Religiously, Calvin stressed the initiative of God in all divine-human relationships. For Calvin, God is active, intervening with mysterious generosity in lives that are hopelessly depraved, overmastering their sinful wills with His grace and power, offering those who deserve to be damned eternal joy, paying the cost Himself, requiring nothing in return. Calvin's is a theology of grace; that not everyone is saved can only mean that God chose not to save them, leaving them to the punishment that their depravity deserves—the corollaries multiply and become problematic, but at the essence of Reformed spirituality is the notion of God's incomprehensible generosity in saving anyone, so that in Christ God Himself fulfilled all of the righteousness and suffered all of the punishment necessary for the salvation of those whom He would call to Himself. Not only is salvation free; it cannot be lost. The doctrine of predestination is, according to the Church of England's Articles of Religion (17), one of "unspeakable comfort," in that the believer's salvation has been determined from before the creation of the world, contingent not upon the believer's own vacillating, sinful will, but upon the immutable will of God. Again, in Coleridge's words, Calvinism is "cruel in the phrases," "but full of consolation to the suffering individual." The phrases of Calvinism have often stood in the way of assessing its personal dimension, which seemed so compelling to Renaissance Christians.

It has been observed that Herbert never worries about Hell, in marked contrast to Donne's obsessive fear of damnation. This is perhaps the clearest evidence of Herbert's Calvinism, the point where dogma touches religious experience. For a Calvinist, Hell is not a possibility for a Christian. Herbert believed in the Perseverance of the Saints, a doctrine that is perhaps the litmus test of a truly Calvinist spirituality.

The dynamics of Calvinism are also the dynamics of Herbert's poetry. "The Collar" is the supreme Calvinist poem, dramatizing the depraved human will that insists on serving itself rather than God, in a state of intrinsic rebellion and growing chaos until God intervenes, intruding upon the human will in a way that cannot be resisted, calling the sinner, effecting a response, and restoring order. For Herbert, God's love is absolutely unconditional, as in "Love(3)":

> Love bade me welcome: yet my soul drew back,
>   Guiltie of dust and sinne.
> But quick-ey'd Love, observing me grow slack
>   From my first entrance in,
> Drew nearer to me.
>
> ("Love [3]," 1–5)

This movement of God's drawing nearer, as the guilty soul draws back, is ever present, both in Herbert's poetry and in Reformation theology.

Herbert's relationship to classical Calvinism is personal rather than dogmatic. Its tenets are taken for granted rather than consciously formulated.

When he departs from Calvin, Herbert generally follows Luther, although in a time when Luther's influence on the English Church was waning. Luther preferred paradox to a logical system. For Luther, if two seemingly contradictory truths were taught in Scripture, both must be upheld; Calvin, on the other hand, tried to reconcile them and, in effect, would often explain one of them away. Herbert follows Luther in his biblicism and in shrinking from such corollaries as Limited Atonement. Herbert often advocates a Lutheran view of the sacraments and of the universality of grace. Herbert may have been influenced by Arminianism—he was a friend of Lancelot Andrewes and debated Predestination with him (Herbert would have had to defend the Calvinist side).[33] Herbert emphasizes God's *love*, as the Arminians did, although he uses the term in much the same way that Calvinists use *grace* (for Herbert, God's love involves action and will, and is entirely unconditional and undeserved).[34] Generally, however, Herbert follows the older school of Reformation thought, preferring Luther and Calvin to both Arminius and the supralapsarian "Calvinists." Herbert's spirituality is essentially that of early Reformation theology, and, as this study will suggest, his is perhaps that movement's clearest and most consistent poetic voice.

ii. Protestant Readings of George Herbert

Herbert is conventionally portrayed as a model of Anglican piety—a characterization that is certainly true. The problem is in understanding the nature of Anglican piety in Herbert's time. Later theological divisions within the Church of England—"High Church" vs. "Low Church," "Anglo-Catholics" vs. "Puritans"—have tended to be read back, without qualification, into Herbert's own day. Moreover, in dealing with doctrines shared by all Christians, and generally avoiding divisive issues, Herbert's poetry is truly *catholic* in every sense of the Apostles' Creed. Christians of all persuasions—the "Puritan" Richard Baxter, the evangelical John Wesley, the Roman Catholic Hopkins, and the more unorthodox Simone Weil— have all valued the spirituality of Herbert's verse. Herbert himself, however, was a clergyman of the Church of England in the early seventeenth century, a period when the church was still dominated by the experience of Martin Luther and the theological synthesis of John Calvin, who may be to the Protestant Reformation what Thomas Aquinas is to Medieval Catholicism.[35] This Protestant tradition has often been minimized by literary historians, partly, no doubt, because of incorrect assumptions about Puritanism. More recently, however, literary critics have been seeing the Protestant spirituality of the seventeenth century more clearly. Herbert's Calvinism, although it is not always labeled as such, is being recognized, if not always fully appreciated or understood.

The relevance of Herbert to Reformed spirituality was immediately apparent to seventeenth-century Calvinists, as Hutchinson shows (after the Restoration and the rise of Anglican Arminianism, Calvinism began to be left to the nonconformists):

> Thomas Hill (1610–65), an unbending Presbyterian, included *The Temple* with only four other poetical works in his extensive library. *The Temple* was a favourite work of Archbishop Robert Leighton (1611–84) [whose Calvinism so impressed Coleridge], who often quoted from it, and it seems to have been the only book of poetry owned by his saintly pupil, Henry Scougal (1650–78), author of one of the earliest Scottish religious classics. Peter Sterry, Cromwell's chaplain, in an undated letter to his son at Eton, counsels him "to read the Scriptures, Mr. Bolton & Mr. Herbert"; his own mystical and poetic prose has phrases reminiscent of Herbert. John Bryan's *Dwelling with God. Opened in Eight Sermons* (1670), one of the few books owned by Bunyan, quotes three poems of "the Divine Poet" in full and selections from seven others. The Nonconformist divines, Philip Henry (1631–96) and his son Matthew (1662–1714), the expositor of Scripture, both spoke of Herbert "with reverence and affection" and often quoted his words.[36]

Richard Baxter and the New England poet Edward Taylor were also strong and noteworthy admirers of Herbert.[37]

During the eighteenth century, despite the neoclassical rejection of "metaphysical" verse, Herbert's poetry was enormously popular among the nonconformist churches. The anonymous *Select Hymns Taken Out of Mr. Herbert's Temple* (1697), based on thirty-two of Herbert's poems, is described as a "widely used Dissenters' hymnal."[38] The biggest revival of Herbert (to risk a pun) came with John Wesley, who edited his poetry and set forty-seven poems from *The Temple* to music, reworking them according to hymn meter. Wesley, however, was an Arminian; though he appreciated Herbert's emphasis on inner spirituality and a personal relationship to Christ, he carefully revised away the more direct references to Calvinist doctrine.[39]

In the meantime, Izaak Walton's "Life" presented Herbert as the model of Laudian piety. The Restoration was accompanied by a strong reaction against Calvinist theology; the cleavage between Anglicans and Puritans (i.e., nonconformists) began to mean something and such conflicts were read back into the period before the War. Walton was in many ways a revisionist, as is increasingly becoming clear,[40] but his portrait of Herbert has had an enormous influence on his reputation and on interpretations of his poetry. Nevertheless, the Established Church after the Restoration still valued Herbert for his Protestantism. "And he that reads Mr. Herbert's Poems attendingly," writes Barnabas Oley, editor of *The Country Parson* (1652), "shall finde not onely the excellencies of Scripture Divinitie, and choice passages of the Fathers bound up in Meetre; but the Doctrine of Rome also finely and strongly confuted."[41]

Only much later did the Church of England lose some of its fear of Rome. The term *Anglican*, meaning an adherent of a more or less Catholic, as against a Protestant theology—so often used in reference to Herbert—was not introduced until 1797, according to the OED. *Anglo-Catholic*, implying an emphasis on the Catholic rather than the Protestant character of the Church of England—a term often used of Herbert—was introduced in 1849. Anglo-Catholicism was essentially a nineteenth-century movement, which then traced its roots back through Laud and eventually, because of his liturgical symbolism, to Herbert. In this century, the Anglo-Catholicism of T. S. Eliot and others has served to emphasize the medieval, Catholic quality of Herbert's verse at the expense of its Protestantism.

Contemporary Herbert scholarship, however, begins with Joseph Summers, who combines the insights of "New Criticism" with penetrating historical scholarship. Summers points out how Walton left out important parts of Herbert's biography—that his stepfather, Sir John Danvers, whom Herbert dearly loved, was one of the regicides, for instance, and that "Herbert's patrons and associates within the Church belonged almost exclusively to the group opposed to Laud."[42] Summers goes on to show through the poetry that "Herbert believed as strongly in predestination and the doctrine of the Covenant of Grace as he believed in the significance and beauty of the ritual."[43] Although he employs the Puritan/Anglo-Catholic dichotomy, Summers shows that neither Herbert nor most churchmen of the time could be categorized so simply.

Although Summers solidly establishes the religious milieu of Herbert's work, another vein of scholarship has aligned him with the traditions of the Medieval Church and with various devotional practices of the Counter-Reformation. Rosemond Tuve, in a challenge to Empson's modernistic reading of Herbert, has shown how Herbert's "original" images are actually part of a rich tradition, which she traces through Christian iconography, liturgy, and emblem books, the meaning of which is essential in understanding Herbert's intention.[44] Tuve's study, which has provoked a great deal of scholarship in the history of Herbert's symbols, was soon followed by the work of Louis Martz, who suggests a relationship between the devotional exercises of Loyola (and, for Herbert, St. Francis de Sales) and the English meditative poem.[45]

The liturgy, the Church Fathers, biblical typology, and the great Christian commonplaces are, of course, common property shared by the Reformers and the rest of Christendom; to emphasize Herbert's Protestantism is not to deny the continuity of the classic Christian doctrines, symbols, and experiences as charted by so many critics. Protestants did employ Roman Catholic devotional materials.[46] In fact, it has been

suggested that Loyola's *Exercises*, part of the Counter-Reformation's response to the appeal of Protestantism among the laity, was part of a larger
Augustinian and Pauline revival of which the Reformation was only a part.
The *Exercises*, like Reformation theology, begin with meditating on one's
sin, moving to a deeper awareness of God's mercy.[47] Calvinists did employ
traditional emblems and typology, as evidenced by the crowded frontis-
piece of Bayly's *Practice of Piety*, with its mitred Aaron and its labeled scenes
from Exodus, although as Barbara Lewalski shows throughout her study,
the Protestants employed typology and emblems in a different way from
the Roman Catholics. This study does not intend to challenge the scholarship of Tuve and others, which seeks to document the continuity of Herbert's symbols with those of the Medieval Church—the Reformation and
the Roman Catholic churches held more in common than they were willing
to admit at the time. Yet, as Rosemond Tuve elsewhere admits, "We simply
find missing in Herbert some of the important ideas of Medieval Catholicism, in their Aquinian formulation particularly" (e.g., the reciprocity and
mutuality of divine and human love; the "participation" of the human
being in and with God).[48] Augustine is more applicable to Herbert than
Aquinas, as Patrick Grant has shown.[49] The Reformation, to a large degree,
was a recovery of Augustine's soteriology; Grant's discussion is helpful in
any "Protestant" reading of Herbert's poetry. Grant is committed, though,
to the medieval approach to Herbert, so that much of his book is taken up
with rather labored tracing of Augustinianism through the Franciscans and
various devotional texts. The direct source of Herbert's Augustinianism—
Calvin, who modified Augustine in important ways—is not studied in
detail. John Mulder, in an article opposing the emphasis on tradition, suggests Pascal as an appropriate model for understanding Herbert. Pascal, of
course, was a Jansenist; that is, in effect, he was a Roman Catholic Calvinist. Mulder offers a brilliant overview of *The Temple* from the perspective of
what is, in effect, Reformed theology.[50] The relevance of Calvin is implicit
in many of the "Medieval" readings of Herbert, although, partly because of
the "Puritan" shibboleth, the French Reformer is often overlooked.

On the other hand, a number of critics have dealt explicitly with Herbert
and Reformation spirituality. Richard Strier has explored how Luther's
doctrine of Justification by Faith illuminates Herbert's poetry. Lawrence
Sasek and Harold Fisch[51] have challenged the stereotypes of "Puritanism,"
and other critics, such as Stanley Stewart,[52] had been employing Calvin to
help understand Herbert's poetry, as Summers suggested. William
Halewood is especially important in demonstrating how the dynamics of
Reformation spirituality—the conflict between the human and the divine
will and their sudden reconciliation by grace—is of major importance, not
only thematically but formally, for seventeenth-century poetry.

A number of dissertations have also helped establish Herbert's position
in terms of Reformed theology. Johnson Donald Hughes, "George Herbert:
His Place in English Church History" (Boston Univ., 1960), employs the

Anglican/Puritan dichotomy but sees the theology of Herbert's poetry as Calvinistic. John Freed, "Salvation/Damnation: The Theology and Personae of George Herbert's *Temple*" (Penn. State, 1970), shows how the Reformed doctrine of revelation functions formally in Herbert's poetry. William Leigh Taylor, "Protestant Theology in George Herbert's *The Temple*" (Univ. of Virginia, 1976), contrasts Herbert's Calvinism to medieval theology, focusing on Herbert's Christology, his legal, contractual language as a metaphor of salvation, and the conflict between God's wrath and God's love, resolved in Christ. Ilona Bell, in " 'When Faith Did Change the Scene': Herbert's Renascence and the Protestant Reformation" (Boston College, 1977), and in her article cited earlier, sees a change in Herbert's poetry, from essentially Catholic meditative goals in his early poetry to a more Protestant spirituality in the later ones. Bell suggests that Herbert reworks the Catholic devotional tradition in his religious poetry just as Donne reworks the Petrarchan conventions in his love poetry. Her provocative study is tainted somewhat by the Anglo-Catholic/Puritan stereotypes, so that Herbert emerges as something of a rebel, an opponent of the Established Church, at the end of his life. Herbert's image as the archetype of Anglican piety need not be challenged in "Protestant" readings of his poetry; it is the nature of that Anglican piety, rather than Herbert's obvious religious conformity, that sometimes needs a revisionary treatment.

Perhaps the most distinguished revisionist in recent years is Barbara Lewalski. Her *Protestant Poetics and the Seventeenth-Century Religious Lyric* offers a sustained corrective to the medieval or Counter-Reformation approach to Herbert, finding in the Protestant view of the Bible and religious symbolism a "new Protestant aesthetics" that she finds to be "the very foundation of Herbert's poetry."[53]

Another major critic who has taken a particular interest in Herbert is Stanley Fish, who is both an important literary theorist and a keen analyst of literary texts. Fish is mainly interested in the process of reading Herbert rather than in Herbert's religious beliefs *per se*, but his criticism—in unveiling the "self-consuming" discovery in the poems that one can do nothing for one's own salvation, for instance—often points implicitly to the spirituality of Calvin and Luther. Fish studies the techniques of Reformation catechisms as they relate to Herbert's method, but he is not so concerned with what those catechisms teach. Fish's understanding of religion is essentially modernist and monistic—there would be no question for Reformed theology of being "absorbed into the deity"; the goal would never be "to stop distinguishing oneself from God." Fish also assumes the intrinsic inadequacy of language for religious expression: "How does one avoid saying amiss if language is itself a vehicle for the making of invidious distinctions?"[54] Reformed theology, on the other hand, as a subsequent chapter will show, holds a very great confidence in language, so that the very Word of God can be conveyed through the words of human beings. More important for poetry is that Fish fairly consistently misreads the tone of Herbert's poetry. In his discussion of "Love (3)" Fish renders an impeccable Calvinist reading of the poem, but he misses the joy implicit in the Reformed doctrine of salvation and obvious, to most readers, in the poem. "Love's smile is like his sweetness," according to Fish; "it sugars a bitter pill."[55]

> [Christ] does not say, "Congratulations, you've passed," but rather, "You still haven't got it right and never will, but come in and sit down anyway." It is easy to see why many readers (including this one) would like it otherwise, would like to reach a "plateau of assurance" and feel some measure of personal satisfaction at having attained it (along with the speaker) after so many false starts and defeated expectations. This is not to say that "Love III" communicates no sense of closure, but that it is a closure which, rather than being earned, is imposed.[56]

Fish's comment on the poem is also an accurate theological rendering of the gospel the poem conveys. Salvation in the poem and in Herbert's theology is always "imposed" and never earned. Human beings never can "get it right," but they are saved anyway. For the Reformers, though, such a realization is not disturbing, as it is to Fish, but it is "good news" to be received with the highest joy and sense of liberation. Reformation theology helps adjust, for a historical critic, some of Fish's inherently subjectivist readings; in doing so, however, it also offers a conceptual, historical basis for some of his discoveries.

Herbert's "Protestantism" is thus well established. The sharp Anglican/Puritan dichotomy still lingers, its inadequacy particularly troubling Herbert scholarship since the poet fits neither stereotype. The most acute critics battle the categories even while they continue to use them (e.g., "It is rather curious that while Herbert would have subscribed to the political and ecclesiastical doctrines of the Laudian Church, his homiletic theory does at several points resemble that of the preachers of the Puritan opposition").[57] At any rate, the importance of specifically Protestant traditions for Herbert's poetry is now clear.

This study, building on the earlier scholarship, seeks to treat Herbert's spirituality in a comprehensive way, focusing on a series of related Reformation doctrines that have specific bearing, formal as well as thematic, on Herbert's poetry. Its purpose is not to place Herbert theologically, nor to align him with any of the doctrinal controversies that he so carefully avoided during his life. Rather, its purpose is to illuminate his poetry by examining some of the basic assumptions of his religious life that also find their way into his poetry. Herbert's assumptions about the human being and God—the conflict between wills, between human depravity and unconditional, irresistible grace—help account for the inner conflict and dynamic of Herbert's verse. Predestination is important thematically, with implications for Herbert's poetic form. For a Calvinist, predestination implies the crucial doctrine of "eternal security," which helps account for the tone of Herbert's poetry, and for the marked differences between Herbert and the other major religious poet of the day, the Arminian John Donne. The chapter on "The Word of God" deals primarily with the theology that underlies both Herbert's imagery—his use of the Bible, his sacramental symbolism, his verbal metaphors—and his vocation as a poet, examining the theory by which God's Word could be conveyed through imaginative human speech. In addition to these specific doctrinal points, Reformation theology requires a certain order of exposition and experience, which is reflected in the sequence of poems in *The Temple*. In the process of justification by faith, law gives way to Christ, just as in *The Temple* the morality of "The Church Porch" gives way to the series of poems on the Passion of Christ. The next stage of the Christian life is sanctification, in which the Christian suffers the conflict between sin and grace, the flesh and the spirit, until the victory of death, apocalypse, and unconditional salvation. Both emotionally and formally, *The Temple* is built upon the assumptions of Reformation spirituality.

Herbert was a poet, not a theologian. Helen Vendler has observed that "in Herbert no human truth or truth of feeling is sacrificed for religious or doctrinal expression."[58] Arnold Stein suggests that "of challenging interest to our own time is Herbert's quiet success in creating lyric forms which endow fixed beliefs, values, and arguments with the full individuality of poetic life and tension."[59] This study does not challenge Herbert's poetic or religious individuality; rather, it is an attempt to define more clearly the "fixed beliefs" that are his starting points in his experience and in his vocabulary. Herbert describes his poetry as "a picture of the many spiritual conflicts that have passed betwixt God and my soul, before I could subject mine to the will of Jesus my master: in whose service I have now found perfect freedom."[60] With poetry of conflict, of religious experience rather than abstract theology, one should not expect either complete consistency or automatic adherence to theological formula. Still, this struggle to submit the will to the will of Jesus, to find freedom not by action but by submission to the active God, what Luther described as "passive righteousness," is at the essence not only of Herbert's poetry but of Reformation spirituality as a whole.

In his "Prayer after Sermon," quoted as the epigraph to this chapter ("The Country Parson," p. 290), Herbert, echoing Romans 8:30, joyfully employs the technical language of Reformation spirituality—"Thou hast elected us, thou hast called us, thou hast justified us, sanctified, and glorified us." Knowing what these terms meant for Herbert is essential in fully understanding him and his poetry. Conversely, understanding Herbert helps recover the experiential side of a vital religious tradition.

— 2 —
"Sinne and Love": The Two Poles of Reformation Spirituality

> Philosophers have measur'd mountains,
> Fathom'd the depths of seas, of states, and kings,
> Walk'd with a staffe to heav'n, and traced fountains:
>   But there are two vast, spacious things,
> The which to measure it doth more behove:
> Yet few there are that sound them; Sinne and Love.
>   —"The Agonie," 1–6

The first sentence of Calvin's *Institutes* sets forth the two broad issues with which Reformation theology was concerned:

> The whole sum in a manner of all our wisdom, which only ought to be accounted true and perfect wisdom, consisteth in two parts, that is to say, the knowledge of God, and of our selves.
>   (*Institutes* 1.1.1.)[1]

Just as Calvin was a distinguished classical scholar, Herbert, as Public Orator of Cambridge University, knew "the ways of learning" thoroughly ("The Pearl," 1); his knowledge of the world, as a Member of Parliament and as a courtier, was undoubtedly both broad and sophisticated.[2] Yet his poetry is circumscribed in its subject matter, so that the scope and range of his poetry are sometimes described as narrow or limited.[3] Herbert's own response to such criticisms is suggested in the epigraph to this chapter. For Herbert, the depths of worldly knowledge are shallow compared to the "vast" depths of human—that is to say, one's own—sinfulness, which is itself swallowed up by the even more "spacious" love of God. Knowledge of human sin and of God's love, both ultimately intersecting in the Passion of Christ, are the focus of Reformation spirituality. Although "few there are

42

that sound them," Herbert in his poetry does sound the depths of self-knowledge and the depths of God's grace, revealing them not as narrow abstractions but as "vast, spacious things" that can fully engage the powers of a master poet. For Herbert, as for the theologians of the Reformation, the concern is exclusively with knowledge of self and knowledge of God, and, most important, the relationship between the two, a knowledge both intellectual and experiential.

Knowledge of God had, of course, always been the province of theology. That self-knowledge is also essential to theology was an innovation or reemphasis of the utmost importance. Medieval religious verse, reflecting the theology of corporate, rather than personal, religious experience, has a sense of selflessness, of anonymity, that is one of its great strengths as religious poetry; but it is in sharp contrast to the "personal" quality that one finds in Herbert's poetry, and in so much of seventeenth-century religious verse.[4] A theology that incorporates knowledge of the self with knowledge of God is intrinsically devotional. When a Jesuit asked an English Protestant, "Where are your books of devotion?", the reply included the theological works of Luther and Calvin.[5] A theology concerned with inner experience as well as abstract knowledge is thus especially useful to poetry. The Reformation doctrines were both highly defined and intensely felt, just as Herbert's poetry is at once highly formalized and deeply personal.[6]

The depravity of the human will and the unconditional love of God are two poles that, together, delimit the theology and the psychology of Reformation spirituality, and they also help define the tension, the conflict, and the resolution of Herbert's verse. The objective doctrines are reflected in Herbert's own understanding of himself and his relationship to God. The intrinsic conflict between the human being and God, resolved by the overmastering intervention of God, represents the core of Reformation spirituality and, as such, it functions as almost a paradigm of George Herbert's verse.

i. Total Depravity and Unconditional Grace

The Protestant emphasis on self-knowledge has no doubt contributed to modern subjectivity and individualism, but self-knowledge for the Reformers was never mere introspection, and it was the opposite of modern self-aggrandizement. "For what man in all the world," asks Calvin, "would not gladly remain as he is—what man does not remain as he is—so long as he does not know himself, that is, while content with his own gifts, and either ignorant or unmindful of his own misery?" (*Institutes* 1.1.1). Knowing oneself is knowing one's weakness, impotence, and "misery," and is in contrast to complacency and pride. It is in this sense of radical honesty and self-awareness that "the knowledge of ourselves not only arouses us to seek God, but also, as it were, leads us by the hand to find him" (*Institutes* 1.1.1). Self-knowledge is itself obtained not by mere introspection but by confrontation with God. "It is certain that man never achieves a clear knowledge of himself unless he has first looked upon God's face, and then descends from contemplating him to scrutinize himself" (*Institutes* 1.1.2). "If it were only a question of the pre-eminent natural endowment of man," says Calvin in another place, "then we might pay regard to the extraordinary gifts which he has received from God; but in so far as he is confronted by God he must crumple up into utter nothingness."[7]

Self-knowledge, paradoxically, is knowledge of one's nothingness; in more technical language, self-knowledge is knowing oneself as a sinner. Sin was understood not so much in terms of external vices or immorality (which may be the "fruit" of sin, just as "good works" were seen as the fruit of a prior inner righteousness) as of an intrinsic inner estrangement from God. This estrangement is such that, according to Luther, "Man cannot of his nature desire that God should be God; on the contrary, he desires that he himself might be God and that God might not be God."[8] The primal rebellion of the Fall[9] is such that it is natural for the human will to assert itself against the will of God. The human will is in bondage to sin. This bondage does not mean that the will and its choices are obliterated. As Calvin explains it, following Luther's distinction between "necessity" and "compulsion," "the will remains, with the most eager inclination disposed and hastening to sin. For man, when he gave himself over to this necessity, was not deprived of will, but of soundness of will." A person will have "sinned willingly, not unwillingly or by compulsion; by the most eager inclination of his heart, not by forced compulsion; by the prompting of his own lust, not by compulsion from without. Yet so depraved is his nature that he can be moved or impelled only to evil" (*Institutes* 2.3.5). Evil, then, is always a function of the active human will. All goodness, on the contrary, comes from the grace of God, who will restrain evil and promote virtue even in unbelievers (3.14.2). "Therefore simply to will is of man; to will ill, of a corrupt nature; to will well, of grace" (*Institutes* 2.3.5).[10]

As Herbert puts it, explaining Valdés with apparent approval, "He means a mans fre-will is only in outward, not in spirituall things" ("Notes on Valdesso," p. 313). The Reformers' rejection of free will is not the same as that of modern determinism. Without questioning commonsensical choices or moral responsibility, the Reformers saw the will as being "in bondage," as Luther terms it, a function of the human being's estrangement from God. This is the sense of Article 10 ("Of Free-Will") of the Anglican Thirty-Nine Articles of Religion:

> The condition of Man after the fall of Adam is such, that he can not turn and prepare himself, by his own natural strength and good works,

to faith, and calling upon God. Wherefore we have no power to do good works pleasant and acceptable to God, without the grace of God by Christ preventing us, that we may have a good will, and working with us, when we have that good will.[11]

According to Aquinas, "the end of our desires is God."[12] Reformation theologians, on the other hand, would deny that human beings really desire God at all; human beings actually desire to be gods themselves, so that their wills are essentially self-serving and in rebellion to the will of God. The desire for God and for His will is itself a manifestation of God's grace, whereby the fallen will is overmastered and remade.

This radical estrangement and rebellion of the human will is, for the Reformers, an introduction to the radical grace of God; the realization of one's sinfulness, the destruction of self-sufficiency, is the only way a person can appreciate, understand, and trust the love of God.

> For we will never have enough confidence in him unless we become deeply distrustful in ourselves; we will never lift up our hearts enough in him unless they be previously cast down in us; we will never have consolation enough in him unless we have already experienced desolation in ourselves. Therefore we are ready to seize and grasp God's grace when we have utterly cast out confidence in ourselves and rely only on the assurance of his goodness. . . . For to the extent that a man rests satisfied with himself, he impedes the beneficence of God. (Calvin, *Institutes* 3.12.8)

If the knowledge of self advocated by Calvin can be summarized as the awareness of sin, the knowledge of God can be summarized as the awareness of grace. To grace, to the direct and undeserved action of God, was ascribed every good thing, from the sustenance of life to the development of arts and sciences (*Institutes* 2.2.14, 16). In particular, however, grace is manifested to the believer as the free gift of salvation. The Gospel, the liberating good news, was that despite the total depravity of the human soul, in Calvin's words, "He comes into our lives taking us just as we are out of pure mercy."[13]

This message of unconditional grace, realized over against the intense awareness of sin, issued in a sense of profound release, a feeling of overwhelming gratitude and adoration. In Herbert's "Prayer Before Sermon," his descriptions of human depravity only heighten the sense of God's incomprehensible generosity:

> O Almighty and ever-living Lord God! Majesty, and Power, and Brightnesse, and Glory! How shall we dare to appear before thy face, who are contrary to thee, in all we call thee? For we are darknesse, and weaknesse, and filthiness, and shame. . . . O write it! O brand it in our

foreheads for ever: for an apple once we lost our God, and still lose him for no more; for money, for meat, for diet: But thou Lord, art patience, and pity, and sweetnesse, and love; therefore we sons of men are not consumed. Thou hast exalted thy mercy above all things, and hast made our salvation, not our punishment, thy glory: so that then where sin abounded, not death but grace superabounded—accordingly, when we had sinned beyond any help in heaven or earth, then thou saidest, "Lo, I come!" ("Prayer Before Sermon," p. 288)

"To be sure," writes Calvin, "all would have been hopelessly lost if the divine Majesty had not condescended to come down to us, seeing that we are not in a position to reach upwards to it" (*Institutes* 2.12.1).[14] That God, out of His love for His hopelessly lost creatures, enters the world in Christ and takes upon Himself the penalty they deserve is, for the Reformers, the definitive fact about His nature. "My God, thou art all love," says Herbert ("Evensong," 29) and with the continual cultivated awareness that one does deserve eternal punishment, the doctrine of "total depravity" serves as a backdrop to accentuate God's boundless generosity and solicitude:

> My God, what is a heart,
> That thou shouldst it so eye and wooe,
> Pouring upon it all thy art,
> As if that thou hadst nothing else to do?
>
> ("Mattens," 9–12)

Herbert is continually celebrating the "superabundance" of God's grace. "Let us . . . poure on him all [the blessings] we can," says God in "The Pulley" (3). In "Gratefulness," Herbert describes how God pours out "Gift upon gift," but human beings are never satisfied—

> . . . much would have more,
> And comes.
>
> (15–16)

Divine grace, the key to all joy and spirituality is, however, a function of the sovereign will of God, not human will. Not everyone is given grace—many are left to the damnation their depravity deserves. Calvin's insistence on this point was largely to establish the wonder of grace when it does come, and the personal, particular quality of God's inscrutable love. Grace is not an impersonal force that functions automatically. Rather, grace is personal, issuing from the volition of a personal God to a particular, marvelously chosen, human being. (The attack on one's self-image in the doctrine of total depravity is countered by the self-esteem fostered by the doctrine of being chosen by God—the psychological implications of the two doctrines cancel or at least balance each other.) The Arminian position that grace is available to everyone, but that it must be chosen by the human will, seemed to the Calvinists to make the human will rather than God's will the active cause of salvation. Arminianism also seemed to depersonalize the whole process of salvation, to make God a collection of conflicting attributes, rather than a person of freedom and will.[15] (In practice, there was little difference in "proclamation of the gospel"; Calvinism agreed that "whosoever will" will be saved [Rev. 22:17], simply that the very will to choose God is a function of grace.) The question of God's fairness in arbitrarily granting His grace to some and denying it to others did not really arise for the early Calvinists. If God were to be "fair," He would damn everyone; He is fair in damning the reprobate (no one has the "right" to be saved)—that He chooses to save anyone is the mystery. That He chooses to save "me" is astonishing. As C. S. Lewis has observed in the passage quoted earlier, the fate of the reprobate did not occupy much of the attention of the early Calvinists. Herbert's "The Water-course" is shocking to modern readers, not only for its doctrine, but for the casual and genial tone in which Herbert articulates the doctrine, extolling the God

> Who gives to man, as he sees fit, $\begin{cases} \text{Salvation.} \\ \text{Damnation.} \end{cases}$
>
> (10)

Even for the believer the soul remains, literally, at the mercy of God. Luther describes grace with a figure also employed by Herbert:

> As the earth itself does not produce rain and is unable to acquire it by its own strength, worship, and power but receives it only by a heavenly gift from above, so this heavenly righteousness is given to us by God without our work or merit. As much as the dry earth of itself is able to accomplish in obtaining the right and blessed rain, that much can we men accomplish by our own strength and works to obtain that divine, heavenly and eternal righteousness. Thus we can obtain it only through the free imputation and indescribable gift of God.[16]

Herbert understands "Grace," in his poem of that title, in identical terms:

> My stock lies dead, and no increase
> Doth my dull husbandrie improve:
> O let thy graces without cease
>   Drop from above!
>
> (1–4)

There can be no righteousness, no "fruits" of good works, apart from the continual grace of God. The estranged soul is dry—"My heart is wither'd like a ground/Which thou dost curse"[17] ("Longing," 8–9). On the other hand, in "The Flower," the "shrivel'd heart" that had gone "quite underground" recovers "greennesse" (8–10), through what was then experienced as "tempests," but is now understood as life-giving rain. Herbert's rendering of the "return" of God in that poem is at once a naturalistic description of the aftermath of a spring storm, a testimony of recovery after despair, and a symbolic description of grace:

> How fresh, O Lord, how sweet and clean
> Are thy returns!
> . . . .
> > After so many deaths I live and write;
> > I once more smell the dew and rain.
> > $(1-2, 37-38)^{18}$

God's overriding grace to the believer, particularly the gift of salvation, is constant, but it is not always experienced. The experience of God's grace can be withheld as freely as it can be granted. Since human will and the Divine will rarely coincide, and in fact tend to be in opposition, grace is not understood as "one's right," as something expected, or owed one by God. "There is no articling with thee," says Herbert ("Artillerie," 31) and grace, however yearned for, always comes as a surprise.

ii. The Self and Grace in Herbert's Poetry

To Reformation thought, the human will and the Divine will are intrinsically opposed, yet they can be reconciled by the intervention of God. Speaking of metaphysical poetry in general, and Donne in particular, William Halewood shows how, in the poetry, "Man's determination to go one way is negated by God's determination that he shall go another."[19] Conflict, which can manifest itself formally in a poem, is assumed by Reformed thought, as is the possibility of sudden reconciliation through an irresistible grace.[20] This conflict between human rebellion and divine grace is portrayed throughout Herbert's poetry; reconciliation comes sometimes in a single poem, other times in the course of a series of poems, but the theological assumptions about the human soul and about God, with the tension between them and the possibility of reconciliation through the action of God, remains constant.

In "Nature," Herbert portrays the Reformation understanding of human depravity in terms of his own self-knowledge:

> Full of rebellion, I would die,
> Or fight, or travell, or denie
> That thou hast ought to do with me.
> > O tame my heart;

> It is thy highest art
> To captivate strong holds to thee.
>
> (1–6)

That Herbert's poetry is full of rebellion ("Affliction [1]"), the desire to die ("Grace"), and even denial that God has anything to do with him ("Deniall"), is no indication that Herbert is wavering in his faith or that his faith is inadequate to his experience. Rather, they illustrate how closely faith and experience come together for Herbert, since such rebelliousness was held by that faith to be inherent in the human soul, forgiven but not eradicated by salvation,[21] and an inevitable part of "Nature." God, though, as in Donne's Sonnet 14, can "captivate strong holds." The continual turmoil of the mind is described in the next stanza:

> If thou shalt let this venome lurk,
> And in suggestions fume and work,
> My soul will turn to bubbles straight,
>   And thence by kinde
>   Vanish into a winde,
> Making thy workmanship deceit.
>
> (7–12)

The poison in the soul, its propensity for rebellion, "lurks," according to the first line; such sin is not always active, but it is always "lurking" in the background. When it is dwelled upon, when "suggestions" draw it out, the rebellion "fumes" in stifled resentment and pride. "Fume," before it became a dead metaphor for repressed rage, originally referred to smoke or to other, usually noxious, exhalations; after exploiting the metaphorical meaning of the word (already common by this time), Herbert returns to the earlier meaning. The "venom" of the first line becomes a poison, or acid, "fuming" in a chemical solution. If God lets this poison continue to boil, "My soul will turn to bubbles straight," until there is nothing left, until the soul with the poison boils away into the air, "vanishes into a winde." The prayer of the next stanza is a confession of the heart's hardness, requiring that either God forcibly inscribe His Law and "fear" of Him in the heart (Heb. 8:10) or "make a new one" (Ezek. 36:26), a conflation of two biblical figures used to describe salvation. The poem is a confession of his own innate incapacity and a prayer for God's action.

"Giddinesse" is another poem on the intrinsic depravity and instability of the human soul.

> Oh, what a thing is man! how farre from power,
>   From setled peace and rest!
> He is some twentie sev'rall men at least
>   Each sev'rall houre.

> One while he counts of heav'n, as of his treasure:
>   But then a thought creeps in,
> And calls him a coward, who for fears of sinne
>   Will lose a pleasure.
>
> Now he will fight it out, and to the warres;
>   Now eat his bread in peace,
> And snudge in quiet: now he scorns increase,
>   Now all day spares.
>
> (1–2)

Human perversity manifests itself in vacillations not only of emotional moods, but of resolutions of the will. "Now he will fight it out" seems to refer to the condition described in the preceding stanza of the sinful thought intruding into his pious reflections. "Coward" in the stanza relates to the metaphor of war in the following stanza, describing not only a spiritual warfare, but the conscience's varying inclination as to its participation in the warfare. When "a thought creeps in," it may be strenuously fought, or it may be quietly tolerated, if not given in to, and both the tempting thought and the various inconstant reactions of the conscience itself testify to the weakness of the soul. After rehearsing more examples of human "giddinesse," Herbert points to both the conflicts and the solution that are fundamental to his poetry:

> Lord, mend or rather make us: one creation
>   Will not suffice our turn:
> Except thou make us dayly, we shall spurn
>   Our own salvation.
>
> (25–28)

Human perversity is such that we would even "spurn/Our own salvation." The "new creation" promised by justification must be continually renewed. God's grace must "make us dayly" or the soul, of itself, will spurn God and even the free gift of salvation. Grace, to have an effect on the totally depraved human nature, must be irresistible.[22]

The doctrine of Irresistible Grace refers specifically to the predestined salvation of an elect soul, a special act of will and power by which the sinner's perverse will is miraculously reoriented to God. On the more ordinary level, of course, human beings do resist God and His grace—that is the definition of sin. Moreover, it is possible to "choose" to follow God, although the volition itself would be interpreted as the gift of God. Those who reject God do so, the Reformers would say, out of their own choice, which, though, is totally predictable given the fact of human sinfulness.

Herbert, in "The Country Parson" (34:283), seems to qualify and expand the conventional Calvinist paradigm of grace:

And all may certainly conclude, that God loves them, till either they despise that love, or despaire of his Mercy: not any sin else, but is within his love; but the despising of Love must needs be without it. The thrusting away of his arme makes us onely not embraced.

In emphasizing God's radical grace, Herbert seems to assert a universal election and to suggest that this grace can be rejected. If so, he is following Luther, whose understanding of grace avoided some of the obvious problematic corollaries of Calvin's system. "It is true that God does not coerce anyone to piety," say the Lutheran confessions, "for those who always resist the Holy Spirit . . . will not be converted."[23] Herbert's statement comes very close to the Lutheran formulation:

The cause of condemnation is that men either do not hear the Word of God at all but willfully despise it, harden their ears and their hearts, and thus bar the ordinary way for the Holy Spirit, so that he cannot work in them; or, if they do hear the Word, they cast it to the wind and pay no attention to it. The fault does not lie in God or his election, but in their own wickedness.[24]

Lutheranism, besides its tolerance for paradox compared to Calvinism's systematic rigor, characteristically treats the experience of salvation from the viewpoint of the human being rather than from the viewpoint of God, as Calvinism tends to. Luther also assumes an organic model of faith, whereas Calvin thinks of a legal-contractual model. For Luther, faith is born, nourished by Word and Sacrament, and if these are "despised," it can die. For Calvin, faith establishes a legal commitment that is irrevocable and binding. Although Herbert is especially fond of the contractual imagery and uses it in a great many of his poems, his sensibility is sometimes closer to the earlier Reformation spirituality, even though the theological influence of Luther was largely replaced by that of Calvin in the seventeenth-century English church.

Still, Herbert's formulation, which emphasizes the action of God, is not Arminian, and it is not necessarily opposed to Calvinism. In the context, "the Parson" is simply trying to assure a Christian of his election. "The despising of Love," the indifference and hostility to spiritual matters, can be seen as the sole mark of the reprobate, whose damnation is always explained in terms of their own will. The damned, whom God chose not to overpower, do thrust God away because they desire to do so. The saved, on the other hand, respond to God's love, not by their own natural will, but by the remade will, created irresistibly as a gift of God. In counseling those unsure of their election, the Reformers were concerned to give assurance, seeing their very anxiety as evidence of grace, since the reprobate would be quite happy to ignore God (see chapter 4). Here the Parson seems to be saying simply that despising God's love and despairing of His mercy are the only sins that could indicate that God's love and mercy are not present. If people do not "despise that Love," they "may certainly conclude that God loves them," since the very openness to God can only come from grace.

At any rate, however Herbert intellectually understood the mysteries of God's action and the human response, his poetry, as William Halewood shows, is consistently "poetry of grace," dramatizing human rebellion reconciled by the intervention of God.

This intrusion of grace into the tumultuous or complacent human soul is reflected again and again in Herbert's poetry and is practically a structural characteristic of his verse. Halewood has observed how Herbert often sets up closed worlds that God suddenly breaks into.[25] In "Artillerie," the speaker's comfortable, insulated repose in his "cell" is bewilderingly broken when a shooting star falls into his lap.[26] The torment expressed in "Deniall," imaged in the poem's formal irregularity, is resolved when God intrudes and "mends my ryme."[27]

The classic example of the collision between the human will's desire for autonomy and the intervening grace of God is "The Collar."

> I struck the board, and cry'd, No more.
> I will abroad.
> What? shall I ever sigh and pine?
> My lines and life are free; free as the rode,
> Loose as the winde, as large as store.

The poem portrays the assertiveness of the human will, desiring autonomy and freedom, divorced from God. The rebellion is not only volitional and moral, but intellectual,[28] as Herbert raises the possibility that his religious impulses come, not from an external God, but from the self.

> Recover all thy sigh-blown age
> On double pleasures: leave thy cold dispute
> Of what is Fit, and not. Forsake thy cage,
> Thy rope of sands,
> Which pettie thoughts have made, and made to thee
> Good cable, to enforce and draw
> And be thy law,
> While thou didst wink and wouldst not see.

> (19–26)

Is the "law" that restricts his "pleasures," with its rulings as to "what is Fit, and not," an artificial construction of the self rather than an eternal, objective demand of God? Are moral restrictions only a "rope of sands," turned by the self into "good cable" that is artificially strong, but actually the construction of "pettie thoughts"? Does the religious and moral life involve "winking" at, or refusing to see this truth? Is not the source of religious life internal rather than external, and therefore should not the self be served?

> He that forbears
> To suit and serve his need,
> Deserves his load.
> But as I rav'd and grew more fierce and wilde
> At every word,
> Me thoughts I heard one calling, *Child!*
> And I reply'd, *My Lord.*
>
> (30–36)

The rebellion melts away at the call of God, who, intervening in the rebellious soul, in a single word of "admonition, acceptance, and love,"[29] effects a response of submission and corresponding love. God's call to His "child" is answered by the recognition of "My Lord," and the proper relationship is thereby restored.

In the vocabulary of Reformed theology, the poem images the "effectual calling," by which God calls the sinner to Himself.[30] The "calling" (35)—the title, of course, is a multilevel pun that includes this sense—is not only an invitation, but it is "effectual." The poem's violent statements and its loose structure that images "the terrible unrest of human self-assertiveness"[31] are themselves resolved as the concluding lines restore metrical, as well as spiritual, order and harmony.[32] God breaks in from the outside, as it were, upon a self that is naturally rebellious, wanting to be its own God. When the true God is experienced, however, the sin is overwhelmed by a love that engenders love as a response. "The Collar" can perhaps be best glossed by Calvin himself, who writes of the human being's "bold and unbridled impulses which contend against God's control. Now, all man's faculties are, on account of the depravity of nature, so vitiated and corrupted that in all his actions persistent disorder and intemperance threaten because these inclinations cannot be separated from such lack of restraint" (*Institutes* 3.3.12). Subsequently, "God designates as his children those whom he has chosen, and appoints himself their Father. Further, by calling, he receives them into his family and unites them to him so that they may together be one" (*Institutes* 3.24.1).

For Herbert, the self, however much it is scrutinized, is always suspect. The human will is intrinsically in conflict with God's will. Resolution comes with the action of God, with the intrusion of a grace that overpowers or melts away all resistance. Human depravity is countered by the grace of God. Reformation spirituality, in all of its complicated structures, is built around these two poles. Law and faith, the double tendency of moralism and antinomianism, the feeling of guilt and self-abnegation balanced by the sense of forgiveness and election, the knowledge that one deserves damnation yet is absolutely assured of salvation—such paradoxes of Reformation spirituality follow from its doctrine of the human being and of God, and they are all manifested in the poetry of George Herbert.

— 3 —
Justification by Faith:
The Theological Sequence of *The Temple*

> First, he preaches the law, and proveth that the whole na-
> ture of man is damned, in that the heart lusteth contrary to
> the will of God. . . . Then preacheth he Christ, the Gospel,
> the promises, and the mercy that God hath set forth to all
> men in Christ's blood; which they that believe, and take it
> for an earnest thing, turn themselves to God, begin to love
> God again, and to prepare themselves to His will, by the
> working of the Spirit of God in them.
> —Tyndale, *The Parable of the Wicked Mammon*

A major issue in George Herbert criticism involves the structure of *The Temple*. Most critics agree that the poems are carefully arranged in a coherent sequence, and that, whether they are ordered according to the architecture of an English church or a Hebrew temple, they reflect an order of Christian experience and the religious life.[1] Herbert's specific understanding of the Christian life was shaped by the theology of his day. Reformation theology, which was particularly concerned with the stages and the process of Christian growth, helps explain the sequence and the ordering of the poems in *The Temple*.

Generally, the spiritual life was held to involve two related and accompanying processes: justification, by which the soul is saved, followed by sanctification, in which the soul is made holy. These two phases of the Christian experience are alluded to directly in the last two lines of "The Altar," the poem that begins and introduces "The Church":

> O let thy blessed SACRIFICE be mine,
> And sanctifie this ALTAR to be thine.

(15–16)

As with the conventional freshman essay in which the last sentence of the first paragraph governs the organization of the essay, these last lines of "The Altar" announce from the very beginning the theological sequence of the poems to follow. Thus, the next poem is entitled "The Sacrifice," which in turn is followed by a series of other poems on Christ and the Atonement. Throughout this first section of *The Temple* Herbert is exploring the relationship between "my hard heart" ("The Altar," 10) and the process by which God lets His "blessed SACRIFICE be mine"—that is, the Reformation doctrine of justification by faith.

The focus of *The Temple* then shifts away from the initial necessity of salvation to the vicissitudes of the Christian experience until death, corresponding to the Reformation doctrine of sanctification. The "hard heart" of the Christian, once justified, must then be broken and remade into something holy, a painful process by which God works to "sanctifie this ALTAR to be thine." (This chapter will discuss the first phase of Reformation spirituality, justification by faith, as it relates to the ordering of *The Temple*. Sanctification will be discussed in chapter 6.)

The doctrine of justification by faith is, according to Rupp, the point of striking unity among Protestants from Luther to Calvin to Hooker;[2] according to Luther "the article of Justification is master and chief, Lord, ruler and judge of every kind of doctrine, and one which preserves and directs every doctrine of the church."[3] Justification, the process of becoming "justified" before God, of becoming accepted despite one's sinfulness, involves both the objective work of God and the inner response of the human being. Archbishop Cranmer, the architect of the *Book of Common Prayer*, refers to three things, "which must concur and go together in our justification":

> Upon God's part, His great mercy and grace; upon Christ's part justice, that is, the satisfaction of God's justice, or price of our own redemption, by the offering of His body and shedding of His blood, with fulfilling of the Law perfectly and thoroughly, and upon our part, true and lively faith in the merits of Jesus Christ, which (faith) yet is not ours, but by God's working in us. . . . Justification is the office of God only, and it is not a thing which we render unto Him, but which we receive of Him; not which we give to Him, but which we take of Him, by His free mercy.[4]

With this insistence on God's initiative, the Reformers taught that in the personal experience of justification, there is the following order: (1) Repentance, in which God gives knowledge of the Law and of one's sinfulness; (2) Faith, in which one attains confidence and trust in the mercy of God as revealed in Christ; (3) Love, in which trust gives way to love of God and His Law.[5] Along with this more or less experiential sequence is the overall structure by which the notion of justification is proclaimed. Tyndale, analyzing the structure of Paul's epistles in the passage quoted as the epigraph to this chapter, sets forth also the logical and rhetorical sequence of Reformation teaching whereby the preaching of the Law is followed by the preaching of Christ. This pattern has already been seen in the discussion of the two poles of Reformed spirituality, in which knowing oneself as a creature of total depravity gives way to knowing God as bearing unconditional grace. Thus it is that in *The Temple*, Herbert begins with a long poem of moral precepts, "The Church-Porch," followed by a series of poems on the atonement of Christ. Herbert first preaches the Law, which, as "The Church-porch," is an essential preparation for the reception of the Gospel of Christ and an eternally valid part of God's "Temple." The Law, however, is introductory to "the church" of the New Covenant, which is the title of the second major section of *The Temple*. "Then preacheth he Christ." The prerequisite of any Christian growth, the concern of most of the later poems, is the response to the historical incarnation and death of Christ, a response defined as justification by faith.

i. The Law

For Reformation theology, it is not true, simply speaking, that good people go to Heaven and that bad people go to Hell. According to the Reformers, there are no good people—salvation is a free gift and can neither be earned nor deserved. Consequently, trust in one's own morality or merit before God is not only deceptive, but may shut out one's true need of forgiveness. Reformation theology revised the traditional relationship between morality and religion. Good works were seen not as conditions for grace, but as results of grace. Just as sinful acts are a symptom of a prior estrangement from God, good works are "the fruits of Faith" (Article 12; "Employment," 25). Since good works come from Christ, it is absurd for a sinful human being to take any credit for them. Moreover, trying to earn salvation by one's good works is self-defeating, since human beings can only fail when faced with God's all-demanding law. Knowing this failure, however, is an important first phase in justification by faith.

The law and morality are important, but they can never, of themselves, bring salvation. Thus Luther stresses the importance of "a precise distinction between these two kinds of righteousness, the active and the passive, so that morality and faith, works and grace, secular society and religion may not be confused. Both are necessary, but both must be kept within their limits."[6] Such a distinction between morality and religion was radical, but it was a logical corollary of the notion that one's own efforts or merit are irrelevant to salvation. Luther denied that he was antinomian, as his critics charged; yet he insisted on distinguishing between the ethical, *per se,* and the religious. Herbert maintains this "precise distinction," consigning his long ethical poem not to "The Church," the division in his volume

dealing with personal religious life, but to "The Church-porch," to a position outside the church itself, keeping the ethical precepts distinct from the
purely religious poems. "The Church-porch" is, however, part of the
edifice, serving theologically as an introduction and as a necessary prelude
to "the Church," just as proclamation of the Law necessarily precedes the
proclamation of grace.

"The Church-porch" is made up of proverbial commonplaces, sometimes profound ethical teaching, and shrewd pragmatic advice about succeeding in the world. This sometimes jarring mixture corresponds to the
first use of the Law, according to Luther, the *usus civilis*.[7] The purpose of
Law on the earthly level is not to justify a sinner before God, but to restrain
evil and to regulate human society.[8] Calvin phrases this understanding
more positively, in a way followed by Herbert. The purpose of civil rule,
according to Calvin, is "to cherish and protect the outward worship of
God, to defend sound doctrine of piety and the position of the church, to
adjust our life to the society of men, to form our social behavior to civil
righteousness, to reconcile us with one another, and to promote general
peace and tranquility" (*Institutes* 4.20.2). Thus Herbert writes about good
manners, social responsibilities, and the church as a social institution—
"how to behave / Thy self in Church" ("Superliminare," 2–3). This social
dimension of Herbert's poem and of Reformation thought will be discussed in chapter 8. The apparent "worldliness" of the poem, and its
exclusion from "the Church" *per se,* are both part of the Reformation understanding of the Law.

Herbert does avoid, though, moralism that is merely bourgeois and self-
serving. The presence of God, though at a distance, looms behind the
precepts—children should be raised with care because they are God's image (102); in giving alms to the poor one can "joyn hands with God to make
a man to live" (376). The secular advice on lust, drinking, swearing, and
wealth is given a deeper resonance because the poet leaves no doubt that at
stake is the eternal soul. God is the author of moral law, however secular or
limited its concerns. The very number of warnings in the poem and the
very often sharp, though unexpected logic of Herbert's advice, showing
the absurdity of sin, attests to the perversity of the human will.

> If God had laid all common, certainly
> Man would have been th'incloser: but since now
> God hath impal'd us, on the contrarie
> Man breaks the fence, and every ground will plough.
>   O what were man, might he himself misplace!
>   Sure to be crosse he would shift feet and face.
>   ("Church-porch," st. 4)

The *usus civilis*, in Reformation thought, gives way to the second use of
the Law, the *usus theologicus*.[10] "Therefore," says Luther, "the true function

and the chief and proper use of the Law is to reveal to man his sin, blindness, misery, wickedness, ignorance, hate and contempt of God, death, hell, judgment, and the well-deserved wrath of God."[10] This essential function of the law, to bring conviction of sin and the kind of self knowledge that for Calvin is essential for knowing God, is implicit in "The Church-porch."

This second use of the law is made explicit in the following poem, "Superliminare," which marks the transition between "The Church-porch" and "The Church." The poem, like the law, contains a threat that seems almost impossible to escape:

> Avoid, Profaneness; come not here:
> Nothing but holy, pure, and cleare,
> Or that which groneth to be so,
> May at his perill further go.
>
> (5–9)

Only righteousness may enter, but those who "groneth to be so" have provision. Still, even the righteous or one who wishes to be righteous may go farther only "at his perill."[11] Stanley Fish points out that the poem first excludes all but the "holy, pure, and cleare," then makes provision for those who lack but earnestly desire righteousness, and then warns both that one may proceed only "at his peril." The poem, says Fish, "proposes conditions and then tells us that they cannot be met, or that if we meet them we are no less subject to the hazards of journeying."[12] The paradox is that of Reformation theology. With perhaps the figure from Gal. 3:24 of the law as a schoolmaster, the poem expresses the essential preparatory function of the law, as it puts the law behind, offering an invitation to a more mystical sweetness:

> Thou, whom the former precepts have
> Sprinkled and taught, how to behave
> Thy self in church; approach, and taste
> The churches mysticall repast.
>
> (1–4)

In the Vulgate and in the Latin writings of Calvin and others, the word for "commandments" is *praecepta*, with the Ten Commandments often referred to as the Ten Precepts.[13] The "former precepts"—the moral advice given in "The Church-porch"—thus stand theologically and structurally, in terms of *The Temple*, for the law. The law, with active human striving, is essential in governing external behavior and social affairs. This secularizing of morality, the emphasis on the *usus civilis* by the Reformers, explains both the "worldly" tone of "The Church-porch" and its exclusion from "The Church" proper. There was also a "third use of the Law," as providing guidelines for Christian behavior. This "third use" was related not to salvation but to sanctification. Christians were expected to be moral, but this was not seen as a condition of salvation but as "the fruit of faith." (That a strong emphasis on grace did, in fact, lead to good works can be sufficiently proven by the fate of the terms "Calvinist" and "Puritan." The very people who put the least emphasis upon human works and merit have become associated with the most scrupulous morality.) With the *usus theologicus*, however, the law brings the essential "knowledge of sin" (Rom. 3:20), the realization that God's demands and one's own spiritual needs cannot be fulfilled by human activity apart from God. This impasse is suggested in "Superliminare," but it must be realized again and again in the religious life, as explored in "The Church." This theological use of the law is part of the spiritual life, because human complacency and self-trust must continually be destroyed.

The problem with trying to attain salvation by one's own good works, of trying to deserve eternal life, is that this very effort can result in a smugness and pride that insulate one from the love and forgiveness of God. "For as long as the presumption of righteousness remains in a man," says Luther, "there remains immense pride, self-trust, smugness, hate of God, contempt of grace and mercy, ignorance of the promises and of Christ. The proclamation of free grace and the forgiveness of sins does not enter his heart and understanding, because that huge rock and solid wall, namely, the presumption of righteousness by which the heart itself is surrounded, prevents this from happening."[14]

In "Humilitie," Herbert shows, in a comical, satirical vein, how in a fallen human being even virtue is tainted, in that it can so easily result in pride. In the poem, the allegorical "Vertues" receive tokens of submission from the various beasts, representing the human passions. The Vertues enforce decorum quite firmly in dealing with "the angrie Lion," "the Fearful Hare," "the jealous Turkie," and so on, but although they can control the passions, the Vertues themselves "fall out" in an unseemly scuffle for the Peacock plume, representing Pride.

> At length the Crow bringing the Peacocks plume,
> (For he would not) as they beheld the grace
> Of that brave gift, each one began to fume,
> And challenge it, as proper to his place,
> Till they fell out: which when the beasts espied,
>   They leapt upon the throne.

> (17–24)

The poem describes the paradox that it is human virtues that are most liable to result in pride, the most deadly of sins. The Vertues, each fuming over "that brave gift . . . as proper to his place," contend with each other so that the passions again rule and the courtly order described in the first two stanzas disintegrates, with Mansuetude, Fortitude, Temperance, and Justice, so nobly introduced, rolling on the floor in an undignified brawl. Only the tears of Humilitie can bring the Vertues to their senses so that they can drive out the beasts. The passions are essentially tractable; the turmoil comes not from the beasts but from the Vertues. Herbert's comic allegory makes the point of how easily human virtue turns to pride, and how the *sine qua non* of virtue is humility and a repentant spirit (which tears invariably represent for Herbert), a humility that is thereby open to God, against whom even virtue can be used as a barrier.

The theological function of the law is supremely illustrated in "Miserie." The speaker describes the utter perversity of humankind.

> Lord, let the Angels praise thy name.
> Man is a foolish thing, a foolish thing,
> Folly and Sinne play all his game,
> His house still burns, and yet he still doth sing,
> *Man is but grasse,*
> *He knows it, fill the glasse.*
>
> (1–6)

The indifferent tone of the last line in light of the somber fact of the stakes involved in human mortality is an example of "folly" that is developed throughout the poem. God demands temperance, but, Herbert remarks incredulously, "why he'l not lose a cup of drink for thee" (8). Human beings sin as if they thought God could not see them sinning. "No man shall beat into his head, / That thou within his curtains drawn canst see" (15–16). The poem then develops the idea of human unworthiness to stand before God.

> My God, Man cannot praise thy name:
> Thou art all brightnesse, perfect puritie;
> The sunne holds down his head for shame,
> Dead with eclipses, when we speak of thee:
> How shall infection
> Presume on thy perfection?
>
> As dirtie hands foul all they touch,
> And those things most, which are most pure and fine:
> So our clay hearts, ev'n when we crouch
> To sing thy praises, make them less divine.
>
> (31–40)

"Man cannot serve thee; let him go" (43). The poem continues in this vein for five more stanzas, in what Reformation theologians would see as accurate descriptions of human depravity. Man is

A lump of flesh, without a foot or wing
To raise him to the glimpse of blisse:
A sick toss'd vessel, dashing on each thing;
Nay, his own shelf:
My God, I mean my self.

(73–78)

The final line of the poem is a startling turn, in which the moral invective, at the interjection "My God," is suddenly and devastatingly applied, not to generalized humanity but to "my self." The external focus condemning other people collapses into a moment of self-discovery. As Calvin insists, one truly recognizes oneself only in confrontation with God. The law, properly used, leads not to abstract moralizing, but to the conviction of sin.

The earlier manuscript version of the poem is significantly entitled "The Publican,"[15] a title that underscores the improper and dangerous use of the law as it complicates and gives added resonance to the poem. The speaker in the poem is inveighing against the sins of humanity, but thereby incurs the danger of the Pharisee in Jesus' parable:

Two men went up into the temple to pray; the one a Pharisee, and the other a publican. The Pharisee stood and prayed thus with himself, God, I thank thee, that I am not as other men are, extortioners, unjust, adulterers, or even as this publican. I fast twice in the week, I give tithes of all that I possess. And the publican, standing far off, would not lift up so much as his eyes into heaven, but smote upon his breast, saying, God be merciful to me a sinner. I tell you, this man went down to his house justified rather than the other: for every one that exalteth himself shall be abased, and he that humbleth himself shall be exalted. (Luke 18:10–14)

The Pharisee's good works cannot "justify" him; only the publican, conscious of his need for mercy as a "sinner," is "justified." The final line of the poem unexpectedly exposes the danger of hypocrisy that is implicit but not recognized throughout the poem. The pattern in the poem is similar to St. Paul's great treatise on the law in Romans. After a catalogue of sins, Paul suddenly indicts not only the sinners but also those who judge them, and on the same grounds:

Therefore thou art inexcusable, O man, whosoever thou art that judgest: for wherein thou judgest another, thou condemnest thyself; for thou that judgest doest the same things. (Rom. 2:1)

The law is valid—the poet's invective against sin is accurate, just as is the Pharisee's denunciation of extortion and adultery. The proper response to the law, however, is neither pride and trust in one's own good works, nor denunciation of the sins of others, but, as with the publican, recognition of oneself as a sinner and one's own need for mercy.

In "Self-condemnation" Herbert undercuts even the tendency to judge the slayers of Christ.

> Thou who condemnest Jewish hate,
> For choosing Barabbas a murderer
> Before the Lord of Glorie;
> Look back upon thine own estate,
> Call home thine eye (that busie wanderer)
> That choice may be thy storie.

>   (1–6)

Herbert then rehearses the ways human beings choose the world ("an ancient murderer," 10) over Christ: you cannot blame the Jews since you also, in your worldliness, choose Barabbas over Christ; you also sell Christ for money, just as Judas did, in your greed and selfishness. Herbert then recalls the point made by St. Paul that even in judging the executioners of Christ, we "judge our selves" (20), leaving us, in the words also of St. Paul "without excuse" (24). The title refers to this self-condemnation of Rom. 2:1, but it also has another sense. The pronouns in the poem shift from second person (the directly accusatory "Thou" in the first stanza) to third person (the more hypothetical "He that . . ." construction in the next two stanzas) to the first person plural ("Thus we prevent the last great day, / And judge our selves" of the final stanza). The poem concludes by involving the speaker himself in the condition he has been attacking. The poem indicts those who judge others without recognition of their own sinfulness, but is not the poet, in inveighing against hypocrites, thereby in danger of the same hypocrisy? The title of the poem, though, is "self-condemnation." Judgment is made to rebound on the one who judges, in this case the poet himself, as indicated by the title. The poem takes its own advice. As with "The Publican," the title indicates a complex awareness of the double danger of sin and of pharisaism. The law, though essential, results in an impasse, issuing not in righteousness, but in awareness of oneself as a sinner.

Herbert's theological understanding of the law is depicted also in "Sinne [1]," where he employs a surprise ending similar to that in "Miserie" in suddenly relocating and internalizing the law:

> Lord, with what care hast thou begirt us round!
>   Parents first season us: then schoolmasters
>   Deliver us to laws; they send us bound
> To rules of reason, holy messengers,
> Pulpits and Sundayes, sorrow dogging sinne,
>   Afflictions sorted, anguish of all sizes,
>   Fine nets and stratagems to catch us in,
> Bibles laid open, millions of surprises,

Blessings beforehand, types of gratefulnesse,
  The sound of glorie ringing in our eares:
  Without, our shame; within, our consciences;
Angels and grace, eternall hopes and fears.
  Yet all these fences and their whole array
  One cunning bosome-sinne blows quite away.

Parents, schoolmasters, ministers "deliver us to laws," but the elaborate structures, both social and psychological, that guard one from sin, the external "fences" that "begirt us round," are blown away, not from outside as expected, but from inside the fortress, by a single sin. The danger is not from without but from within. The greatest safeguards, the severest threats, or the most generous promises of reward cannot prevent a fallen soul from sinning. When this is realized, when the locus of sin is recognized not as being from without, but from within one's own "bosome," then the solution may be recognized.

ii. Christ

Following the pattern of Reformation thought, the preaching of the law ("The Church-porch") is followed by the preaching of Christ (the series of poems on Jesus culminating in "Easter Wings"). The understanding of grace, of free forgiveness, is not separable for the Reformers from the historical incarnation and atonement of Christ, who gave Himself up to suffer and die at the hands of sinners.[16] In the poems on the passion of Christ, the fact of human sin is intensified as it is portrayed as the cause and means of Christ's agony, the suffering of which is the supreme example of God's love and free, unmerited grace. The human response to Christ's passion, developed in the poems along with the narrative, signals the response to Christ that was defined by the Reformers as justifying faith. This series of poems is unified not only thematically and logically, but formally as well, as the poems repeat, comment upon, and respond to the preceding poems, melding the series into a very tight theological unity.

After the poem of the law, "The Church-porch," and the introductory "The Altar," comes "The Sacrifice," a long poem that is in many ways the keystone of Herbert's *Temple*, just as its subject is the keystone of Christian theology. In this poem human sinfulness and depravity are heightened, as human action is directed against the suffering Christ. It is clear, however, that Christ does not have to suffer—He remains, in every stanza of the poem, the omnipotent God, who by His will subjects Himself to human will, that is, to sin. The tensions in the poem are not only between Christ and His tormentors, but between Christ's passivity and His omnipotence, a tension accounted for in the poem by the evocation of a boundless grace that overrides everything that His tormentors deserve.

The poem portrays the awesome inversion implicit in the doctrines of the Incarnation and the Atonement. "I suffer binding, who have loos'd their bands" (47). Christ, "who all things else command[s]," obeys Herod. What is thereby highlighted is the sinfulness of humankind, the perversity of the apostle who valued an ointment at three hundred coins and was willing to sell his master for only thirty (13–20), the "spite" of "Mine owne deare people" who prefer a murderer to the Prince of Peace (101–20).[17] The congruent descriptions of Christ's divinity and generosity only intensify the sense of human sin and of judgment.

> They buffet me, and box me as they list,
> Who grasp the earth and heaven with my fist,
> And never yet, whom I would punish, miss'd:
> > Was ever grief like mine?
>
> > > (129–32)

Rosemond Tuve shows the undercurrent threat of judgment that runs throughout the poem. The sense that divine punishment is both deserved and possibly imminent is a major theme of the poem,[18] but the emphasis throughout seems to be on the fact that the punishment is not given, that God does not defend Himself, nor treat the offenders as they obviously deserve. In nearly every stanza, the contrast is between the malice of His tormentors and the corresponding generosity of God. They spit on Christ, whose own spittle healed the blind (133–36); they give Christ vinegar, who gave them manna (237–40); they tear up Christ's mantle, which healed the sick (241–44). This "disparity between man's behavior toward God and God's behavior toward man"[19] reveals at the same moment not only humanity's radical sinfulness, but God's radical grace. Moreover, the manifestations of human sinfulness toward Christ are often allusions to the types and symbols of redemption.

> With clubs and staves they seek me, as a thief,
> Who am the way of truth, the true relief;
> Most true to those, who are my greatest grief:
> > Was ever grief like mine?
>
> > > (37–40)

Ironically, it is appropriate that they seek Him, who is the Way (John 14:16). The rabble, in crying for Christ's crucifixion, "wish *my blood on them and theirs*" [Matt. 27:25] (107).

> See how spite cankers things. These words aright
> Used, and wished, are the whole worlds light:

> But hony is their gall, brightnesse their night:
> Was ever grief like mine?
>
> (109–12)

The words that have been taken as a curse (and as a justification for anti-Semitism), Herbert points out, are exactly the appropriate response. Appropriation of the blood of Christ, with the acknowledgment of personal responsibility for sin implicit in the statement, is precisely how sin is expiated. Those who crucify Christ, however, fail to distinguish honey from gall, light from darkness—they "know not what they do" (Luke 23:34)—and Herbert brilliantly exploits the consequent irony. Scornfully, the soldiers array Christ in a scarlet robe ("Which shews my bloud to be the only way" [158]), put on His head a crown of thorns (Adam's curse [165–68]), and cry *"Hail King"* (173).

> Yet since mans scepters are as frail as reeds,
> And thorny all their crowns, bloudie their weeds;
> I, who am Truth, turn into truth their deeds.
>
> (178–80)

The sarcasm of the soldiers in calling Him King is doubly ironic since their intended sarcasm turns out to be truth. Despite their "scoffes or scornfulnesse" (174), Christ turns their deeds into truth, as the garments intended as insults become both types of salvation and symbols of human weakness, which Christ puts on. The taunts at the cross are similarly "turned into truth." When He is mockingly asked to "come down," He replies, "Alas, I did so, when I left my crown" (221–22) in Heaven. Being executed with robbers, He comments that He is, in fact, a thief—"What have I stollen from you? death" (231). Throughout the poem are references to the Old Testament types of salvation—the Paschal lamb (59), the emancipation from Egypt (10), the manna (6, 11, 239), the water struck from the rock (122, 169–71), types of salvation applied very directly to Christ's executioners.[20]

Herbert renders human sin and Christ's sufferings in such a way that the rebellious human will is subsumed into God's plan of salvation. Herbert, in a typical Reformation emphasis, ascribes the crucifixtion itself to God's sovereignty over all events.

> The Princes of my people make a head
> Against their Maker: they do wish me dead,
> Who cannot wish, except I give them bread:
> Was ever grief like mine?
>
> (5–8)

They wish Christ dead, but they cannot even wish apart from the gift of God. "They use that power against me, which I gave" (10). Herbert continually uses the word *give,* emphasizing with Calvin that every single faculty of life is due to the grace of God.[21]

> Then they condemn me all with that same breath,
> Which I do give them daily, unto death.
>
> (69–70)

The very breath by which Christ is sentenced to death is itself His gift. The pathos of the poem, in which Christ's blood is "curing all wounds, but mine; all, but my fears" (27), is not negated, but rather intensified by the realization that Christ is still in control. In the poem, "God holds his peace at man, and man cries out" (187). Despite the hints of punishment and even reprobation, that God's grace is selectively denied to some while others receive it (133–35, 141–43), the point throughout the poem is the contrast between active human sin against God and the unconditional love of Christ, who is precisely "Most true to those, who are my greatest grief" (39).

This opening series of poems on Christ is punctuated by poems of response, so that there is an interplay in "The Church" between the historical events of Christ and the individual soul's appropriation of them. "The Sacrifice" is followed by "The Thanksgiving," which portrays a personal reaction to Christ's passion as it alludes to and comments on the previous poem (as in its discussion of the preceding poem's refrain in 1–10). Although in "The Thanksgiving" and in the following poem, "The Reprisall," the soul has an impulse to outdo Christ or to pay Him back for His suffering, to earn salvation, both poems emphasize that Christ's suffering and atonement are so complete that there is nothing more to be done.

> Shall I be scourged, flouted, boxed, sold?
> 'Tis but to tell the tale is told.
>
> (7–8)

Scourging and so on are punishments due to sin, but Christ has already suffered them for the speaker. Despite the frenetic desire to "do something" in response to Christ's passion, Herbert indicates the futility or irrelevance of any human works in light of Christ's death.

> Then for thy passion—I will do for that—
> Alas, my God, I know not what.
>
> (49–50)

Just as Christ has been treated in an opposite way to what He deserved, so will the sinner:

> Shall thy strokes be my stroking? thorns, my flower?
> Thy rod, my posie? crosse, my bower?
>
> (13–14)

Herbert's second poem on Christ, "The Agonie," similarly defines both sin and love in terms of the single atonement of Christ:

> Philosophers have measur'd mountains,
> Fathom'd the depths of seas, of states, and kings,
> Walk'd with a staffe to heav'n, and traced fountains:
>   But there are two vast, spacious things,
> The which to measure it doth more behove:
> Yet few there be that sound them; Sinne and Love.
>
> Who would know Sinne, let him repair
> Unto Mount Olivet; there shall he see
> A man so wrung with pains, that all his hair,
>   His skinne, his garments bloudie be.
> Sinne is that presse and vice, which forceth pain
> To hunt his cruell food through ev'ry vein.
>
>   (1–12)

The seriousness of sin can be known only by the seriousness of its cure. Sin is what torments Christ, what caused His agony in the Garden. It is the pressure, rendered by Herbert in almost psychological terms, that made Christ sweat blood.

> Who knows not Love, let him assay
> And taste that juice, which on the crosse a pike
> Did set again abroach; then let him say
>   If ever he did taste the like.
> Love is that liquour sweet and most divine,
> Which my God feels as bloude; but I, as wine.
>
>   (13–18)

Both sin and love are defined by the blood of Christ. What God experiences as suffering—human sin taken on out of love at the Atonement—the human soul receives back as the sweetness of grace. Blood is transformed, for the Christian, into wine (a Protestant sacramental symbol reversing the traditional figure of wine transforming into blood). On God's part is the suffering for sin; all the Christian need do, according to Reformation theology, is to receive God's love. The figure answers the previous question in "The Thanksgiving" (13–14) affirmatively: His strokes at the scourging are to be "my stroking," a caress; His thorns, "my flower"; His blood, the sinner's wine.

Following "The Agonie" is "The Sinner." As if in answer to the former poem's "Who would know Sinne" (7), "The Sinner" portrays the knowledge of personal sin that Calvin says is essential. The soul contains "But shreds of holiness, that dare not venture / To show their face" (6–7). Even one's holiness cannot stand before God. For Calvin, sin was such as to damage even the image of God, in which human beings were created:

Therefore, even though we grant that God's image was not totally an-
nihilated and destroyed in him, yet it was so corrupted that whatever
remains is frightful deformity. Consequently, the beginning of our recovery of salvation is in that restoration which we obtain through Christ.
(*Institutes* 1.15.4)

The prayer in "The Sinner," "Lord restore thine image" (12), not only
echoes Calvin's understanding of sin but marks "the beginning of our
recovery of salvation," as Christ's death, the subject of this sequence of
poems, is being appropriated by the speaker who is commenting on and
responding to them.

After the acknowledgment of sin in "The Sinner" is a poem on the cure
for sin, "Good Friday," a meditation on the enormity of Christ's "grief,"
recapitulating the refrain of "The Sacrifice" as a solution for sin. The poem
ends in a prayer, with the classical Protestant emphasis, for Christ to dwell
in his heart:

> Sinne being gone, oh fill the place,
> And keep possession with thy grace.
> (29–30)

The following poem, "Redemption," depicts the Reformation's complex
understanding of the human condition and the action of Christ. The colloquial rhythm and the unserious tone of the poem belie the real seriousness
of the quest:

> Having been tenant long to a rich Lord,
>   Not thriving, I resolved to be bold,
>   And make a suit unto him, to afford
> A new small-rented lease, and cancell th'old.
>
> (1–4)

"Not thriving" under the Old Covenant of the law is an understatement,
reflecting not so much "knowledge of sin" as personal unease. The pilgrim
seeks the Lord in heaven, but he is not there, so he seeks him in all the
places appropriate for a "rich Lord"—"In cities, theaters, gardens, parks,
and courts" (10). The search for God, though, whether in Heaven or on
earth, is futile insofar as the seeker depends upon his own efforts. It is the
human will that desires the "great resorts"—God's will is something different. The search for God is inherently thwarted by the seeker's misdirected
will.

> At length I heard a ragged noise and mirth
>   Of thieves and murderers: there I him espied,
>   Who straight, *Your suit is granted*, said, & died.
>
> (12–14)

After searching futilely in all the wrong places, he finds his lord where he leasts expects him—among sinners. He is saved, as it were, despite and even previous to his efforts. The Lord could not be found "In heaven at his manour" (5) because he had already left for earth. As Patrick Grant points out, when the speaker finally does see his lord, his "request is granted before he has time to make it."[22] The lord dies before the supplicant can even speak, thereby granting the request in a way contrary to what the speaker could expect, and at the same time anticipating or "preventing" his very search. The ironies are those of God's foreknowledge and predestination, as the rather complacent tenant's casual random search ends with Christ finding him and granting his request by dying.

In "Sepulchre," in which Herbert returns to the narrative sequence of the passion, the historical description of Christ's burial merges with personal appropriation of Christ's death, becoming a meditation on grace.

> O blessed bodie! Whither art thou thrown?
> No lodging for thee, but a cold hard stone?
> So many hearts on earth, and yet not one
>   Receive thee?
>
>   (1–4)

The rejection of Christ at the crucifixion is conflated with the sinner's exclusion of Christ. In the poem, Herbert develops his earlier theme of the heart's harboring transgressions and "thousands of toyes," with little room for Christ ("The Sinner"). The hardness of the human heart is such that even stones are more willing and more appropriate to receive Christ.

> And as of old, the law by heav'nly art
> Was writ in stone, so thou, which also art
> The letter of the word, find'st no fit heart
>   To hold thee.
>
>   (17–20)

The stanza alludes to Christ's being able to write the law in the tables of stone (Exod. 31:18), but it does not yet allude to the law written "in fleshy tables of the heart" (2 Cor. 3:3). There is no heart fit, yet, as so often in Herbert, the final lines reveal a solution even as they intensify the sense of human depravity.

> Yet do we still persist as we began,
> And so should perish, but that nothing can,
> Though it be cold, hard, foul, from loving man
>   Withhold thee.
>
>   (21–24)

Grace, in this poem, is irresistible. The human heart obstinately and perversely persists in its self-destructive sin, excluding Christ, and in fact,
murdering him (11–14). Yet it is impossible, ultimately, to exclude Christ.
That the "cold, hard, foul" heart could do so, would argue a potency that it
does not have. Though "our hard hearts have took up stones to brain thee"
(13), Christ's love cannot be thwarted, even by the sin that put Him to
death. That no heart is fit (19), that all deserve to perish (22), cannot
withhold Christ from loving man. His love is coupled with power that, in
the final line, breaks into the poem, demolishing all of the objections to His
coming that make up most of the poem.[23]

The preceding poems, depicting not only Christ's passion but the speak--
er's interaction and involvement with the atonement of Christ, involve
what Calvin calls "participation in Christ" and "partaking in his death"
(*Institutes* 3.3.9). The Easter poems that follow not only complete the series
on the life of Christ, but signal the justification of the believer. "If we share
in his resurrection," says Calvin, "through it we are raised up into newness
of life to correspond to the righteousness of God" (*Institutes* 3.3.9).

> Rise heart; thy Lord is risen. Sing his praise
>   Without delayes,
> Who takes thee by the hand, that thou likewise
>   With him mayst rise:
> That, as his death calcined thee to dust,
> His life may make thee gold, and much more, just.
>   ("Easter," 1–6)

The heart, described as harder than stone in the preceding poem, "Sepulchre," has been "calcined to dust" and, just as it has been buried with
Christ (or rather, in terms of the previous poem, Christ has been buried in
it), it can "share in his resurrection." Christ, in the Divine initiative, "takes
thee by the hand," and in so doing, by the spiritual alchemy of the atonement, turns the "stone" of the heart into gold. The three components of
justification referred to by Cranmer are complete, in terms of *The Temple*,
with this poem—the grace of God, the work of Christ, and the response of
faith. The believer, by faith in the atonement of Christ, is made "just" (6).

The remainder of "Easter" is a celebration of the resurrection, and also a
song of praise for justification that looks forward to the rest of *The Temple*.
Christ on the Cross, described with such pathos in the earlier poems, from
this perspective is described in a very different way:

> Awake, my lute, and struggle for thy part
>   With all thy art.
> The crosse taught all wood to resound his name,
>   Who bore the same.

His stretched sinews taught all strings, what key
Is best to celebrate this most high day.

(7–12)

The grisly figure of the tautness of Christ's body stretched on the cross is conflated with the stretching of the strings on a lute. The agony of the crucifixion, in light of the resurrection and the victory of salvation, is transformed into joyous music. This inversion of tone from the earlier poems applies also to the attitude toward the Reformation doctrine of the sufficiency of Christ's atonement. Whereas "The Thanksgiving" expresses a perhaps ironic frustration that the speaker's desire to grieve, weep, and suffer for Christ has been already accomplished for him, here again Christ precedes him, but the tone is lyrical and celebratory:

I got me flowers to straw thy way;
I got me boughs off many a tree:
But thou wast up by break of day,
And brought'st thy sweets along with thee.

(19–22)

That Christ has "got up" before he did, and that Christ brings his own "sweets," so that offerings of flowers or of anything else are not really needed, are here far from being a matter for frustration. The very cosmos can add nothing to Christ.

The Sunne arising in the East
Though he give light, & the East perfume;
If they should offer to contest
With thy arising, they presume.

(19–22)

The "Contest" with Christ's passion described in "The Reprisall"—"Yet thy wounds still my attempts defie" (7),—the attempt to measure off good works against Christ's sacrifice, is thus revealed, gently, as presumption.

"Easter" is also a poem about poetry. The poet responds to the resurrection of Christ, which makes his heart "just" (6), by means of art:

Awake, my lute, and struggle for thy part
With all thy art.

(7–8)

Struggle and art are conjoined in Herbert, as critics have observed,[24] and the poem suggests that the source of his music, with its agony and joy, its conflict and its order, is the figure of Christ, crucified, as it were, on the lute. ("The crosse taught all wood to resound his name, / Who bore the same. / His stretched sinews taught all strings, what key / Is best.") Herbert conceived his poetry as a means of participation with Christ (see "The Quidditie," 11–12).

> Consort both heart and lute, and twist a song
> Pleasant and long:
> Or since all music is but three parts vied
> And multiplied;
> O let thy blessed Spirit bear a part;
> And make up our defects with his sweet art.
>
> ("Easter," 13–19)

As in other of Herbert's poems on his poetry, the heart must be involved with the music, as is God Himself:

> Whereas if th'heart be moved,
> Although the verse be somewhat scant,
> God doth supplie the want.
>
> ("A true Hymne," 16–18)

The lines in "Easter" refer to God's "part" in the song, the trinity in the chord, Christ's sinews in the lute string. The arts and sciences, according to Calvin, themselves come from the grace of God, as another example of His all-giving power and involvement in the world (*Institutes* 2.2.14–16), and here the response of praise is itself indistinguishable from God's working. The musical metaphor refers also to the process of justification and sanctification, by which God "makes up our defects with his sweet art." God's art is the process by which he "makes up our defects," the plan of salvation that He works upon the soul. "It is thy highest art / To captivate strong holds to thee" ("Nature," 5–6). The "song / Pleasant and long" that Herbert plans, in conjunction with God's art, can refer not only to the song within the poem (of 19–30), but to *The Temple* itself, which rehearses in various ways the event and its significance celebrated in this poem:

> Can there be any day but this,
> Though many sunnes to shine endeavour?
> We count three hundred, but we misse:
> There is but one, and that one ever.
>
> (27–30)

Christ's resurrection, by which "we are raised up into newness of life," is underscored by "Easter-wings," which in the first stanza relates the resurrection to the fall of Adam, and in the second, the steps by which that fall and that salvation are reiterated in the speaker's own life. The poems on baptism are meditations on God's prevenient grace—"Thou didst lay hold, and antedate / My faith in me" ("H. Baptism [2]," 4–5)—the rite being seen in the Protestant sense as a seal of salvation, that even before an infant can make a decision, God acts in the sacrament of baptism to engraft the child to Himself, and it is thus an important promise that salvation is now assured:

> In you Redemption measures all my time,
> And spreads the plaister equal to the crime.
> You taught the Book of Life my name, that so
> Whatever future sinnes should me miscall,
> Your first acquaintance might discredit all.
>   ("H. Baptism [1]," 10–14)

The justified soul has been written in the book of Life. Whatever happens from this point, salvation is secure, and any future sins are already forgiven.

This poem points forward in an important way to the more difficult experiences described in the poems that follow. Calvin's discourse on rebirth in Christ, in which he speaks of sharing in Christ's resurrection (*Institutes* 3.3.9) points out that such regeneration is a continual process, and Calvin follows immediately with a series of sections to the effect that believers, though saved, are still sinners (*Institutes* 3.3.10–15) and that "there still remains in them a continuing occasion for struggle whereby they may be exercised and . . . better learn their own weakness" (*Institutes* 3.3.10). Similarly, the poems of justification and baptism are followed in *The Temple* by "Nature," "Sinne (1)" and "Affliction (1)." The process these poems describe—the struggles of sanctification, the next phase of the Christian life—will be discussed in a later chapter, but the subsequent poems in *The Temple* continually refer back to this first series, to the fact of Christ's atonement, to the prior experience of justification, and to the consequent assurance of salvation "Whatever future sinnes should me miscall."

iii. The Imputation of Righteousness

Elsewhere Herbert focuses on specific aspects of the doctrine of justification by faith. Thus the poem "Faith" expresses in a tone of bemused wonder the paradoxes of grace:

> I owed thousands and much more:
> I did beleeve that I did nothing owe:
> And liv'd accordingly; my creditor
> Beleeves so too, and lets me go.
>   (13–16)

"Faith puts me there with him, who sweetly took/Our flesh and frailtie, death and danger" (23–24). "If blisse had lien in art or strength, / None but the wise or strong had gained it" (25–26). As it is, "grace fills up uneven nature" (32).[25] The poem also alludes to a doctrine that is common to Herbert's poetry and important in Reformation theology:

> When creatures had no reall light
> Inherent in them, thou didst make the sunne
> Impute a lustre, and allow them bright,
>   And in this shew, what Christ hath done.

> (33–36)

With justification, Christ's righteousness is "imputed" to the one who clings in faith to Him. Christ indwells the believer and the believer is engrafted into Christ, so that God in judgment sees not the sinner but Christ. God declares the believer righteous, looking not at his sins, but at Christ's merit, which the believer is able to claim. Just as to Christ is imputed the believer's sin, so to the believer is imputed Christ's righteousness.[26]

This doctrine is why, in "Judgement," the poet is able to write so light-heartedly on the traditionally harrowing prospect described in the first stanza:

> Almightie Judge, how shall poore wretches brook
>   Thy dreadfull look,
> Able a heart of iron to appall,
>   When thou shalt call
> For ev'ry mans peculiar book?

> What others mean to do, I know not well,
>   Yet I heare tell,[27]
> That some will turn thee to some leaves therein
>   So void of sinne,
> That they in merit shall excell.

> But I resolve, when thou shalt call for mine,
>   That to decline,
> And thrust a Testament into thy hand:
>   Let that be scann'd.
> There thou shalt finde my faults are thine.

When the book of his deeds is required, rather than looking for "some leaves" that might be void of sin, he will turn in a New Testament. He can claim the record of Christ's deeds as recorded in the Gospels as his own before the Almighty Judge. Moreover, his own sins have themselves been claimed by Christ ("there thou shalt finde my faults are thine") who alone is to judge the earth (John 5:22). "No mean assurance, this," comments Calvin, "that we shall be brought before no other judgement seat than that of our Redeemer, to whom we must look for our salvation!" (*Institutes* 2.16.18). The "Testament" is not only the record of Christ's righteousness and atonement, but the Covenant between God and humanity by which the relationship is assured. The poem can be best glossed by Calvin:

> But when consciences are disquieted as to how they can find God gracious, what they are to answer and what can be the ground of their confidence, when they are summoned before the judgment seat of God, there they should not begin to calculate the requirements of the law but must plead as their righteousness the one Christ who surpasses all the perfection of the law. (*Institutes* 3.19.2 [Niesel])

The contrast between the prospect of a horrible judgment and the release from fear through the imputation of Christ is similarly portrayed in "Justice (2)."

> O Dreadfull Justice, what a fright and terror
> Wast thou of old,
> When sinne and errour
> Did show and shape thy looks to me,
> And through their glasse discolour thee!
> He that did but look up, was proud and bold.
>
> The dishes of thy ballance seem'd to gape,
> Like two great pits;
> The beam and scape
> Did like some torturing engine show;
> Thy hand above did burn and glow,
> Daunting the stoutest hearts, the proudest wits.
>
> But now that Christs pure vail presents the sight,
> I see no fears:
> Thy hand is white,
> Thy scales like buckets, which attend
> And interchangeably descend,
> Lifting to heaven from this well of tears.
>
> For where before thou still didst call on me,
> Now I still touch
> And harp on thee.
> Gods promises have made thee mine;
> Why should I justice now decline?
> Against me there is none, but for me much.

The final line alludes to Romans 8, the great text of justification and assurance:

If God be for us, who can be against us? . . . who shall lay any thing to the charge of God's elect? It is God that justifieth. Who is he that condemneth? It is Christ that died, yea rather, that is risen again, who is even at the right hand of God, who also maketh intercession for us. Who shall separate us from the love of Christ? (Rom. 8:31ff.)

What before seemed an instrument of torture now seems like buckets in a well ("of tears," i.e., repentance), descending in judgment only to lift up again to heaven. The law of justice is not completely done away with for the Reformers; rather, their interest was on its function. "Before thou still didst call me"—the law, in its full weight, is important in "calling" the sinner to Christ, in fact, in lifting him up to Heaven. The horror of the law is due to seeing it through the "glasse" of "sinne and errour" (3–4). Seeing it through "Christs pure vail," he sees the beauty of the law. The hand of justice is not burning (11); it is only white (15) in its purity, although from the perspective of sin such purity would be experienced as burning. With Christ as an intercessor and with God's promises, there is no reason to decline justice (or the law of the Old Covenant), which now is to be touched, dwelt upon, and celebrated. Christ outweighs human sin, and the balance is now in the believer's favor.[28] Seeing the law through "Christs pure vail" seems to suggest the symbol of "putting on Christ" as a garment, which is the common symbol for the imputation of righteousness. The figure in the poem is of a person looking out at the law. The law is not veiled; rather, the speaker is veiled by Christ.

Luther distinguishes between "active righteousness," that of the law, and "passive righteousness," in which the believer simply allows Christ to work in him. "Resting in Christ" is difficult, since the self perversely insists upon law, desiring to be justified through its own efforts, bearing its own guilt. Faith involves self-surrender to an active God, trusting Christ to forgive sins and to produce the "fruit" of good works, apart from fear, guilt, and self-righteousness. "Resting in Christ" is a favorite metaphor of Herbert, expressing the ideal relationship between the soul, weary with futile activity, and the radically active, solicitous God, in whom the believer, by the self-surrender of Faith, can enjoy the security and peace of unconditional grace, allowing God to do the work requisite for salvation. Attaining this kind of surrender is a theme throughout *The Temple*, culminating in "Love (3)." "Rest" as a metaphor for "passive righteousness" occurs in isolated poems throughout *The Temple*. In "H. Communion," Herbert writes of God "Making thy way my rest" (9). In "Trinitie Sunday," the prayer is "That I may runne, rise, rest with thee" (9) (the normal order of a day would involve rising first, but Herbert is making the metaphors align structurally with the persons of the Trinity developed throughout the poem—"rise" corresponds to the Son, the Redeemer; "Rest" to the Holy Spirit, the Comforter and Sanctifier). In "The Pulley," "rest" is to be found only with God. Behind Herbert's use of the term is the profound corollary of justification by faith. According to Calvin, "Christ died and rose again that we might have eternal Sabbath . . . that we might rest from our own human works and allow the spirit of God powerfully to work within us."[29]

In "Even-song," the figure of rest as a metaphor for the ideal relationship between the soul and God receives its most extensive development. The poem is a celebration of the evening and hence, of the rest and sleep brought by night. As is typical of Herbert, another level of meaning is operating throughout.

> Blest be the God of love,
> Who gave me eyes, and light, and power this day,
> Both to be busie, and to play
> But much more blest be God above,
>   Who gave me sight alone,
> Which to himself he did denie:
> For when he sees my waies, I dy:
> But I have got his sonne, and he hath none.
>
> (1–8)

God gives everything—eyes, light, power, the ability to work and to play are all seen as direct gifts of God, what Calvin would call "common grace." By the fourth line, the meditation shifts to the "special grace" of God's saving purpose in Christ.[30] The figure of Christ healing the blind is contrasted with a complex figure of God denying sight to Himself. The line alludes to the incarnation and the crucifixion, with perhaps a reference to what happened at the crucifixion—"the sun was darkened" (Luke 23:45), introducing also the characteristic play "sun/son" that Herbert is so fond of. In the context of the stanza, the line refers to the imputation of righteousness, whereby God does not "see my waies"; rather, the believer's sins are "hid" in Christ (Col. 3:3; see also Herbert's poem of that title). In giving up his "sun," God graciously leaves Himself in darkness; the believer, however, has the "sun," so that the darkness of "my waies" is canceled by Christ's light. The meditation on the close of the day thus becomes also a meditation on Christ and on salvation:

> What have I brought thee home
> For this thy love? have I discharged the debt,
> Which this dayes favour did beset?
> I ranne; but all I brought, was fome.
>   Thy diet, care, and cost
> Do end in bubbles, balls of winde;
> Of winde to thee whom I have crost,
> But balls of wilde-fire to my troubled minde.
>
> (9–16)

He has paid nothing back for these favors. He tried, but in vain—"all I brought, was fome." God's graces, lavished on him, "end in bubbles, balls of winde." God receives only "winde" in return, but the futile efforts are "balls of wilde-fire to my troubled minde," as the conscience, desiring so much to show gratitude to God, is tormented by its failures. This is a note sounded deeply and often in Herbert's poetry. The impulse to pay God back is a natural response to God's generosity and can be a proper motivation for good works as a response to grace. Nevertheless, this impulse can also turn into a rejection of the kind of rest God's grace requires, a substitution of "active" for "passive righteousness." In the soul tormented by "wilde-fire," God intervenes:

> Saying to man, *It doth suffice:*
> *Henceforth repose: your work is done.*
>
> (19–20)

As in "The Collar," God's solicitous, overwhelming grace brings recognition as to who God is, and a response of submission that restores the relationship:

> My God, thou art all love.
> Not one poore minute scapes thy breast,
> But brings a favour from above;
> And in this love, more than in bed, I rest.
>
> (29–32)[31]

"Aaron" is Herbert's most comprehensive treatment of the theme of justification by faith. The first stanza depicts God's ideal, expressed in terms of the symbolism of Aaron's garments.

> Holinesse on the head,
> Light and perfections on the breast,
> Harmonious bells below, raising the dead
> To leade them unto life and rest:
> Thus are true Aarons drest.
>
> (1–5)

The invocation of Aaron, the priest of the Old Covenant, and the expressed need for his garments and the purity they symbolize, corresponds to the Reformation understanding of the law. Complete moral purity, insisted upon by the law, is necessary in order to be acceptable to God. This fact must be realized before one can accept the New Covenant. Thus, "Aaron" begins by "preaching the law," the response to which signals its function, the *usus theologicus:*

Profanenesse in my head,
Defects and darknesse in my breast,
A noise of passions ringing me for dead
Unto a place where is no rest:
Poore priest thus am I drest.

(6–10)

Contrasting himself with Aaron, the speaker point by point measures himself against the law, a procedure reinforced by the structure of the poem, which allows complete parallelism through its repeated rhyme words. On Aaron's head is the symbol of holiness; in the "Poore priest's" head is "profanenesse." In place of "light and perfections," the speaker's heart contains "defects and darknesse"; in the place of harmony, noise. Instead of leading others to salvation, the speaker feels himself headed for judgment, for eternal death in hell—"a place where is no rest." After this rigorous exercise in self-knowledge, with its horrible conclusion, the alternative of Christ is lifted up.

Onely another head
I have, another heart and breast,
Another musick, making live not dead,
Without whom I could have no rest:
In him I am well drest.

(11–15)

The speaker, not denying the condition of his own head, breast, and so on, realizes that he has another head, that he has been engrafted into Christ (Col. 1:18–22). "Justified by faith is he," says Calvin, "who, excluded from the righteousness of works, grasps the righteousness of Christ through faith, and *clothed in it*, appears in God's sight not as a sinner but as a righteous man (*Institutes* 3.11.2 [my italics]). Aaron's garments do not fit; Herbert changes to Calvin's and St. Paul's metaphor of being clothed in Christ.[32]

Christ is my onely head,
My alone onely heart and breast,
My onely musick, striking me ev'n dead;
That to the old man I may rest,
And be in him new drest.

(16–20)

Sanctification, the process of dying to self and clinging more and more to Christ, is signaled in this stanza in which Christ becomes "my *onely* head," "my *onely* musick," and with a double emphasis "my *alone onely* heart and breast." The "old man" of sin (Eph. 4:22), is being suppressed, as faith, as dependence on Christ, increases.

> So holy in my head,
> Perfect and light in my deare breast,
> My doctrine tun'd by Christ, (who is not dead,
> But lives in me while I do rest)
> Come people; Aaron's drest.
>
> (21–25)

The perfections described in the first stanza, are reiterated and fulfilled in the final stanza, just as Christ fulfilled the Old Law not only in his own righteousness, but in the righteousness He bestows on those who have faith in Him. Still, there is a change. The substantives of the first stanza—"Holiness," "light and perfections"—become adjectives. The speaker does not *have* holiness, but he *is* holy. He does not have perfection, but he is perfect. The distinction is that between righteousness that is possessed and righteousness that is imputed and internalized. The internalization of the external law is also signified by the shift in prepositions from "on" ("Holinesse on the head"), to "in" ("So holy in my head").[33] Similarly, there is a shift in emotion. The word *light* is identical as a noun and as an adjective, but in the final stanza, yoked with *Perfect,* it is an adjective, and can only mean that the speaker's heart now feels "light." The burden of sin and the law (with all of its heavy turbans, robes, and metalwork) is gone, replaced with a feeling of "lightness" (by means, of course, of the "light" that is Christ, who now indwells the believer). The self-condemnation of the beginning of the poem, entirely appropriate for the Reformers and necessary for the later emotional release, is transformed, for the speaker can now speak of "my deare breast." The new psychological self-acceptance signified by the adjective "deare" applied, for once, to himself[34] comes from the experience of being loved by Christ, and of loving Christ, of accepting the freedom from guilt that the Atonement offers.

Christ "is not dead"—the allusion to the resurrection implies not only Christ's resurrection within the regenerate soul as in "Easter," but also his continued activity, as He "lives in me while I do rest." The self does not have to "work," to struggle in either good deeds or self-condemnation. Good works come not from self-oriented activity, but from surrender of the human will to the will of Christ, which is accomplished not by striving, but by submission. "Rest" in the poem involves both resting "to the old man" (19), of allowing Christ to "strike dead" (18) the unregenerate nature, and the more positive resting in Christ, of active trust and faith in Christ's work and indwelling presence.

The poem, in conveying both the sequence of justification and some of its most subtle nuances, can be aptly glossed by John Calvin:

This is a wondrous way of making just, so to clothe the lost with the righteousness of Christ that they are not afraid when faced by the judgement which they deserve, and while they themselves rightly condemn themselves, they find that they are declared righteous in virtue of some authority outside themselves. (*Institutes* 3.11.11 [Niesel])

They "rightly condemn themselves," as Herbert condemns himself throughout *The Temple*, but "they are not afraid." The "making just," the being "declared righteous," is accomplished by "some authority outside themselves," just as in Herbert's poetry God figuratively intervenes in the self with an often surprising declaration. In "Aaron," the complicated Reformation doctrines of the law, conviction of sin, justification by faith, imputation of righteousness, and "resting in Christ" coalesce, the complicated interrelationships still intact, as Herbert forms them into poetry.

— 4 —
"Unspeakable Comfort": The Doctrine of Predestination

The godly consideration of Predestination and our Election in Christ, is full of sweet, pleasant, and unspeakable comfort to godly persons, and such as feel in themselves the working of the Spirit of Christ, mortifying the works of the flesh, and their earthly members, and drawing up their mind to high and heavenly things, as well because it doth greatly establish and confirm their faith of eternal salvation to be enjoyed through Christ, as because it doth fervently kindle their love towards God.
—Article 17 of *The Thirty-Nine Articles of Religion* of the Church of England

The doctrine of predestination, that God chooses whom He will save and effects that salvation by His power over all things, including the human will, was seen by most early Reformed theologians as a corollary of justification by faith. If human merit or effort means nothing in salvation, it follows that salvation is caused solely by God. It was also clear for Calvin, although Luther and other theologians would not go this far, that since not everyone is saved, God must have chosen not to save them, since He can override even the most sinful will (God's refusal of salvation to some was termed "reprobation"). The understanding of salvation by grace, itself an example of God's absolute sovereignty over the universe, merged with a doctrine of God's providence that ascribed literally everything to God's action.

Although predestination is popularly identified solely with John Calvin, the doctrine, in some form, has been common in Christian theology. Various teachings in the Bible stress God's sovereignty over all events, especially those having to do with salvation. The theology of predestination, as a corollary of grace, was worked out in detail by Augustine, from whom Calvin borrowed the greater part of his doctrine. Thomas Aquinas, no less than Calvin, argued for predestination, reprobation, election, and a form of perseverance, insisting that the number of those who would be saved is already fixed.[1] To some theologians, such as Ambrose, Origen, and Jerome, predestination meant simply that God could foresee the merit that human beings would acquire. Aquinas went farther, emphasizing the causality of predestination, teaching that God does predestine to life or to destruction, insofar as He determines to bestow His grace so that salvation can be merited. Calvin differed from Aquinas in a significant way by rejecting the concept of merit altogether, insisting upon an "unconditional election," whereby there are no conditions whatsoever upon God's "free gift" of salvation, offered not to those who merit it, but to sinners.

Calvin's major innovation in the doctrine, differing from both Aquinas and Augustine, is in turning predestination into a doctrine of assurance. If salvation is based not on human choice, but on God's, then it is impossible to fall from grace, to lose one's salvation, so that whatever sins or doubts a believer falls into, God will nevertheless complete His work of sanctification and will receive the believer into Heaven. It is in this sense that the Church of England held predestination to be a doctrine of "unspeakable comfort."

Walton says of Herbert's friendship with Lancelot Andrewes that "there fell to be a modest debate betwixt them two about predestination and sanctity of life."[2] Andrewes was an Arminian, so that if there was a debate, Herbert would be taking the Calvinist position.[3] For Herbert, predestination was a corollary of grace, and the foundation of the believer's assurance. Herbert's sense of security before God, in such contrast to the Arminian Donne, is related directly to Calvin's doctrine of predestination and the perseverance of the saints. Calvin's related idea of God's sovereignty over all events is central to Herbert's portrayal of the relationship between God and His creation. Moreover, the assumption of predestination manifests itself in the form and the strategy of many of his poems.

i. Providence and God's Sovereignty

The doctrine of predestination involves mainly an understanding of salvation. Calvin went farther in developing the implications of God's sovereignty and in applying predestination to the relationship between God and the creation. Calvin was radical in assigning every seemingly contingent or "natural" event to the direct causality of God. In this regard, Herbert followed Calvin almost point by point. Herbert's nature poetry, his sense of how the world is governed, and his understanding of the meaning of contingent events, are all informed by his view of divine providence.

"To make God a momentary Creator," says Calvin, "who once for all finished His work, would be cold and barren, and we must differ from profane men especially in that we see the presence of divine power shining as much in the continuing state of the universe as in its inception" (*Institutes* 1.16.1). Similarly, Herbert's Parson, in reasoning with an atheist, "conceives not possibly, how he that would beleeve a Divinity, if he had been at the Creation of all things, should lesse beleeve it, seeing the Preservation of all things; for Preservation is a Creation, and more, it is a continued Creation, and a creation every moment" ("Country Parson," 34:281). In his chapter "The Parson's Consideration of Providence," Herbert lists three categories by which God's power is exerted "in everything which concerns man": (1) "sustaining power" by which "he preserves and actuates every thing in his being; so that corne doth not grow by any other vertue, then by that which he continually supplyes, as the corne needs it"; (2) governing power, by which, for example, God arranges the seasons, the weather, and so on, for the corn to grow; (3) spiritual power, "by which God turnes all outward blessings to inward advantages" ("Country Parson," 30:270–71).[4] Similarly, Calvin asserts not only that God is the sustaining Creator, but that "he is also everlasting Governor and Preserver—not only in that he drives the celestial frame as well as its several parts by a universal motion, but also in that he sustains, nourishes, and cares for, everything he has made, even to the least sparrow" (*Institutes* 1.16.1 [Matt. 10:29]). Herbert's first two categories are the same as Calvin's, and the third is implicit in the *Institutes*. Like Herbert, Calvin insists that even the most "natural" processes, such as the growing of food and the sustenance of animals, are to be seen as instances of God's direct, providential care for His creatures (*Institutes* 1.16.7).

Herbert's understanding of nature is thus far different from that of his brother Edward, the forerunner of Deism. Calvin explicitly rejects the idea of a God who created the universe only to leave it to run its course. God does not "idly observe from heaven what takes place on earth," but rather, "he governs all events" (*Institutes* 1.16.4).[5] In "The Church Militant," "The smallest ant or atome knows thy power" (3).[6] The infinity of a God who governs every single detail of the universe simultaneously is perhaps a key to Calvin's continual insistence that God and His ways cannot be fully comprehended by the radically limited human mind. "And truly God claims, and would have us grant him, omnipotence—not the empty, idle, and almost unconscious sort that the sophists imagine, but a watchful, effective, active sort, engaged in ceaseless activity" (*Institutes* 1.16.3). The intricacy of God's management, the vastness and variety of His continual working, and yet His solicitude in listening to one person's prayer is celebrated in "Praise (3)":

> Thousands of things do thee employ
> In ruling all
> This spacious globe: Angels must have their joy,

> Devils their rod, the sea his shore,
> The windes their stint: and yet when I did call,
> Thou heardst my call, and more.
>
> (19–24)

Herbert's long poem "Providence" is his most extensive development of the theme. Michael McCanles cites the regularity of the poem's form (pentameter quatrains rhyming abab)—a regular, traditional form of the sort Herbert seldom used—played against enjambment and continual shifts of caesura, "thereby imitating the natural world's asymmetry under God's mastering it in total harmony."[7] For Herbert, the natural world is not orderly in the sense defined by eighteenth-century philosophers—Nature is not symmetrical or simple and there is no attempt at an "argument from design." Rather, what Herbert is celebrating in the poem is Nature's asymmetry, its superfluity, its lavish differences. Nature illustrates for Herbert not a cosmic watchmaker, but a God who is incomprehensibly active and utterly free in what He does:

> To show thou art not bound, as if thy lot
> Were worse than ours, sometimes thou shiftest hands.
> Most things move th'under-jaw; the crocodile not.
> Most things sleep lying; th'Elephant leans or stands.
>
> (137–44)

Exceptions are testimonies of God's freedom, so that His creation exuberantly defiies human categories. "Frogs marry fish and flesh; bats, bird and beast; / Sponges, non-sense and sense; mines, th'earth & plants" (135–36). This incredible diversity, however, is governed and made harmonious by the "skill and art" of God.

> We all acknowledge both thy power and love
> To be exact, transcendent, and divine;
> Who dost so strongly and so sweetly move,
> While all things have their will, yet none but thine.
>
> For either thy command or thy permission
> Lay hands on all: they are thy right and left.
> The first puts on with speed and expedition;
> The other curbs sinnes stealing pace and theft.
>
> Nothing escapes them both; all must appeare,
> And be dispos'd, and dress'd, and tun'd by thee,
> Who sweetly temper'st all. If we could heare
> Thy skill and art, what musick would it be!
>
> (29–40)

Herbert's line, "All things have their will, yet none but thine," expresses the essence and the paradox of God's control. The contingency of natural causes, and even ostensibly free human choices, are all nevertheless directed by God and integrated into His plan. In the poem Herbert demonstrates how the diversity of nature is nevertheless made harmonious:

> Sheep eat the grasse, and dung the ground for more:
> Trees after bearing drop their leaves for soil.
>
> (69–70)

The plenitude of creation is such that even opposites can coexist, each with its own purpose:

> How harsh are thorns to pears! and yet they make
> A better hedge, and need less reparation.
> How smooth are silks compared with a stake,
> Or with a stone! Yet make no good foundation.
>
> (121–24)

Calvin says that "the universe was established especially for the sake of mankind" (*Institutes* 1.16.6), and in Herbert's poem God's planning of nature is expressed in terms of mankind's benefit. The human will also, paradoxically, is governed by God's providence.

> O sacred Providence, who from end to end
> Strongly and sweetly movest, shall I write,
> And not of thee, through whom my fingers bend
> To hold my quill?
>
> (1–4)

The very physical act of writing the poem Herbert ascribes to providence, which is thus both the subject and the creator of the poem. In the *Institutes* Calvin continually insists upon both human responsibility and God's sovereign purpose. Herbert's paradox, "while all things have their will, yet none but thine," is similar to that of Augustine, quoted by Calvin, whereby God "does with the very wills of men what he wills."[8] Although this poem celebrates God's providential control of nature, its understanding of God's effective will and His overall governing and harmonizing of ostensible chaos is applicable as well to how God governs the human being.

"God so attends to the regulation of individual events, and they all so proceed from his set plan," says Calvin, "that nothing takes place by chance" (*Institutes* 1.16.4). Again, he insists that "Nothing happens except what is knowingly and willingly decreed by him" (*Institutes* 1.16.3). The concepts of chance and fortune are rejected (*Institutes* 1.16.2). Something of Calvin's attack on fortune may be suggested in "The World":

> Love built a stately house; where *Fortune* came,
> And spinning phansies, she was heard to say,

That her fine cobwebs did support the frame
Whereas they were supported by the same:
But *wisdome* quickly swept them all away.

(1–5)

Although it may appear that fortune supports the world, in fact, fortune itself is supported by the "frame" built by love. The visual image Herbert sets up—do the cobwebs hold the frame together, or does the frame hold the cobwebs together?—could be accounted for in terms of either fortune or providence. Both would explain the evidence, if fortune were not of such insubstantial material in contrast to the solid frame of the house built by love. Calvin makes a distinction between points of view in explaining the appearance of chance. "However all things may be ordained by God's purpose and sure distribution, for us they are fortuitous" (*Institutes* 1.16.9). From the human perspective one does experience chance happenings, but behind them is the solidity of what God has built. Fortune is illusory, a function of merely human "phansies," which are swept away by *"wisdome."*

Just as the doctrine of God's providence rules out the possibility of chance, it also rules out the idea that everything is governed by general, dependable laws of nature.[9] Thus, Herbert observes that country people tend to assume "that all things come by a kind of naturall course; and that if they sow and soyle their grounds, they must have corn; if they keep and fodder well their cattel, they must have milk, and calves." The Parson, on the other hand, "labours to reduce them to see Gods hand in all things, and to believe, that things are not set in such an inevitable order, but that God often changeth it according as he sees fit, either for reward or punishment" ("Country Parson," 30:270).[10] The hand of providence is thus seen not merely in the orderliness of things, as in later world views with their assumptions of a mechanistic universe and a purely transcendent deity, but most especially in their disorder. Herbert refers any "accident" to the direct working of God. "If God have sent any calamity either by fire, or famine, to any neighboring Parish," the Parson assembles his people "and exposing to them the uncertainty of humane affairs, none knowing whose turne may be next, and then when he hath affrighted them with this, exposing the obligation of charity" ("Country Parson," 19:253). Herbert further describes the purpose of such unexpected actions of God:

And it is observable, that God delights to have men feel, and acknowledg, and reverence his power, and therefore he often overturnes things, when they are thought past danger; that is his time of interposing: As when a Merchant hath a ship come home after many a storm, which it hath escaped, he destroys it sometimes in the very Haven; or if the goods be housed, a fire hath broken forth, and suddenly consumed them. Now this he doth, that men should perpetuate, and not break off their acts of dependence. ("Country Parson," 3:271)[11]

Again, what human beings truly need is to depend upon God. For this reason, God "overturnes things," so as to destroy human complacency and self-sufficiency.

The danger of Calvin's doctrine of providence, which ascribes every single action in some way to the will of God, is that it comes close to suggesting that God causes evil, and that the human will, with its responsibility, is obliterated. Indeed, not only are natural occurrences governed by God, according to Herbert, but also the policies of nations, as in "The Church Militant":

> Almightie Lord, who from thy glorious throne
> Seest and rulest all things ev'n as one:
> The smallest ant or atome knows thy power,
> Known also to each minute of an houre:
> Much more do common-weals acknowledge thee,
> And wrap their policies in thy decree,
> Complying with thy counsels, doing nought
> Which doth not meet with an eternall thought.
>
> (1–8)

Calvin admits that even "thieves and murderers and other evildoers are the instruments of divine providence, and the Lord himself uses these to carry out the judgments that he has determined with himself" (*Institutes* 1.17.5). Yet Calvin strenuously insists that the evildoers are still responsible for their actions. In regard to evil deeds, God "by no means commands us to do them; rather we rush headlong, without thinking what he requires, but so raging in our unbridled lust that we deliberately strive against him. And in this way we serve his just ordinance by doing evil, for so great and boundless is his wisdom that he knows right well how to use evil instruments to do good. . . . Thus, since the matter and guilt of evil repose in a wicked man, what reason is there to think that God contracts any defilement, if he uses his service for his own purpose?" (*Institutes* 1.17.5). In other words, according to Wilhelm Niesel, in the exercise of divine providence, "God takes into account the fact that we are men gifted with reason and will-power. All that we are able to devise and set in motion is integrated into His plan."[12]

This same tension between divine causality and human responsibility is at the heart of Calvin's most controversial doctrine, reprobation. If salvation is contingent solely upon God's will toward those He has chosen, it follows that condemnation likewise depends upon God's will and choice. If there is a predestination to eternal life, based on God's election, there must also be a predestination to damnation, based also on God's election. Such a conclusion was rejected by the Lutherans and was carefully avoided in the Thirty-nine Articles of the Church of England. Herbert, though, concurs, although very cautiously, with Valdés, who insisted that "Neither *Pharaoh*, nor *Iudas*, nor those who are *vessels of wrath*, could cease to be such." Comments Herbert: "This doctrine however true in substance, yet needeth discreet, and wary explaining" ("Notes on Valdesso," pp. 313–14). Herbert seems to assume reprobation in the conclusion of "The Watercourse," in which God "gives to man, as he sees fit, $\begin{cases} \text{Salvation.} \\ \text{Damnation.''} \end{cases}$

Yet the poem, as well as Calvin's doctrine, is more complex than it appears. Calvin insists that God is just to the reprobate, that they receive no punishment that they do not deserve.[13] What Calvin focuses on throughout his thought is that although everyone deserves to be damned, God inexplicably gives some of them eternal life. Salvation is not owed to anyone; it is always a free gift. There is no question of God's not being fair in that He does not save everyone: rather, He would be fair if He condemned everyone. Salvation is the abrogation of justice; reprobation, the carrying out of what is fair. Thus, again, sin and its consequent punishment were regarded as functions of the human will, for which the individual has full responsibility. In the words of a contemporary scholar, "Damnation, as it were, is entirely man's doing; but salvation belongs essentially to God."[14] On one hand is God's election; on the other, human choice. Calvin affirms both poles of the paradox, as does Herbert in "The Watercourse."

> Thou who dost dwell and linger here below,
> Since the condition of this world is frail,
> Where of all plants afflictions soonest grow;
> If troubles overtake thee, do not wail:
> For who can look for lesse, that loveth $\begin{cases} \text{Life?} \\ \text{Strife?} \end{cases}$
>
> (1–5)

Herbert's alternate line endings imply that the condition of the world is appropriate for both those who love "Life" and those who love "Strife." That the world is "frail," that the fertility of its living plants is outmatched by the growth of afflictions, places the world in opposition to those who love life. "If troubles overtake thee . . . who can look for lesse?" Those who love life only "linger here below" anyway; troubles are to be expected, not bewailed. Similarly, "who can look for lesse, that loveth Strife?" They have what they love. The condition of the world, its instability and violence, is simply the outcome of that strife which some persons consciously pursue. There is a hint of reaping what one sows in the expression of troubles "overtaking" the one who loves strife. The human condition is miserable for lovers of strife because they deserve it and because a world of conflict is, by definition, what they love. The human condition is miserable for lovers of life because, by definition, they can never be satisfied in a world of death. The condition of misery is the same for both; the difference is that lovers of strife are at home in it. The problem is how those who love life may find an escape from the world of death.

But rather turn the pipe and waters course
To serve thy sinnes, and furnish thee with store
Of sov'raigne tears, springing from true remorse:
That so in pureness thou mayst him adore,
Who gives to man, as he sees fit, $\begin{cases} \text{Salvation.} \\ \text{Damnation.} \end{cases}$

(6–10)

Herbert's metaphor of branching pipes of water is itself paralleled in Calvin:

Water is sometimes drunk from a spring, sometimes drawn, sometimes led by channels to water the fields, yet it does not flow forth from itself for so many uses, but from the very source, which by unceasing flow supplies and serves it. In like manner, the flesh of Christ is like a rich and inexhaustible fountain that pours into us the life springing forth from the Godhead into itself. Now who does not see that communion of Christ's flesh and blood is necessary for all who aspire to heavenly life? (*Institutes* 4.17.9)

Those who "aspire to heavenly life"—that is, those who love life in Herbert's poem—receive it when Christ "pours into us the life springing forth from the Godhead." The water in the poem thus symbolizes not only grace, but life, the same life that is aspired to in the first stanza. Interestingly, the human being himself must "turn the pipe," whereupon "waters course / To serve thy sinnes," the verb *course* suggesting the rapidity, eagerness, and abundance of grace and of its source. Even tears of repentance are thereby "furnished" for him, and they are "sov'raigne tears" (tears of the sovereign), "springing from true remorse" ("was ever grief like mine?"). Repentance is itself a gift—the tears of repentance are themselves from Christ, and a function of the purifying water that is grace and life.

The last line is startling in its effect. The human being is said to "turn the pipe," and the life-giving water "courses" accordingly. Now, with the final line it is stated that the tap is actually controlled by God. As Calvin says elsewhere, again using the same metaphor that Herbert must have borrowed, channels of water call to mind their source: "God may sufficiently witness his secret grace to us, provided only the pipe, from which water abundantly flows out for us to drink, does not hinder us from according its due honor to the fountain" (*Institutes* 3.24.3). God ultimately controls the flow of water—from His end, as it were—although from the human perspective there is the experience of choosing and acting to appropriate grace. The poem thus portrays two choices: on the human side, between life and strife, and on God's part, between salvation and damnation. God's choice is prior; in the terms of the metaphor, God must open the valve before any water can be conveyed. The pipes are full; from the earthly point of view, the "call" is extended to everyone, but only those who love "life," who have a prior desire for the water, will respond to the means of salvation offered by Christ.[15]

God's gift is prior to its appropriation. In terms of the poem, "Salvation" is both parallel to and synonymous with "Life"; "Damnation" similarly corresponds to "Strife." In the poem, those who love life receive it as salvation, and those who love strife receive it as damnation. Both are "gifts" of God, contingent only upon His will—given "as he sees fit." Calvin and Herbert would not see any unfairness in God's giving damnation to the reprobate. "If troubles overtake thee, do not wail: / For who can look for lesse, that loveth strife?" Even those who love life can look for no less. What the poem focuses on is the marvelous fact that God chooses to save anyone. Paradoxically, if someone is saved, the responsibility is God's. If someone is damned, the responsibility belongs to the self. The emphasis in the poem is how "waters course / To serve thy sinnes"; the difficult doctrine of reprobation is only casually mentioned, but it does not imply, for Herbert, that God is responsible for sin. That responsibility for damnation, although not salvation, rests with the self is made clear in the poem immediately following. "Self-condemnation," after rehearsing the ways in which Christ is rejected, concludes with a symbol of the Last Judgment:

> Thus we prevent the last great day,
> And judge our selves. That light which sin & passion
> Did before dimme and choke,
> When once those snuffes are ta'ne away,
> Shines bright and cleare, ev'n unto condemnation,
> Without excuse or cloke.
>
> (19–24)

The light that saves is also the light that damns. Yet, at the same time, we "judge our selves" and remain "without excuse or cloke."

For Herbert, God is sovereign, active in every detail of the world's—even a rebellious world's—governance, and He is the first and final cause of salvation. Calvinism may minimize human freedom, but it does so to exalt God's freedom, as expressed in the plenitude and even the apparent randomness of His creation, no less than in His free choice of whom to save.

ii. The Perseverance of the Saints

Although predestination, when logically pursued, leads to difficult doctrines such as reprobation, it originally had a much different function and was perceived as a doctrine that could offer absolute assurance of salvation. Developments within the Calvinist tradition itself unsettled this assurance, obscuring the fact that Calvin saw himself as writing for "poor consciences that seek steadfast assurance of eternal life" (*Institutes* 1.7.1 [Norton]).[16] The theology of grace, with its corollary of predestination, promised the believer a salvation that could not be lost, issuing in feelings not of insecurity—of worrying whether one was of the elect or not—but of confidence.[17] As a modern church historian observes, "Salvation in which man has even the smallest hand is thereby invested with a degree of doubt. But salvation which from beginning to end is entirely the work of God is invested with complete assurance: God's work, it cannot fail or be frustrated."[18] "It is impossible," writes Calvin, "that those who really belong to the elect people should finally perish or sink unsaved. For their salvation is founded on such sure and firm bases that, even if the whole structure of the world tottered, that certainty itself could not dissolve. . . . The elect can no doubt sway or fluctuate, nay even fall; but they will not perish because the Lord will always stretch out His arm to save them."[19] In "Miserie," Herbert castigates the human race for its perversity, but even here he writes of the doctrine of perseverance:

> They quarrell thee, and would give over
> The bargain made to serve thee: but thy love
> Holds them unto it, and doth cover
> Their follies with the wing of thy milde Dove,
>   Not suff'ring those
>   Who would, to be thy foes.
>
>   (25–30)

However much human beings, even the elect, will rebel at serving God, His love "Holds them unto it," covering their sins, and, by His sovereign control, does not allow them to be His enemies even if they want to be.

It is one of the great ironies of theological history that a doctrine once established to assure the believer of salvation eventually worked to unsettle that assurance. Whereas the old insecurity would involve worrying about dying in a state of mortal sin and going to hell, the new insecurity would involve worrying about whether one is of the elect. Later Calvinists began devising complicated tests to try to find evidence of their election. The most general test, for a movement initiated by Luther's and Calvin's theology of *sola gratia*, became attention to one's good works. Good works began to be so emphasized as the evidence of election that the theology originally attacked as dangerously permissive[20] has since been attacked as oppressively moralistic. Also among Calvin's successors grew an emphasis on personal feelings in the work of grace. Calvin, on the other hand, consistently "pointed away from the feelings of the individual to scripture, Christ, the church, and the sacraments for the assurance of salvation." "This," continues Basil Hall, "represents the essential factor in the division

between Calvin's own thought and the development of English Protestantism which is miscalled Calvinism."[21] Thus Calvin insisted that "we
shall not find assurance of our election in ourselves; and not even in God
the Father, if we conceive him as severed from his Son. Christ, then, is the
mirror wherein we must, and without self-deception may, contemplate our
own election" (*Institutes* 3.24.5). Given the doctrine of total depravity,
neither good works nor introspection can ever give assurance—one must
not look at the self, but at Christ, who unfailingly draws the elect to
Himself. As Calvin observes,

> When a Christian looks into himself he finds cause to be afraid or even to
> despair; but since he is called to communion with Christ he must in so
> far as assurance of salvation is concerned, regard himself as a member of
> the body of Christ so that he is in a position to appropriate all of the
> benefits of Christ's passion. Thus he will win a sure hope of eternal
> perseverance when he considers that he belongs to Him who cannot fall
> or fail.[22]

These very words, expressing a Christocentric rather than introspective
view of assurance, are echoed in "The Holdfast": "What Adam had, and
forfeited for all, / Christ keepeth now, who cannot fail or fall" (13–14).

In Herbert's day, the deviations from Calvin's teachings were already
apparent in what Hall calls the "English Protestantism miscalled Calvinism." Herbert, on the whole, is more conservative, following the early
Reformers rather than the theologians contemporary with him, following
Calvin rather than the Calvinists, and resting in "a sure hope of eternal
perseverance." "The Country Parson," though, in counseling the doubtful,
*"urgeth them to do some pious charitable works, as a necessary evidence and fruit of
their faith"* ("The Country Parson," 15:249).[23] In one poem, "Perseverance,"
excluded from *The Temple*, Herbert does doubt his salvation, but the poem
is so thoroughly in accord with Calvin's teachings, both in the problem it
poses and in the solution it finds, that it is the exception that proves the
rule of Herbert's assurance:

> My God, the poore expressions of my Love
> Which warme these lines & serve them vp to thee
> Are so, as for the present I did moue,
>   Or rather as thou mouedst mee.
>
>   (1–4)

It is providence "through whom my fingers bend / To hold my quill"
("Providence," 3–4). The poet is realizing that he can take no credit for any
of his "good works." Even in writing a poem in praise of God, the action is
not his, but God's.

> But what shall issue, whether these my words
> Shall help another, but my judgment bee,
> As a burst fouling-peece doth saue the birds
> But kill the man, is seald with thee.

                                                                    (5–8)

Herbert is well aware of Calvin's teaching that even the works of the ungodly are used by God for His good purposes (*Institutes* 1.18). Even if "my words / Shall help another," he is thinking, that is no guarantee that he himself is saved. "What shall issue . . . is seald with thee." God's choice is already "seald" and it is impossible to know what that choice is. Herbert has thus embarked on what Calvin calls "the dangerous sea" of doubting one's election (*Institutes* 3.24.4), and the "deadly abyss" threatens to engulf him.

> ffor who can tell, though thou hast dyde to winn
> And wedd my soule in glorious paradise,
> Whether my many crymes and vse of sinn
>   May yet forbid the banes and bliss?
>
> Onely my soule hangs on thy promisses
> With face and hands clinging vnto thy brest,
> Clinging and crying, crying without cease,
>   Thou art my rock, thou art my rest.

                                                                    (9–16)

There is no measuring of "the fruits of salvation"—in fact, he has them, according to the second stanza, but the knowledge of them is such that "his conscience feels more fear and consternation than assurance." Rather than seeking assurance from himself, however, the poet does precisely what Calvin advises in the midst of such torment. He clings to Christ. He "hangs on thy promisses." "For it is his will," writes Calvin in discussing such doubts, "that we be content with his promises and not inquire elsewhere whether he will be disposed to hear us" (*Institutes* 3.24.5). In the emotional turmoil of his doubting, he clings to the only point of stability—the "rock" that is Christ. As he questions his salvation throughout the poem, his soul is nevertheless anchored. The word "onely" that begins the last stanza can function as a conjunction, signaling a contrast with the rest of the poem (I am tormented that I may not be of the elect, only I am clinging to Christ). Or, it may function as an adverb (only my soul is clinging to Christ, while the rest of me is tormented). The stanza portrays a soul's desperate and saving faith that rehearses again and again, "without cease," the fact that its emotions would deny. The soul, unstable in itself, is clinging to the rock (the Lord as "the rock of our salvation," Ps. 95:1). The self, in turmoil, recognizes that Christ is also "rest." The dependence imaged in the last stanza—a crying child clinging to its mother—describes a faith whose consolation is implict although not always recognized, just as a child may cry in insecurity while in its mother's arms. The poem thus affirms the believer's ultimate security, whatever the temptations of moods and emotions. This one poem in which Herbert questions his salvation is given a title, "Perseverance", that point directly to Calvin's doctrine of eternal security, "The Perseverance of the Saints."

Reformation spirituality stresses the assurance of salvation. In the Lutheran tradition, which sharply differs from Calvinism in its insistence that anyone may be saved and on the objectivity of the sacraments as means of grace, worry about election or reprobation was excluded. Even in English and Reformed circles, though, the stress was on the security of the believer, even amidst doubts and inner conflicts. To the objection that the doctrine of election would seem to deny salvation to some who endeavored to live a godly life, Calvin asks, "Whence could such endeavor arise but from election?" (Institutes 3.23.12). Following this reasoning, the very fact that one is worried about salvation, or is experiencing conflict or doubt, was seen, paradoxically, as evidence of election. According to John Bradford, since a Christian's life is characterized by the inner conflict between the indwelling Holy Spirit and the flesh, the simple fact of inner struggle is evidence that the Holy Spirit is present within the believer's heart:

> This battle and strife none have but the elect "Children of God": and they that have it are the elect "children of God" "in Christ before the beginning of the world" [2 Tim. 1:9], whose salvation is as certain and sure as is God Himself; for they are given to Christ, a faithful shepherd, who hath so prayed for them lest they should perish that we know His prayer is heard: yea, He promiseth so to keep them that "they shall not perish" [John 10:28, 17:9ff.]. And therefore they ought to rejoice, and herethrough comfort themselves in their conflicts, which are testimonials, and most true, that they are the elect and dear "children of God"; for else they could not nor should not feel any such strife in them.[24]

The reprobate, then, are those who endure no spiritual conflict, since the flesh remains unopposed. Or, as Herbert puts it in "Business": "Who in heart not ever kneels,/Neither sinne nor saviour feels" (37–38). Those who do not feel sin, by the same token cannot feel the Savior. Those who do feel sin, conversely, do so by the ministry of the Holy Spirit (John 16:8).

Richard Hooker, the most authoritative Anglican theologian, whose rejection of Calvinist church polity is complemented by his affirmation of Calvin's view of justification and perseverance, argues similarly to those who are tormented by their lack of faith:

Well, to favour them a little in their weakness; let that be granted which they do imagine; be it that they are faithless and without belief. But are they not grieved for their unbelief? They are. Do they not wish it might, and also strive that it may, be otherwise? We know they do. Whence cometh this, but from a secret love and liking which they have of those things that are believed? No man can love things which in his own opinion are not. And if they think those things to be, which they shew that they love when they desire to believe them; then must it needs be, that by desiring to believe they prove themselves true believers. For without faith, no man thinketh that things believed are. Which argument all the subtilty of infernal powers will never be able to dissolve.[25]

The certainty of salvation preached by Bradford and Hooker does not preclude doubt—rather, it insists that doubt and other forms of spiritual instability are inevitable and to be expected. "Now the minds of all men being so darkened as they are with the foggy damp of original corruption," writes Hooker, "it cannot be that any man's heart living should be either so enlightened in the knowledge, or so established in the love of that wherein his salvation standeth, as to be perfect, neither doubting nor shrinking at all. If any such were, what doth let why that man should not be justified by his own inherent righteousness?"[26] The "distrustful suggestions of the flesh," and especially the mistaking of emotion for faith, will cause spiritual vacillations and even doubting.

Yet they which are of God do not sin either in this, or in any thing, any such sin as doth quite extinguish grace, clean cut them off from Christ Jesus; because the "seed of God" [1 John 3:9] abideth in them, and doth shield them from receiving any irremedial wound. Their faith, when it is at the strongest, is but weak; yet even then when it is at the weakest, so strong, that utterly it never faileth, it never perisheth altogether, no not in them who think it extinguished in themselves. . . . For that which dwelleth in their hearts they seek, they make diligent search and inquiry. It abideth, it worketh in them, yet still they ask where; still they lament as for a thing which is past finding: they mourn as Rachel, and refuse to be comforted, as if that were not which indeed is, and as if that which is not were; as if they did not believe when they do, and as if they did despair when they do not.[27]

Hooker could here be describing Herbert in his most agonized poems of affliction, but Herbert, like the theologians, sees the basis for an assurance of salvation in God's fiat and in His promises as expressed in Scripture—not in the vacillations of human emotions. Assurance for Luther, Calvin, and Hooker was objective, not subjective; in fact, subjective feelings were understood as often obscuring the believer's true security, which is to be apprehended by faith in God's declaration, rather than by confidence in the fickleness of the "flesh."

Herbert's poem on the subject, "Assurance," portrays the doctrine of perseverance, founded upon the doctrines of justification and grace, and also the conflict between the emotions and faith. The speaker in the poem does not feel saved—the poem portrays a turning away from the self to a reliance on the objective work of God, in whom alone assurance of salvation can be found.

> O spitefull bitter thought!
> Bitterly spiteful thought! Couldst thou invent
> So high a torture? Is such poyson bought?
> Doubtlesse, but in the way of punishment.
> When wit contrives to meet with thee,
> No such rank poyson can there be.
>
> Thou said'st but even now
> That all was not so fair, as I conceiv'd,
> Betwixt my God and me, that I allow
> And coin large hopes, but that I was deceiv'd:
> Either the league was broke, or neare it;
> And, that I had great cause to fear it.
>
> And what to this? what more
> Could poyson, if it had a tongue, expresse?
> What is thy aim? wouldst thou unlock the doore
> To cold despairs, and gnawing pensivenesse?
> Wouldst thou raise devils? I see, I know,
> I writ thy purpose long ago.
>
> (1–18)

The "spitefull bitter thought" that seems so poisonous to Herbert is that "the league," the Covenant between the soul and God, could be broken. If this is possible, then the relationship with God is not a secure one. The "large hope" he has in God threatens to give way to fear. The vehemence with which Herbert describes any thought that would even suggest that his relationship with God is somehow contingent or conditional is an index to the powerful and bitter feelings unleashed when the Arminians began challenging the Calvinist notion that one cannot fall from grace. If everything in salvation is not the work of God, if salvation is in any way contingent upon the works or choices of the self, then assurance vanishes, unlocking "the doore / To cold despairs, and gnawing pensivenesse."

> But I will to my Father,
> Who heard thee say it. O most gracious Lord,
> If all the hope and comfort that I gather,
> Were from my self, I had not half a word,

> Not half a letter to oppose
> What is objected by my foes.

(19–24)

In this stanza the address and the attention of the poem turns from the self to God.[28] "Hope and comfort" are not to be found in the self at all, which can by no means deny any of the charges against it. Rather, assurance is found in terms of God's unalterable covenant:

> But thou art my desert:
> And in this league, which now my foes invade,
> Thou art not onely to perform thy part,
> But also mine; as when the league was made
> Thou didst at once thy self indite,
> And hold my hand, while I did write.

(25–30)

According to the tenet of justification, with its doctrine of the imputation of Christ's righteousness, "thou art not onely to perform thy part, / But also mine," so that the works of Christ are, as it were, transferred to the account of the believer. Herbert, however, goes farther, ascribing even the inception of the covenant, the initial faith of the believer, to the direct causality of God:

> . . . when the league was made
> Thou didst at once thy self indite,
> And hold my hand, while I did write.

To the Arminians, the believer's subscription to God's covenant is a free choice. Melanchthon saw man and God as cooperating in the act of salvation.[29] Calvin, on the other hand, taught that God, in effect, performs both parts. In Herbert's poem, not only does God commit Himself to the Covenant, signing His name to the "league," but He also signs the speaker's name—or rather, holds "my hand, while I [do] write." The doctrine that God provides everything necessary to salvation—not only good works, but even faith itself—results in a salvation that cannot be lost:

> Wherefore if thou canst fail,
> Then can thy truth and I: but while rocks stand,
> And rivers stirre, thou canst not shrink or quail:
> Yea, when both rocks and all things shall disband,
> Then shalt thou be my rock and tower,
> And make their ruine praise thy power.

(31–36)

Only if God can fail is salvation endangered. Whether one stands like a rock or "stirres" like a river, as the speaker has been doing, God, unlike human beings, can "not shrink or quail." "Salvation is founded on such sure and firm bases that, even if the whole structure of the world tottered, that certainty itself could not dissolve" (Calvin, *Institutes* 3.24.6 [first ed.; Niesel]). In the apocalyptic dissolution of the universe, God's salvation will remain firm and, in fact, become fully manifest. Salvation and its perpetuity is a function of God's power, which cannot be resisted or undone.

> Now foolish thought go on,
> Spin out thy thread, and make thereof a coat
> To hide thy shame: for thou hast cast a bone
> Which bounds on thee, and will not down thy throat:
> What for it self love once began,
> Now love and truth will end in man.
>
> (37–42)

The "bitterly spitefull thought" of the first stanza becomes merely "foolish." The poison, perhaps suggesting a venomous spider, gives way to a figure of spinning out thread, suggesting spiderwebs, Bacon's symbol for futile introspection and subjectivism.[30] The coat spun out of the self contrasts with the symbol of imputed righteousness—being clothed in Christ. The bone cast by the adversary sticks in his own throat. By being made to reflect on his unworthiness, the speaker comes to see that he can do nothing for his salvation and that therefore he can trust God to do everything. The final couplet capsulizes Calvin's doctrine of election and sanctification. The inception of a person's salvation can be ascribed to no other cause than the inscrutable purpose of God ("what for *it self* love once began"), but what is once begun will be carried out to completion. The final couplet echoes a familiar text of Christian confidence: "Being confident of this very thing, that he which hath begun a good work in you will perform it until the day of Jesus Christ" (Phil. 1:6). The process cannot fail, because its outcome is predestined by God.

"Assurance," like "Perseverance," is a poem of conflict between the certainty of salvation as understood by faith and the conflicting feelings and impulses of the "flesh." Both poems can be aptly glossed by Hooker: "The simplicity of faith which is in Christ taketh the naked promise of God, His bare word, and on that it resteth. This simplicity the serpent laboureth continually to pervert, corrupting the mind with many imaginations of repugnancy and contrariety between the promise of God and those things which sense or experience or some other foreconceived persuasion hath imprinted."[31] There is, to be sure, often violent struggle in Herbert's poetry. The conflict, though, is not a contest between "the good Angel," and "the bad Angel," with the human soul at stake, as in the morality plays, but a conflict between the flesh and the spirit in a person already infallibly saved. Even in Herbert's most agonized poems of affliction and rebellion, the question of his soul's destiny is never really at issue. At the worst, Herbert will pray for death—"Remove me, where I need not say, / *Drop from above*" ("Grace," 23–24)—not from any suicidal despair, but from desire to escape the infirmities of the flesh to be with God, an expectation grounded on his confidence in salvation.

Herbert's belief in "Eternal Security" is important, not only in understanding the poems of struggle, but also in accounting for some of the most characteristic qualities of his religious verse. In marked contrast to medieval religious poets and to Donne, Herbert never emphasizes the threat of hell. Although Herbert clearly believes in a state of eternal punishment, hell is simply not a possibility for the true Christian. Although Calvin is quite generally associated with "hellfire and damnation," in fact it is Herbert's neglect of hell in his personal religious poetry that is one of the best evidences of his Calvinist assumptions. Calvin rebukes those who "tremble and remain anxious throughout life—as if God's righteous vengeance which the Son of God has taken upon himself, still hung over us" (*Institutes* 2.16.5). Edwin Sandys (1516–88), in discussing the doctrine of perseverance with some of its scriptural sanctions, draws implications that seem directly applicable to Herbert. In his sermon on Luke 1:74 ("That we being delivered out of the hand of our enemies might serve him without fear"), Sandys, a Calvinist Archbishop of the Church of England, urges a particular quality of spirituality:

Him we must serve "without fear." . . . The believing Christian, the regenerate child of God, who through faith in Christ is certain of his deliverance from the devil and from hell, assured of remission of sins and of life everlasting in the death and resurrection of Jesus Christ our Saviour, he serveth in the reverent fear of love, and not in that dreadful fear of death and everlasting damnation, wherewith the reprobate mind is daunted. He feareth not death, for he is sure of life: he feareth not damnation, for he is assured of salvation: he believeth that which Christ hath promised, and doubteth nothing of the obtaining of that which Christ hath procured for him. He is surely persuaded with St. Paul that neither death, nor life, nor tribulation, nor affliction, nor anything present, or to come, shall separate him from the love of God which is in Christ Jesus [Rom. 8:38]. But this certainty of God's love towards him in Christ, and the testimony of his love towards God again, casteth out all fear of eternal punishment. For ye have not, saith the Apostle, received again in the spirit of bondage unto fear, but ye have received the spirit of adoption, by which we cry Abba, Father! This Spirit testifieth with our spirit that God is our gracious Father, and if He our Father, we His children, and if His children, heirs of his glorious kingdom [Rom. 8:15ff.]. . . . And this certainty of our salvation the Spirit of God testifieth to our spirit, whereby we put away all servile fear of punishment, being assured of God's constant favor and eternal love towards us; who never

leaveth unfinished that which He hath begun, nor forsaketh him whom
he hath chosen.[32]

Besides Herbert's lack of fear before God, the doctrine of assurance helps
account for the tone of the poetry, which is not only confident, but sometimes brash. The doctrine that one cannot fall away from salvation makes
possible an intimacy with God that often seems startling in its honesty and
its confidence. "Each one of us," writes Calvin, "by trusting in the grace of
Christ must have confidence in prayer and frankly dare to invoke God."[33]
Herbert "frankly dares" to address God in ways unthinkable apart from his
security in Christ.

Another function of the assurance of salvation is what Calvin describes
as Christian freedom, in particular, the freedom of the conscience, whereby
the soul is freed from burdensome moralisms based on salvation by works.
Avoiding antinomianism and moral permissiveness, Calvin nonetheless
insists on the "repose" of the conscience in light of grace (*Institutes 3.19.7*).
Herbert urges the same thing in "Conscience:"

> Peace pratler, do not lowre:
> Not a fair look, but thou dost call it foul:
> Not a sweet dish, but thou dost call it soure:
>   Musick to thee doth howl.
> By listening to thy chatting fears
> I have both lost mine eyes and eares.
>
> Pratler, no more, I say:
> My thoughts must work, but like a noiselesse sphere;
> Harmonious peace must rock them all the day:
>   No room for pratlers there.
> If thou persistest, I will tell thee,
> That I have physick to expell thee.

(1–12)

The "physick" that can expel the overscrupulous conscience is the blood of
Christ, as developed in the remaining two stanzas. Calvin, in a whimsical
vein not always associated with him, similarly describes the oversensitive
conscience, whose "chatting fears" can end in a slavery that denies both
God's gifts and the liberation offered in Christ:

> For when consciences once ensnare themselves, they enter a long and
> inextricable maze, not easy to get out of. If a man begins to doubt
> whether he may use linen for sheets, shirts, handkerchiefs and napkins,
> he will afterwards be uncertain also about hemp; finally, doubt will even
> arise over tow. For he will turn over in his mind whether he can sup
> without napkins, or go without a handkerchief. If any man should con-
> sider daintier food unlawful, in the end he will not be at peace before

God, when he eats either black bread or common victuals, while it occurs to him that he could sustain his body on even coarser foods. If he boggles at sweet wine, he will not with clear conscience drink even flat wine, and finally, he will not dare touch water if sweeter and cleaner than other water. (*Institutes* 3.19.7)

That to Herbert the soul is infallibly saved and cannot fall from grace helps explain the confident tone of his poetry, a confidence that is not negated by the intensity of his poems of anguish. The anguish is, at least intellectually, controlled by the conviction that estrangement from God can never be final. The doctrine functions as a foundation on which other poems of his rest, or, to use Herbert's own metaphor, it functions as the floor of "the Church." Joseph Summers sees "The Church-floore" as a hieroglyph picturing "the marvellous art of God in decreeing the perseverance of the saints."[34]

> Mark you the floore? that square & speckled stone,
>   Which looks so firm and strong,
>   Is *Patience:*
>
> And th'other black and grave, wherewith each one
>   Is checker'd all along,
>   *Humilitie:*
>
> The gentle rising, which on either hand
>   Leads to the Quire above,
>   Is *Confidence:*
>
> But the sweet cement, which in one sure band
>   Ties the whole frame, is *Love*
>   And *Charitie.*
>
>   Hither sometimes Sinne steals, and stains
>   The marbles neat and curious veins:
> But all is cleansed when the marble weeps.
>   Sometimes Death, puffing at the doore,
>   Blows all the dust about the floore:
> But while he thinks to spoil the room, he sweeps.
>   Blest be the *Architect,* whose art
>   Could build so strong in a weak heart.

The poem, as revealed in the final word, is not merely an allegorized description of a church building, but a description of the internalized church God builds within the individual heart, the "Temple of the Holy Ghost," "which temple ye are" (1 Cor. 3:17, see also vv. 9–16, 6:19). Sin does inevitably come into the believer's life, as Calvin strenuously insists,[35] but the "architecture" is such that repentance is inevitable and "all is cleansed when [not "if"] the marble weeps." The warfare between the spirit and flesh ends at death, when the flesh becomes dust. Thus, Death, "while he thinks to spoil the room," actually completes the process of sanctification and the final victory over sin. The heart itself is weak, still subject to sin and death, but the structure built by God is strong:

> Blest be the *Architect,* whose art
> Could build so strong in a weak heart.

The floor of the church is built of patience and humility—traditional virtues for the sojourning Christian—but "The gentle rising, which on either hand / Leads to the Quire above, / Is *Confidence.*" Patience and humility seem at first sight to be in opposition to confidence. The Reformers were not unaware of the danger that confidence of one's election without patience and humility could result in presumption and pride, and they warned about the dangers of "carnal security," with its complacency and self-sufficiency. Herbert's metaphor places patience and humility as the very substance of the Christian's duty, but what leads patience and humility upward is confidence, "the gentle rising" that inevitably leads to the Heavenly choir. What Summers calls "the structure of salvation" described in this poem is held together "in one sure band" by love, a word used by Herbert not only in its moral and emotional sense, but also as the name of God (e.g., "The World," "Discipline," "Love [3]").[36] Salvation, for Herbert, is as indestructible as the church that the poem describes. It is invulnerable to sin and death and, despite the weakness of the human heart, is sustained and preserved by the love and providence of God.

If the doctrine of the assurance of salvation issues in a confidence that looks forward in time to "the Quire above," it also implies the importance of retrospection. If one has experienced justification in the past, then one is infallibly saved now, no matter how "unsaved" one might feel in the present. Thus Herbert's poetry often refers back to previous times of grace as a means of consolation. Perhaps the clearest example is in "The Discharge," in which the poet is trying to quell his typically contentious heart:

> Busie enquiring heart, what wouldst thou know?
> > Why dost thou prie,
> And turn, and leer, and with a licorous eye
> > Look high and low;
> And in thy lookings stretch and grow?
>
> Hast thou not made thy counts, and summ'd up all?
> > Did not thy heart
> Give up the whole, and with the whole depart?
> > Let what will fall:
> That which is past who can recall?

> Thy life is Gods, thy time to come is gone,
>> And is his right.
> He is thy night at noon: he is at night
>> Thy noon alone.
> The crop is his, for he hath sown.
>
> And well it was for thee, when this befell,
>> That God did make
> Thy businesse his, and in thy life partake:
>> For thou canst tell,
> If it be his once, all is well.
>
> (1–20)

To the "busie" self that threatens to "stretch and grow" in its rebellion against God, the poet, in effect, replies that it is too late. The heart has already given itself up to Christ—"That which is past who can recall?" "Thy life is Gods, thy time to come is gone, / And is his right." The seed sown cannot be taken back by the sower. "That God did make / Thy businesse his" suggests not only God's interference, but, playing on the word *busie,* (1) the futility of salvation by works. God partakes in a human life and "If it be his once, all is well." As the poem continues into a meditation on time, anxiety, and grief, the final line affirms a positive reliance on God's promise and providential control that is necessary in light of the uncertainty of the world:

> Away distrust:
> My God hath promised; he is just.

Similarly, "The Glance" portrays the practice of, in the midst of spiritual anguish, remembering one's initial consciousness of salvation:

> When first thy sweet and gracious eye
> Vouchsaf'd ev'n in the midst of youth and night
> To look upon me, who before did lie
>> Weltring in sinne;
> I felt a sugred strange delight,
> Passing all cordials made by any art,
> Bedew, embalme, and overrunne my heart,
>> And take it in.
> Since that time many a bitter storm
> My soul hath felt, ev'n able to destroy,
> Had the malicious and ill-meaning harm,
>> His swing and sway:
> But still thy sweet originall joy,
> Sprung from thine eye, did work within my soul,
> And surging griefs, when they grew bold, controll,
>> And got the day.
>
> (1–16)

The "bitter storm" would indeed be "ev'n able to destroy" if it had its "swing and sway," but of course it does not. The "sweet originall joy" of grace once given, a function of "thy first glance so powerful" (17), is still able to "work within my soul."

The paradigm suggested in this poem of "surging griefs" in conflict with and finally controlled by "sweet originall joy" is perhaps applicable to Herbert's poetry as a whole. In the course of *The Temple*, poems of joy and confidence alternate with poems of spiritual desolation. The mixture of moods in Herbert's poetry, and its connection to the doctrine of assurance, is suggestively treated by Calvin. In prayer, according to Calvin, one should be both "cast down and overcome" and at the same time confident in "the firm assurance of God's favor." Calvin admits that "these are indeed things apparently contrary," but, he observes, "repentance and faith are companions joined together by an indissoluble bond, although one of these terrifies us while the other gladdens us, so also these two ought to be present together in prayers."

> But "assurance" I do not understand to mean that which soothes our mind with sweet and perfect repose, releasing it from every anxiety. For to repose so peacefully is the part of those who, when all affairs are flowing to their liking, are touched by no care, burn with no desire, toss with no fear. But for the saints the occasion that best stimulates them to call upon God is when, distressed by their own need, they are troubled by the greatest unrest, and are almost driven out of their senses, until faith opportunely comes to their relief. For among such tribulations God's goodness so shines upon them that even when they groan with weariness under the weight of present ills, and also are troubled and tormented by the fear of greater ones, yet, relying upon his goodness, they are relieved of the difficulty of bearing them, and are solaced and hope for escape and deliverance. It is fitting therefore that the godly man's prayer arise from these two emotions, that it also contain and represent both. (*Institutes* 3.20.11)

The doctrine of assurance does not prevent Herbert from experiences of spiritual desolation, nor does desolation prevent him from believing in his infallible salvation. Suffering and conflict were seen as inevitable in the conflict between the flesh and the spirit that accompanied the process of sanctification. Despite the poems of anguish, Herbert's doctrine of assurance manifests itself not only in the general tone of confidence, but also in his more strident voice, in which Herbert is able to insist boldly that God keep to his bargain.

The relationship between the doctrine of perseverance and Herbert's poetry is further suggested in "The 23d Psalme," in which Herbert goes beyond his source in emphasizing and embellishing the doctrine:

> Or if I stray, he doth convert
>   And bring my minde in frame:
> And all this not for my desert,
>   But for his holy name.

$$(9\text{--}12)$$

When the Christian sins, God will continually "convert" him. God deals with the "straying" self by conversion, by action that will "bring my minde in frame," a line that expresses well the reordering that takes place, both thematically and formally, in poems such as "The Collar." "All this," of course, is not "for my desert," but for the glory of God, to Whom alone is ascribed all the work of salvation.

> Surely thy sweet and wondrous love
>   Shall measure all my dayes,
> And as it never shall remove,
>   So neither shall my praise.

$$(21\text{--}24)$$

The stanza recalls a line from another poem of assurance, "Holy Baptisme (1)": "In you Redemption measures all my time" (10). The word *measure* in Herbert's day could imply encircling or limiting, suggesting the protective function of grace. The more general meanings of apportioning by measure and of close comparison to an unvarying standard also express aspects of grace, which is meted out as it is needed, and which, in the Redemption, is a constant large enough to "measure all my dayes," a love that "never shall remove."

iii. Predestination and Poetic Form

Describing the two poles of George Herbert criticism, Stanley Fish suggests that "rather than swinging back and forth between the poet of order and stability and the poet of change and surprise, Herbert criticism should ask the question posed by its own shape and history: how is it that a poet and the poetry he writes can be restless and secure *at the same time?*"[37] Fish gives his own answer to the question in terms of catechistic theories and affective stylistics, but at least another way to account for the paradox is in terms of the doctrine of predestination. The experience of restlessness and instability, assumed to be part of the process of sanctification, is countered by the doctrine of eternal security, and by the faith that in the midst of turmoil God is nevertheless in control. Patrick Grant points out "that many of Herbert's best poems certainly show a fascination with the secret interior workings of God's plan and with man's instrumentality for an end already determined."[38] That the end is already determined, is, of course, a doctrine of Reformed theology. "The secret interior workings of God's plan" correspond closely to the "interior workings" of the poetic craftsman, who orders his felt experiences, chaotic though they may be, according to an objective design. In Herbert's case, the objective, intellectual design would correspond to the religious doctrines that he believes, intellectually, to be true. In Herbert's poems, as in Reformed soteriology, the solution has been determined and is generally implicit from the beginning. Over and over again, the speaker in Herbert's poetry goes through his turmoil and rebellion, but discovers, through multilevel ironies, that he has never escaped God's providential, saving design.

The irony of "The Collar," in which the imagery employed to express rebellion has a double-edged religious meaning, is well known. The speaker's complaint that his only reward is "a thorn / To let me bloud" (7–8) and his desires for a crown (14–15) recall directly Christ's crown of thorns. The imagery of "harvest," "fruit," and "crown" alludes also to traditional eschatological symbols, pointing to the end of time, at which Christians will receive their rewards.[39] The speaker's desire for wine and corn (10–13) assumes a complicated resonance when they are recognized also as sacramental symbols. The yearning to be "free as the rode" is made startlingly ironic when "rode" is recognized as a pun on "rood," the cross of Christ. Herbert at a single stroke offers both an evocative image of human freedom, the "open road" of Walt Whitman and Jack Kerouac, and, in the very act of doing so, the more complex ideal of Christian freedom through the cross. The cross, the crown of thorns, the sacrament, stand as both a criticism of the speaker's impertinence and an ever-present but unrecognized solution to his needs and desires. As Grant points out, "the seeming self-determinations of man are merely the instruments of God's foreordained mercy. In the very assertion of his freedom the speaker is made ironically to allude . . . to the very means by which his rebellion will effect the opposite of what he intends."[40]

> But as I rav'd and grew more fierce and wilde,
> > At every word
> Me thoughts I heard one calling, *Child!*
> > And I reply'd, *My Lord.*

> > > > > > (33–36)

The phrase *at every word* (34) is often neglected: the calling of God, the resolution of the turmoil, revealed here to the reader only at the end of the poem, is stated to have been, in fact, continuous throughout the poem. Even in the midst of the rebellion ("*As* I rav'd . . ."), God is calling the speaker "*Child*" "At every word" of the poem. The irresistible grace that binds the child to his Lord is operative even in the midst of the ostensible rebellion, as also implied in the double-edged imagery. The very form of the poem, with the final quatrain, is shown, in retrospect, to be not so chaotic as it appears. Although it may seem that "My lines . . . are free" (4), the seemingly erratic line lengths are shown to be simply various arrangements of the four types of lines established by the regularity of the final quatrain (lines of 5, 2, 4, and 3 feet). The regular rhyme scheme of the conclusion helps one to notice that even in the earlier "chaotic" part of the poem, every line, eventually, is made to rhyme with some other line, however far removed. "There has been a pattern there," observes Grant, "but only by the intervention of the Lord do we see it."[41] The speaker and the reader experience turmoil, disorder, and confusion—this corresponds to life as it is experienced in time. From the viewpoint of eternity, however, the contingencies of human experience are all made to correspond to the preordained and infallible plan of God. The form of "The Collar" images precisely the world view of Reformed spirituality.

Besides the pattern of predestination, the poem dramatizes the corollaries of the depravity of the human will—human beings of themselves do not want to serve God—and the irresistible power of grace. In this regard, Herbert himself provides the best gloss of "The Collar," referring in "Miserie" to the foolishness of even "the best of men":

> They quarrell thee, and would give over
> The bargain made to serve thee: but thy love
> Holds them unto it, and doth cover
> Their follies with the wing of thy milde Dove,
> Not suff'ring those
> Who would, to be thy foes.
>
> (25–30)

"Affliction (1)" is Herbert's other great poem on a "quarrell" with God, on an attempt to "give over / The bargain made to serve thee," and here again, looming behind the emotions of rebellion, are the evidences of God's saving plan. The position of the poem in "The Church," the third poem after the baptism sequence that initiates the Christian life and the process of sanctification, highlights its theme, the growth of a new Christian. Although a very personal, even autobiographical poem, its intense emotions, as in "The Collar," are given an ironic resonance, by the scriptural and doctrinal allusions that point to the continual fulfillment of God's plan of sanctification:

> When first thou didst entice to thee my heart,
> I thought the service brave:
> So many joyes I writ down for my part,
> Besides what I might have

> Out of my stock of naturall delights,
> Augmented with thy gracious benefits
>
> I looked on thy furniture so fine,
>   And made it fine to me:
> Thy glorious household-stuffe did me entwine,
>   And 'tice me unto thee.
> Such starres I counted mine: both heav'n and earth
> Payd me my wages in a world of mirth.
>
>   (1–12)

Although God's initiative in the relationship is established in the first line, the stanzas are "me-centered" in a way that is very unusual in Herbert. In these two stanzas, the first-person pronoun occurs in every line but one (6); especially noticeable is the large number of possessives, the range of qualities that the speaker is laying claim to possessing: "my heart," "my part," "What I might have," "my stock of naturall delights," "Such starres I counted mine," "my wages." The first stanza refers to three sources of the happiness that he enjoys: there is the joy the speaker feels in his new employment, "*Besides* what I might have / Out of my stock of naturall delights," a reference, perhaps, to his own talents and pleasures, "*Augmented* with thy gracious benefits." The grace of God receives one line of compliment in these twelve lines, but it is presented as an augmentation added to the other benefits, rather than as the source and center of them all. It might be reading too closely, of course, to question these lines or to read in them a hint of irony—even when the speaker begins to consider that God's "household-stuffe," the church, belongs to him ("Such starres I counted mine")—were it not for the very clear scriptural and doctrinal allusion at the end of the second stanza: "both heav'n and earth / Payd me my wages in a world of mirth." If there was one thing on which seventeenth-century Protestants would agree, it would be that the only "wages" anyone earns is death. "For the wages of sin is death; but the gift of God is eternal life through Jesus Christ our Lord" (Rom. 6:23). "Wages," what the soul deserves, is always opposed to "gift," what is freely bestowed, regardless of merit. The point was continually emphasized by the early Protestants. The implicit criticism of the young Christian characterized in the poem is that he seems to think he deserves happiness. Happiness there may be from God's "gracious benefits," but the concept that "heav'n," not to mention "earth," owes him "wages in a world of mirth," is certainly ironic. The wages dues to human beings is death; to insist on the wages one deserves is at worst a prideful lack of awareness of one's sinfulness, and at best a comic misunderstanding of the situation. The last lines of the first two stanzas contrast with each other: "Augmented with thy gracious benefits"; "Payd me my wages in a world of mirth." The speaker is confusing God's free gifts to sinners with wages he feels he deserves, an impression reinforced by the number of "possessions" that he is claiming.

The context of this misapprehension, and the place of initial joy in the Christian life is given by an even more direct scriptural allusion:

> At first thou gav'st me milk and sweetnesses;
>> I had my wish and way:
> My dayes were straw'd with flow'rs and happinesse;
>> There was no moneth but May.
> But with my yeares sorrow did twist and grow,
> And made a partie unawares for wo.
>
> (19–24)

Herbert's choice of milk as a symbol for the ease and joys of the early years in God's service is a direct scriptural allusion, which establishes the underlying theme of Christian growth:

> And I, brethren, could not speak unto you as unto spiritual, but as unto carnal, even as unto babes in Christ. I have fed you with milk, and not with meat: for hitherto ye were not able to bear it. (1 Cor. 3:1–2)
>
> For every one that useth milk is unskilful in the word of righteousness: for he is a babe. But strong meat belongeth to them that are of full age, even those who by reason of use have their senses exercised to discern both good and evil. (Hebrews 5:13–14)

A "babe in Christ" is first fed milk, but as he grows, he must be made to digest "strong meat." The speaker wonders why his earlier pleasures in serving God have been taken away; the answer is implicit in the very complaint: "At first thou gav'st me milk. . . . But with my years" the more serious and painful spiritual nourishment begins. Although when God gave him milk, "I had my wish and way," that is hardly the point of the Christian life, which involves submission to God's will, to God's "wish and way," not the servant's. Although before, "my thoughts reserved / No place for grief or fear" (15–16), such naiveté gives place to the "strong meat" of spiritual warfare: "My flesh began unto my soul in pain" (25).

The pain and frustration described in the next stanzas are genuine and poignant; yet the poem maintains an undercurrent of ironic self-criticism. The two stanzas on the poet's sickness are concluded by a line that describes his vulnerability to afflictions—"I was blown through with ev'ry storm and winde" (36)—which also alludes to the New Testament:

> That we henceforth be no more children, tossed to and fro, and carried about with every wind of doctrine. (Eph. 4:14)
>
> For he that wavereth is like a wave of the sea driven with the wind and

tossed. . . . A double minded man is unstable in all his ways. (James 1:6, 8)

Again, the reference is to spiritual children, those who have not yet grown up in the faith, so that they are shaken and discomfited by every "wind" of emotion or human thought. The speaker's "double-mindedness" is hinted at in the next two stanzas, as his real attitude to serving God becomes clear:

> Whereas my birth and spirit rather took
> The way that takes the town;
> Thou didst betray me to a lingring book
> And wrap me in a gown:
> I was entangled in the world of strife,
> Before I had the power to change my life.
>
> Yet, for I threatned oft the siege to raise,
> Not simpring all mine age,
> Thou often didst with Academick praise
> Melt and dissolve my rage.
> I took thy sweetned pill, till I came where
> I could not go away, nor persevere.
>
> (37–48)

The speaker complains that he has no freedom. God "betrays" him, "wraps" him up, "entangles" him, "Before [he] had the power to change [his] life." If he did have the power to change his life, he would choose not God, but "The way that takes the town." God is in control, however. Nor is God the tyrant that lines 37–42 imply; God works by managing to "Melt and dissolve my rage," offering him a "sweetned pill," the very sweetness of which is scorned. The young speaker, very proud of "my birth and spirit," finds himself in academia (the "book" and "gown" would not refer to the priesthood, but to Cambridge) where his unhappiness is assuaged somewhat by the "Academick praise" he received as a successful student. Even here, however, the pride is evident; he is solaced not by submission to God, but by the feeding of his own ego, concerned not to praise God, but to be praised himself.

As the bitterness builds, the complaints are concluded and summarized in a statement of momentous irony:

> Thus doth thy power crosse-bias me, not making
> Thine own gift good, yet me from my wayes taking.
>
> (53–54)

What the speaker does not realize is that God must take "me from my wayes" in order to make His gift good—in fact, taking him from his ways is the gift. "My birth and spirit rather took / The way that takes the town," presumably the sort of sophisticated worldliness Herbert elsewhere condemns (e.g., "The Quip," "Dotage," "Vanitie [2]"). One's birth involves original sin; one's "spirit" is depraved. Salvation is deliverance from one's own ways, even when one is perfectly happy with them ("There is a way that seemeth right unto a man, but the end thereof are the ways of death" [Prov. 16:25]). Herbert's metaphor for this process is theologically precise, and the pun, repeated and thoroughly explored in "The Crosse," is almost certainly intended: "Thus doth thy power crosse-bias me." His will is "crossed"; his direction is changed by the cross. Salvation involves the thwarting of one's will, which "by birth and spirit" is inclined to sin as the poem itself demonstrates, occurring only when God's power works to cross-bias the soul.

From this point, the speaker begins to ask the right questions.

> Now I am here, what thou wilt do with me
> > None of my books will show:
> I reade, and sigh, and wish I were a tree;
> > For sure then I should grow
> To fruit or shade: at least some bird would trust
> Her household to me, and I should be just.
>
> > > > > (55–60)

Now the speaker, completely defeated, begins to think of God's will ("what thou wilt do with me") rather than his own. Helen Vendler observes that the desire to be a tree suggests an opposition between the continuous effort involved in will, contrasted with the effortlessness of simply being.[42] Moreover, the desire for fruit, the birds living in the branches, and particularly the connection to being "just" suggests another biblical symbol, again one that relates to the growth of the Christian:

> The kingdom of heaven is like to a grain of mustard seed, which a man took, and sowed in his field: which indeed is the least of all seeds: but when it is grown, it is the greatest among herbs, and becometh a tree, so that the birds of the air come and lodge in the branches thereof. (Matt. 13:31–32)

Elsewhere (Matt. 17:20) the mustard seed is described as a symbol of faith. Faith is expected to issue in fruit and, for the Reformers, in being made "just" ("The just shall live by faith" [Rom. 1:17], Luther's central slogan). The stanza portrays the speaker as simply giving up—a necessary experience as Herbert shows in many of his poems—expressing a desire for faith. The mustard-seed parable is a reminder however, that only a very little faith is enough, that the seed of faith, as Hooker observed, can never be rooted out and that such faith is in a continual process of growing, until it "becometh a tree" in which even the birds of the air can find refuge. The irony is that the speaker, through his frustrations and defeats, and the painfully small seed of faith, is growing, by the very conflicts, to fruit and shade and toward being made just.

The final stanza recapitulates, heightens, and resolves the earlier conflict. All through the poem the speaker has wanted God's will to conform to his will. Now the pretense of wanting to serve God, ironically developed in the first four stanzas, is unmasked:

> Well, I will change the service, and go seek
> Some other master out.
>
> (63–64)

Perhaps now the speaker begins to realize what would happen if God's will did conform to his will. The speaker has not been complaining that he has been forgotten by God; his complaint is that "thou troublest me" (61). What would it be like if God did stop troubling him, if he were "clean forgot"?

> Ah my deare God! though I am clean forgot,
> Let me not love thee, if I love thee not.
>
> (65–66)

If God's will did conform to his own, a will that wants only to break away from Him, he could not love God at all. Something in him (the "seed" of faith, the Holy Ghost) loves God even against his will ("Ah my deare God!"). He cannot "change the service," because such things, even the question of whether he loves God, are in God's hands. His own rebellion ("if I love thee not"), is itself dependent upon God's permission ("let me not love thee").

In "Affliction (1)," as in "The Collar," the outcome of the struggle is predetermined, or rather predestined, both by the poet's craftsmanship and by his theological assumptions. The experience of the will as dramatized in the poems is not negated; rather, it is ironically commented upon as it is shown to unwittingly conform to God's (and the poet's) saving design.

A paradigm of the formal implications of predestination can be seen in "Jesu":

> JESU is in my heart, his sacred name
> Is deeply carved there: but th'other week
> A great affliction broke the little frame,
> Ev'n all to pieces: which I went to seek:
> And first I found the corner, where was *J*
> After, where *ES,* and next where *U* was graved.
> When I had got these parcels, instantly

> I sat me down to spell them, and perceived
> That to my broken heart he was *I ease you,*
> And to my whole is *JESU.*

As Stanley Fish observes, the poem begins with everything needed for the solution. The relationship is already established and portrayed as inviolable: "JESU is in my heart, his sacred name / Is *deeply* carved there." The "heart" and with it the solution fall apart by "a great affliction." The poem portrays the process by which the original and implicit solution falls back into place, and is recognized, so that the poem ends precisely where it began.[43] While the speaker is engaged in "spelling" out the true presence of Christ in his fragmented life, Jesus, as Fish points out, is everywhere in the poem: "As the first and last word of the poem, he is its frame, and he is also the frame (body), that is broken in line 3. It is because his frame is first broken and then 'graved' (put into the grave) that hearts broken as his was can be eased."[44]

As in "The Collar" and "Affliction (1)," and Reformed theology, salvation is announced from the very beginning and "at every word." Salvation, however, is not always, or is only eventually, perceived, although it has directed the final outcome.

Herbert's more narrative poems also exhibit the patterns of predestination. "Redemption" shows how a random search has been directed by the foreknowledge of God. Similarly, in "Christmas," the speaker, both with body and mind ("my horse and I") seeking "pleasures," stops at a random inn (the poem makes a point of its randomness—"the next inne I could find") where he finds the Lord waiting for him, "expecting" him:

> After all pleasures as I rid one day,
> My horse and I, both tir'd, bodie and minde,
> With full crie of affections, quite astray,
> I took up in the next inne I could find.
>
> There when I came, whom found I but my deare,
> My dearest Lord, expecting till the grief
> Of pleasures brought me to him, readie there
> To be all passengers most sweet relief?

(1–8)

Though the preceding actions seem, at the time, to be random, the confrontation with Christ is predestined.

The doctrine of predestination and its corollaries manifest themselves in the organization and the underlying ironic framework of the lyrics. As in "Heaven," the echo poem, the questions in Herbert's poetry are generally framed so that the answer is inherent in the question. Stanley Fish comments that "there are any number of formulas that will allow us to talk about Herbert's poetry, but each of them is a rewriting of the contradiction that exists at its heart, the contradiction between the injunction to do work—to catechize, to raise altars, to edify souls, to rear temples, to write poems—and the realization, everywhere insisted upon, that the work has already been done."[45] Fish, focusing on the paradox itself, offers another useful formula for talking about Herbert's poetry. All of the "rewritings" of the paradox—including that of Fish—are simply noticing the traces and the formal implications of Calvinism, which may have managed to inspire a "work ethic," but always insisted "that the work has already been done."

The theology of predestination, the assurance that God is in control of all the contingencies of human experience and that salvation is certain, is important both thematically and formally for Herbert's verse and his imagination. Rudolf Otto has shown how predestination, as a religious idea grounded in the "numinous," tends to manifest itself in conjunction with expressions of free will:

> "Predestination" in this sense . . . has nothing whatever to do with the "unfree will" of "Determinism." Rather, it finds very frequently precisely in the "free will" of the creature the contrast which makes it stand out so prominently. "Will what thou wilt and how thou canst; plan and choose; yet must all come about as it shall and as is determined." That is the earliest and most genuine expression of the matter. In the face of the eternal power man is reduced to naught, *together with* his free choice and action. And the eternal power waxes immeasurable, just because it fulfills its decrees *despite* the freedom of human will.[46]

Herbert's poetry often dramatizes the will—usually, in accordance with Reformation thought, the sinful will—showing how, as Niesel summarizes Calvin, "All that we are able to devise and set in motion is integrated into His plan."[47] The relationship between the speaker in the poem, who is limited and in time, and the poet who controls the poem from the outside, crafting the experience according to objective belief and artistic form, is itself analogous to predestination. God, like the poet, is intimately involved in, but is also apart from, the creation. Human life and a poem, viewed temporally, from the inside, may seem random or contingent, but viewed *sub specie aeternitatis*, from the outside, there are traces of an overreaching control.

— 5 —

Calvinist and Arminian:
The Theological Difference between Herbert and Donne

> If ever book was calculated to drive men to despair, it is Bishop Jeremy Taylor's on Repentance. It first opened my eyes to Arminianism, and that Calvinism is *practically* a far, far more soothing and consoling system.
> —Samuel Taylor Coleridge, *Notes on English Divines*

Despite their similarities as "metaphysical poets," Donne and Herbert are very different. As the two major religious poets of their day, Herbert and Donne, for all their friendship and mutual respect, write from a different kind of religious experience. Louis Martz has noted the contrast between "Donne's instability and Herbert's deeply achieved security."[1] Margaret Blanchard has surveyed the differences between the two exceptionally well, citing Donne's fear of damnation, his tendency to address the self rather than Christ, and his tendency to express a formal rather than a personal relationship with God, all in direct contrast to Herbert.[2] After her incisive and sophisticated comparison, Blanchard suggests several reasons why Donne "was more removed from and more fearful of his God" than Herbert:

Numerous seventeenth century characteristics tended to sever men from God: a theological over-emphasis of doctrinal and intellectual aspects of religion (minimizing the imaginative appeal of Christ's human life); the dogma of justification by faith alone and the resultant stress on steady, unwavering faith (giving rise to despair, guilt and fear of damnation); the sense of "otherness of God" throughout the Protestant Reformation; the emphasis of the legalistic aspects of God and de-emphasis of His immanence; the loss of the "historical concrete," and particularly the rejection of traditional Eucharistic dogma, the continuous-incarnational aspect of Christ's presence in time.[3]

The real problem, she says, is not why Donne was so negative in his spirituality, but why Herbert was so different. Elsie Leach suggests that Donne's fear of judgment is Calvinist and Herbert's confidence in God's love is Arminian.[4] Leach is right in seeking a theological, rather than a merely temperamental difference to account for the very different religious poetry of the two men, but her answer is precisely the opposite of what it should be. In fact, Herbert is the Calvinist and Donne is the Arminian.[5] The sense of security and confidence in Herbert's poetry derives from the Calvinist doctrine of the perseverance of the saints, which insists that salvation is the sole work of God and therefore that it can never be lost. The sense of insecurity and desperation in Donne's poetry derives from the Arminian position that salvation is in some way contingent upon the human will and that therefore one can fall away from grace.

i. Arminianism and Calvinism

Again, Calvin's theological synthesis was practically definitive in England until well into the seventeenth-century. His system of church government and theory of the sacraments were hotly debated by Anglicans, Lutherans, and others, but his central understanding of grace and of salvation was accepted and, in fact, assumed by most Protestants, not as "Calvinism," implying a separate party, but as simply the Reformed, biblical faith. However, an alternative Protestant theology did arise, which would, by the Restoration, eventually supplant Calvinism in Anglican thought; its groundwork was laid by the Dutch cleric Jacobus Arminius (1560–1609), and like Calvin's soteriology, it was to develop in a number of different ecclesiastical and theological directions, characterizing the traditionalist Laud, the separatist Milton, and the evangelical Wesley.

Arminianism may have been an important theological corrective to the weaknesses of Calvinism, but its liberalizing effects were not without costs. Calvinist predestination threatens to imply that God is responsible for evil. The doctrine of limited atonement seems to restrict the scope of Christ's sacrifice and of God's love and seems to be denied by Scripture (1 John 2:2). Another weakness of Calvinism is that it can tend toward antinomianism—if salvation is by grace alone, if grace can not be merited and if salvation, once given, cannot be lost, why should one act morally? Arminianism vindicated God by shifting responsibility for salvation or damnation to human choice, rather than to the choice of God, and reintroduced the importance of personal morality which, if the will is free, is both possible and necessary in a Christian. By shifting the locus of salvation to the human will, rather than to the will of God, Arminianism was conceptually liberating, but practically it placed a heavy burden on the individual soul.[6]

The crucial objection of the Calvinists was to the Arminian notion that one can lose one's salvation. "The theological controversies in Cambridge between 1595 and 1600," says H. C. Porter, "revolved round the nature of the 'comfortable certainty of true faith' and its connection with God's decree of election. William Barrett, by raising the issues of the possible loss of justifying faith, of the limits to the Christian assurance of salvation, and of the quality of justifying faith itself, struck at the heart of the Calvinist certainty."[7] This "Calvinist certainty," affirmed by Herbert and explicitly rejected by Donne, is the central theological and emotional difference between the two religious poets.

ii. Donne's Arminianism

Donne's theological position is notoriously difficult to pin down. If Donne is an Arminian, he is very different from later Arminians such as Jeremy Taylor and John Wesley. Donne strenuously affirms justification by faith alone and his sermons are eloquent in celebrating God's grace. In many ways Donne exemplifies Reformation spirituality, as contrasted to later Protestant thought. He often sounds Calvinist or Lutheran in his sermons and, for example, in "Batter My Heart." Yet in Donne's thought the tightly knit structure of Reformation theology, as articulated by Luther and systematized by Calvin, begins to unravel. Although Donne affirms human depravity and God's election, Calvin's corollary of limited atonement is unequivocally rejected, as is Calvin's understanding of irresistible grace and the perseverance of the saints. Commentators wrestling with the complexity of his theological positions agree in affirming his originality. Calling Donne an Arminian, pure and simple, probably oversimplifies his position.[8] Still, in terms of the five points by which Calvinists and Arminians defined each other since the Synod of Dort (1618), and especially on the question of whether salvation can be lost, Donne would tend to be in the Arminian camp, with Herbert in the Calvinist.

In a consideration of the five points mentioned earlier, the complexity of Donne's religious beliefs and their Arminian drift become clear: Donne believes strongly in human sinfulness, as his writings on the misery and hopelessness of the human condition clearly show; but, unlike Calvinists, he does believe that a measure of free will survived the fall. Unlike later Arminians, Donne did not believe that the will could *effect* salvation, but he did insist that the will must *accept* salvation,[9] and that this is a genuine free choice. For Calvinists, one is saved, as it were, against one's will, and even acceptance of God is possible only by His grace.

Although Donne often writes of election in what seems to be a Calvinist way,[10] he also severely questions its implications.[11] Donne's teachings on predestination and the unconditional quality of election are complex, or perhaps not fully integrated. While according to one study Donne is said to have "actually departed more decisively from Calvinist predestinarianism than any other English divine,"[12] another study sees him as rejecting only the supralapsarian school of Calvinism (that the decree of election preceded the creation and the fall) while affirming the infralapsarian position (that the decree of election was after the creation and God's foreknowledge of the fall.)[13] Part of the difficulty may be that Donne is playing the different theological positions against each other, employing the same kind of paradox, irony, and tortuous convolutions that characterizes all of his "metaphysical" imagery. Thus Donne will often sound Calvinist when he is actually expressing Arminian notions at the same time. Thus *Holy Sonnet* 1 (2), concludes with the terrifying thought

> That Thou lov'st mankind well, yet wilt not choose me,
> And Satan hates me, yet is loath to lose me.
>
> (13–14)[14]

The lines seem to emphasize the exclusivity of God's election associated with Calvinism. Actually, though, it expresses Arminian Universalism, which stresses God's love for all mankind, so that God does not choose individuals whom He will save—of course, this is what the line literally says. Arminians do believe "Thou . . . wilt not choose" the individual, except insofar as God chose to offer all of mankind a chance to be saved; rather, the individual must choose God. Calvinists would believe the opposite: God condemns mankind as a whole, but chooses the individual.

At any rate, Donne explicitly repudiates the doctrine of limited atonement, which suggests that not everyone can be saved:

They are too good husbands, and too thrifty of Gods grace, too sparing of the Holy Ghost; that restraine Gods generall propositions, *Venite omnes* [Matt. 11:28], let all come, and *Vult omnes salvos* [1 Tim. 2:4], God would have all men saved, so particularly, as to say, that when God sayes *All*, he meanes some of all sorts, some Men, some Women, some Jews, some Gentiles, some rich, some poore, but he does not meane as He seems to say, simply All. Yes, God does meane, simply *All*, so as that no man can say to another, God meanes not thee, no man can say to himselfe, God meanes not me.[15]

Donne is no less adamantly opposed to the more comforting Calvinist doctrine of irresistible grace. "Trust not to an irresistible grace that at one time or other God will have thee, whether thou wilt or no."[16] Donne is insistent on the inviolability of the human will even in the act of salvation. "God saves no man without, or against his will."[17]

Here again, one of his poems seems to contradict this denial of Calvinism, "Batter My Heart" (*Holy Sonnet* 10[14]) seems a celebration of irresistible grace, of the Calvinist God who breaks strongholds and ravishes.[18] Although the imaginative and devotional appeal of Reformation spirituality is still evident in the poem, its view of the human will is essentially Arminian. In the poem, the speaker's will is directed to God, but it is hemmed in by sin. "I . . . labour to admit you" (5–6), because "dearly I love You" (9). According to the Calvinist schema, though, the will is rebellious, but it is hemmed in by God. Thus, in "The Collar," the will is portrayed as laboring to exclude God. In Donne's poem, the speaker wishes that God would be more forceful, but in fact, He is not; "You / As yet but knock, breathe, shine, and seek to mend" (1–2). God knocks on the door, as if the sinner must open the door to admit Him, a conceptual contrast with Herbert's "Love (3)," in which God opens the door to admit the sinner. In Donne's poem, the speaker does love God but is frustrated by the sinfulness of his life, which he feels excludes him from God's presence. According to a Calvinist, though, loving God is assurance that one is already loved by God, whose acceptance is unconditional and irrevocable.

Perhaps one of the strengths of Donne's religious poetry comes from his standing at a transition point between Calvinism and Arminianism, between the view that God accomplishes everything for salvation and the view that the burden lies essentially on the self. Donne still finds the earlier position very attractive—he yearns for God to be the ravisher—but he does not really believe in it. This tension between the two kinds of spirituality manifests itself in the complexity of his theological positions and in the richness of his religious verse.

Donne's essential Arminianism is revealed most clearly in his rejection of the perpetuity of salvation, in which he departs most decisively from Calvinist orthodoxy. This final point suggests the practical and psychological implications of both systems, and it is the issue of perseverance that most clearly distinguishes Donne from Herbert.

Donne does reject what was perceived as the Roman Catholic position, which would deny the believer any assurance whatsoever that he will be saved. In one sermon Donne associates, in an interesting way, the Calvinist doctrine of reprobation with the Roman Catholic denial of assurance:

> To conceive a cruell God, a God that hated us, even to damnation, before we were, (as some, who have departed from the sense and modesty of the Ancients, have adventured to say) or to conceive a God so cruell, as that at our death, or in our way, he will afford us no assurance, that hee is ours, and we his, but let us live and die in anxiety and torture of

conscience, in jealousie and suspition of his good purpose towards us in the salvation of our soules, (as those of the Romane Heresie teach) to conceive such a God as from all eternity meant to damne me, or such a God as would never make me know, and be sure that I should bee saved, this is not to professe God to be terrible in his works; for, his Actions are his works, and his Scriptures are his works, and God hath never done, or said anything to induce so terrible an opinion of him.[19]

Donne's own non-Calvinist understanding of assurance—the "peace of conscience, the undoubting trust and assurance of Salvation"—is developed in a sermon in which he first rejects the Roman dependence on works and denial of absolute assurance, in favor of the Reformers' emphasis on the assurance of faith. The believer is assured of salvation insofar as he has faith and, as Donne significantly adds, "as long as he continues so." Donne then attacks those "which would reform the Reformers," who hold that "if ever you had faith, you are safe for ever." This rhetorically oversimplified doctrine of the perseverance of the saints is rejected in favor of "conditional assurance":[20]

Deceive not your selves then, with that new charme and flattery of the soule, that if once you can say to your selves you have faith, you need no more, or that you shall alwaies keepe that alive. . . . So that it is not enough to say, I feele the inspiration of the Spirit of God, He infuses faith, and faith infused cannot be withdrawn; but as there is a Law of faith, and a practice of faith, a Rule of faith, and an example of faith, apply thy selfe to both.[21]

For Donne, assurance is conditional, based on continued faith and in continual repentance for sins. In a sermon on one of the penitential Psalms, Donne observes that "*David* gives no man rule nor example of other assurance in God, than in the remission of sins. Not that any precontract or election makes our sins no sins, or makes our sins no hindrances in our way to salvation, or that we are in Gods favour at that time when we sin, nor returned to his favor before we repent our sin."[22] For the Calvinist, even future sins are totally atoned for already at the cross. "Redemption measures all my time," as Herbert puts it, so that the decree of election, in effect, makes final forgiveness certain. "You taught the Book of Life my name, that so / What ever future sinnes should be miscall, / Your first acquaintance might discredit all" ("H. Baptisme [1]," 10, 13–14).

Donne not only lacks the Calvinist assurance by which sins are unconditionally forgiven by the action and decree of God, but he also lacks what assurance could be found in a Roman Catholic doctrine of relative merit. For Donne, any sin signifies a lack of faith, so that even small sins can be as dangerous as "mortal sins." It is a greater infirmity to be defeated by pygmies than by giants, says Donne. Past victory over great sins means nothing if one then succumbs to sins that are more trivial, a point he illustrates with the figure of a swimmer, after having "swom over a tempetuous sea," drowning, at last, in a "shallow and standing ditch."[23] Sin, for Donne, must be scrupulously watched for and guarded against:

> By disarming thy selfe, by devesting thy garisons, by discontinuing thy watches, meerly by inconsideration, thou sellest thy soul for nothing, for little pleasure, little profit, thou frustratest thy saviour of that purchase, which he bought with his precious blood, and thou enrichest the Devils treasure.[24]

Salvation remains uncertain—after swimming the ocean one might still drown in a standing ditch. The believer must be in a continual state of self-scrutiny and repentance. Hell is a continual possibility and the possibility of falling away from grace is a continual nightmare:

> *Horrendum est*, when Gods hand is bent to strike, *it is a fearfull thing, to fall into the hands of the living God*; but to fall out of the hands of the living God, is a horror beyond our imagination.[25]

A Calvinist, on the other hand, would deny that it is possible to fall out of the hands of the living God. For Donne, the possibility is ever present in his imagination, and it looms behind much of his religious poetry.

Donne believes that an individual is assured of salvation only "as long as he continues in faith" and repents of his sins, only as long as his will is aligned with God's. The problem, though, is that Donne sees himself as being as "inconstant" to God as he was to his mistresses:

> Oh, to vex me, contraryes meete in one:
> Inconstancy unnaturally hath begott
> A constant habit; that when I would not
> I change in vowes, and in devotions.
> As humorous is my contritione
> As my prophane love, and as soone forgott:
> As ridlingly distempered, cold and hott,
> As praying, as mute; as infinite, as none.
> I durst not view heaven yesterday; and to day
> In prayers, and flattering speaches I court God:
> To morrow I quake with true feare of his rod.
> So my devout fitts come and go away
> Like a fantastique Ague: save that here
> Those are my best dayes, when I shake with feare.
>
> (*Holy Sonnet*, 3[19])

Vacillations of moods become of the utmost importance to Donne because on them depends his eternal salvation. "What if this present were the worlds last night?" (9[13],1). What if he dies before he can repent? "Tis late to aske abundance of thy grace, / When we are there" (4[7],11–12).

> I have a sinne of feare, that when I have spunne
> My last thred, I shall perish on the shore;
> Sweare by thy selfe, that at my death thy Sunne
> Shall shine as it shines now, and heretofore;
> And, having done that, Thou hast done,
> I have no more.
> ("A Hymne to God the Father," 13–18)

The question of dying in a state of grace is one of Donne's most urgent themes.[26] Donne trains like a spiritual athlete for death.

For Donne to be assured, paradoxically, he must be in a continual state of repentance and unease:

> O might these sighs and tears returne againe
> Into my breast and eyes, which I have spent,
> That I might in this holy discontent
> Mourne with some fruit, as I have mourn'd in vain.
> (*Holy Sonnet* 3[3], 1–4)

Such "holy discontent" is essential if grace depends not solely upon the sovereign will of God, as in Calvinism, but in the human act and emotion of repentance. This is not to say that Donne is a Pelagian, or an Arminian like Jeremy Taylor, who puts far more trust in the human will than Donne would allow.[27] Donne does believe that one is saved by grace. "Yet Grace, if thou repent, thou canst not lacke" (*Holy Sonnet* 2[4], 9). The conditional clause is, of course, significant. A Calvinist would not make grace contingent upon repentance, but would make repentance contingent upon grace. Repentance itself is a gift of God. According to Herbert, God will either "stop our sinnes from growing thick and wide, / Or else give tears to drown them, as they grow" ("H. Baptisme [1]," 7–8).

Donne is himself aware of the difficulties in his theological position, which insists on the necessity of grace, but does not permit grace to do everything. He sometimes questions his own Arminianism:

> Yet Grace, if thou repent, thou canst not lacke;
> But who shall give thee that grace to beginne?
> (*Holy Sonnet* 2 [4], 9–10)

The conditional clause ("if thou repent") intrudes itself between grace, offered as an alternative to damnation ("yet grace . . ."), and its abundance ("Thou canst not lacke"). In the next line the conditional clause itself is scrutinized: Is not the very act of repenting the action of grace? The poem closes by positing two alternatives:

> Oh make thy selfe with holy mourning blacke,
> And red with blushing, as thou art with sinne,
> Or wash thee in Christs blood, which hath this might
> That being red, it dyes red soules to white.

A more assured religious poet may have used "and" in place of "or"—repent *and* Christ will cleanse you. Donne presents the two terms as alternatives: "make thy selfe" repentant *"or* wash thee in Christs blood."[28] Salvation becomes a function of the self or Christ, of repentance or atonement. Donne is perhaps caught between the poles. Too much of an Augustinian to trust the will and too much of an Arminian to trust grace alone, Donne denies himself any confidence.

iii. Their Poems to Each Other: The Anchor and the Seal

The differences between the religious poetry of Donne and Herbert are obvious. Of the twenty-four Holy Sonnets, nineteen deal with the imminent possibility of hell. For a Calvinist, hell is not a possibility for an elect Christian, and even in the most intense poems of spiritual anguish, Herbert does not feel himself threatened by damnation. For Herbert, salvation is secure, forgiveness is unconditional, grace is irresistible. In a sermon on the parable in Luke 14:23, Donne develops the figure of Christ as the Master of the feast. Donne stresses the imperturbability of the Master:

> The Master of the feast invited many; solemnly, before hand; they came not: He sent his servants to call in the poore, upon the sudden; and they came; so he receives late commers. And there is a *Compelle intrare.* He sends a servant to compell some to come in. But that was but a servants work, the Master onely invited; he compelled none. We the servants of God, have certaine compulsions, to bring men hither; the denouncing of Gods Judgements, the answers of the Church, Excommunications and the rest, are compulsories. The State hath compulsories, too, in the penall Laws. But all that is but to bring them into the house, to church. . . . But to salvation, onely the Master brings—and (in that Parable) the Master does onely invite; he compells none.[29]

In Herbert's treatment of the same figure in "Love (3)," the Master is active, drawing nearer to the guilty soul, insisting upon taking all of the responsibility for his sin, and, finally, compelling him to join the feast: "You must sit down, sayes Love." Calvinists felt that Arminian universalism depersonalized salvation, making God inactive, a passive reservoir of grace to be tapped or refused. Arminian soteriology seemed to make God more distant and detached. Even the doctrine of limited atonement (Calvinists prefer the term *particular* atonement) worked to preserve this intimacy. Arminians may be on solid ground theologically in emphasizing that

Christ died for everyone; Calvinists, on the other hand, may be on solid ground psychologically in emphasizing that "Christ died for me."[30] In fact, Herbert seems to come as close as he ever comes to the doctrine of limited atonement[32] in insisting upon the irresistibility of grace and the intrinsic efficacy of Christ's sacrifice:

> Besides, thy death and bloud
> Show'd a strange love to all our good:
> Thy sorrows were in earnest; no faint proffer,
> Or superficiall offer
> Of what we might not take, or be withstood.
>
> ("Obedience," 26–30)

Paradoxically, Calvinism, for all of its harshness, offers Herbert a sense of security and intimacy with God. In writing of the last judgment, Herbert confesses that "I see no fears" ("Justice [1]," 14), and his apocalyptic poems at the end of "The Church" are joyful and even whimsical in tone. He anticipates with the greatest yearning beholding God face to face:

> What wonders shall we feel, when we shall see
> Thy full-eyed love!
> When thou shalt look us out of pain,
> And one aspect of thine spend in delight
> More then a thousand sunnes disburse in light,
> In heav'n above.
>
> ("The Glance," 19–24)

For Donne, in marked contrast to Herbert, God remains terrifying:

> My body, and soule, and I shall sleepe a space,
> But my ever-waking part shall see that face,
> Whose feare already shakes my every joynt.
>
> (*Holy Sonnet* 3[6], 6–8)

In comparing the religious positions of the two poets, one can do no better than to consider the poem Donne wrote to Herbert, "To Mr. George Herbert, with my Seal, of the Anchor and Christ," and Herbert's reply.[32]

> A sheafe of Snakes used heretofore to be
> My seal, the Crest of our poore family.
> Adopted in Gods Family, and so
> Our old Coat lost, unto new armes I go.
> The Crosse (my seal at Baptism) spred below,
> Does, by that form, into an Anchor grow.
> Crosses grow Anchors; Bear, as thou shouldst do
> Thy Crosse, and that Crosse grows an Anchor too.

> But he that makes our Crosses Anchors thus,
> Is Christ, who there is crucifi'd for us.
> Yet may I, with this, my first Serpents hold,
> God gives new blessings, and yet leaves the old;
> The Serpent, may, as wise, my pattern be;
> My poison, as he feeds on dust, that's me.
> And as he rounds the Earth to murder sure,
> My death he is, but on the Crosse, my cure.
> Crucifie nature then, and then implore
> All Grace from him, crucified there before;
> When all is Crosse, and that Crosse Anchor grown,
> The Seal's a Catechism, not a Seal alone.
> Under that little Seal great gifts I send,
> Wishes, and prayers, pawns, and fruits of a friend.
> And may that Saint which rides in our great Seal,
> To you, who bear his name, great bounties deal.

The Anchor is a traditional symbol of hope, especially of the hope of salvation (Heb. 6:19–20). For Donne, "Crosses grow Anchors," but the emphasis throughout the poem is on the cross borne, not by Christ, but by the believer. "Bear, as thou shouldst do / Thy Crosse, and that Crosse grows an Anchor too." In other words, the locus of hope is in the sufferings of the individual, although it is only through Christ that the individual's sufferings can be so transformed ("But he that makes our Crosses Anchors thus, / Is Christ who there is crucifi'd for us"). In Calvinism, the basis of assurance is placed in history, in the irrevocable past (the crucifixion, the decree before the creation of the world); for Donne, the basis of assurance is in the continuing experience of the individual Christian. Donne's poem characteristically is a meditation on sin; the Serpent— symbolizing Satan, Donne's own nature as expressed in his family crest, with the traditional symbolism of sin being nailed to Christ's cross—is as much the subject of this poem as the Anchor, the symbol of assurance. Donne's departure from Calvinism is especially pronounced in this poem:

> Crucifie nature then, and then implore
> All grace from him, crucified there before.

Donne's ordering of nature and grace, so precisely established by two "thens" in a single line, would be seen by a Calvinist as being exactly upside-down. A Calvinist would insist that imploring "All Grace from him, crucified there before" must come first; then, and only then, can the sinful nature be crucified in the process of sanctification. Even in a poem on the ostensible subject of Christ's cross turning into the Anchor of hope, Donne cannot escape his preoccupation with sin and the sense that salvation is somehow contingent upon his own efforts and failures.

Herbert's reply in effect corrects Donne's understanding of his own symbolism:

> Although the Crosse could not Christ here detain,
> Though nail'd unto't, but he ascends again,
> Nor yet thy eloquence here keep him still,
> But onely while thou speak'st; This Anchor will.
> Nor canst thou be content, unlesse thou to
> This certain Anchor adde a Seale, and so
> The Water, and the Earth both unto thee
> Doe owe the symbole of their certainty.
> Let the world reel, we and all ours stand sure,
> This holy Cable's of all storms secure.
>
> (1–10)[33]

The first four lines compliment Donne's eloquence, as they subtly challenge his doctrine. Herbert first establishes how Christ's suffering on the cross gives way to the glory of the Ascension, perhaps insinuating that just as Christ could not be detained by His cross, neither should Christians be detained by theirs. At any rate, Herbert does say that while Donne's cross-centered poetry creates the illusion of Christ "here" on the cross, Christ, in fact, has ascended into heaven, in triumph and power. Herbert perceptively sketches the possibilities and limitations of art—Donne's eloquence does, in a sense, capture Christ, "But onely while thou speak'st." Art can create an important temporary illusion, but it is to be contrasted to the objectivity of faith. The first clause, extending for four lines, with its complicated syntax and ambiguity, is balanced by three words of simplicity and certainty: "This Anchor will." That is, this Anchor, Hope, will keep Christ with us. For an Anglican inclined to the theology of Calvin, the theological virtue of hope would connote not merely wishful thinking, but the assurance of salvation. Thomas Wilson, a contemporary of Herbert, in his *Christian Dictionary* defined hope as "an assured expectation of all promised good things of this life; especially, of heavenly glorie." For Herbert the cross is, specifically, an anchor, which infallibly establishes the Christian even in the chaotic storms of intellect, introspection, and emotional afflictions:

> Let the world reel, we and all ours stand sure,
> This holy Cable's of all storms secure.

Herbert's understanding of the anchor as a symbol of eternal security is made even more explicit in another poem on Donne's seal:

> When winds and waves rise highest, I am sure,
> This *Anchor* keeps my *faith*, that, me secure.

Both Donne and Herbert would agree that faith keeps "me secure." The question is, what keeps faith secure? Is faith contingent upon the human will? Can heaven be lost, as Donne believes and fears? For Herbert, faith itself is grounded outside of the believer in the objective work of God: "This *Anchor* [i.e., the Cross] keeps my *faith* . . . secure." The believer's security does depend upon faith, as Donne agrees, but for Herbert faith itself is "anchored" securely by Christ.

While establishing that the anchor is a natural symbol of the believer's inviolable salvation, Herbert is also developing the implications suggested by the seal, the physical object itself that Donne was writing about and that he sent to him. In Calvinist terminology, the word *seal* has reference to the act by which God irrevocably certifies the soul's salvation. *Seal*, to Wilson, connotes "the firme stablenesse of Gods free predestination to life," a work of the Spirit "assuring every elect believer of his own adoption and salvation by Christ [2 Tim. 2:19; Eph. 1:13]." Thus Herbert's reply to Donne is especially pointed:

> Nor canst thou be content, unlesse thou to
> This certain Anchor adde a Seal.

Donne cannot be content, suggests Herbert, unless he adds to the anchor of hope the notion of the seal of salvation. Donne is impressing on the hot wax ("The Water, and the Earth")[34] the seal of the anchor, imaging, perhaps unwittingly, "the symbole of their certainty."

In Donne's poem, snakes give way to crosses, which give way again to snakes that must be crucified; crosses will turn to anchors, but the focus of the poem is on the cross here and now, which the believer must carry. Herbert explores the figurative meaning of the anchor symbol itself, which Donne does not do, finding in it and in the very concept of sealing a letter symbols of assurance. Herbert's reply is both a celebration of and an argument for the Calvinist doctrine of the perseverance of the saints. Throughout his reply, phrases and images are repeated that speak, in such marked contrast to the tenor of Donne's poem, of certainty and security: "This Anchor will," "this certain Anchor," "the symbole of their certainty," "we and all ours stand sure," "of all storms secure," "in great Loves Commonweal (where nothing should be broke)," "I am sure," "This Anchor keeps my *faith*, that, me secure."

Herbert's reply, with its indirection and tact, is highly reminiscent of the theological counseling procedure described in "The Country Parson" (24:280–83). Whenever the Parson finds someone troubled theologically, "he fortifyes, and strengthens with his utmost skill." Such theological problems are of two kinds, both of which might seem applicable to Donne: "either they think, that there is none that can or will look after things, but all goes by chance, or wit" (i.e., they deny predestination in the sense of providence—Donne in his emphasis on free will might be thought to over-stress the potentialities of "wit"); "or else, though there be a great Gover-nour of all things, yet to them he is lost, as if they said, God doth forsake and persecute them." To the first, the Parson unveils God's action of "pres-ervation," how God preserves the physical creation at every moment, then proceeding to the fulfillment of the prophecies in Scripture. The implica-tion is that God can similarly "preserve" His human creatures, and that the promises of Scripture are reliable—both points relating to the doctrine of the perseverance of the saints. "But if he sees them neerer desperation, then Atheisme; not so much doubting a God, as that he is theirs; then he dives unto the boundlesse Ocean of Gods Love, and the unspeakable riches of his loving kindnesse," showing with Hooker that the very con-sciousness of sin is itself evidence of God's love. However, the Parson must argue "without opposing directly (for disputation is no cure for Atheisme)"; rather, the points are casually "woven into his discourse, at severall times and occasions," and applied with "dexterity," just as they are in his poems to Donne.

This is not to say that Herbert was arguing with Donne or that he was explicitly counseling him—Herbert was not yet in orders, and Donne was a distinguished Dean. Rather, the two sets of poems highlight the emotional and doctrinal differences between the two poets as they both meditate upon the same symbols.

iv. Lamb in the Wolf's Skin, Wolf in the Lamb's Skin

Both the Arminianism of Donne and the Calvinism of Herbert result in religious poetry of the highest order. Despite their obvious similarities, as "metaphysical" poets, as Christians, and as seventeenth-century Anglican Protestants, there is nevertheless a real theological difference, which mani-fests itself in the particular strengths and weaknesses of both religious poets.

There is a sense in which Donne's religious poetry is more exciting than Herbert's. The speaker of Donne's poetry remains always on the knife edge between salvation or damnation. More is at stake for Donne. There is a nervousness, an urgency, that makes for compelling religious verse. Con-flict is continuous, resulting in complicated tensions, in a dynamism born of intense self-scrutiny and desperate wrenchings of the will.

On the other hand, there is relatively little variety or scope in Donne's religious verse. For Donne, faith must be continually renewed and the saving encounter with Christ endlessly repeated. Over and over again in the "Holy Sonnets," the speaker faces damnation, then turns to Christ. There is little thematic progression in the sonnets; rather, the sequence of justification by faith is replayed, with variations, again and again. Sin is followed by grace, which is followed by sin, in a cycle that is broken by death. Another weakness of Donne's religious poetry is that it tends to focus on the self rather than on God. Donne's poetry, although not his sermons, does tend to be introspective rather than transcendent in its focus.[35] Donne's theology requires an intense kind of self-scrutiny, a heightened awareness of sin and vacillations of the will, that makes for great poetry, but it also makes extremely difficult the kind of self-forgetfulness required in most religious experience.

Herbert, on the other hand, writes out of an intimacy with God, an intimacy at least partly issuing from a confidence in the inviolability of their relationship. Herbert addresses God in a variety of tones, from adoration to levity, from the impudent to the hostilely bitter, from anger to love. This tonal range and the underlying unity of devotion that is evident in *The Temple* can perhaps be partially accounted for by Herbert's conviction that nothing he can say or do can separate him from God. There is also a theological breadth that is missing in Donne's poetry (although, again, not in his sermons). Herbert writes of justification, but he then goes on to write of other aspects of the religious life. Both poles of the religious relationship are explored; the self, portrayed with great emotional honesty, and also God, as a felt reality, transcendent and numinous, yet immanent and personal. Literary evocations of God are notoriously liable to fail, and Herbert is one of the few poets to succeed, both religiously and imaginatively.

Herbert's poetry, though, is static compared to Donne's. Any conflicts are either over before they begin (as in "The Collar," framed by the past tense) or they are quickly resolved either in the individual poem or in the sequence of *The Temple.* The ultimate question of salvation or damnation is never raised by Herbert—the issue has been taken out of his hands, and has been settled, as it were, long ago. The will is less active in Herbert; in fact, it is generally an obstacle to the "passive righteousness" required by his theology. Yet, although Herbert's theology and his poetry are more static than Donne's, this stasis perhaps allows him to write of the substance of the religious life rather than merely the desire for it. Although Herbert's stasis may make his poetry seem less emotional than Donne's, it also, perhaps, allows him to be more "artful."

It is paradoxical that Herbert's confidence in and intimacy with God are due, at least in part, to Calvinism, with its harsh doctrines of total depravity and limited atonement, and that Donne's uncertainty and even torment should be due to the seemingly more liberal and humane doctrines that characterize Arminianism, with its insistence on free will and the possibility that anyone can be saved. However, no less an authority, both in poetry and in religion, than Coleridge has pointed to the same paradox:

Arminianism is cruel to individuals, for fear of damaging the race by false hopes and improper confidences, while Calvinism is horrible for the race, but full of consolation to the suffering individual. . . . Calvinism (Archbishop Leighton's for example) compared with Taylor's Arminianism, is as the lamb in the wolf's skin to the wolf in the lamb's skin: the one is cruel in the phrases, the other in the doctrine.[36]

Arminianism, by rejecting complacency and by holding out the possibility of salvation to everyone, is both beneficial and comforting applied to humankind as a whole, but in placing the burden of salvation or damnation on the human will, in all of its frailty, it is "cruel to individuals." Calvinism, which preaches that God chooses the few whom He will save, leaving the nonelect to eternal punishment, is indeed "horrible for the race," but the very notion of a grace that is irresistible, unconditional, and irrevocable is "full of consolation to the suffering individual." Herbert is a lamb clothed in the wolf's skin of Calvinism. Donne is a wolf, gnawing his own flesh, clothed in the enlightened theology of Arminianism. Calvinism "is cruel in the phrases," with its dreadful language of depravity and reprobation; Arminianism has gentle phrases (free will, universal atonement), but is cruel "in the doctrine." Coleridge, perhaps faced with the incapacity of his own will, his inability, for instance, to simply choose to stop taking opium, saw the consolation in a theology that based salvation not on the contingency of human will and efforts, but on the omnipotent will and unceasing effort of God.

—— 6 ——
Sanctification:
The Theological Sequence of *The Temple*

> And indeed, this restoration does not take place in one
> moment or one day or one year; but through continual and
> sometimes even slow advances God wipes out in his elect
> the corruptions of the Flesh, cleanses them of guilt, conse-
> crates them to himself as temples renewing all their minds
> to true purity that they may practice repentance throughout
> their lives and know that this warfare will end only at
> death.
>
> —Calvin, *Institutes 3.3.9*

Herbert himself described *The Temple* as "a picture of the many spiritual conflicts that have passed betwixt God and my soul, before I could subject mine to the will of Jesus my master: in whose service I have now found perfect freedom."[1] Herbert, in discussing his poetry, is making direct reference to a key notion of Reformation spirituality, the process of sanctification. Salvation of the soul is but the first phase of God's work; the soul must then be made holy, as Herbert acknowledges at the outset in the last lines of "The Altar" ("O let thy blessed SACRIFICE be mine, / And sanctifie this ALTAR to be thine"). God will save, and He will also "sanctifie." When the soul is justified by faith, it is regenerated by the indwelling Holy Spirit; human nature, though—"the Flesh"—is still depraved. God and the soul are in conflict, a conflict of wills, until "I could subject mine to the will of Jesus my master." According to Wilson's *Christian Dictionary*, paralleling Herbert, sanctification is "a freedome from the tyranny of sinne, into the liberty of holynesse, begun heere, and daily to be encreased till we be perfect." Conflict between God and the soul eventually, according to Herbert, issues in "perfect freedom." Herbert's poetry, then, by his own description, is a "picture" of sanctification.[2]

The Reformation doctrine of sanctification helps explain the conflicts in Herbert's poetry. The vacillation of moods, the warfare between spirit and flesh, the sense in which both good works and guilt can be a snare, the role of suffering in the Christian life, are all thoroughly treated by Reformation theologians in ways that illuminate Herbert's poetry.

Sanctification, which is essentially the Reformation doctrine of the Christian life, is especially useful in understanding the ordering of the poems in *The Temple.* The poem on the law, "The Church-porch," is followed by a clearly ordered sequence of poems on Christ. Thereafter the poems have proved harder to classify as a coherent, linked series, with poems of exaltation alternating with poems of spiritual desolation. At the close of the volume, a thematic sequence seems to reemerge with a series of poems on death and the apocalypse. According to Reformation theologians, sanctification involves exactly the kind of conflict and vacillation that characterizes the large middle section of *The Temple.* Sanctification is concluded by death, in which the fallen "flesh" becomes dust, leaving the spirit victorious, a point that explains not only the sequence but the tone of the final poems on death. The process of sanctification is emphasized and reiterated, on a larger scale, in "The Church Militant" and in the final poem of *The Temple.*

i. The Polarity of Reformation Spirituality and of The Temple

Despite the doctrine of the perseverance of the saints, "the minds of the godly," as Calvin observes, "are rarely at peace" (*Institutes* 3.2.7). Reformation spirituality affirms both human depravity and unconditional grace, doctrines that imply both humility and confidence, desolation and joy. The difficulties of the Christian life—the problems of changing moods, suffering, doubt, and recurring sin—were major concerns of the theologians. There is, though, no question of failing at sanctification, which is predestined and which always accompanies justification.[3] It is a process caused by God in which the believer is made to die to self so as to depend totally on Him. Sanctification does imply moral reformation, as the sinful will is subjugated to the righteous will of God, but it also achieves its effect by moral and spiritual failure. "The more a man is marked by the spirit of holiness," says Calvin, "the more must he realize how far he is yet from the attainment of perfect righteousness, and is thus led to trust only in God's pure mercy.[4] Niesel comments that "in this regard progress is properly the recognition of our lack of progress."[5]

"For whomever the Lord had adopted and deemed worthy of his fellowship," according to Calvin, "ought to prepare themselves for a hard, toilsome, and unquiet life, crammed with very many and various kinds of evil" (*Institutes* 3.8.1). Human nature is still depraved, even after salvation.

The indwelling Holy Spirit and the providence of God will bring it to perfection, but the process will, inevitably, go against the inclinations of the self. "Obviously, if everything went according to their own liking, they would not know what it is to follow God" (*Institutes* 3.8.4). If the human nature is depraved, it will inevitably be in conflict with God, and human nature will be defeated in the contest, often in a very painful way. The kind of suffering and even failure which Calvin continually insists upon, is, however, purposeful. "Not without hard struggle is each one able to persuade himself of what all confess with the mouth: namely, that God is faithful" (*Institutes* 3.2.15). "Hard struggle," paradoxically, is the only way to learn God's faithfulness and love.

Thus the poems in "The Church" that follow the series on justification through Christ record an extremely wide range of moods, from exaltation to near despair. This very vacillation points to the doctrine of sanctification, picturing all of the varying moods and afflictions that the process of being made holy was believed to involve. The Christ poems are concluded by poems of sacramental commitment, "Holy Baptisme" (1) and (2), the rite that begins the Christian life. The three poems immediately following are startling in such a context: "Nature" ("Full of rebellion, I would die"), "Sinne (1)" ("Yet all these fences and their whole array / One cunning bosome-sinne blows quite away") and "Affliction (1)" ("Well, I will change the service"). Such poems of seeming failure coming immediately after the justification and baptism poems may seem out of place, or at least not purposefully arranged, but the very same sequence is evident in *The Institutes,* in which the almost lyrical section on rebirth in Christ is followed immediately by five sections proving that believers will still sin.[6] In *The Temple,* these negative poems are followed by "Repentance," "Faith," "Prayer (1)," "The H. Communion," "Antiphon (1)"—a hymn of praise— and "Love (1) and (2)." As indicated by the titles alone, Herbert is clearly depicting in this sequence a reconciliation with God. Sin is followed by repentance, which gives way to the various modes of communion with God, and finally to love, which involves an emotional, joyful response to God, based on the recognition of God's identity. Yet these seven poems of affirmation are followed by another poem of dejection, "Employment (1)" ("I am no link of thy great chain" [21]), followed, again, by two poems of affirmation and communion, "The H. Scriptures (1) and (2)." This pattern of alternation repeats itself in various configurations until, with "Death," Herbert begins a series on the Apocalypse. This mixing of positive and negative experiences is often the subject of individual poems (such as "Whitsunday"). The large group of poems between "H. Baptisme (2)" and "Death," is not, strictly speaking, a sequence, and despite inner grouping of poems, their arrangement may be somewhat arbitrary; but the very irregularity of their ordering helps to image the conflicts and vacillations that were understood as being inherent in the Christian life.[7] McCanles describes Herbert's arrangement of the poems as a "sine wave of heights and depths."[8] The scientific metaphor is very close to Hooker's description of the Christian life, which also applies to the structure of *The Temple:* "The higher we flow the nearer we are unto an ebb."[9]

The poems of sanctification, dealing with the Christian life, are introduced and announced by the baptism poems, which look backward, to baptism and to the cross, and forward, to the poems of struggle and defeat that follow:

> As he that sees a dark and shadie grove,
>   Stayes not, but looks beyond it on the skie;
>   So when I view my sinnes, mine eyes remove
> More backward still, and to that water flie,
> Which is above the heav'ns, whose spring and vent
>   Is in my deare Redeemers pierced side.
>   O blessed streams! either ye do prevent
> And stop our sinnes from growing thick and wide,
> Or else give tears to drown them, as they grow.
>   In you Redemption measures all my time,
>   And spreads the plaister equall to the crime.
> You taught the Book of Life my name, that so
>   What ever future sinnes should me miscall,
>   Your first acquaintance might discredit all.
>
> ("Holy Baptisme [1]")

The water of baptism is conflated with the biblical image of waters above the heavens (Gen. 1:6–8). Falling water is, for Herbert, a symbol of grace (cf. "Grace"), with the wounds of Christ being the outlet for the water that is stored in heaven. If salvation is based not on human experience but on the finished work of Christ on the cross, then assurance in times of difficulty and sin comes from looking back to what has already been irrevocably bestowed. One can look back to one's baptism,[10] to the historical execution of Jesus, to one's election "before the Foundation of the world" (Eph. 1:4). Such retrospection is important in divorcing the contingencies of the human condition from the certainty of salvation. Structurally, in terms of *The Temple*, the poem points in two directions: to the preceding poems on "my deare Redeemer," and to the following poems describing the believer's "future sinnes." The certainty of salvation, so firmly set down in this poem, is meant to frame and give perspective to the poems that follow. "What ever future sinnes should me miscall" are already discredited. Since he is irrevocably saved, God will take care of his sins, either by stopping them, as in "The Collar," or by giving the gift of repentance. The speaker's name has already been inscribed in the "Book of Life," so his vision "stayes not" on his sins. For Herbert, "Redemption measures all my time." That is, the "Redemption" imaged in the preceding Christ-sequence "measures all my time," imaged in the succeeding poems. The affirmation of this poem is meant to govern and to accompany the poems of failure that follow.

"H. Baptisme (1)" speaks both of failure and of security. Similarly, Reformation spirituality requires both humility and confidence: knowledge of one's total depravity is balanced by the assurance of salvation. This theological paradox also helps to account for the polarity in the following section of Herbert's verse. "The more severe we are towards ourselves, and the more sharply we examine our own sins," writes Calvin, "the more we ought to hope that God is favorable and merciful towards us" (*Institutes* 3.3.15). In other words, by realizing one's own incapacity, the soul can be led to a firmer dependence on God. Self-abnegation and assurance thus complement one another. Calvin quotes St. Bernard:

> Sorrow for sins is necessary if it be not unremitting. I beg you to turn your steps back sometimes from troubled and anxious remembering of your ways, and to go forth to the tableland of serene remembrance of God's benefits. Let us mingle honey with wormwood that its wholesome bitterness may bring health when it is drunk tempered with sweetness. If you take thought upon yourselves in your humility, take thought likewise upon the Lord in his goodness.[11]

Herbert likewise, in the poems that follow, "mingles honey with wormwood," alternating between sorrow and serenity, thoughts of self and thoughts of God, striving in this section of *The Temple* for a "wholesome bitterness . . . tempered with sweetness."

ii. *The Flesh and the Spirit: The Reformation* Psychomachia

A major aspect of Reformation thought, which helps account for the polarity in this section of *The Temple*, is the inner conflict between the "old man" of sin and the regenerated "new man," both of which are contending within the believer. The Holy Spirit indwells the believer; the "flesh," the depraved human nature, still remains, so that the spirit—comprising the human soul indwelled by the Holy Spirit—and the flesh—both physical weakness tainted by the fall and the depraved human will—are in continual conflict with each other. "The flesh lusteth always contrary to the spirit," as explained by Article IX of the Thirty-nine Articles. "And this infection of nature doth remain, yea in them that are regenerated; whereby the lust of the flesh . . . (which some do expound the wisdom, some sensuality, some the affection, some the desire of the flesh), is not subject to the Law of God." Sanctification is the process by which the spirit attains victory over the flesh, a victory complete only upon death, when the flesh, with its infirmities, is dissolved, so that the conflict ends with the regenerated self made completely holy.[12] This continual battle between the old nature and the new nature, the flesh and the spirit, not only involves the moral sphere but was also seen as an explanation for emotional turmoil and for doubt. According to Lewis Bayly, "the *truest faith* hath oftentimes the *least feeling,* and *greatest doubts;* but so long as thou *hatest* such doubtings, they shall not be laid unto thy charge; for they belong to the *flesh,* from which thou art *divorced.* When thy flesh shall *perish,* thy weak inward man, which *hates* them, and *loves* the Lord Jesus, shall be saved."[13]

This conflict between the old nature and the new is a continual theme in Herbert's poetry. Its terms are drawn clearly in the second baptism poem, which, with "H. Baptisme (1)," completes the introduction to the series on sanctification. The first stanza refers to the poet's baptism as an infant, a meditation on God's action of grace, which even precedes conscious faith.

> Since, Lord, to thee
> A narrow way and little gate
> Is all the passage, on my infancie
> Thou didst lay hold, and antedate
> My faith in me.

The second stanza explores the requirement that "Except ye be converted, and become as little children, ye shall not enter into the kingdom of heaven" (Matt. 18:3ff.).

> O let me still
> Write thee great God, and me a childe:
> Let me be soft and supple to thy will,
> Small to my self, to others mild,
> Behither ill.

In the third stanza, the flesh is opposed to the soul, and "the growth of flesh" is contrasted, unfavorably, to "Childhood." This is simply another traditional formulation of the dichotomy between the spirit and the flesh, the old man and the new man. John Bradford describes the conflict of sanctification as a struggle between a giant (the old man of sin) and a child (the new man, born again in Christ).[14] The childlike innocence and submission required by Christ applies to the converted soul, the "inward man" ("Except ye be converted and become as little children"), which is in contention with the "flesh":

> Although by stealth
> My flesh get on, yet let her sister
> My soul bid nothing, but preserve her wealth:
> The growth of flesh is but a blister,
> Childhood is health.

Herbert is not advocating perpetual childishness.[15] Rather, he is introducing the protagonists of the Reformation *psychomachia* in very traditional, yet imaginatively realized terms. "The growth of flesh," of depraved human nature, is definitely a disease, in these terms, and is opposed to the sanctity of that part of the soul which has been "born again" and is promised salvation—"Childhood is health." The poem admits that "by stealth" the flesh will "get on," but this does not effect the security of the soul, whose "wealth" is to be "preserved" by God. Just as "H. Baptisme (1)" serves as a transition between justification and sanctification, introducing the paradox of sin and assurance, "H. Baptisme (2)" completes the introduction to the sanctification poems by specifying a theological and symbolic framework for the conflicts that are to follow.[16]

The battle is not conceived as simply a conflict between two aspects of the self, but as a struggle between the sinful self and God, Who, as the Holy Spirit, indwells the regenerated heart. In "The Reprisall," Christ is described as a wrestler, with whom the speaker is struggling. The poem ends in a succinct statement of what sanctification involves, expressed in terms of the familiar conflict between the "old man" and the "new": "In thee I will overcome / The man, who once against thee fought" (14–15). The man who once fought against Christ is still fighting in this poem. The speaker prays for "a disentangled state and free" (6), and this disentangling is at least alluded to in these lines, in which the "I" is disassociated from "the man" who still opposes God. Although the disentangled soul is now imagined as wrestling not with Christ but with "the old man" of sin, the latter will be overcome only "in thee," in Christ, who is still left wrestling with a contentious self. The conflict posited by the Reformation doctrine of sanctification is complex in its psychology. The conscious self will tend to be a function of both "the inward man" of faith and "the old man" of sin, so that sanctification will sometimes assume the form of a struggle with the self and sometimes the form of a struggle with God.

Whereas the morality plays presented the spiritual warfare as a struggle between "the good Angel" and "the bad Angel," with the human soul at stake, the Reformation presented the warfare as an internal struggle between two contradictory aspects of the self, the outcome of which is assured. In two poems "Decay" and "Sion," Herbert places this *psychomachia* in the larger context of the way God formerly dealt with his people. In "Decay" Herbert contrasts the Old Covenant, in which God dealt with His people in external terms, to the New Covenant, in which God dwells within the believer's heart.

> Sweet were the dayes, when thou didst lodge with Lot,
> Struggle with Jacob, sit with Gideon,
> Advise with Abraham, when thy power could not
> Encounter Moses strong complaints and mone.
>   Thy words were then, *Let Me alone.*

> One might have sought and found thee presently
> At some fair oak, or bush, or cave, or well:
> Is my God this way? No, they would reply:
> He is to Sinai gone, as we heard tell:
>   List, ye may heare great Aarons bell.

"Sweet were the dayes," says Herbert, when God related to His people externally, face-to-face. The localized God of holy places is, in many ways, easier to find. The first stanza alludes to Moses' successfully persuading God to change His mind (Exod. 32:9–14), even though God first told Moses to "Let me alone" (32:10). Although the episode is a good example of how "sweet were the dayes" when God related so directly with His people, Herbert gives the three words a new emphasis. In Exodus, God's statement, "Let me alone," comes first, then, in light of "Moses strong complaints and mone," the Lord repents. In Herbert's version the repentance is described first, so that God's initial response is given an unusually strong emphasis, reinforced by the italics, the position as the last words in the stanza, the rhythmic inversion of the third foot, and the strong rhyme with "Mone." Thus, in describing the sweetness of the Old Covenant and its face-to-face encounter with God, Herbert also suggests that alienation, the "otherness," that face-to-face relationships presuppose. In the context of the allusion to Exodus, Moses is interceding for the people who have been worshiping the Golden Calf. The Lord's statement, *"Let me alone,"* describes the alienation of human beings from God due to sin, and the nature of divine judgment. The parallel line[17] in the second stanza, "List, ye may heare great Aarons bell," similarly suggests the dangers under the Old Covenant. The bells, according to Exod. 28:35, "shall be upon Aaron to minister: and his sound shall be heard when he goeth in unto the holy place before the LORD, and when he cometh out, that he die not." The bells were to protect Aaron from being killed by the awesome holiness and power that resided in the Tabernacle.

> But now thou dost thy self immure and close
> In some one corner of a feeble heart:
> Where yet both Sinne and Satan, thy old foes
> Do pinch and straiten thee, and use much art
>   To gain thy thirds and little part.

Under the New Covenant, God enters flesh to suffer at the hands of "Sinne," not only in the Incarnation, but also as an indwelling presence in the sinful believer's heart. At this point Herbert begins describing the familiar *psychomachia*. God graciously limits Himself to enter the lists against sin on behalf of human beings. God's possession in the heart is seemingly quite small—it is "some one corner of a feeble heart," "thy thirds and little part." Moreover Sinne and Satan "Do pinch and straiten thee," as if they were able to crowd out the self-limited, suffering Omnipotence.

> I see the world grows old, when as the heat
> Of thy great love, once spread, as in an urn
> Doth closet up it self, and still retreat,
> Cold Sinne still forcing it, till it return,
>   And calling *Justice,* all things burn.

The conflict between God and sin is resolved with the Apocalypse, the dissolution of all things. Herbert here generalizes sin in terms of "The world," much as he does in "The Church Militant," but the process he describes applies also to the conquest of sin in the "feeble heart." Under the New Covenant, the heat of God's love is intensified by His self-limitation and His suffering at the hands of "Cold sinne." The heat of love is contracted and intensified, becoming so hot that it becomes destructive, whereupon love manifests itself as justice against sin, whereupon "all things burn." At the dissolution of the body, the sinful flesh is destroyed, just as at Judgment Day sin is vanquished. The Holy Spirit is often defeated, seemingly, in the conflict with sin (see "Eph. 4:30 *Grieve not the Holy Spirit, Etc.*"), but ultimate victory, though it comes under the aspect of destruction, is assured.

"Decay" is directly paralleled by "Sion," which also begins by lauding the glory of the Old Covenant and concludes with the indwelling God fighting sin in the process of sanctification:

> Lord, with what glorie wast thou serv'd of old,
> When Solomons temple stood and flourished!
>   Where most things were of purest gold;
>   The wood was all embellished
> With flowers and carvings, mysticall and rare:
> All show'd the builders, crav'd the seers care.
>
> Yet all this glorie, all this pomp and state
> Did not affect thee much, was not thy aim;
>   Something there was, that sow'd debate:
>   Wherefore thou quitt'st thy ancient claim:
> And now thy Architecture meets with sinne;
> For all thy frame and fabrick is within.

The eternal physical Temple of Solomon is thus contrasted with the spiritual temple—the Holy Spirit dwelling "within" the believer (1 Cor. 3:16–17).

> There thou art struggling with a peevish heart,
> Which sometimes crosseth thee, thou sometimes it,

> The fight is hard on either part.
> Great God doth fight, he doth submit.

God's "Architecture"—the internal temple—"meets with sinne," struggling "with a peevish heart." Sometimes the heart "crosseth" God, when it sins. Sometimes God "crosseth" the heart, as in "Affliction (1)": "Thus doth thy power cross-bias me" (53).

From the human point of view, in the struggle of sanctification the conscious self is torn between its desire for God and its desire for sin. "The Knell"[18] aptly describes the soul's dilemma in the face of this conflict.

> Now is the season,
> Now the great combat of our flesh & reason:
>   O help, my God!
>   See, they breake in,
> Disbanded humours, sorrows, troops of sinn,
>   Each with his rodd.
>
>   (6–12)

Confronted with this spiritual battle between his sinful flesh and his reason, the mark of the Divine Image, the soul is "perplexed" and inconsistent:

> The Bell doth tolle:
> Lord help thy servant whose perplexed soule
>   Doth wishly look
>   On either hand
> And sometimes offers, sometimes makes a stand,
>   Strugling on th'hook.
>
>   (1–6)

The "perplexed soule" looks wistfully at both sides of the conflict, sometimes sallying into the attack, sometimes halting where he is. Both the inner vacillations and the concept of assurance seem to come together in the final image of the stanza. The speaker describes himself as "strugling on th'hook," a figure that describes the pain and resistance that he must often feel, but also that he has been "caught" by the Fisher of men.

Herbert's most ingenious explicit treatment of this conflict between the old man of sin and the new man of the Holy Spirit is "Coloss. 3.3 *Our life is hid with Christ in God.*"

> *My* words & thoughts do both express this notion,
> That *Life* hath with the sun a double motion.
> The First *Is* straight, and our diurnall friend,
> The other *Hid* and doth obliquely bend.

One life is wrapt *In* flesh, and tends to earth:
The other winds towards *Him,* whose happie birth
Taught me to live here so, *That* still one eye
Should aim and shoot at that which *Is* on high:
Quitting with daily labour all *My* pleasure,
To gain at harvest an eternall *Treasure.*

The "double motion" corresponds to the twin tendencies of the flesh and of the spirit, described here as two separate lives: "One life is wrapt *In* flesh, and tends to earth: / The other winds towards *Him.*" Nevertheless, even in light of this conflict or tension in the two lives of the self, "Our life is hid with Christ in God," a fact that is in the midst of the struggle, just as the motto from the Scripture is imbedded in the poem. The life of the flesh is obvious; "The other *Hid* and doth obliquely bend." In other words, although the spiritual life is hidden, it is infallibly present, just as the motto is hidden in the seemingly random lines of the poem. Moreover, the spiritual life, however obscure, has the power to "obliquely bend" the "straight" motion of the flesh. Formally, in mathematical language, a "double motion" is resolved by an oblique vector. Theologically, the conflict of sin and grace is resolved in Christ. The oblique motto, adapted from Col. 3:3, *"My Life Is Hid In Him That Is My Treasure,"* signifies the doctrine of imputation, whereby the believer, engrafted into Christ, receives the benefit of His righteousness, while Christ takes upon Himself all of the believer's sins. The believer's own life is hidden in Christ; his own sins and conflicts are hidden by the passion of Christ, which alone is the basis of salvation. The text, which Herbert had painted at Bemerton Church,[19] resolves the two contradictory "lives," the one sinful, the other godly, in terms of the assurance of salvation.

Besides such relatively straightforward dramatizations of the battle between the flesh and the spirit in particular poems, the concept was a basic psychological assumption that was used to diagnose a wide range of spiritual problems. Richard Hooker gives four causes of religious dejection,[20] all of which seem applicable to Herbert and can be seen as variations of the "infirmity of the flesh" interfering with the spiritual life:

(1) Physical causes, such as illness, can result in spiritual depression (e.g., "Josephs coat," "The Crosse").

(2) Comparing oneself to others or to oneself at another time can result in irrelevant discouragement (e.g., "Affliction [1]").

(3) Mistaking emotions for faith. Some, according to Hooker, "in heaviness of spirit suppose they lack Faith, because they find not the sugared joy and delight which indeed doth accompany Faith, but so as a separable accident, as a thing that may be removed from it; yea there is a cause why it should

be removed. . . . Too much joy even spiritually would make us wantons" (e.g., "The Glimpse," "The Temper [2]").[21]

(4) Focusing on "distrustful suggestions of the flesh." Introspection, focus on the self rather than Christ, will tend to create doubts and anguish (e.g., "Assurance," "Perseverance").

Hooker goes on to insist that faith, the work of the spirit, cannot be destroyed, even though believers, from the infirmity of the flesh, sometimes cannot even recognize it in themselves. "Their faith, when it is at the strongest, is but weak; yet even then when it is at the weakest, so strong, that utterly it never faileth, it never perisheth altogether, no not in them who think it extinguished in themselves."[22]

Because of the weakness of the flesh, therefore, the emotions are deceptive. Luther and Calvin strongly opposed the Anabaptist "enthusiasts" because of their dependence upon subjective "motions" and Herbert opposed the similar tendencies in "Valdesso." Herbert is continually opposing his feelings with the objective truth of God's promises. This has already been seen in "Assurance," and "Perseverance," and it occurs throughout the poems of spiritual depression ("A Parodie," "The Glimpse"). Thus in "Temper (2)," the departure of joy is related directly to the battle between the Holy Spirit and the flesh:

> It cannot be. Where is that mightie joy,
> > Which just now took up all my heart?
> > Lord, if thou must needs use thy dart,
> Save that, and me; or sin for both destroy.
>
> The grosser world stands to thy word and art;
> > But thy diviner world of grace
> > Thou suddenly dost raise and race,
> And ev'ry day a new Creatour art.
>
> O fix thy chair of grace, that all my powers
> > May also fix their reverence:
> > For when thou dost depart from hence,
> They grow unruly, and sit in thy bowers.
>
> Scatter, or binde them all to bend to thee:
> > Though elements change, and heaven move,
> > Let not thy higher Court remove,
> But keep a standing Majestie in me.

The poem does not at all imply that salvific grace comes and goes, as Sr. Thekla infers;[23] rather, it is a prayer for the subjugation of the flesh, a complaint not against God, but against the unruliness of human emotions. The prayer is that God either "scatter" the poet's emotions or "binde them all to bend to thee." The prayer is for "a standing Majestie," for the Holy

Spirit to rule his sinful flesh. The poem is not about salvation but about sanctification, as indicated not only in the conflict between the spirit and the flesh but also in the title—"Temper," which, according to the OED, in the seventeenth-century refers to character, specifically to mental composure (as in "losing one's temper"), and also to the process by which metal is hardened.

This spiritual warfare and its consequences are treated in specific poems, and they are assumed in much of the spiritual "instability" portrayed throughout *The Temple*. Given the human condition, understood as a continual inner struggle between the flesh and the spirit, depravity and grace, the Christian life was seen as intrinsically dynamic. "The life of a Christian man is a continual effort and exercise in the mortification of the flesh, till it is utterly slain, and God's Spirit reigns in us" (Calvin, *Institutes* 3.3.20). Spiritual growth is not a matter of gradual evolution or progress, but of conflict.

iii. Bearing the Cross and the Hidden God

The process of sanctification involves negative spiritual experience as well as positive. In fact, sanctification involves the breaking of the self so that it can receive Christ more fully. As such, it involves suffering. Reformation thought fully sounds these experiences, as does Herbert's poetry. One may isolate three different but related areas that involve the gracious, but painful chastening of God: (1) the self must be broken of its tendency to depend upon its own merit, its desire to earn salvation by good works rather than to rest in the unconditional grace of God; (2) the self must face physical and emotional suffering, so as to break off its dependence on "the Flesh" and to increase its dependence upon God; (3) the self must be faithful to what Luther describes as "the Hidden God," the *deus absconditus*, so that one walks by faith and not by sight, submitting one's will to God's will even when it seems inscrutable and when God seems absent.

The impulse to "atone for the atonement,"[24] to bypass the free gift of God either by assuming that one deserves God's favor or by insisting on suffering for one's own sins, is a subtle danger of the flesh, which, as Luther says, understands nothing except the law.[25] In several of the poems, such as "The Thanksgiving" and "The Reprisall," Herbert dramatizes something of a competition between the speaker's "good works" and the all-sufficient merit of Christ.[26] The process of stripping oneself of all pretense of merit is portrayed in "The Holdfast," which point by point rejects any dependence on human effort, which unwittingly is an obstacle to grace:

> I threatned to observe the strict decree
> Of my deare God with all my power & might.
>
> (1–2)

The blustering tone of these lines, the antagonistic "threatned," and the perhaps ironic inflation implied in "all my power & might," suggest the problems inherent in basing salvation on one's own righteousness, a notion dramatically corrected by the next line: "But I was told by one, it could not be" (3). Believers will still sin, as Calvin insists. Unfortunately, human "power & might" simply cannot measure up to the "strict decree" of God.

> Yet I might trust in God to be my light.
> Then will I trust, said I, in him alone.
> Nay, ev'n to trust in him, was also his.
>
> (4–6)

Salvation is through faith, but for Herbert, in a rebuke to Arminianism, even faith is a gift of God.

> We must confesse that nothing is our own.
> Then I confesse that he my succour is:
> But to have nought is ours, not to confesse
> That we have nought. I stood amaz'd at this,
>
> Much troubled, till I heard a friend expresse,
> That all things were more ours by being his,
> What Adam had, and forfeited for all,
> Christ keepeth now, who cannot fail or fall.
>
> (7–14)

Human beings, like Adam, will continually "fail or fall." The requisite works, faith, and repentance and the Paradise that they lead to are kept by Christ, and are thus assured. The realization that a person contributes nothing to salvation is at first troubling, as is Calvinism, until the connection is made in the poem with the assurance of salvation. Insofar as the soul depends upon itself, this assurance is lost sight of. Stanley Fish regards "The Holdfast" as "the quintessential Herbert poem."[27] As Fish explains it, the speaker will agree to anything as long as some sphere of responsibility remains to him. What he will not do is admit that nothing is required of him, for to do so would be to give up his sense of personal worth, the feeling that he was in some way "needed."[28] The point of the poem is that it is only in the realization "that we have nought" that one is impelled to "holdfast" to God, as is made clear in the context of the Psalm to which the title alludes:

> My flesh, and my heart faileth: but God is the strength of my heart, and my portion forever. . . . It is good for me to hold me fast by God, to put my trust in the Lord God (Ps. 73:25, 27).[29]

Only when the flesh and the heart fail does the Psalmist recognize that "God is the strength of my heart," and this movement from personal failure to trust in God occurs again and again in Herbert's poetry.

Thus, in "The Crosse," the poet's very desire to serve God is thwarted by what the poet sees as God's direct action.

> What is this strange and uncouth thing?
> To make me sigh, and seek, and faint, and die,
> Until I had some place, where I might sing,
>   And serve thee; and not onely I,
> But all my wealth and familie might combine
> To set thy honour up, as our designe.
>
> And then when after much delay,
> Much wrastling, many a combate, this deare end,
> So much desir'd, is giv'n, to take away
>   My power to serve thee; to unbend
> All my abilities, my designes confound,
> And lay my threatnings bleeding on the ground.
>
> One ague dwelleth in my bones,
> Another in my soul (the memorie
> What I would do for thee, if once my grones
>   Could be allow'd for harmonie).
>   (1–16)

Herbert's belief in the sovereignty of God over all events leaves him no question as to who is responsible for his affliction—he did not believe in chance, fate, or microbes. After years of struggle over the question of his vocation, Herbert finally entered the priesthood, whereupon, the poem suggests, he was stricken with debilitating sickness.[30] The irony of his sickness's coming at the time when he had finally found his vocation is especially bitter. To Herbert, God has both given him the vocation and taken away his power to fulfill it (9). Herbert's poem, while it complains about how God is treating him, is no less severe, however, in regard to his own desires to serve God. The first stanza, in linking "not only I, / But all my wealth and familie" to the honor of God, may be somewhat ironic in confounding human honor (wealth, family) with that of God, but in the second stanza Herbert clearly returns to the imagery he so often uses in writing about his desire to do good works on God's behalf. As in "The Thanksgiving" and "The Reprisall," he is pictured as wrestling with God. Although the "much wrastling, many a combate" seemed to have been over, the stanza ends with the protagonist thrown and defeated. As in "The Holdfast" ("I threatned to observe the strict decree / Of my deare God"), his "threatnings" lie "bleeding on the ground."

> Besides, things sort not to my will,
> Ev'n when my will doth studie thy renown;
> Thou turnest th' edge of all things on me still,
>   Taking me up to throw me down.
>   (19–22)

The phrase *my will*, occuring twice in two lines, is emphasized by repetition, the rhyme words ("me still"), and, most important, by its contrast with the final four words that resolve the poem.

> To have my aim, and yet to be,
> Further from it then when I bent my bow;
> To make my hopes my torture, and the fee
>   Of all my woes another wo,
> Is in the midst of delicates to need,
> And ev'n in Paradise to be a weed.
>
> Ah my deare Father, ease my smart!
> These contrarieties crush me: these crosse actions
> Doe winde a rope about, and cut my heart:
>   And yet since these thy contradictions
> Are properly a crosse felt by thy sonne,
> With but foure words, my words, *Thy will be done.*
>
> (25–36)

In the poem, "my will" is opposed to "thy will." "My wealth and family," "my power," "my abilities," "my designs," "my aim," make up most of the poem, but at the end, Christ's words become "my words," and self-will, however good its intentions, is reoriented to submission to the will of God. The poet's will is "crossed": it is thwarted; it is confronted with the cross of Christ, who more fully faced the "contradictions" of line 25–30 and who anticipated the poet's own suffering; and the poet is given his own cross to bear (Luke 9:23), which must be faced with the words Christ used when He faced His cross (Matt. 26:42). Submission to God's will involves the thwarting of "my will," even when the latter is piously intent on achieving great things for God. Even virtuous desires, paradoxically, can stand in the way of submission to God, in which case it becomes necessary for God "to take away / My power to serve thee; to unbend / All my abilities" (9–11).

Just as there is a tendency for the flesh to hold on to good works as an attempt to merit God's favor, there is also the tendency to hold on to guilt. Human nature, still under the law, finds it difficult to accept the unconditional quality of God's love, so that it continually seeks to put conditions on grace and to resist forgiveness. "Love (3)" is the best example: "Love bade me welcome: yet my soul drew back, / Guiltie of dust and sinne" (1–2). The first line is exactly divided between the welcome of love and the soul drawing away. The entire poem is built upon these poles, amounting to an argument between guilt and unconditional love. This argument is also the subject of "Dialogue":

> Sweetest Saviour, if my soul
> Were but worth the having
> Quickly should I then controll
> Any thought of Waving.

> But when all my care and pains
> Cannot give the name of gains
> To thy wretch so full of stains,
> What delight or hope remains?

(1–8)

"Waving" can have two complementary meanings, as Hutchinson points out.[31] It can mean "wavering," so that the stanza could be paraphrased as follows: If my soul were worth anything I should be able to control the wavering, the vacillation of my life. As it is, "all my care and pains" result in nothing, I can make no progress I am so stained with sin. Or the word can mean "waiving," a term in harmony with other legal metaphors in the poem, meaning "declining the offer." Hutchinson paraphrases the stanza, "If I thought my soul worth thy having, I would not hesitate to surrender it, but, since all my care spent upon it cannot give it worth (*gains*, 6), how can I expect thee to benefit by acquiring it?"[32]

> *What, child, is the ballance thine,*
> *Thine the poise and measure?*
> *If I say, Thou shalt be mine;*
> *Finger not my treasure.*
> *What the gains in having thee*
> *Do amount to, onely he,*
> *Who for man was sold, can see;*
> *That transferr'd th' accounts to me.*

(9–16)

"This is not so much an answer," observes McCanles, "as an attempt to undercut the presuppositions of the speaker's argument."[33] The figure of the scales involves a mercantile metaphor, referring to the cost of the soul, but it also recalls the scales of judgment of "Justice (2)." In effect, the first speaker, who is judging and condemning himself, is reminded that judgment is not his prerogative, that God does the judging. Salvation is a matter of the divine decree: *"If I say, Thou shalt be mine; / Finger not my treasure."* Salvation is contingent only upon what "I say." "Thou shalt be mine" connotes choice and election, and the reasons for God's inexplicable grace are hidden in the unfathomable counsel of God (13–16).

With *"Finger not my treasure,"* the speaker's anxieties, as McCanles says, "become suddenly reduced to fussiness and impertinent meddling."[34] McCanles surely misreads the poem's tone when he suggests that "the speaker's spiritual agony is really a kind of sleazy curiosity, superimposed on and fused with Christ's irritated assertion of absolute possession of a soul saved."[35] The tone of the lines is established by the interjection *"Child,"* which, as in "The Collar," is admonitory, a gentle suggestion of spiritual immaturity, but, more important, a word of affection. The speaker underestimates God's love for him. The soul, although "full of stains," is God's "*treasure.*" McCanles is right, though, in seeing the irrelevance of the soul's anxiety. "Not only is the speaker saved, but his salvation is already safely written up in the account book."[36] The speaker still argues:

> But as I can see no merit,
>   Leading to this favour:
> So the way to fit me for it
>   Is beyond my savour.

(17–20)

Where the first two stanzas refer to salvation, the last two stanzas refer to sanctification—"the way to fit me for it." Just as no merit is involved in acquiring God's grace, His "favour," the process of sanctification, by which the soul is perfected, is beyond human understanding.

> As the reason then is thine;
> So the way is none of mine:
> I disclaim the whole designe:
> Sinne disclaims and I resigne.

(21–24)

The speaker faces the Calvinist dilemma—if the reason for God's "favour" lies not in his own merit, but solely in God's will, and if the "Way to fit me for it," the process of moral improvement, likewise "is none of mine," belonging solely to the action of God, then what is one to do? The speaker simply gives up. The legal terminology means that the speaker renounces his part in "the whole designe" of salvation and sanctification. That is to say, as Herbert is careful to point out, "Sinne disclaims." The attitude is one of stubborn intractibility; renouncing salvation because of guilt is theologically identical to basing salvation on merit. Ironically, however, the speaker's giving up, resigning, in the face of God's action, is precisely what Christ is asking of him:

> *That is all, if that I could*
>   *Get without repining;*
> *And my clay, my creature, would*
>   *Follow my resigning:*
> *That as I did freely part*
> *With my glorie and desert,*
> *Left all joyes to feel all smart——*
>   Ah! no more: thou break'st my heart.

(25–32)

Renunciation of the self's role in salvation is all Christ is asking, if the renunciation could be complete, without the "repining" for the old covenant of works dramatized in this poem. The model for self-renunciation is Christ (Phil. 2:5ff). Christ, who truly had them, freely parted with "glorie and desert"; should not "my clay" do likewise in parting with his feeble self glory, and his insistence on basing life or death on his own "desert"? Christ is not only giving him a model, but, by recounting his own passion, He is specifying the true cost of the soul, the weight on the balance-scale, the price of "my treasure." *"What the gains in having thee / Do amount to, onely he, / Who for man was sold, can see."* When the speaker is vividly reminded of what Christ has done, when he is shown the cost and the implications of Christ's unconditional love for him, his defenses collapse. "Ah! no more: thou break'st my heart." "It is just the breaking of his own heart at Christ's resignation that the speaker has been resisting," observes McCanles. "Suddenly, at the end, the poem breaks loose from the malign dialectic between false humility and false pride, and opens into the infinite space of Christ's gift of salvation, a space that no words can encompass."[37]

Whether it is dominated by a pride that thinks it can replace Christ's sacrifice by its own merits, or by a guilt that thinks it can never deserve salvation, the heart must be broken, as in "Dialogue" as well as in other poems such as "The Altar," before it can fully accept God's love. Sanctification is painful and always deflating to the self, which is made to put away both pride and guilt, the opposite but complementary emotions of the doctrine of "merit," in order to accept holiness as a free, unmerited gift.

Suffering is also an important part of sanctification. "The two highest points of life, wherein a Christian is most seen," says Herbert in "The Country Parson," "are Patience, and Mortification; patience in regard of afflictions, Mortification in regard of lusts and affections, and the stupifying and deading of all the clamorous powers of the soul" ("Country Parson," 3:227). Herbert's "mortification" is similar to what Calvin described in a chapter title, "The Sum of the Christian Life: The Denial of Ourselves" (*Institutes* 3.7). Virtue is defined in terms of absolute self-renunciation, in which the depraved human will gives way to the righteous will of God. By mortification of the self, the "clamorous powers of the soul" so vividly portrayed in "The Collar" are stilled, and the soul learns not to trust in itself, but only in God. Herbert's other category, "Patience," he relates explicitly to "afflictions," the title of five of his poems. Calvin described suffering as "Bearing the Cross" (*Institutes* 3.8).[38] Christ himself suffered the torment of the cross. "Why should we exempt ourselves, therefore, from the condition to which Christ our Head had to submit, especially since He submitted to it for our sake to show us an example of patience in himself?" (*Institutes* 3.8.1). By patience, Herbert and Calvin did not mean stoicism, which Calvin explicitly discussed and rejected. Pain must be painful, to paraphrase Calvin, if there is to be any virtue in overcoming it (*Institutes* 3.8.8). Those who would deny or suppress human emotion go against Christ, who wept, experienced fear, and knew sorrow (*Institutes* 3.8.9). Suffering is not only inevitable in a Christian life, but it is an intrinsic part of sanctification, of being made holy like Christ.

The problem of suffering is complicated and deepened by the conviction of God's total sovereignty over all events. Everything that happens was ascribed to the action and the will of God. To Reformation theologians nothing is accidental; there is no such thing as chance.

> Especially let that foolish and most miserable consolation of the pagans be far away from the breast of the Christian man; to strengthen their minds against adversities, they charged these to fortune. Against fortune they consider it foolish to be angry because she was blind and unthinking, with unseeing eyes wounding the deserving and the undeserving at the same time. On the contrary, the rule of piety is that God's hand alone is the judge and governor of fortune, good or bad, and that it does not rush about with heedless force, but with most orderly justice deals out good as well as ill to us. (Calvin, *Institutes* 3.7.10)

Calvin's radical view of providence, if it does not tend to make God responsible for evil, at least highlights God's inscrutability. When Herbert is sick, thwarted, or depressed, he does not blame microbes, his bad luck, or external circumstances, but bypasses all secondary causes to question the sovereign God Himself.[39] In adversity, writes Calvin, "believers comfort themselves with the solace that they suffer nothing except by God's ordinance and command, for they are under his hand" (*Institutes* 1.16.3). Herbert is quoted in his sickness as praying, "Lord, abate my great affliction, or increase my patience: but Lord, I repine not; I am dumb, Lord, before thee, because thou doest it."[40] In suffering, the human will is directly confronted and opposed by the will of God, and the human will may respond in rebellion or submission. Calvin sees the function of suffering as breaking the dependence on the flesh and bringing the soul into a deeper knowledge of God:

> Our Lord had no need to undertake the bearing of the cross except to attest and prove his obedience to the Father. But as for us, there are many reasons why we must pass our lives under a continual cross. First, as we are by nature too inclined to attribute everything to our flesh— unless our feebleness be shown, as it were, to our eyes—we readily esteem our virtue above its due measure. And we do not doubt, whatever happens, that against all difficulties it will remain unbroken and unconquered. . . . He can best restrain this arrogance when he proves to us by experience not only the great incapacity but also the frailty under which we labor. Therefore, he afflicts us either with disgrace or poverty, or bereavement, or disease, or other calamities. Utterly unequal to bearing these, in so far as they touch us, we soon succumb to them. Thus humbled, we learn to call upon his power, which alone makes us stand fast under the weight of afflictions. But even the most holy persons, however much they may recognize that they stand not through their own strength but through God's grace, are too sure of their own for-

titude and constancy unless by the testing of the cross he bring them into a deeper knowledge of himself. (*Institutes* 3.8.2).

Confidence in the flesh must be broken. "Calamities" prove human frailty, and by failure in dealing with them, one is made to call upon God. "Even the most holy persons," however, who do recognize their dependence on God, can be too sure of their own courage and faith, unless suffering brings them into a deeper knowledge of God. Calvin's theodicy, to appropriate Stanley Fish's term, is radically *self-consuming;* the self, whether complacently proud of its own abilities, or secure in its own holiness, must face the test of the cross. Although suffering is seen positively as destroying the self, Calvin, the sheep in wolf's clothing, characteristically relates this self-destruction to the assurance of salvation:

> And it is of no slight importance for you to be cleansed of your blind love of self that you may be made more nearly aware of your incapacity; to feel your own incapacity that you may learn to distrust yourself; to distrust yourself that you may transfer your trust to God; to rest with a trustful heart in God that, relying upon his help, you may persevere unconquered to the end; to take your stand in his grace that you may comprehend the truth of his promises; to have unquestioned certainty of his promises that your hope may thereby be strengthened. (*Institutes* 3.8.3)

Moreover, writes Calvin, "the more we are afflicted with adversities, the more surely our fellowship with Christ is confirmed" (*Institutes* 3.8.1).

God's discipline is painful, not pleasant. In "Discipline," God's wrath and His love are seemingly in conflict with one another. Herbert, to whom all experiences are ultimately due to the causality of God, is frank in his complaining, although he also implies that in suffering, God's wrath and His love are reconciled in the work of sanctification.

> Throw away thy rod,
> Throw away thy wrath:
> O my God,
> Take the gentle path.
>
> (1–4)

One of Lewis Bayly's consolations to those in "extremitie of paine" is "that these are the *scourges* of thy heavenly *Father,* and the rod is in his *hand.*"[41] Elsewhere Herbert similarly questions God's discipline, urging Him to "take the gentle path": "Art thou all justice, Lord? / Shows not thy word / More attributes?" ("Complaining," 11–13). In "Discipline," Herbert does not question the justice of God's dealing with him so harshly; rather, he is asking that God manifest His other quality of mercy. However, when the poem begins developing the difference between love and judgment, the categories significantly blur:

> Then let wrath remove;
> Love will do the deed:
>   For with love
> Stonie hearts will bleed.
>
> Love is swift of foot:
> Love's a man of warre,
>   And can shoot,
> And can hit from farre.
>
> Who can scape his bow?
> That which wrought on thee,
>   Brought thee low,
> Needs must work on me.
>
>   (17–28)

What the speaker desires as a "gentle path" becomes "a man of warre," turning the conventional figure of cupid with his bow into an archer "swift of foot" like Achilles, from whom no one can escape and who makes hearts bleed. The "man of warre" epithet is from Exod. 15:3, the context of which describes in graphic terms the carnage God wrought against the Egyptians:

> The Lord is a man of war: the Lord is his name. Pharaoh's chariots and his host hath he cast into the sea: his chosen captains also are drowned in the Red Sea. The depths have covered them: they sank into the bottom as a stone. Thy right hand, O Lord, is become glorious in power: thy right hand, O Lord, hath dashed in pieces the enemy. And in the greatness of thine excellency thou hast overthrown them that rose up against thee: thou sentest forth thy wrath, which consumed them as stubble. (Exod. 15:3–7)

The biblical epithet describing God's wrath is turned by Herbert into an epithet of God's love: "Love's a man of warre." Herbert's metaphors suggest that love, no less than wrath, is violent and devastating. Love does cause suffering; in fact, says Herbert, it is love that caused God Himself to suffer:

> Who can scape his bow?
> That which wrought on thee,
>   Brought thee low,
> Needs must work on me.

Again, human suffering is related to the suffering of Christ. If love "brought thee low" in the Incarnation and Atonement, this same love "needs must work on me" in bringing the speaker low, a term that implies both suffering and humility. The violently nongentle metaphors for God's love suggest that God's wrath and His love are identical. In fact, the dominating image of God's rod is an allusion to Heb. 12:6, which likewise subordinates God's anger to His love: "For whom the Lord loveth he chasteneth, and scourgeth every son whom he receiveth." What is experienced as God's wrath is at the same time the work of His love.

That such discipline contributes to the speaker's sanctification is also made clear in the poem:

> For my hearts desire
> Unto thine is bent:
>   I aspire
> To a full consent.
>
> (5–8)

The human will is "bent" to the will of God. The only aspiration is to be able to make "a full consent" to God. The self afflicted by God's rod is becoming subjugated to God's Word:

> Not a word or look
> I affect to own,
>   But by book,
> And thy book alone.
>
> (9–12)

The progress of sanctification is slow and painful, but it is certain:

> Though I fail, I weep:
> Though I halt in pace,
>   Yet I creep
> To the throne of grace.
>
> (13–16)

Though the Christian will fail, he will always be brought to repentance. The taut syllabic verse, which requires intense poetic restraint, is itself an image of discipline—two five-syllable lines followed by an even shorter three-syllable line capture perfectly the sense of "halting in pace," of creeping slowly, yet inexorably, to the throne of grace. The latter image is another allusion to Hebrews, in which the Christian, on the basis of Christ's empathy and acceptance, is urged to "come boldly unto the throne of grace, that we may obtain mercy, and find grace to help in time of need" (4:16). Despite the tentativeness, the argument with God that runs throughout the poem is very bold, a boldness that, as in Hebrews, rests upon the assurance of salvation. The speaker of the poem, despite his

achieved submission and the implicit recognition of God's love, is not
particularly solaced, nor is his pain any the less. The poem concludes with
an almost exasperated complaint, contrasting the perfection of God to the
weakness of man, whose very frailties both require and should temper
God's discipline:

> Throw away thy rod,
> Though man frailties hath,
>   Thou art God:
> Throw away thy wrath.
>
>   (29–32)

Yet in the very terms with which he is complaining, Herbert is showing his
recognition that suffering is purposeful, that the rod is being held by a
loving Father. Calvin similarly discusses the figure of the Father's rod,
concluding, as Herbert would agree, that "in the very harshness of tribulations we must recognize the kindness and generosity of our Father toward
us, since he does not even then cease to promote our salvation. For he
afflicts us not to ruin or destroy us, but, rather, to free us from the condemnation of the world" (*Institutes* 3.8.6).

Herbert's understanding of suffering is treated more fully and more
dispassionately in "Affliction (5)":

> My God, I read this day,
> That planted Paradise was not so firm,
> As was and is thy floting Ark, whose stay
> And anchor thou art onely, to confirm
>   And strengthen it in ev'ry age,
>   When waves do rise, and tempests rage.
>
>   (1–6)

The Ark (typologically the church)[42] is, paradoxically, more stable than
Paradise, although it is "floting" in a seemingly formless sea, subject to the
"tempests rage."[43] Despite the chaos of experience, the Christian is secured
by the anchor of Christ, the traditional symbol upon which Donne and
Herbert exchanged poems. For Herbert, the anchor is a symbol of the
believer's security amidst all tribulations.

> Let the world reel, we and all ours stand sure,
> This holy Cable's of all storms secure.
>   ("In. Sacram Anchoram Piscatoris," 9–10)
>
> When winds and waves rise highest, I am sure,
> This *Anchor* keeps my *faith,* that, me secure.
>   ("Another Version," 3–4)

In "Affliction (5)" the ark is more firm than Paradise because in Eden, although there were no "tempests" or afflictions, there was the possibility of falling. The Christian, although subject to Adam's curse of a life of hardship, is ultimately secure.

> At first we liv'd in pleasure.
> Thine own delights thou didst to us impart:
> When we grew wanton, thou didst use displeasure
> To make us thine: yet that we might not part,
>   As we at first did board with thee,
>   Now thou wouldst taste our miserie.
>   (7–12)

In Eden, life was pure pleasure, and God's "own delights" were freely given to human beings. With sin, however, God employs "displeasure" as a means "to make us thine." Herbert clarifies why the ark, with all of its storms, is more firm than Paradise. So that we may not part from God, as we did in Eden, when we "did board" with God in uninterrupted communion, God boards with us, in the Incarnation, and "tastes our miserie," which is the fruit of sin.

> There is but joy and grief;
> If either will convert us, we are thine:
> Some Angels us'd the first; if our relief
> Take up the second, then thy double line
>   And sev'rall baits in either kinde
>   Furnish thy table to thy minde.
>   (13–18)

One might say the same of the mood of Herbert's poetry—"There is but joy and grief." Both emotions are spiritually important, and both serve as "baits" to reestablish the communion between the soul and God depicted by Herbert through his symbol of the Banquet (cf. "Love [3]").

> Affliction then is ours;
> We are the trees, whom shaking fastens more,
> While blustring windes destroy the wanton bowres,
> And ruffle all their curious knots and store.
>   My God, so temper joy and wo,
>   That thy bright beams may tame thy bow.
>   (19–24)

But, because of sin, affliction, not pleasure, is ours. In this final stanza, Herbert brilliantly conflates the symbol of the Garden with the symbol of the ark in the storm. "We are the trees"—the imagery places us, in effect, back in Eden—but now the trees, rather than the ark, are facing the tempest. The storm destroys wantonness and artificiality, but only establishes the trees more firmly. The final couplet is a prayer not only for "wo" to be tempered, as in "Discipline," but also a recognition that "joy" must be tempered as well. As in "Discipline," it is a request that God "tame thy bow." The bow here, however, is not only a symbol of God's devastating power but, in terms of the Noah's ark allusions that run throughout the poem, it is God's bow which He set in the clouds, the rainbow, the seal of God's promise not to destroy (Gen. 9:13–15). The story of the Flood in the poem is concluded by the image of a rainbow. The tempests will not destroy completely, but in the clouds will appear God's bow, no longer strung for battle, but "tamed" and transfigured by the "bright beams" of light that shine through.

In this poem, Herbert's understanding of the interplay between joy and grief, desperation and security, is perhaps overly intellectualized. In other poems, when the pain is being experienced rather than analyzed, the emotions are not so easily resolved. Yet, for Herbert, "Storms are the triumph of his art" ("The Bag," 5), and the realization that the darkness and seeming chaos of an emotional storm is actually the purposeful art of God is an important theme in Herbert's poetry. Latimer suggests that human depravity is such that without suffering a human being would live in utter self-dependent complacency, forgetting about God altogether:

There is nothing so dangerous in the world as to be without trouble, without temptation. For look, when we be best at ease, when all things go with us according unto our will and pleasure, then we are commonly most farthest off from God. For our nature is so feeble that we cannot bear tranquillity; we forget God by and by.[44]

Latimer's point is similar to the theme of "The Pulley," in which satisfaction, "Rest," is denied human beings on the grounds that if that final gift were granted, they would "rest in Nature, not the God of Nature" (14). Suffering and unease are necessary to break complacency, to force a soul to become dependent on God.

There is another level of suffering, though, that is the most intense kind of desolation for a person of faith—the experience of the absence of God. Herbert, as with other religious writers and persons of faith, plumbs "the dark night of the soul." "No one who has not been profoundly terrified and forsaken prays profoundly."[45] Luther's comment may well be extended to religious poetry: no one who has not been profoundly terrified and forsaken writes profoundly, and Herbert, like Luther and other Reformation thinkers, charts the experience of God's absence with as much depth as he records the experience of God's presence.

Luther's theology of faith led to his concept of *"Deus absconditus,"* the hidden God:

> Faith has to do with things not seen [Heb. 11:1]. Hence in order that there may be room for faith, it is necessary that everything which is believed should be hidden. It cannot, however, be more deeply hidden than under an object, perception, or experience which is contrary to it. Thus when God makes alive he does it by killing, when he justifies, he does it by bringing down to Hell. . . . thus God hides his eternal goodness and mercy under eternal wrath, his righteousness under iniquity.[46]

Thus it is not unusual that Herbert writes of God's hiddenness, and when he does so, he plunges into the deepest waters of Reformation spirituality, confronting directly the inscrutable will of God, upon which, to the Reformers, everything depends.

"God does not afflict directly by coming near," writes Luther, "but He afflicts by withdrawing and leaving it to the creatures."[47] Herbert's poem "Longing" is perhaps his most intense, most unqualified, poem on the withdrawal of God, the sense that God is absent:

> My throat, my soul is hoarse;
> My heart is wither'd like a ground
>   Which thou dost curse.
>   My thoughts turn round,
> And make me giddie; Lord, I fall,
>   Yet call.
>
> (7–12)

His throat is hoarse from praying, as is his soul, in the familiar metaphor of a parched ground in need of the waters of grace. The allusion to Adam's curse (Gen. 3:17), may help account for his condition as due to sin, but although, like Adam, "I fall," he is desperately calling for succor. The thought that God is not responding to him is dizzying, disorienting. Herbert describes a spiritual vertigo—"My thoughts turn round, / And make me giddie" and like anyone spun around and around, he falls, but he still calls to God. Yet no one seems to be listening.

> Let not the winde
> Scatter my words, and in the same
>   Thy name!
>
> (22–24)

He is praying in Christ's name, a powerful allusion to Jesus' promise that "whatsoever ye shall ask in my name, that I will do" (John 14:13). The wind that scatters his words also scatters the name of Christ.

> Lord Jesu, thou didst bow
> Thy dying head upon the tree:
> O be not now
> More dead to me!
> Lord heare! *Shall he that made the eare,*
> *Not heare?*
>
> (31–36)

Herbert is phenomenologically precise—the point for him as for many "death of God" theologians is not whether God still exists, but whether God is "dead to me." As in other poems ("Affliction [1]," "The Collar") when the speaker verges on total rejection of God, there is an emotional backlash followed by some sort of affirmation: "Lord heare! *Shall he that made the eare, Not heare?*" Herbert generally uses italics in this manner to indicate another voice that enters the poem, usually the Word of God intruding into the poem and resolving the turmoil, as in "The Collar." The italicized words, a quotation from Ps. 94:4, may well function in this way, a reminder that his prayers are being heard, if not answered. The quotation can also function as a proof-text, reminding God of His promise. If so, Herbert is boldly quoting God's own scriptures back at Him, holding God to His Word.

> Behold, thy dust doth stirre,
> It moves, it creeps, it aims at thee:
> Wilt thou deferre
> To succour me,
> Thy pile of dust, wherein each crumme
> Says Come?
>
> (37–42)

Again, Herbert's meanings go in different directions. The stirring dust may be an ironic allusion to the Resurrection, as in "Dooms-day": "Summon all the dust to rise, / Till it stirre, and rubbe the eyes" (3–4), which, especially in connection to what may be an allusion to the second coming of Christ (42), may be another indirect suggestion of relief. The sense of the stanza, though, portrays a human being moving so slowly, yet aiming for God, longing in every particle of his being for God. The dust can only creep feebly along, aspiring to a distant point; it is dependent, as always in Reformation thought, not on its own efforts, but on God to "Come."

In his confusion, the speaker questions his understanding of providence, positing two equally distressing alternatives:

> Hast thou left all things to their course,
> And laid the reins
> Upon the horse?
>
> (44–46)

Has God given up His control of things, letting them run uncontrolled? Or is the opposite true: "Is all lockt? Hath a sinners plea / No key?" (47–48). Is the universe "lockt," all determined, to the point that prayer can change nothing? Either God controls nothing, or He controls everything. In the speaker's present mood, both possibilities are devastating.

It is important that Herbert never questions his belief in God. His prayers, which do not cease even though he seems to receive no answer, attest to the intensity of his faith. The problem is that there is a gap in the relationship, that God has seemingly withdrawn serenely into Heaven, leaving the speaker alone in his misery:

> Thou tarriest, while I die,
> And fall to nothing: thou dost reigne,
> And rule on high,
> While I remain
> In bitter grief: yet am I stil'd
> Thy childe.
>
> (55–60)

The bitter tone is unmistakable, despite the overtones of God's love, which, as in "The Collar," insists on still calling the speaker *"Child!"*, connoting a permanent relationship. It is most significant that even in this extreme mood of dejection, of feeling forsaken by God, the poet never doubts his salvation, and in fact the poem contains an especially clear statement of the Calvinist doctrine of eternal security:

> Lord, didst thou leave thy throne,
> Not to relieve? how can it be,
> That thou art grown
> Thus hard to me?
> Were sinne alive, good cause there were
> to bear.
>
> But now both sinne is dead,
> And all thy promises live and bide.
> That wants his head;
> These speak and chide,
> And in thy bosome poure my tears,
> As theirs.
>
> (61–72)

"Were sinne alive," there would be good reason for God to forsake him, but as it is, he is irrevocably saved—"Now both sinne is dead / And all thy promises live and bide." Sin no longer has dominion over him, as far as his acceptance before God is concerned; instead, God's "promises" are active.[48] In the poem, sin "wants his head"—sin is decapitated, as it were (alluding perhaps to Gen. 3:15, which was taken as a prophecy of how Christ would "bruise" the head of the serpent). The promises, on the other hand, "speak and chide." It is significant that the promises—such as the scripture he has just quoted (35–36)—are not speaking to and chiding the poet; rather, as the next line indicates, they seem to be speaking to and chiding God Himself. God's promises pour the poet's tears into God's bosom, as if they were the promises' own tears. This final couplet in the stanza, evoking the complexities of Christ's intercession and imputation, strongly underscores the paradoxical principle that it is on the basis of God's promises and the inviolability of salvation that the poet is able to complain to God. The poet is not worried about his salvation but is pleading with God on the basis of a promise already given.

There is nothing the poet can do to change his condition—all depends solely on the action of God, which is being implored throughout the poem.

> My love, my sweetnesse, heare!
> By these thy feet, at which my heart
> Lies all the yeare,
> Pluck out thy dart,
> And heal my troubled breast which cryes,
> Which dyes.
>
> (79–84)

The poet loves God, "My love, my sweetnesse." The imagery of the poem also implies that God loves him, with the restrained but precise allusion to the dart of Cupid, the God of Love. As in "Discipline," God's bow and His darts are devastating, but they are also signs of His covenant. In this sense the "troubled breast" is so because of God's dart, which also, by the Cupid imagery, would be the cause for his own love of God ("My love, my sweetnesse"). The plea to "pluck out thy dart" would thus seem to imply that if God ceased troubling him, by taking out the arrow from his heart, he would paradoxically cease to love God. At any rate, the poem, for all of its theological awareness, makes no attempt to use the doctrines as a means to mitigate or to deny the emotional desolation and longing that are the subject of the poem. The doctrines of assurance and the experience of being forsaken are in tension with each other, both affirmed, with each pole of the religious life, here in conflict, giving depth and complexity to the other.[49]

Herbert may feel sometimes that God is absent, but, as he develops in "A Parodie," he knows intellectually that it is not possible for God to completely forsake him.

> Souls joy, when thou art gone,
> And I alone,
> Which cannot be,

> Because thou dost abide with me,
>   And I depend on thee;
>
> Yet when thou dost suppresse
>   The cheerfulnesse
>   Of thy abode,
> And in my powers not stirre abroad,
>   But leave me to my load:
>
> O what a damp and shade
>   Doth me invade!
>   No stormie night
> Can so afflict or so affright,
>   As thy eclipsed light.

(1–15)

The first two lines of the poem are directly negated by the next two. It feels sometimes as if God is gone—"which cannot be / because thou dost abide with me." What actually happens, says Herbert, is that God will sometimes "suppress / The cheerfulnesse / Of thy abode," leaving him solely in his own "powers." The light is "eclipsed," but not extinguished—"thou dost but shine lesse cleare." It is in this sense alone that God can be said to withdraw:

> Ah Lord! do not withdraw,
>   Lest want of aw
>   Make Sinne appeare;
> And when thou dost but shine lesse cleare,
>   Say, that thou art not here.
>
> And then what life I have,
>   While Sinne doth rave,
>   And falsely boast,
> That I may seek, but thou art lost;
>   Thou and alone thou know'st.
>
> O what a deadly cold
>   Doth me infold!
>   I half beleeve,
> That Sinne sayes true: but while I grieve,
>   Thou com'st and dost relieve.

(16–30)

Sin "falsely" claims that God is irrevocably "lost" to him, but Herbert, at most in his poetry, only "half beleeves" it. In the "stormie night" of affliction, in the "deadly cold" moods of desolation, "what life I have" may be obscured even to the poet himself, but all that is important is that "Thou and alone thou know'st." Herbert thus again paraphrases what was apparently one of his favorite texts—"*Coloss. 3.3. Our life is hid with Christ in God.*" One's "life" may be hidden even from oneself, but the life is nevertheless secure, insofar as it is "hid" in God. The Christian may not know his own security, but "thou know'st."

"The Search" is also about the absence of God, and, like "Affliction [1]" and "The Crosse," it becomes a confrontation with God's inscrutable will. After seven stanzas lamenting the absence of God, who no longer seems to hear his prayers, the poet stumbles onto the answer:

> Where is my God? what hidden place
> Conceals thee still?
> What covert dare eclipse thy face?
> Is it thy will?
>
> (29–32)

God's will is the only concealment that could "eclipse thy face." The next three stanzas affirm the omnipotence and the inscrutability of God's will:

> O let not that of any thing;
> Let rather brasse,
> Or steel, or mountains be thy ring,
> And I will passe.
>
> Thy will such an intrenching is,
> As passeth thought:
> To it all strength, all subtilties
> Are things of nought.
>
> Thy will such a strange distance is,
> As that to it
> East and West touch, the poles do kisse,
> And parallels meet.
>
> (33–44)

Yet, in considering God's will, the poet begins to see that just as omnipotence can inviolably conceal God, it can also inviolably bring Him near. The doctrine of God's inviolable will as the cause of whether humans experience him, can, in other contexts, imply reprobation, but its reverse side is eternal security: "Be not Almightie, let me say, / Against, but for me" (51–52). The present tense at the beginning of the poem, describing his unanswered prayers, and the imperatives of the stanzas of supplication, give way to the future tense:

> When thou dost turn, and wilt be neare;
> What edge so keen,
> What point so piercing can appeare
> To come between?
>
> (53–56)

"Thou . . . wilt be neare"; although He does not seem near at the moment, He will inevitably return, and their intimacy will be as absolute as their seeming alienation.

> For as thy absence doth excell
> > All distance known:
> So doth thy nearnesse bear the bell,
> > Making two one.
>
> > (57–60)

The sense of feeling forsaken and the sense of intimacy with God are both ascribed to God's sovereign will, which is both the efficient and the final cause. The purpose of the affliction is to make faith possible, to cause the depraved human will to accept the will of God. The inscrutability of God's will does not mean that it is arbitrary, although it may seem so from the limited human perspective; rather, it is radically righteous.[50] God's will is inscrutable simply because it is the very boundary of logic, beyond which it is impossible to speculate:

> For his will is, and rightly ought to be, the cause of all things that are. For if it has any cause, something must precede it, to which it is, as it were, bound; this is unlawful to imagine. . . . When, therefore, one asks why God has so done, we must reply: because he has willed it. But if you proceed further to ask why he so willed, you are seeking something greater and higher than God's will, which cannot be found. Let men's rashness, then, restrain itself, and not seek what does not exist, lest perhaps it fail to find what does exist. (Calvin, *Institutes* 3.23.2)

God's "deep judgments," as Calvin says, "swallow up all our powers of mind" (*Institutes* 3.23.1). "Thy will such a strange distance is, / As that to it / East and West touch . . . and parallels meet" (41–44).

The unfathomable depths of God's righteous will are countered, however, by the unfathomable depths of the human sinful will. In "Justice (1)," the poet's questioning of God significantly leads to questioning of himself:

> I cannot skill of these thy wayes.
> *Lord, thou didst make me, yet thou woundest me;*
> *Lord, thou dost wound me, yet thou dost relieve me:*
> *Lord, thou relievest, yet I die by thee:*
> *Lord, thou dost kill me, yet thou dost reprieve me.*
> But when I mark my life and praise,
> Thy justice me most fitly payes:
> For, *I do praise thee, yet I praise thee not:*
> *My prayers mean thee, yet my prayers stray:*
> *I would do well, yet sinne the hand hath got:*
> *My soul doth love thee, yet it loves delay.*
> I cannot skill of these my wayes.

If God's will is inscrutable, so is the human will. In "Sinne (2)," Herbert shows how the very concept of sin is impossible to objectify:

> O that I could a sinne once see!
> We paint the devil foul, yet he
> Hath some good in him, all agree.
> Sinne is flat opposite to th' Almightie, seeing
> It wants the good of *vertue*, and of *being*.
>
> *(1–5)*

Herbert solves the theological problem, in a rather sophisticated way, not only by alluding to Augustine's analysis of evil as nonbeing, but also by seeing the popular images of devils as external projections from the inner recesses of the human soul. "Yet as in sleep we see foul death, and live: / So devils are our sinnes in perspective" (9–10). No less striking, however, is the reason Herbert gives for why it is so difficult to have a clear conception of sin, to truly understand and imagine what sin is:

> But God more care of us hath had:
> If apparitions make us sad,
> By sight of sinne we should grow mad.
>
> *(6–8)*

As John Mulder observes, commenting on the poem, "The blindness to God's purpose is finally an act of God's mercy."[51]

In his discussion of the *deus absconditus*, the Hidden God, Luther describes how God "does not delay or keep aloof forever. Indeed, He manages all things in such a manner that the Word seems to be altogether of no account and nothing. But out of this nothing and out of what is of no account He makes everything through a very great and amazing change, so that what previously appeared to be *everything* perishes and is reduced to nothing."[52] Luther could be glossing "The Flower," which follows three of the most intense poems of spiritual suffering ("The Search," "Grief," "The Crosse"):

> How fresh, O Lord, how sweet and clean
> Are thy returns! ev'n as the flowers in spring;
> To which, besides their own demean,
> The late-past frosts tributes of pleasure bring.
> Grief melts away
> Like snow in May,
> As if there were no such cold thing.
>
> *(1–7)*

The near despair, in Luther's words, which "previously appeared to be *everything* perishes and is reduced to nothing," melting like snow, "As if there were no such cold thing."

And now in age I bud again,
After so many deaths I live and write;
I once more smell the dew and rain,
And relish versing: O my onely light,
It cannot be
That I am he
On whom thy tempests fell all night.

(36–42)

God may hide himself. His purposes may be inscrutable, and they may work at cross purposes to the human will, but His design, in the words of Cranmer, is to "show Himself to be the God of His people, when He seems to have altogether forsaken them; then raising them up when they think He is bringing them down and laying them low; then glorifying them when He is thought to be confounding them; then quickening them when He is thought to be destroying them."[53] God's actions are thus certain to be misinterpreted; their purpose, however violent the means, is sanctification—raising up, glorifying, quickening.

iv. Death and Apocalypse: The Final Poems

Sanctification ends with death. The connection between the physical death of the flesh and the final triumph of the spirit is dramatized in "The World":

Love built a stately house; where *Fortune* came,
And spinning phansies, she was heard to say,
That her fine cobwebs did support the frame,
Whereas they were supported by the same:
But *Wisdome* quickly swept them all away.

Then *Pleasure* came, who, liking not the fashion,
Began to make *Balcones, Terraces,*
Till she had weakned all by alteration,
But rev'rend *laws,* and many a *proclamation*
Reformed all at length with menaces.

Then enter'd *Sinne,* and with that Sycomore,
Whose leaves first sheltred man from drought & dew,
Working and winding slily evermore,
The inward walls and Sommers cleft and tore:
But *Grace* shor'd these, and cut that as it grew.

(1–15)

The poem has a "double motion," as in "Coloss. 3.3" immediately following. There is progress in each stanza, with belief in Fortune (rendered with the typical Calvinist contempt) giving way to Wisdom, Pleasure giving way to laws, sin giving way to grace; yet, at the same time, the series is one of progressively more serious failures. When the cobwebs are cleared away by Wisdome, Pleasure begins to make more fundamental structural alterations in "the stately house." Pleasure is then dealt with by the "menaces" of "rev'rend *laws*," but the success of wisdom and morality mean little, because the very foundation and support of the house are undermined by sin and guilt.[54] Grace does shore up the walls and trim back the sycomore/ fig tree, but the "stately house" is by now structurally unsound.

> Then *Sinne* combined with *Death* in a firm band
> To raze the building to the very floore:
> Which they effected, none could them withstand.
> But *Love* and *Grace* took *Glorie* by the hand,
> And built a braver Palace than before.
>
> (16–20)

This final stanza is startling; sin and death, despite all the good offices of Wisdom, Law, and Grace, seem at first victorious in completely destroying Love's "stately house." This destructive work, however, becomes a means by which an unsound structure is razed so that love may build "a braver Palace than before." Death is not the end, but, as the wages of sin which destroys the old nature, a prelude to the new creation. Love and grace, already active in the poem, are joined, apocalyptically, by glorie, so that the "stately house," once destroyed, is rebuilt as a "Palace," an even "braver" structure. The forward-backward movement in the poem, with its sequence of damage followed by patch-work repairs followed by greater damage, a pattern similar in many ways to the "progression" of poems in *The Temple*, ends as the ostensible victory of death makes possible a final restoration.[55] Similarly, the process of sanctification, with its spiritual warfare, its heights and depths, is brought to a definite conclusion in *The Temple*, with the series of poems on death and the apocalypse.

The concluding poems in "The Church" are introduced by "A Wreath," which recapitulates and images in its form the "double motion," the halting progress of sanctification. The positioning of this summary poem, immediately before "Death," reinforces the theological structure of "The Church," in which sanctification is completed at death:

> A Wreathed garland of deserved praise,
> Of praise deserved, unto thee I give,
> I give to thee, who knowest all my wayes,
> My crooked winding wayes, wherein I live,
> Wherein I die, not live: for life is straight,
> Straight as a line, and ever tends to thee,
> To thee, who art more farre above deceit,
> Then deceit seems above simplicitie.

> Give me simplicitie, that I may live,
> So live, and like, that I may know, thy wayes,
> Know them and practise them: then shall I give
> For this poore wreath, give thee a crown of praise.

The poem is frustrating to read with its repetitive two steps forward, one step backwards motion, but its halting progress is a hieroglyph of sanctification. The poem images "My crooked winding wayes" which are contrasted with life, which is "straight as a line, and ever tends to thee." The "wayes" of a sinful human being may be tortuous, but time is inexorably straight, and it does bring the believer, despite any personal lack of progress, closer and closer to God. In fact, the poem does show progress. In the first three lines the "wreathings" are mere repetitions ("of deserved praise, / Of praise deserved"; "unto thee I give, / I give to thee"). When God's knowledge is being described, the repeated term becomes qualified or even inverted ("who knowest all my wayes, / My crooked winding wayes," "wherein I live, / Wherein I die, not live"), showing an increase and even a reversal of self-knowledge at the confrontation with God. The next four lines, describing the "straightness" of God's ways, are interwoven but in such a way that the syntax of the sentence is scarcely interrupted and the effect, for once, is of unimpeded progress ("For life is straight, / Straight as a line, and ever tends to thee, / To thee, who art more farre above deceit, / Then deceit seems above simplicitie"). The final four lines, a prayer, show qualities being added to the interwoven term ("That I may live, / So live and like"; "that I may know, thy wayes, / Know them and practise them"). A growing Christian, one who is being sanctified, comes to know God's ways, but also to practice them, to not only live a certain way, but to "like" doing so. The final four lines repeat the terms and the line endings of the first four lines, although reversed like a mirrored image, but there is a definite advance: To God's knowledge of his ways (3–4), is added his knowledge of God's way (10–11); the "poore wreath" of praise becomes a crown.

The process of sanctification having been portrayed in "The Church" and summarized in "A Wreath," Herbert then begins the new series with "Death":

> Death, thou wast once an uncouth hideous thing,
>   Nothing but bones,
>   The sad effect of sadder grones:
> Thy mouth was open, but thou couldst not sing.

$$(1-4)$$

Human beings are generally too shortsighted, seeing only the temporal process of "Flesh being turn'd to dust, and bones to sticks" (8). Fleshly bodies are seen as "The shells of fledge souls left behinde" (11). In light of

Christ, however, and the assurance of a resurrection to bliss, death can
now be addressed in a quite different way:

> But since our Saviours death did put some bloud
> Into thy face;
> Thou art grown fair and full of grace,
> Much in request, much sought for as a good.
>
> For we do now behold thee gay and glad,
> As at dooms-day;
> When souls shall wear their new array,
> And all thy bones with beautie shall be clad.

(13–20)

"Fair and full of grace" is both a conventional descriptive epithet and a
theological statement. Now death is full of God's grace. As in "The World,"
death is a necessary prelude to the new creation (Rev. 21:1–5), as the
building is razed so that love may build "a braver Palace, then before," and
"the dead shall be raised incorruptible" (1 Cor. 15:52). That "gay and glad"
should be associated with "dooms-day," with all of its usual ominous connotations, may seem somewhat jolting, although it is easily explained by
Herbert's assurance of salvation. More startling is the way the poem manages to portray the most macabre images in a tone that is light and even
amused. In the first stanza, a corpse or a skull, with its slack, open mouth,
is chided for not being able to sing. The poem describes two views of
death: one, before Christ, as it were, and the other "since our Saviours
death did put some bloud / Into thy face" (an image that is both witty and
theologically precise). The poem itself assumes the latter point of view,
seeing death from the perspective of salvation.

The following poems, with the traditionally horrifying titles of "Dooms-
day" and "Judgment" are in the same confident, even whimsical mood.
The former poem opens with an almost comic scene of resurrected bodies
rubbing their eyes and nudging each other, each one amazed that the *other*
person now lives:

> Come away,
> Make no delay.
> Summon all the dust to rise,
> Till it stirre, and rubbe the eyes;
> While this member jogs the other,
> Each one whispring, *Live you brother?*

(1–6)

The final stanza sharply contrasts the human condition in the temporal
world to the eschatological promise:

> Come away,
> Help our decay.
> Man is out of order hurl'd,
> Parcel'd out to all the world.
> Lord, thy broken consort raise,
> And the musick shall be praise.

(25–30)

Human beings are subject to decay, to the dissolution of death and the chaos of the world. The prayer is for the Lord to raise "thy broken consort," a multilevel figure referring to the Church as the Bride, the consort, of Christ (Rev. 21:2), broken, but now raised in wholeness, and to "broken consort" as a musical term, referring to the harmony of a multitude of different instruments.[56]

After "Dooms-day" comes "Judgement," another example of Herbert's serious humor, in which the "dreadful look" of the "Almightie Judge," "able a heart of iron to appall" (1–3), begins to scrutinize the records of each soul's works (Rev. 20:12). While some of the "poore wretches" will try to find at least some pages that are "void of sinne, / That they in merit shall excell" (9–10), the speaker resolves to boldly go up to God's throne

> And thrust a Testament into thy hand:
> Let that be scann'd.
> There thou shalt finde my faults are thine.

(13–15)

The final, explicitly apocalyptical poem is "Heaven," portraying through a purposefully restrained form the ineffable experiences of Heaven, hinting at them, anticipating them, in terms of human questions and desires:

> Then tell me, what is that supreme delight?
>   *Echo.*   Light.
> Light to the mind: what shall the will enjoy?
>   *Echo.*   Joy.
> But are there cares and businesse with the pleasure?
>   *Echo.*   Leisure.
> Light, joy, and leisure; but shall they persever?
>   *Echo.*   Ever.

(13–20)

The final poem of "The Church," "Love (3)," is the capstone of *The Temple*, recapitulating and resolving once and for all the paradoxes of sin and grace, guilt and love, that are Herbert's continual themes. The Banquet (the wedding feast, the Prodigal Son's reception, the countless metaphors of being fed and serving) signifies in Christ's teaching the Kingdom of

Heaven, a Kingdom prefigured in the Eucharist, as in any reception of grace, to be fully realized in the perfect communion of Christ and the saints in heaven. The placing of the poem after the series on sanctification, with the depiction of longing and frustration, and immediately after the apocalyptic poems, gives "Love (3)" a special place in the theological context of *The Temple*. Latimer's sermon on the Great Banquet of Matt. 22:1–14 suggests why this poem is fitting as the culmination of the earlier poems of sanctification:

> This feast, this costly dish hath its sauces; but what be they? Many, the cross, affliction, tribulation, persecution, and all manner of miseries: for like as sauces make lusty the stomach to receive meat so affliction stirreth up in us a desire to Christ. For when we be in quietness we are not hungry, we care not for Christ: but when we be in tribulation, and cast into prison, then we have a desire to Him; then we learn to call upon Him; then we hunger and thirst after Him; then we are desirous to feed upon Him.[57]

Although the speaker in "Love (3)" does not at the time exactly portray a hunger for Christ, the concept is similar to that of Luther, who, like Herbert, puts more emphasis on God's initiative:

> For this God disciplines His saints in wonderful ways. Indeed, He sends trials & dangers of every kind upon them, but in such a manner that when the trials are over, He may refresh them & bury them up with the richest comforts.[58]

Critics seem unanimous in attesting to the sense of "closure" that the poem gives to "The Church."[59] The feast portrayed in "Love (3)" is the goal of all the preceding poems.

Moreover, the poem brings together Herbert's understanding of human sin and God's unconditional love, themes that have been underlying concerns throughout *The Temple*, in a definitive way. Just as there are few religious poems so positive or joyful in their message and in their effects, so there are few poems that are so Calvinistic.

> Love bade me welcome: yet my soul drew back,
> Guiltie of dust and sinne.
> But quick-ey'd Love, observing me grow slack
> From my first entrance in,
> Drew nearer to me, sweetly questioning,
> If I lack'd any thing.

(1–6)

Again, the human being continually draws away from God, but the initiative is taken by God, who responds by drawing even nearer:

> A guest, I answer'd, worthy to be here:
> > Love said, You shall be he.
> I the unkinde, ungratefull? Ah my deare,
> > I cannot look on thee.
> Love took my hand, and smiling did reply,
> > Who made the eyes but I?
>
> > > > (7–12)

The speaker, "Guiltie of dust and sinne," knows that he is not "worthy to be here." His acceptance is based not on his worth, but on the declaration of love: "You shall be he." Stanley Fish is basically correct in saying that the words "You shall be he" "do not mean either that the speaker *is* worthy, or that he shall be in the future, but that he is *declared* worthy. . . . The question of merit is not adjudicated; it is simply set aside. Merit is not attributed to the speaker, nor is he found to be without it; rather, he is told that its determination has been made without reference to his desert."[60] (In the doctrine of sanctification, however, there is a sense in which a Christian "shall be" worthy in the future, as the personality and even the body are remade with the Resurrection of the Body.)

> Truth Lord, but I have marr'd them: let my shame
> > Go where it doth deserve.
> And know you not, sayes Love, who bore the blame?
>
> > > > (13–15)

The question of guilt is not quite so simple as Fish describes—it has not been "simply set aside." Love does not deny that the speaker is "Guiltie of dust and sinne"; rather, Love has taken the blame and the punishment it deserves upon Himself in the Incarnation and the Atonement. Yet the soul insists upon seeing salvation as something that can be earned, worked for, or at least repaid: "My deare, then I will serve" (16). The speaker agrees to stay, but he wants to serve Christ, rather than to simply let Christ serve him.

> You must sit down, sayes Love, and taste my meat:
> > So I did sit and eat.
>
> > > > (17–18)

This is similar to Herbert's rendition of "The 23d Psalme," "Nay, thou dost make me sit and dine" (17). Love's insistence, perhaps command ("You *must* sit down"),[61] results in the speaker's simply accepting the unimaginable benefits that are inexplicably offered him, *gratis*, by the fathomless generosity of God.

The final poems in the volume leave the topic of "The Church" as it exists in the believer's heart, to describe "The Church Militant" as it exists in the world, but they also serve to emphasize and further define the theme of sanctification. "The Church Militant" depicts the conflict between sin and religion, which is essentially the same conflict explored on the personal level in the earlier poems, here manifested corporately, in history and in the world.[62] The first part of "The Church Militant" (9–100) depicts the progress of religion, of the church. The poem then takes up the progress of sin (101–258). That both religion and sin have been enormously successful at the same time is an incisive paradox—again, Herbert is portraying sanctification in terms of a "double motion." The final part of the poem (259–79) discusses the two in terms of each other:

> Yet as the Church shall thither westward flie,
> So Sinne shall trace and dog her instantly:
> They have their period also and set times
> Both for their vertuous actions and their crimes.
>
> (259–62)

The struggle with sin and the religious life depicted in "The Church" applies also to the corporate history of "The Church Militant." Spiritual growth, as well as the growth of the church, is continually "dogged" by sin. Both sin and the church, however, continually draw "more neare / To time and place, where judgement shall appeare" (276–77). "Judgement may meet them both & search them round" (269). Despite the frustration that the success of religion is matched by the success of sin—culminating in the poem with sin triumphing as religion—the victory of religion is predestined and the tone remains celebratory. That the vicissitudes of history are firmly under the control of God is established strongly in the very first lines of the poem:

> Almightie Lord, who from thy glorious throne
> Seest and rulest all things ev'n as one:
> The smallest ant or atome knows thy power,
> Known also to each minute of an houre:
> Much more do Common-weals acknowledge thee,
> And wrap their policies in thy decree,
> Complying with thy counsels, doing nought
> Which doth not meet with an eternall thought.
>
> (1–8)

Throughout the poem the account of history is punctuated by a refrain that points directly to God's control and God's mysterious will:[63]

> *How deare to me, O God, thy counsels are!*
> *Who may with thee compare?*

The refrain is sometimes jarring, as when it juxtaposes God's "counsels" with the rise of Antichrist (205–10), but the poem, with its discordant subject matter held together by the refrain, images precisely the Reformed doctrine of how history, no less than the individual Christian life, is directed by the sovereign purpose of God.

The final poem in *The Temple*, "L'Envoy," returns the conflict with "Sinne" to the individual, personal level. The tone is strident, a return to and a recapitulation of spiritual warfare from a personal point of view:

> *King of Glorie, King of Peace,*
> With the one make warre to cease;
> With the other blesse thy sheep,
> Thee to love, in thee to sleep.

> (1–4)

The poem begins with a prayer for the *"King of Peace"* to put an end to the warfare, and for the *"King of Glorie"* to accomplish the final glorification, with His sheep loving Him and "resting in Christ." Herbert thus begins "L'Envoy" where he concluded "The Church," but he feels constrained to return his readers to the battle with Sinne, which is not yet concluded. The invective, the curse, is reserved for that manifestation of Sinne which would deny the spiritual realities that are the substance of *The Temple*, specifically, the continuing efficacy of Christ's Atonement for the believer:

> Let not Sinne devoure thy fold,
> Bragging that thy bloud is cold,
> That thy death is also dead,
> While his conquests dayly spread;
> That thy flesh hath lost his food,
> And thy Crosse is common wood.
> Choke him, let him say no more,
> But reserve his breath in store,
> Till thy conquests and his fall
> Make his sighs to use it all,
> And then bargain with the winde
> To discharge what is behinde.

> *Blessed be God alone,*
> *Thrice blessed Three in One.*

The poem reiterates the *psychomachia*, opposing "his conquests" (Sinne's) to "thy conquests" (God's). The subjugation of sin is ascribed to the action of God. Dramatizing the struggle of sanctification in heightened terms, the speaker curses Sinne, speaking of its fall, then blesses God. Herbert could not dispense with the theme of sanctification on this side of the grave.

"The Church" follows the process in an individual Christian life to its apocalyptic conclusion, but living Christians are part of "The Church Militant," and as the term "Militant" implies, are still participants in the warfare.

The doctrine of sanctification, involving what may be termed the religious psychology of Reformation thought, offered Herbert a way to understand and to order his own experiences. Herbert's description of *The Temple* as "a picture of the many spiritual conflicts that have passed betwixt God and my soul, before I could subject mine to the will of Jesus my master," is thus a precise statement not only of the theme of his poetry, but of the theological and structural principle by which it is ordered.

—— 7 ——
The Word of God: Revelation and Proclamation

The *Word* in Characters, God in the Voice.
> —Vaughan, "H. Scriptures," 8

By his Word, God alone sanctifies temples to himself for lawful use.
> —Calvin, *Institutes* 4.1.5

If the doctrines of predestination and sanctification suggest formal models for explaining the external organization and the internal conflict of Herbert's verse, the doctrine of the Word helps explain its texture—the biblical and sacramental imagery, the concept of language—and its nature as religious verse. That Christ reveals Himself through language, through the Holy Scriptures, and that He is conveyed through original human utterance, as in preaching, was a major conceptual emphasis of Reformation theology. The doctrine of revelation and proclamation is thus especially relevant to verbal art, to poetry. Herbert's calling as an Anglican priest was to be a "minister of the word," a vocation he fulfilled in his poetry no less than in his parish.

"The Reformation is a matter of the word alone."[1] Thus Gerhard Ebeling sums up the complexities of Reformation spirituality. The term "the Word of God" had a number of senses, each of them involving God's action in revealing, communicating, and expressing Himself to humankind through the fact and symbol of language. Christ, above all, is the Incarnate Word, the *logos*, the full, concrete manifestation of God, who assumed human life to save sinners. Second, "the Word of God" is the Bible, God's revelation of Himself and His message of reconciliation in Christ through language. Third, "the Word of God" is preaching, whereby the Scriptures and Christ's offer of salvation are communicated through the language of human beings who proclaim God's Word to others. "In each case the word is active, saving and judging."[2] The term had specific reference to the Gospel, defined in Thomas Wilson's dictionary as "the glad and joyfull tydings of Remission of sinnes, & eternall salvation by faith in Christ." God's "Word," which was also used in describing the promises of God and the decree of salvation, was thus connected to God's saving action and to the assurance of salvation.[3] The concept of God's Word was thus a central unifying metaphor around which the whole of Reformation theology and practice was arranged.[4]

The Reformation is sometimes heralded as the beginning of modern subjectivism, replacing the authority of the church with that of personal religious experience. Actually, however, the early Reformers saw themselves as simply subordinating one objective authority, the church, to a greater objective authority, the Word.[5] The experience oriented "enthusiasts" were condemned by the early Reformers, although they would later have a great impact upon Protestantism. The reforming of the Church involved first of all a reemphasis and a reinterpretation of the Bible. Luther's conversion was through meditation on a single verse from the Scripture (Rom. 1:17); his new realization that the just shall live by faith caused him to reinterpret the entire Bible in this light. As Luther describes it, "a totally other face of the entire Scripture showed itself to me," as every passage he turned to unveiled and confirmed "the gospel."[6]

The iconoclasm of some of the more radical reformers is an especially important example of the Reformation's insistence on the priority of the word—in fact, of language itself—in Christian spirituality. Zwingli and his compatriots seem to have had nothing against art as such;[7] rather, the biblical prohibition of "graven images" was obeyed rather than the tradition of the medieval church.[8] At stake was not only the question of authority, but the primacy of language in Christian thought and worship. Garside summarizes Zwingli's argument:

> To begin with, men can learn nothing of the content of God's Word from an image. "Why," Zwingli rhetorically asks, "do we not send images to unbelievers so that they can learn belief from them?" Precisely because we would be required to explain what they mean, which in turn requires knowledge of the Word. "If now you show an unbelieving or unlettered child images, then you must teach him with the Word in addition, or he will have looked at the picture in vain." For if "you were newly come from the unbeliever and knew nothing of Christ and saw Him painted with the apostles at the Last Supper, or on the Cross, then you would learn nothing from this same picture other than to say 'He who is pictured there was a good-looking man in spite of it all.'" . . . One may have images of Christ, but they are powerless; the "story must be learned only from the Word, and from the painting one learns nothing except the form of the body, the movements or the constitution of the body or face.[9]

The universal Protestant insistence that worship be conducted and the Bible translated in the vernacular languages was a major conceptual change from the medieval church, marking perhaps more dramatically than anything else the new emphasis, not only on the Word, but on words themselves.

When the crucifixes and statues of the Virgin Mary were removed from the churches, they were generally replaced by a different kind of icon, the open Bible. Herbert himself urged that the church be decorated by paintings, not of visual religious scenes, but of texts of Scripture ("Country Parson," 13:246). Whereas Roman Catholicism had stressed the sacraments as the means of grace, the Reformation stressed the Word as the means of grace.[10] By means of the Scriptures, by means of preaching, the message of reconciliation and the person of Christ Himself are conveyed to the hearers.[11] The sacraments were still "means of grace," but they were themselves brought under the verbal metaphor, so that they became understood as "visible words," conveying in the most concrete and immediate form the Gospel of Christ.[12]

This theological emphasis on the metaphor of the Word has clear aesthetic implications. Donne interestingly summarizes the Reformation preference for the aural over the visual, when he observes that "the eye is the devils doore. . . . But the eare is the Holy Ghosts first doore" (*Sermons*, 8:228). Lust and envy enter the soul through the eyes, and one can sin through the other senses, but it is through the ear, through the hearing of God's Word, that the Holy Ghost enters. Herbert goes so far as to recommend that in church one worship with eyes shut: "In time of service seal up both thine eies. . . . Those doores being shut, all by the eare comes in" ("The Church-Porch," 415, 418).[13] The Protestant Church, while seemingly rejecting the visual arts, became a great patron of the aural ones such as music. The iconoclasts themselves employed music in their worship. Although Zwingli, who was a musician, did not approve of musical instruments in church, the song—a synthesis of music and "the Word"—was a universal trait of Reformation worship.[14]

The Church of England, of course, did not go so far as Zwingli in systematically replacing physical icons with verbal ones—nor did most other Protestants. Still, the *Book of Common Prayer*, which is so important in Herbert's poetry, is a thoroughly "Reformed" document, both in ritual and in sacramental doctrine.

Besides helping to understand, for example, Herbert's sacramental imagery, the exaltation of "the Word" helps account for other features of Herbert's art. Denis Donoghue is impressed by "the confidence which the speaker reposes in the language in which he participates."

What is remarkable in this poem ["Decay"] is not Herbert's use of domestic figures to express metaphysical relations, but the confidence with which he uses them; his assumption that whatever he wants to say can be entrusted to these homely terms.[15]

Donoghue's comments on Herbert's "domestic figures" are reminiscent of Herbert's own comments on the Bible. "The Holy Scripture . . . condescends to the naming of a plough, a hatchet, a bushell, leaven, boyes piping and dancing; showing that things of ordinary use are not only to serve in the way of drudgery, but to be washed, and cleansed, and serve for lights even of Heavenly Truths" ("Country Parson," 21:257). Herbert is recommending the use of such familiar and concrete illustrations in teaching parishioners complex ideas, a method he probably employed in his sermons,[16] and which is characteristic of his poetry. Herbert's poetry may thus be shaped by the Bible in more fundamental ways than by his countless scriptural allusions. His "confidence" in language may itself be due to his belief in the Word. The belief that God reveals Himself—not only intellectually, but sacramentally—through the medium of language may be related also to Herbert's own exploration of language. Herbert, in his poetry, with all of its complex wordplay, "sucks" meanings from a word, as he advocates doing with the words of Scripture ("The H. Scriptures [1]" and "Country Parson," 4:228), exploring a word in all of its implications and configurations for the "hony" of revelation.[17]

The doctrine of the Word also helps account for the intimacy between the speaker and God portrayed in Hebert's religious verse, and for various formal characteristics of particular poems. Margaret Blanchard points out that a major difference between the poetry of Herbert and that of Donne is that "God speaks to Herbert whereas the Divine in Donne does not speak."[18] Contrasting the auditory imagery in Herbert to the visual imagery of Donne, Blanchard shows the psychological connection between the process of speaking and hearing and the experience of intimacy.[19] This sense of dialogue in the poem expresses itself formally. "The poet is not alone," observed Mulder, "for he receives instruction from without by a series of messages: something found, received, read, overheard; he is taught by friends, bystanders, or a chance meeting in the way; and sometimes God addresses him directly."[20] Indeed, God addresses him directly in many of these encounters under various forms, whether the poet is actively deciphering what he discovers to be God's Word, as in "Jesu,"[21] or whether he is interrupted by an unexpected "word" from God, as in "The Collar." In each case, the dynamics of revelation animate Herbert's poetry.

i. The Incarnate Word

Rosemond Tuve has aptly described Herbert's poetry as "Christocentric."[22] Nearly all of Herbert's poems either address Christ directly, or are about Christ in some way. The mode of Christ's presentation in the poetry can be clarified by Reformation theology and its differences with medieval and Counter-Reformation thought. The important issue for Herbert is how Christ can be communicated by means of human language—how the incarnate Word is conveyed through the written word of the Scriptures, the proclaimed word of preaching, the visible word of the sacrament, and finally, the word of the poet, which involves them all.

The Reformation slogan "Christ alone" meant that salvation and forgiveness of sins are centered not in penitence or in any other mediators, but in the person and work of Christ. In the years preceding the Reformation, according to church historians, "Christ was popularly regarded as a strict judge, to be placated with satisfactions or absolutions."[23] The conceptual shift by which Christ was experienced as the source of unconditional forgiveness and love was an important by-product of early Reformation spirituality. With the Counter-Reformation, the Roman church began to modify the presentation of Christ, as expressed, for example, in the awe-inspiring icons of *Christ Pantokratōr*, encouraging devotion to a very human and tender Christ. It is in this light that Martz and others have noted Herbert's lack of interest in the "personality" of Christ, as compared to the Catholic devotional manuals.[24] Indeed, Herbert writes relatively little about Jesus' life as portrayed in the Gospels, with the significant exception of the passion, which he treats in great detail. More often Christ is presented not biographically, but as a living presence. Martin Luther's evocation of how Christ should be imagined relates especially well to Herbert: "Christ should be so set forth that thou shouldst see nothing beside him, and shouldest think that none can be more to thee or present within thee than he is: for he sitteth not idly in heaven, but is present with us working and living in us."[25] William Mueller observes that Donne, in his depiction of God, focuses "on his existence rather than his essence . . . on his activity in the world of man."[26] Herbert is concerned with Christ existentially; Christ is not a literary character, whom he is writing *about,* a literary treatment that assumes detachment. The Christ of Herbert's poetry, continually breaking out of or defying human categories of understanding (e.g., "Dialogue," "Love [3]"), is a person with whom the speaker shares a relationship. In Herbert, as Ilona Bell points out, "Christ speaks as the mediator, not as the suffering man."[27] Yet, as mediator, Christ is exalted in the context of a deep and personal intimacy.

Since the human mind is depraved, human beings can know nothing about God, except what He reveals. Mere human speculation about God apart from the revelation of Christ, in whom God fully manifests Himself, is futile:

All thought about God which does not proceed from the fact of Christ is a fathomless abyss which utterly engulfs our faculties. A clear example of this is furnished not only by Turks and Jews who under the name of God worship their fantasies but also by the Papists. The principle of their theological schools, that God in Himself is the object of faith, is generally known. Hence they philosophize at length and with much subtlety about the hidden majesty of God while overlooking the fact of Christ.[28]

Calvin's critique of scholasticism is very similar to Herbert's in "Divinitie":

> As men, for fear the starres should sleep and nod,
>   And trip at night, have spheres suppli'd;
> As if a starre were duller than a clod,
>   Which knows his way without a guide:
>
> Just so the other heav'n they also serve,
>   Divinities transcendent skie:
> Which with the edge of wit they cut and carve.
>   Reason triumphs, and faith lies by.
>
> Could not that Wisdome, which first broacht the wine,
>   Have thicken'd it with definitions?
> And jagg'd his seamless coat, had that been fine,
>   With curious questions and divisions?
>
> But all the doctrine, which he taught and gave,
>   Was clear as heav'n, from whence it came.
>
>   (1–14)

The stars do not depend upon astronomers' understanding their motions for them; neither does God or His action depend upon the definitions of theologians. In neglecting the way reason attempts to "cut and carve" the study of faith, Herbert has recourse to "the fact of Christ." "Wisdome" is not an abstraction in this poem, but a person, and a very concrete person who "broacht the wine" and wore a "seamlesse coat." The personification of wisdom as Christ derives doubtless from Prov. 8:22–31, which describes the preexistence, the personality, and the role in creation of wisdom—a passage taken as a parallel to the description of the Word, the *logos,* of John 1.[29] There can be no knowledge of God apart from Christ, who is Himself wisdom and the Word of God. This is not to say that there can be no propositional knowledge about God; in the words of Christ, as recorded in the Scriptures, God himself reveals "doctrine," which Herbert describes as coming from heaven. In focusing upon Christ as "Wisdome," and as the Word of God, Herbert necessarily, for the Reformers, must depend on the written word of the Scriptures as testifying to and recording the "doctrine" of the Incarnate Word. Thus Herbert's poem, while ridiculing human philosophy and presenting wisdom concretely in the person of Christ, quotes verses of Scripture (Mark 12:29, 30; 13:33; Matt. 7:12), contrasting their clarity to the oversubtle intellectualizing of human beings, who would prefer to make the Word of God problematic rather than face its lucid demands:

> *Love God, and love your neighbours. Watch and pray.*
>   *Do as ye would be done unto.*
> O dark instructions; ev'n as dark as day!
> Who can these Gordian knots undo?
>
>   (17–20)

Italics in Herbert's poetry generally indicate another speaker, usually God, intruding into or contrasting with the dominant voice of the poem. Here, the words of Scripture, the words of Christ, contrast with the futility of human speculation. There can be no knowledge of God apart from His Word.

According to Lewis Bayly, "Christ is called the *Word:* first, because the conception of a *Word* in mans *mind,* is the nearest thing, that in *some sense* can shadow unto us the manner how he is *eternally begotten* of his Father's *substance.* . . . Secondly, because that by *him,* the Father hath from the beginning declared *his Will* for our salvation. . . . Thirdly, because he is the *chief argument* of all the *Word of God*" (*The Practice of Piety,* p. 7). For Herbert, Christ is all anyone needs to know of the Deity. As has been seen in "Divinitie," it is not possible for Herbert to write about the Incarnate Word apart from the Scriptures, which were themselves taken to be the means by which Christ is communicated.

ii. The Written Word

As God is present in Jesus, so, for Calvin, is Jesus present in the Scriptures.[30] In each case, God adapts Himself to human nature by becoming flesh in human history and then by recording and perpetuating this fact and its purpose in human language. "We must read scripture," says Calvin, "with the intention of finding Christ therein."[31] The Bible is not only a source of knowledge, but the means by which God speaks directly to human beings, a communication that is experiential and sacramental. "When by the power of the Spirit it effectually penetrates our hearts, when it conveys Christ to us, then it becomes a word of life converting the soul" (*Institutes* 1.9.3).[32] This Christocentric view of Scripture, that the Incarnate Word is manifested in the written Word, is important to remember in regard to Herbert's view of the Bible and its role in his poetry. For Herbert, Christ is "the letter of the word" ("Sepulchre," 17–20).

In the Church of England the Bible was given a central place. Henry's reformation may have been more political than theological, but his provision for vernacular Bible reading in church was of the utmost significance.[33]

Cranmer's *Book of Common Prayer* provided for daily liturgical readings, designed so that the Old Testament would have been read through in the course of a year, the New Testament would have been read in its entirety three times in the course of the year, and the entire Psalter would have been read every month.[34] In addition, the habit of individual Bible reading would usually involve reading a chapter before leaving the bedchamber, a chapter at noon, a chapter at night—a program which, with the monthly reading of the Psalter and the addition of six remaining chapters reserved for New Year's Eve, provided that the entire Bible be read through personally once every year.[35] Protestant books of devotion often consisted simply of quotations from Scripture topically arranged.[36] In fact, the paucity of original books of Protestant devotion and meditation, as compared to those of the Counter-Reformation, may be due to the supreme place held by individual Bible-reading in individual devotions. Herbert, who grew up in a household particularly devoted to the Scriptures and to the daily services,[37] which he himself would attend as a student and conduct as a priest, who studied the Bible thoroughly in his course of "divinitie," and who pored through it in his own devotions, was saturated intellectually and imaginatively with the biblical text.

Calvin conceived of his theology as simply a systematic exposition of the teachings of Scripture.[38] Indeed, if the Bible is God's revelation of Himself in propositions of language, and if human beings, through their fallen reason, can add nothing to what God says of Himself, the role of theology is radically circumscribed. Theology becomes hermeneutics; the difference between Calvin and Arminius turns on their different interpretation of certain key Scriptures.[39] Calvin's most "dreadful" doctrines (the term is his—*Institutes* 3.23.7), were themselves his attempt to reconcile various Scriptures. He pursues the confessedly difficult and dangerous implications of predestination only, he says, "because it pleased God to publish it" (*Institutes* 3.21.3, cf. 1–2).

The Bible was not simply a collection of doctrines, though; reading the Bible was experienced as an intensely personal confrontation with God Himself. The Bible's impact on a sensitive Christian such as Herbert was not only intellectual, but also experiential and imaginative, as Harold Fisch has observed:

> For Tyndale, the Scottish covenanters, for Milton and Herbert, the reading of Scripture was not a matter of accepting dogmas, it was a matter of being exposed to a direct, even blinding spiritual illumination. . . . The tremendous effect which the Bible had upon men, the awe, the terror, and ecstasy which it undoubtedly inspired, should be sufficient to convince the sceptic that the men of the Reformation were concerned with real and mighty facts of experience. . . . Moreover, the Scriptures, as well as being the Word of God, was literature. It enlightened the eyes, but it also nourished the literary imagination.[40]

Thus the comment about Herbert's devotion to the Bible in the Printer's Preface to *The Temple* is not surprising:

> Next God, he loved that which God himself hath magnified above all things, that is, his Word: so he hath been heard to make solemne protestation, that he would not part with one leaf thereof for the whole world, if it were offered him in exchange.

The Bible, by presenting God through the medium of language, is the master text behind Herbert's poetry.

The doctrine of the Scriptures is one of the relatively few theological issues Herbert discusses at length. Herbert's "Brief Notes on Valdesso's *Considerations*" is a commentary on Ferrar's translation of a work by Juan Valdés, a Spanish Catholic exiled by the Inquisition for his advocacy of "Lutheran" principles such as "Justification by Faith."[41] As such, Valdés was popular among Protestants, serving as an example, in the words of Herbert, "that God in the midst of Popery should open the eyes of one to understand and expresse so clearly and excellently the intent of the Gospell in the acceptation of Christ's righteousness (as he showeth through all his considerations) a thing strangely buried, and darkened by the Adversaries, and their great stumbling-block" (pp. 304–5). Herbert also praises his reverence for Christ and his moral precepts; yet Valdés is also a Catholic and, what is more, a mystic, whose emphasis on the individual's illumination by the Holy Spirit brings him very close to the "enthusiasts,"[42] the Protestant sects and mystics condemned by Reformation theology as dangerously heterodox. Herbert's commentary (the full title of which is "Brief Notes *relating to the dubious and offensive places in the following* considerations") is essentially a critique of Valdés from the perspective of Reformation spirituality. Specifically, Herbert continually complains that Valdés "slights the Scripture too much" (p. 306), and that "his opinion of the scripture is unsufferable" (p. 318).

For example, Valdés suggests that when a neighbor is in need, the Christian's impulse or "motion" to help comes from God, the indwelling Holy Spirit; conversely, "when they doe not perceive any motion" they understand "that God would have them to remain quiet, assuming that in this case it is God's will for the Christian to refrain from helping." Herbert's response is devastating: "In indifferent things there is roome for motions and expecting of them; but in things good, as to relieve my Neighbour, God hath already revealed his Will about it" (p. 313). God's objective Word says, "love thy neighbor" (Luke 10:17); that is God's will and His final, authoritative direction for His people. He does not communicate Himself primarily through feelings, but through His Word. God's will, as revealed in Scripture, is to be sharply distinguished from human will; ethics and truth are grounded in the objective declaration of God in Scripture, not in the variable and deceptive feelings of the self.

Similarly, Herbert objects to Valdés' teaching of illumination, whereby the "candle" of the Scriptures gives way to the "sunbeames" of the Holy Spirit, so that "the light of the holy spirit . . . being come, a man hath no need to seek that of Holy Scripture." The problem here, according to Herbert, is that "he opposeth the teaching of the spirit to the teaching of the scripture, which the holy spirit wrot. Although the holy spirit apply the scripture, yet what the scripture teacheth, the spirit teacheth" (p. 317). Personal illumination or revelation can have no precedence over Scripture; indeed, the test of revelation is whether it is consonant with and points to Scripture. Herbert elsewhere cites the example of Acts 10, in which the content of Cornelius's vision was to send for Peter, Christ's apostle, author of the epistles, and thus deliverer of God's Word. "*Cornelius* had revelation, yet *Peter* was to be sent for, and those that have inspirations must still use *Peter*, God's Word" (p. 310). Citing 2 Pet. 1:17–21, Herbert goes on to observe that Peter himself "preferres the Word before the sight of the Transfiguration of Christ. So that the Word hath the precedence even of Revelations and Visions" (p. 318).

For Herbert, as for Luther and Calvin, it is impossible to separate the Scriptures from the God who inspired them:

All the Saints of God may be said in some sence to have put confidence in Scripture, but not as a naked Word severed from God, but as the Word of God: And in so doing they doe not sever their trust from God. But by trusting in the word of God They trust in God. Hee that trusts in the Kings word for anything trusts in the King. (Pp. 306–7)

The Scriptures are not only supremely authoritative, they are inexhaustible. "The H. Scriptures . . . have not only an Elementary use, but a use of perfection, neither can they ever be exhausted, (as Pictures may be by a plenarie circumspection) but still even to the most learned and perfect in them, there is somewhat to be learned more" (p. 309). On this subject, Herbert includes a quasi-poetic hieroglyph (p. 310):

In the Scripture are $\begin{cases} \textit{Doctrines, these ever teach more and more.} \\ \textit{Promises, these ever comfort more and more.} \end{cases}$

Rom. 15.4.

Comments Herbert on this schematic diagram of the inexhaustible quality of the Scriptures, using Valdés' figure of a servant who is promised in a letter a thousand ducats from his master:

For as the servant leaves not the letter when he hath read it, but keeps it by him, and reads it againe and againe, and the more the promise is delayed, the more he reads it, and fortifies himselfe with it; so are wee to doe with the Scriptures, and this is the use of the promises of the Scriptures. But the use of the Doctrinall part is more, in regard it presents us not with the same thing only when it is read as the promises doe, but enlightens us with new Considerations the more we read it. (P. 310)

Herbert's doctrine of the Bible is most fully summarized in "The Country Parson," in the chapter entitled "The Parsons Knowledg" (3:228–29). After three sentences on the usefulness of knowledge about agriculture and so on, the chapter focuses on knowledge of the Scripture. That a chapter on "The Parsons Knowledg" should be almost completely taken up by a discussion of Scripture is, of course, in the Reformation tradition of *sola scriptura*, of the written Word as the source and content of all religious knowledge:

> They say, it is an ill Mason that refuseth any stone: and there is no knowledg, but, in a skilfull hand, serves either positively as it is, or else to illustrate some other knowledge. . . . But the chief and top of his knowledge consists in the book of books, the storehouse and magazine of life and comfort, the holy Scriptures. There he sucks, and lives. ("The Country Parson," 3:228).

The Parson, according to Herbert, finds four kinds of knowledge in the Scriptures: "Precepts for life, Doctrines for knowledge, Examples for illustration, and Promises for comfort."

Herbert, though, turns immediately to the crucial question of hermeneutics, an issue that takes up the remainder and the bulk of the chapter. If Scripture is the source of all religious knowledge, the question of how the words of Scripture are to be interpreted was a major concern of the early Reformers, who were challenging first of all the interpretations and the teaching authority of the medieval church, as well as the subjectivism of the "Enthusiasts." Against the former, Luther and Calvin argued that the Scriptures are essentially clear and have no need of *a priori* theological teaching for their interpretation ("Divinitie"). Therefore, the Scriptures should be accessible to every Christian, to whom the Holy Spirit can minister, through the Scriptures, on a personal level. On the other hand, such individualism opened up the danger of "private interpretation" (cf. 2 Pet. 1:20), and the proliferation of sects based upon capricious and subjective interpretations of the Bible. Against the "enthusiasts," the argument was to insist that the Scriptures provide an objective, not a subjective authority.

Herbert's hermeneutics well summarize the Reformation concern that the Bible be both experienced on a subjective level and understood as an authority outside the self:

> But for the understanding of these [the Precepts, Doctrines, Examples, and Promises]; the means he useth are first, a holy Life, remembering what his Master saith, that *if any do Gods will, he shall know of the Doctrine,*

John 7. and assuring himself that wicked men, however learned, do not know the Scriptures, because they feel them not, and because they are not understood but with the same spirit that writ them. The second means is prayer, which if it be necessary even in temporall things, how much more in things of another world, where the well is deep, and we have nothing of our selves to draw with? Wherefore he ever begins the reading of the Scripture with some short inward ejaculation, as, *Lord, open mine eyes, that I may see the wondrous things of thy Law.* &c. [Ps. 119:18]. ("Country Parson," 3:228–29)

Herbert here closely parallels Calvin, who writes, in another context, of "ever so learned men, endowed with the highest judgment, [who] rise up in opposition and bring to bear and display all their mental powers in this debate" over Scripture.

But even if anyone clears God's Sacred Word from men's evil speaking, he will not at once imprint upon their hearts that certainty which piety requires. . . . For as God alone is a fit witness of himself in his Word, so also the Word will not find acceptance in men's hearts before it is sealed by the inward testimony of the Spirit. The same Spirit, therefore, who has spoken through the mouths of the prophets must penetrate into our hearts to persuade us that they faithfully proclaimed what had been divinely commanded. (*Institutes* 1.7.4)

The Holy Spirit is necessary to interpret what the Holy Spirit wrote. According to Herbert, "Wicked men, however learned" can never "feel" nor understand the Scriptures because they lack the Holy Spirit. "We have nothing of our selves to draw with." The very understanding of Scripture depends, as with all else, on the action of God.

This is not to say, however, that a Christian, in whom the Holy Spirit dwells and is active, is thereby free to interpret the Scripture according to his own inner "motions." Calvin continues his argument by insisting upon the objective, transcendental quality of the Holy Spirit, disassociating the work of the Spirit from the judgments of the self: "Therefore, illumined by his power, we believe neither by our own nor by anyone else's judgment that Scripture is from God; but above human judgment we affirm with utter certainty (just as if we were gazing upon the majesty of God himself) that it has flowed to us from the very mouth of God by the ministry of men" (*Institutes* 1.7.5).

This theoretical objectivity, that Scripture, with its all-embracing authority, rests "neither by our own nor by anyone else's judgment," is maintained, for Reformation theologians, by a very practical principle of hermeneutics. "Scripture," says Calvin, "is self-authenticated" (*Institutes* 1.7.5); he might also have said that Scripture is self-interpreting, a principle summarized by Herbert:

The third means is a diligent collation of Scripture with Scripture. For all Truth being consonant to it self, and all being penn'd by one and the self-same Spirit, it cannot be, but that an industrious, and judicious comparing of place with place must be a singular help for the right understanding of the Scriptures. To this may be added the consideration of any text with the coherence thereof, touching what goes before, and what follows after, as also the scope of the Holy Ghost. When the Apostles would have called down fire from Heaven, they were reproved, as ignorant of what spirit they were. For the Law required one thing, and the Gospel another: yet as diverse, not as repugnant: therefore the Spirit of both is to be considered, and weighed. ("Country Parson," 3:229)

Herbert is describing the central hermeneutic contribution of Reformation thought, as first developed by Luther, a principle known as "the analogy of faith." William Whitaker (1548–95), a Cambridge Professor of Divinity, explains it as follows:"[in interpreting the Bible,] one place must be compared and collated with another, the obscurer places with the plainer or less obscure. For though in one place the words may be obscure, they will be plainer in another. . . . All our expositions should accord with the analogy of faith."[43] Difficult places in Scripture must be interpreted according to the clear ones. No text may be removed from its context; no teaching of the Bible can be exalted at the expense of other teachings. By the faith that the Bible is unified and noncontradictory, in Herbert's words, that it is "consonant to it self, all being penn'd by one and the self-same Spirit," the Bible becomes a complex and self-interpreting system. In "The H. Scriptures (2)," Herbert describes "the analogy of faith":

> Oh that I knew how all thy lights combine,
>   And the configurations of their glorie!
>   Seeing not onely how each verse doth shine,
> But all the constellations of the storie.
> This verse marks that, and both do make a motion
>   Unto a third, that ten leaves off doth lie:
>   Then as dispersed herbs do watch a potion,
> These three make up some Christians destinie.
>
> (1–8)

Although "the analogy of faith" stressed the literal meaning of Scripture above the traditional allegorical readings, typology and even the medieval fourfold interpretation (historical, allegorical, moral, mystical) were not rejected. In fact, for Herbert, the various biblical types and symbols seem to have been part of "the constellations of the storie" that he could trace throughout the Bible and that he employed in his own poetry. Rather, the Reformers, by adding the hermeneutic assumption of a closed system, offered a principle of verification. Luther himself summarizes the fourfold levels of meaning in Scripture, but concludes with the principle that "no allegory, tropology, or anagogy is valid, unless the same truth is expressly stated historically elsewhere. . . . but one must indeed take in an allegorical sense only what is elsewhere stated historically, as mountain in the sense of righteousness in Ps. 36:6."[44] Thus, although a Protestant like Herbert may well see in the Song of Solomon a type of the church or even the Virgin Mary,[45] he would be unlikely to see Esther, a maiden interceding for the people, as a type of the Virgin Mary, since the notion of Mary's intercession is nowhere, he would say, literally affirmed in Scripture.[46] The analogy of faith does not go against Herbert's obvious manipulation of biblical symbols. If anything, it gives his typology direction and precision by insisting, in terms of Herbert's poem, that each star, each verse or biblical image, shines not only in itself, but also in "constellations" of a greater, though complex, unity.[47]

Barbara Lewalski has explored in depth the differences between medieval and Protestant typology and the importance of the latter to George Herbert. Again, the Protestants believed that the Old Testament saints were saved by grace through faith, just as the New Testament saints were. The Old and the New Covenants, for all their differences, made up a continuum. This means that the Old Testament does not simply symbolize the New Testament meaning; rather, according to Lewalski, it embodies that meaning. Whereas medieval exegetes would see the crossing of the Red Sea as an allegory of Baptism, pointing ahead as a shadow of what would eventually be instituted fully in the Church, Reformation readers of Scripture would see the Red Sea crossing as, in effect, an actual Baptism, an example, not merely a symbol, of the means God employs in freeing human beings from every kind of slavery into the freedom of the Gospel, as passing through the waters conveys death, burial, and rebirth. Both the Old Testament and the New convey the Gospel. God dealt with Abraham and David in the same way that He deals with any believer, even today. Thus Lewalski shows how, for the Protestant, the antitype of biblical symbolism is not simply Christ, but the contemporary Christian. Conversely, the Protestants tended to see their own lives as following the patterns laid out in the people and events of Scripture.[48] For Herbert, the biblical figure of Aaron with his symbolic robes made him think not only of the intercessory role of Christ and the New Testament priesthood, but, more profoundly, of himself ("Aaron").

The Scripture addresses the believer in a highly personal way, yet the Reformers took care to emphasize that Scripture, taken as a whole, resists private interpretations, and in effect can interpret and comment upon itself. Another way of insuring the objectivity of biblical interpretation is through the church, the "communion of saints":

> The fourth means are Commenters and Fathers, who have handled the places controverted, which the Parson by no means refuseth. As he

doth not so study others, as to neglect the grace of God in himself, and what the Holy Spirit teaches him; so doth he assure himself, that God in all ages hath had his servants, to whom he hath revealed his Truth, as well as to him; and that as one countrey doth not bear all things, that there may be a Commerce; so neither hath God opened, or will open all to one, that there may be a traffick in knowledg between the servants of God, for the planting both of love, and humility. Wherefore he hath one comment at least upon every book of Scripture, and ploughing with this, and his own meditations, he enters into the secrets of God treasured in the holy Scriptures. ("Country Parson," 3:229).

The Reformers did insist upon the teaching role of the church; the difference with the Catholic position is that, for the early Protestants, the church is itself grounded upon Scripture, rather than *vice versa*, so that the true church, guided by the Holy Spirit, can teach nothing contrary to the express teachings of Scripture. Yet this does not at all imply for Herbert any sort of "private" interpretation. Since the Church is built upon the apostolic testimony (Eph. 2:20), "the Word"—later written down and drawn up into the canon of Holy Scripture but incarnate in Christ and proclaimed as the Gospel, which first called members into the Church—necessarily is prior in time and in authority. Thus Herbert advises the Country Parson, when arguing with the "Papist," to concentrate on the authority of Scripture over against the authority of the Church apart from Scripture. The "Papist" should be asked "whether it [the church] be a rule to itself, whether it hath a rule, whether having a rule it ought not to be guided by it?" ("Country Parson," 24:263). The rationale for Herbert is that the Holy Spirit ministers not only to himself but also to other "Servants of God," from whom he can learn. As he points out in "Brief Notes on Valdesso," "the teaching of the Spirit," whether through an individual or the church, will correspond to "the teaching of the Scripture, which the holy spirit wrot" (p. 317). Herbert sees a unity of testimony, described in terms similar to that of the analogy of faith, "a traffick in knowledge between the servants of God," in which an individual's understanding of the Scripture is checked against that of another Christian's, just as one biblical text is to be collated with another.[49]

Herbert's poems on the Scriptures describe the kind of devotional experience he finds in them:

> Oh Book! infinite sweetnesse! Let my heart
>   Suck ev'ry letter, and a hony gain,
>   Precious for any grief in any part;
> To cleare the breast, to mollifie all pain.
> Thou art all health, health thriving till it make
>   A full eternitie: thou art a masse
>   Of strange delights, where we may wish & take.

> Ladies, look here; this is the thankfull glasse,
> That mends the lookers eyes: this is the well
>> That washes what it shows. Who can indeare
>> Thy praise too much? thou art heav'ns lidger here,
> Working against the states of death and hell.
>> Thou art joyes handsell: heav'n lies flat in thee,
>> Subject to ev'ry mounters bended knee. ("The H. Scriptures"
>> [1])

For Herbert, that God reveals himself through the written Word is another function of the Incarnation. The Scriptures are heaven's ambassador (with a pun on "ledger" so that the ambassador is a written text).[50] In this text, as with the Incarnate Word, the infinite and transcendent empties itself to accommodate human beings—"heav'n lies flat in thee." Through the Scriptures "heav'n," with its secrets, is made accessible, although only through prayer and submission:

> Thou art joyes handsell: heav'n lies flat in thee,
> Subject to ev'ry mounters bended knee.

The conventional notion that one can "mount" to Heaven is here corrected in terms of Herbert's Reformation theology and by his sustained spatial imagery. One can reach heaven not by one's own efforts but by the gift ("handsell") of God—in this case, by recognizing that heaven is, in effect, no longer out in the sky, but that, by divine accommodation, it "lies flat" in God's Word. That the Bible was seen as the very utterance of God meant that every word was holy and charged with meaning. "Let my heart / Suck ev'ry letter, and a hony gain, / Precious for any grief in any part." The "infinite sweetnesse" that is so gained, however, does not come cheaply. The function of Bible reading for the early Reformers was twofold, tying in to the two poles of Reformation spirituality: to increase the awareness of one's sinfulness by confronting God's Law, and then to understand the scope of God's forgiveness and the assurance of salvation through the Gospel. The Bible reveals not only God, but also the self:

> Ladies, look here; this is the thankfull glasse,
> That mends the lookers eyes: this is the well
>> That washes what it shows.

Herbert describes the Scriptures as a mirror in which one's true self can be discerned, but it is a mirror that "mends the lookers eyes." The Bible exposes the reader's ("the lookers") sin, but in doing so, as a means of grace, it begins the process of mending.[51] The point is deepened as Herbert changes the figure of the mirror to a reflecting well "that washes what it shows," so that the Scriptures are associated with the well of the Holy

Spirit (John 4:14; 7:38–39) and the cleansing waters of the well of salvation (Isa. 12:1–3). This reflexive quality of the Scriptures is underscored in "The H. Scriptures (2)":

> Such are thy secrets, which my life makes good,
>> And comments on thee: for in ev'ry thing
>> Thy words do finde me out, & parallels bring,
> And in another make me understood.
>
> (9–12)

Although Herbert says that his life is a comment on Scripture, the conventional hermeneutical problems are neatly reversed. The problem is not understanding the Scriptures; rather, the Scriptures "make me understood." The point is not how the reader interprets the Scriptures, but rather how the Scriptures interpret the reader.[52] "Thy words do finde me out."

Herbert's biblicism is illustrated throughout his poetry, from explicit doctrinal statements to more complex symbolic treatments of how the Scriptures function. In "To all Angels and Saints" Herbert rejects praying to Mary or to other denizens of heaven for the simple reason that

> our King,
> Whom we do all joyntly adore and praise,
>> Bids no such thing:
> And where his pleasure no injunction layes,
> ('Tis your own case) ye never move a wing.
>
> (16–20)

Herbert is here advocating a "strict constructionist" view of how to apply Scripture. it is not enough that one avoid whatever Scripture forbids, but one may only do what the Scripture enjoins. Although all of the Reformers rejected prayer to the saints, Herbert is nearly Zwinglian in his insistence that "All worship is [God's] prerogative" (21), and that therefore a Christian, even the saints in heaven, should "never move a wing" without an express "injunction" from God. Herbert's stand is based not on strong personal feelings, but on Scripture alone. In fact, he will gladly pray to the saints if any one can show him where he is told to in Scripture: "We are ever ready to disburse, / If any one our Masters hand can show" (29–30).

Elsewhere Herbert expresses his understanding of Scriptures through symbols. For example, the shooting star that falls into the speaker's lap in "Artillerie" seems to be a symbol, among other things, for the Holy Scriptures. Not only does Herbert describe the Bible as a "book of starres" at length in "The H. Scriptures (1)," but in his Latin poem, "In S. Scripturas," Herbert compares it to a falling star, in ways that directly parallel "Artillerie":

Heu, quis spiritus, igneúsque turbo
Regnat visceribus, meásque versat
Imo pectore cogitationes?
Nunquid pro foribus sedendo nuper
Stellam vespere suxerim volantem,
Haec autem hospitio latere turpi
Prorsùs nescia, cogitat recessum?
Nunquid mel comedens, apem comedi
Ipsâ cum dominâ domum vorando?
Imò, me nec apes, nec astra pungunt:
Sacratissima Charta, tu fuisti
Quae cordis latebras sinúsque caecos
Atque omnes peragrata es angiportus
Et flexus fugientis appetitûs.
Ah, quàm doctra perambulare calles
Maenadrósque plicásque, quàm perita es!
Quae vis condidit, ipsa nouit aedes.

("Lucus," 5:411)

[O what spirit, what fiery whirlwind
Takes my bones and stirs
My deepest thoughts? When I was resting
Near my door not long ago,
And it was evening, did I
Swallow a falling star? And is it
Trying to escape, not knowing how
In this disgraceful lodging to be hidden?
Have I in sipping honey
Consumed the bee, in eating up
The house eaten up the mistress of the house?
Not bee, not star has penetrated me.
Most Holy Writ, it's you who've traveled through
All the dark nooks and hidden pleats
Of the heart, the alleys and the curves
Of flying passion. Ah, how wise and skilled you are
To slip through these paths, windings, knots.
The spirit that has reared the building
Knows it best.

(trans. McCloskey, p. 85)]

In "The H. Scriptures (1)" Herbert, drawing on Ps. 119:103, describes the sweetness of honey that he is able to suck out of every letter (1–2). Here the honey has a bee in it. In the latter poem, the star of "The H. Scriptures (2)" leaves heaven to enter into his life in a personal and painful way, just as the falling star in "Artillerie" interrupts the speaker's complacent revery with a demanding message. Although in "Artillerie" the star is described as symbolizing "good motions," the connection of the two poems cannot be doubted, extending as it does not only to the falling star symbol, but to the dramatic setting itself ("When I was resting / Near my door . . . / And it was evening"; "As I one ev'ning sat before my cell"). Again, Herbert is emphasizing in both poems the Bible's capacity to penetrate the façades and defenses of the self, and to create self-knowledge through the Holy Spirit, who knows the soul so intimately. In this perspective, the speaker in "Artillerie" should perhaps not be so surprised to hear "of speech in stars" (10), in that the Bible, God's heavy artillery, speaks with powerful specificity.

Another symbol for the Scriptures seems to be "the silk twist" in "The Pearl," a figure that may well have been taken directly from Calvin's *Institutes*. The poem devotes a stanza each to the complexities of learning, honor, and pleasure, concluding with an affirmation of faith:

> I know all these, and have them in my hand:
> Therefore not sealed, but with open eyes
> I flie to thee, and fully understand
> Both the main sale, and the commodities;
> And at what rate and price I have thy love;
> With all the circumstances that may move:
> Yet through these labyrinths, not my groveling wit,
> But thy silk twist let down from heav'n to me,
> Did both conduct and teach me, how by it
>   To climb to thee.
>
>   (31–40)

The labyrinth metaphor, of course, derives ultimately from the myth of Theseus, who was led out of the minotaur's maze by a cord provided by Ariadne.[53] This myth, however, provided one of Calvin's favorite and most reiterated images for the complexity and futility of the human mind and its endeavors. "For each man's mind is like a labyrinth," says Calvin (*Institutes* I.v.12),[54] who also speaks of the "labyrinth of the world" (*Institute* 3.6.2). The confidence with which the speaker of the poem announces that he knows the way of learning, honor, and pleasure, is perhaps undercut by the possibilities that these "wayes" may well be labyrinths from which it is impossible to escape, mazes that can result only in one's getting hopelessly lost. The final stanza claims not only worldly and intellectual knowledge, but knowledge of God. The speaker claims to "fully understand" the terms of his salvation, "at what rate and price I have thy love." This confident knowledge of theology is well and good, but it too is described as a labyrinth. According to Calvin, the knowledge of God, theology itself, "is for us like an inexplicable labyrinth unless we are conducted into it by the thread of the Word" (*Institute* 1.6.3). In the poem, the earlier confidence is qualified as the stanza turns upon the word *Yet* (37), acknowledging that "these" kinds of knowledge are all "labyrinths." "My groveling wit" is then opposed to "thy silk twist let down from heav'n to me." The silk twist has been variously interpreted as faith, as being reminiscent of Jacob's ladder and thus a type of Christ, and so on,[55] but the parallel to Calvin's "thread of the Word" which alone can conduct one out of the "inexplicable labyrinth" is extremely close. Moreover, the "silk twist let down from heav'n" is said to "teach me, how by it / To climbe to thee." That the function of the twist is to teach, a mode of learning contrasted to that of "my groveling wit" and to the "I know" statements of the earlier stanzas, seems to point very clearly to the doctrine of the Holy Scriptures.

Another symbolic representation of the Bible is especially important in its strategic placing in *The Temple*. Coming as it does immediately before "Love (3)," the echo poem "Heaven" gives to the "holy leaves" of Scripture a climactic position in Herbert's poetic sequence. That the poem is about the Bible is not immediately obvious, but Rickey is doubtlessly right when she argues that the "echo" refers to the Holy Scriptures.[56]

> O who will show me those delights on high?
>   *Echo.*   I.
> Thou, Echo, thou art mortall, all men know.
>   *Echo.*   No.
> Wert thou not born among the trees and leaves?
>   *Echo.*   Leaves.
> And are there any leaves, that still abide?
>   *Echo.*   Bide.
> What leaves are they? impart the matter wholly.
>   *Echo.*   Holy.
> Are holy leaves the Echo then of blisse?
>   *Echo.*   Yes.

(1–12)

The first part of the poem is the speaker's discovery of the means by which he can be instructed. The echo claims to be able to show him "those delights on high." The speaker blithely assumes that the voice is mortal. "No," he is told—the voice is qualitatively different from other human utterance. He then begins questioning the voice, and learns that it has something to do with "leaves," with a written text. The Echo he is addressing he finally identifies as "holy leaves." The answers become more and more direct and clear, until, by accepting the self-authenticating "Yes," the speaker begins to employ the echo to "show me those delights on high," and his questions are fully answered:

> Then tell me, what is that supreme delight?
>   *Echo.*   Light.
> Light to the minde: what shall the will enjoy?
>   *Echo.*   Joy.
> But are there cares and businesse with the pleasure?
>   *Echo.*   Leisure.

> Light, joy, and leisure; but shall they persever?
> *Echo.*   Ever.

Of course, on one level the answers are inherent in the questions, and the Scriptures are thus portrayed as an echo of human language. Rickey compares this poem to a similar echo poem by Lord Herbert of Cherbury, George Herbert's unorthodox brother, which is, in effect, "dramatizing God as an echo of man."[57] In the case of "Heaven," however, as Rickey shows, the Echo does know more than the human speaker, serving as providential revelation through the medium of human language. The poem thus also suggests the relationship between Man's Word and God's Word. The Scriptures are presented as the echo of "bliss," originating not from earth ("among the trees and leaves") but from "Heaven." The poem's title suggests how God's Word from Heaven comes to earth, where it is reflected back—echoed—in the language and writings of the prophets and apostles, as supernatural truth is conveyed by means of ordinary human language. The apocalyptic sequence of which it is a part ("Death," "Dooms-day," "Judgement," "Heaven") has been discussed already, but it is significant that the poem entitled and ostensibly about "Heaven" is not about pearly gates, nor even directly about the beatific vision, but about the Scriptures. As his subject moves him closer and closer to the transcendent, Herbert pulls back, away from his own poetic speculations, to point to Scripture, which alone is the proper source of any heavenly knowledge. Calvin urges just this procedure in the passage Herbert employs in "The Pearl":

> For we should so reason that the splendor of the divine countenance, which even the apostle calls "unapproachable" [1 Tim. 6:16], is for us like an inexplicable labyrinth unless we are conducted into it by the thread of the Word. (*Institutes* 1.6.3)

At this crucial point in "The Church," the poet, like the theologian, rejects the role of teacher, referring his reader to the only reliable guide:

> O Who will show me those delights on high?
> *Echo.*   I.

The poet, at this point, is no longer asserting, but questioning. Although the questions are answered, the ineffable experience of heaven is rendered not in emotional, experiential terms but propositionally, in suggestive and tantalizing restraint; heaven must be mediated through the Word.

The specific impact of the Bible on Herbert's verse has been well treated by other critics.[58] As has already been apparent, the Bible is part of the very texture of Herbert's poetry, with its countless allusions to Scripture.[59] Herbert rejects the conventional reliance on classical mythology and secular allegory to rely on the Scriptures alone,[60] a practice in the tradition of Protestant biblicism.

Besides Herbert's continual use of biblical types, narratives, and symbols, his other, seemingly nontraditional imagery may well have been influenced by the practice of the Bible. In discussing techniques of catechizing, Herbert speaks of the device of "making what hee [the catechumen] knows to serve him in that which he knows not":

> This is the skill, and doubtlesse the Holy Scripture intends this much, when it condescends to the naming of a plough, a hatchet, a bushell, leaven, boyes piping and dancing; shewing that things of ordinary use are not only to serve in the way of drudgery, but to be washed and cleansed, and serve for lights even of Heavenly Truths. ("Country Parson," 21:257)

Herbert cultivates this "skill" in his poetry and also "condescends" to imagery drawn from commonplace experiences, presenting the Kingdom of Heaven in terms of an ordinary inn ("Love [3]"), or presenting holiness through the act of sweeping the floor ("The Elixer"). Such "lowly" images in religious verse may violate classical decorum, but Herbert's own practice of employing "things of ordinary use" as "lights even of Heavenly Truths" is based on an even higher authority.[61]

Herbert's multilayer language may also have something to do with what was perceived as the richness inherent in every single inspired word of the Scriptures. Herbert disapproved of Donne's and Andrewes's practice of dissolving the text into its components, preaching on what in effect was a single word out of Scripture ("the words apart are not scripture, but a dictionary" ["Country Parson," 7:235]). Still, Herbert desires to "Suck ev'ry letter, and a hony gain, / Precious for any grief in any part" ("The H. Scriptures [1]," 2–3). The critic of Herbert's poetry must similarly "suck ev'ry letter" to uncover the multilevel complexities of Herbert's diction.[62] Again, Herbert's manifest delight in puns and wordplay is anticlassical (Dryden alludes to Herbert in "Macflecknoe" as one who, along with making poems in the shape of wings and altars, will "torture one poor word ten thousand ways" [207–8]). Treating language as an inexhaustible source of complex and multilevel meanings, however, may well have its sanction in the biblical tradition of commentary and devotions. Such linguistic and semantic richness seems cultivated in Herbert's own aesthetic, so that his description of reading the Bible seems also to apply to his poems—both of which "present us not with the same thing only when it is read. . . , but enlightens us with new considerations the more we read it" ("Brief Notes on Valdesso," p. 310).

Similarly, the very structuring and arrangement of *The Temple* seems to reflect "the analogy of faith." Herbert's poems are like the Bible in that individual images and themes refer back and forth to each other through-out the text, so that a single poem can be elucidated by other poems and by its context. Herbert's own principles of biblical exegesis ("an industrious, and judicious comparing of place with place. . . . the consideration of any text with the coherence thereof, touching what goes before, and what follows after" ["Country Parson," 4:229]) are now being applied by critics to Herbert's poetry with the purpose of "seeing not onely how each verse doth shine, / But all the constellations of the storie" ("The H. Scriptures [2]," 3–4).[63] Again, Herbert's perception of the biblical text may well be reflected, not only imaginatively and thematically, but in the very form and arrangement of his verse.

In "Christmas," Herbert suggests the relationship between his poetry and the Bible as God's Word:

> The shepherds sing;—and shall I silent be?
>   My God, no hymne for thee?
> My soul's a shepherd too,—a flock it feeds
>   Of thoughts, and words, and deeds.
> The pasture is thy word: the streams, thy grace
>   Enriching all the place.
> Shepherd and flock shall sing, and all my powers
>   Out-sing the day-light houres.
>
> (15–22)

"The pasture is thy word," with God's grace giving it life. From the pasture of God's Word, the soul feeds its flock—"thoughts, and words, and deeds"—and from this nourishment "Shepherd and flock . . . and all my powers" join in song, in poetry. According to this poem, Herbert sees his imagination and his poetry as being nourished, in an intimate and essential way, by the Scriptures. The written Word is not only a source of images and symbols for Herbert, but it is also his theological keystone and perhaps the major focus of his devotional life.

Moreover, the Bible is a written text that can inspire other written texts. The notion that God's communication with human beings is not primarily through mystical experiences but through words helps to explain Herbert's confidence in the capabilities and richness of language. "Scripture itself," observes Rosalie Colie, "like these poems, is also dazzlingly intricate and blindingly clear."[64] Herbert's comment in "Discipline" is thus perhaps not so much an abject negation of the self as a simple description of Herbert's theological, devotional, and poetic dependence upon the Bible:

> Not a word or look
> I affect to own,
>   But by book,
> And thy book alone.
>
> (9–12)

iii. Proclamation of the Word

As Herbert announces in the very first stanza of *The Temple,* the aim of his poetry is the same as that of a sermon:[65]

> Harken unto a Verser, who may chance
> Ryme thee to good, and make a bait of pleasure.
> A verse may find him, who a sermon flies,
> And turn delight into a sacrifice.
>
> ("The Church-porch," 3–6)

Herbert, significantly, did not confuse the two. Poetry is not essentially didactic but aesthetic, working through "pleasure" and "delight." Herbert, though, intends his poetry to "find" someone, to bring the reader to "good," to transform aesthetic "delight" into the religious joy of a "sacrifice." That this particular poem, "The Church-porch," does lead into "The Sacrifice," the poem on Christ's atonement, has been discussed already, but nearly all of his poems open up in some way to the "sacrifice" of Christ. In the homiletic theory of the Reformation, God's "Word"—the Gospel of Christ as revealed in Scripture—may be communicated through original human utterance. Herbert's poetry, in a way similar to his sermons, conveys "the Word."

"For, among the many excellent gifts with which God has adorned the human race," writes Calvin, "it is a singular privilege that he deigns to consecrate to himself the mouths and tongues of men in order that his voice may resound in them" (*Institutes* 4.1.5). God's Word consists of a living person, Jesus Christ, and a written text, the Holy Scriptures, but it also "resounds" in "the mouths and tongues" of human beings.

In fact, according to the early Protestants, a person is ordinarily drawn to faith through someone else's preaching or oral exposition of the Gospel. Lewis Bayly calls preaching "the *ordinary* means by which the Holie Ghost begetteth *faith* in our hearts" (p. 196); to Latimer it is "God's instrument of salvation."[66] Tyndale describes the supernatural workings of God's Word, conflating Christ and the Scriptures with their proclamation through a human agency:

> God worketh with His Word, and in His Word: and when His Word is preached faith rooteth herself in the hearts of the elect, and as faith entereth, and the Word of God is believed, the power of God looseth the heart from the captivity and bondage under sin, and knitteth and coupleth him to God and to the will of God.[67]

The preaching of God's Word was, quite literally, seen as a means of grace, binding the hearer to Christ, not only begetting faith, but conveying assurance and strength in the process of sanctification.

Besides this sacramental view of preaching, sermons also had an intellectual function. Despite a long homiletic tradition, the church of the late Middle Ages had neglected preaching.[68] There were various reasons—the clergy was often relatively uneducated and in the popular mind the sacraments and the liturgy, although in an unfamiliar language, were thought to communicate grace automatically, with no *a priori* need of explanation or understanding. The Reformers, on the other hand, insisted that the individual Christian, no matter how simple, must personally understand the Christian faith and the worship service. "It was no longer thought to be enough," according to a church historian, "if a simple Christian could say a prayer or two by heart with proper reverence. He must know something of the theory of prayer, and some theology, so that he could pray with the understanding also."[69] Thus Walton records how Herbert would painstakingly explain the worship service to his parishioners.[70] For the Country Parson, according to Herbert, there are "three points of his duty, the one, to infuse a competent knowledge of salvation in every one of his Flock; the other, to multiply, and build up this knowledge to a spirituall Temple; the third, to inflame this knowledge, to presse, and drive it to practice, turning it to reformation of life, by pithy and lively exhortations" ("Country Parson," 21:255).

Herbert comments that, for the first point, catechizing is essential; the purpose of sermons, in an analogy to poetry, is to "inflame." The model of catechizing has been well-employed in understanding Herbert's poetry.[71] Skillful catechizing, according to Herbert, "exceeds even sermons in teaching: but there being two things in sermons, the one Informing, the other Inflaming; as Sermons come short of questions in the one, so they farre exceed them in the other. For questions cannot inflame or ravish, that must be done by a set, and laboured, and continued speech" ("The Country Parson," 21:257). Catechizing teaches; sermons "inflame." The purpose of a sermon is not only to teach, but to persuade, to appeal not only to the mind but to the soul. Similarly, the purpose of a poem, according to Sidney, is to teach and to delight. Herbert, who desired to "turn" this "delight into a sacrifice," would probably agree that the purpose of poetry is not only to teach but also to "inflame." That "inflaming" and "ravishing" are effected not by a spontaneous overflow of feeling but by "a set, and laboured" process of craftsmanship is the testimony of a master poet.

Similarly, Herbert's advice on how to deliver a sermon ("The Country Parson," 7:232–33) seems to apply just as well to delivering a poem: "When he preacheth, he procures attention by all possible art," such as "by earnestnesse of speech, it being naturall to men to think, that where is much earnestness, there is somewhat worth hearing." That "earnestness" can be a carefully crafted poetic illusion is well known, although not always applied to Herbert. Herbert urges a manner of "earnestness" as a rhetorical tool to procure attention, a means to a more important end.

Herbert also stresses the need to be concrete in sermons, an awareness that he sustains throughout his poetry: "Particulars ever touch, and awake more than generalls," a principle that brings him to recommend specifically artistic modes of discourse: "Sometimes he tells them stories . . . for them also men heed, and remember better than exhortations; which though earnest, yet often dy with the sermon." The necessary artfulness of a sermon is, however, only a means by which "the Parson procures attention; but the character of his sermon is Holiness; he is not witty, or learned or eloquent, but Holy," a quality however that is itself conveyed, among other means, by an attention to language analogous to the poetic process: "by dipping, and seasoning all our words and sentences in our hearts, before they come into our mouths, truly affecting, and cordially expressing all that we say." The sermon, for Herbert, is an art form.

Critics have observed two different styles in the sermons of seventeenth-century England. The sermons of Donne, on the one hand, are highly rhetorical and "metaphysical" in their complex symbolism, full of learning, yet emotional in their impact. Other sermons, such as those by William Perkins, are in the "plain style," striving for clarity rather than complexity, appealing to the intellect rather than to the emotions. That these two styles or methods of composing and delivering a sermon were both prevalent is certainly true. It is probably a misnomer to identify the former as "Anglican" and the latter as "Puritan."[72] The terms, again, are hopelessly vague, but even if they are accepted, it can be shown that even extreme "Puritans" were quite capable of sounding like Donne (one thinks of Jonathan Edwards and Edward Taylor). Conversely, Herbert, a staunch Episcopalian usually put in the "Anglican" camp, nevertheless advocates the "plain style" of preaching:

> The Parsons Method in handling of a text consists of two parts; first, a plain and evident declaration of the meaning of the text, and secondly, some choyce observations drawn out of the whole text, as it lyes entire, and unbroken in the Scripture it self. This he thinks naturall, and sweet, and grave. Whereas the other way of crumbling a text into small parts, as the Person speaking, or spoken to, the subject, and object, and the like, hath neither in it sweetnesse, nor gravity, nor variety, since the words apart are not Scripture, but a dictionary, and may be considered alike in all the Scripture. ("The Country Parson," 7:234–35)

Hutchinson (p. 557) says that this is one of the earliest criticisms of the "metaphysical" style of preaching such as that practiced by Lancelot Andrewes, and that Herbert's comments were employed in later "Calvinist" critiques. At his first sermon at Bemerton, according to Walton, Herbert "delivered his sermon after a most florid manner, both with great learning and eloquence; but, at the close of this sermon, told them, 'That should not be his constant way of preaching; for since Almighty God does not intend to lead men to heaven by hard questions, he would not therefore fill their heads with unnecessary notions; but that, for their sakes, his language and his expressions should be more plain and practical in his future sermons.'"[73] Herbert could preach in the "metaphysical" manner, but his concern was to communicate to a specific audience, in this case to a country parish;[74] the so-called Anglican or metaphysical preachers were generally of the court, addressing a more sophisticated audience, a consideration that may account for the stylistic difference in seventeenth-century sermons better than theological generalizations.

As has often been observed, Herbert, following his advice to preachers, writes in a "poetic Plain style," rejecting conventional ornamented verse in favor of a studied simplicity and clarity.[75] Behind the starkness of his verse, though, critics have observed complicated allusions and prodigious learning that gives his poetry a resonance that is all the richer and more complicated for its subtlety and restraint. This quality in Herbert's verse is directly related to the concern articulated by William Perkins, the "Puritan" theorist, who teaches that the minister "must privately use at his libertie the arts, Philosophy, and variety of reading, whilest he is in framing his sermon: but he ought in publicke to conceale all these from the people, and not to make the least ostentation." Such an insistence upon wide learning (he "must" use it), coupled with the notion that this learning must be artfully concealed, has aesthetic implications for poetry no less than for sermons. Herbert would agree with Perkins that *"humane wisdome* must be conceald, whether it be in the matter of the sermon, or in the setting forth of the words: because the preaching of the word is the *testimony of God."*[76]

Herbert's homiletic theory describes the sermon as a work of art; the same artistry he employs in his sermons he employs in his poetry.[77] Human learning, rhetoric, and conscious design are important in both art forms, but in both cases they are not to call attention to themselves, but to the Word of God. Herbert's poems, like his sermons, "inflame or ravish" by means of "a set, and laboured, and continued speech" ("Country Parson," 21:257). God's Word—the message of salvation, the person of Christ, the text and meaning of the Holy Scriptures—is to be communicated through the agency, creativity, and personality of human beings.

Herbert's ideas about preaching the Word of God receive their fullest treatment in "The Windows":

> Lord, how can man preach thy eternall word?
>   He is a brittle crazie glasse:
> Yet in thy temple thou dost him afford
>   This glorious and transcendant place,
>   To be a window, through thy grace.

> But when thou dost anneal in glasse thy storie,
>   Making thy life to shine within
> The holy Preachers; then the light and glorie
>   More rev'rend grows, & more doth win:
>   Which else shows watrish, bleak & thin.
>
> Doctrine and life, colours and light, in one
>   When they combine and mingle, bring
> A strong regard and aw: but speech alone
>   Doth vanish like a flaring thing,
>   And in the eare, not conscience ring.

The symbol of a stained glass window allows Herbert to precisely express how God's "eternall word," in all of its complex senses, is conveyed to human beings.

How the symbol functions is suggested in "Love-joy," another poem on a stained glass window:

> As on a window late I cast mine eye,
> I saw a vine drop grapes with *J* and *C*
> Anneal'd on every bunch. One standing by
> Ask'd what it meant. I, who am never loth
> To spend my judgement, said, It seem'd to me
> To be the bodie and the letters both
> Of *Joy* and *Charitie*. Sir, you have not miss'd,
> The man reply'd; it figures *JESUS CHRIST.*

The window[78] presents Jesus Christ (the Incarnate Word) through language ("*J* and *C*," the written Word), and through the biblical and sacramental symbol of the vine ("visible Words" discussed in the next section, below). The speaker interprets what he sees, applying the objective word on the level of human experience—"Joy and Charity" (the proclaimed Word).[79] "*JESUS CHRIST,*" however, is the light in the window, by whom all the symbols are illuminated.

In "The Windows," the figure of the stained glass window is internalized. The preacher is the window. Just as a stained glass window, in itself, consists of drab pieces of leaded glass, the preacher is "a brittle crazie glass"—both are nothing without the light that must shine through them. Herbert superimposes the symbol of the windows on the doctrines of justification and sanctification. "Thou dost anneal in / glass thy storie"—just as scenes from the life of Christ are "anneal'd" in glass, so, in justification, is Christ's life inscribed in the soul. Thus "thy life" shines not only in the windows but, as the indwelling Christ, "within the holy Preachers." The preacher, though, must allow Christ's life to grow within him; he must be "holy"—"the light and glorie / More rev'rend grows"— that is, he must be sanctified.

The question is, "how can man preach thy eternall word?" The Word is

Christ, but He is manifested through "thy storie"—the scenes from the Bible as annealed in the stained glass window. Moreover, the "eternall Word" is the Gospel that the preacher must proclaim to sinners. The poem's concern is to "win" souls (9), for the Word to "ring" not merely "in the eare," but deeper, in the conscience (15). Herbert, in "The Elixer," articulates the problem in terms of the same symbol:

> A man that looks on glasse,
>   On it may stay his eye;
> Or if he pleaseth, through it passe,
>   And then the heav'n espie.
>
> (9–12)

One may look only upon the surface of the glass and fail to look through it to the truth that it conveys.[80] In "The Windows," the stained glass must not only be colored but must also be translucent, or else the light "shows watrish, bleak, & thin." The preacher must preach the Bible, just as the windows depict the stories of Christ, but his effectiveness depends upon his own sanctification, the degree to which the Word is apparent in his life,[81] and the "illumination" of the Holy Spirit. Herbert distinguishes between "speech alone," which does not convert souls, and the "eternall Word," which is the light of Christ conveyed through "the brittle crazie glass" of human speech.

Herbert is not only the preacher of "the Windows," but also an artist, who himself "anneals" images from the Scripture into his poetry, combining and mingling "Doctrine and life, colours and light." Whether or not the "temple" of line 3 can refer to *The Temple* as a whole, he may well have conceived his poetry—variegated, yet unified—as "a brittle crazie glasse," through which the Word of God may shine. The metaphor of God's "shining" through the human being and particularly the human voice is itself employed by Calvin, whose commendation of both speaking and singing may well be relevant, not only to "The Windows," but to Herbert's art as a whole:

> Since the glory of God ought, in a measure, to shine in the several parts of our bodies, it is especially fitting that the tongue has been assigned and destined for this task, both through singing and through speaking. For it was peculiarly created to tell and proclaim the praise of God. (*Institutes*, 3.20.31)

iv. The Sacraments: Visible Words

One church historian has drawn attention to how the Reformation, in its worship and in its sacramental life, employed "the retention of old forms for the expression of the new type of faith."[82] Luther's reforms of the Mass involved translating it into the vernacular and revising out any elements that did not point to Christ. Invocations to the Saints and to the Virgin Mary were excised (see Herbert's "To all Angels and Saints" for the rationale), as were other theologically objectionable usages, but the basic structure of the Mass was retained, as were liturgical practices such as the sign of the cross, the use of the crucifix and other symbols, the church year, and so on, all of which were felt by Luther to draw the worshiper closer to Christ. Other Reformers, such as Zwingli, were more radical in their desire to change worship completely away from that associated with the medieval church. What should be retained and what changed was a matter of controversy. It should be emphasized, though, that even "reformed" churches, that is, those which leaned to Calvin rather than to Luther, often practiced a relatively "high" liturgy.[83] The Anglican *Book of Common Prayer* is part of the tradition, exemplified on the Continent, especially among the Lutherans, of a conservative order of worship in the context of the new theology.[84] There was certainly controversy in England over the liturgy, with many people objecting to various "vestiges of popery" such as vestments, wedding rings, and so on. Herbert participated in the debate with his "Musae Responsoriae," defending the Anglican customs against Andrew Melville, the Scottish presbyterian. Herbert consistently prefers the more conservative liturgy, with its rich symbolism and ceremony.

A more significant question, though, had to do with the reinterpretation of the sacraments. Luther insisted on the fundamental importance of the Real Presence of Christ in the Eucharist. Zwingli, on the other hand, insisted that the Lord's Supper is only symbolic. Calvin, mediating between the two positions, held that the physical bread and its spiritual effects are to be distinguished. This debate split the Reformation. The Church of England tried to avoid the divisiveness of the issue by including in the *Book of Common Prayer* language that could appease all parties. This latitude is reflected in Herbert's poetry, which employs imagery drawn from all parties; in his poems explicitly on Holy Communion, he follows the distinctions urged by Calvin as preserved in the Prayer Book, but elsewhere he goes farther, recognizing in the sacrament, in Lutheran terms, the Real Presence of Christ. On the function of the sacraments, though, most Protestants agreed—they were seen as "visible words," concrete manifestations of the Gospel of free forgiveness through Christ's sacrifice, and as such they permeate Herbert's poetry.

Before I discuss how the Reformers and Herbert viewed the mode of Christ's presence in the sacrament, it will be helpful to begin with the points of agreement and how the "old forms" were reinterpreted in light of Reformation spirituality. The sacraments, in Reformation usage, were seen as part of the ministry and the doctrine of the Word.[85] In this regard, the definition of Augustine was adopted and elaborated by the early Protestants: "The word is added to the element and there results the sacrament, as if itself also a kind of visible word."[86] The sacraments, both baptism and the Lord's Supper, defined as "visible words," are thus tangible expressions of the same proclamation that is inherent in the historical Christ, the Holy Scriptures, and the preaching of the Word. This proclamation in every case is the Gospel, the message of salvation through the atonement of Christ. Baptism involves being born again. The Eucharist means that Christ's broken body is offered to sinners. The function of the sacraments, among other things, was to make the Gospel immediately tangible, personal, and objective. This was the understanding of Cranmer, the author of *The Book of Common Prayer*, who also suggests the relationship between the Scriptures, preaching, and the sacraments:

> Our Saviour Christ hath not only set forth these things most plainly in His holy Word, that we may hear them with our ears, but He hath also ordained one visible sacrament of spiritual regeneration in water, and another visible sacrament of spiritual nourishment in bread and wine, to the intent that as much as is possible for man we may see Christ with our eyes, smell Him at our nose, taste Him with our mouths, grope Him with our hands, and perceive Him with all our senses. For as the Word of God preached putteth Christ into our ears, so likewise these elements of water, bread, and wine, joined to God's Word, do after a sacramental manner put Christ into our eyes, mouths, hands, and all our senses.[87]

For Cranmer, the sacraments convey Christ through "all our senses," in the same way that preaching conveys Christ through hearing. The Word and the Sacraments are both "means of grace"—they communicate the Gospel of Christ and produce faith. For the Reformers, Holy Communion was not a sacrifice offered by human beings to God, as in Roman Catholicism, but a means of "nourishment" given by God to human beings. Again the vectors are reversed, in what could be the paradigm of Reformation spirituality: God acts; human beings receive. Bread does not become God (an ascent of matter); God becomes bread (the descent of the spirit).

As tangible manifestations of the Gospel, the sacraments were experienced as personal "pledges" and "seals" of God's promise, and were thus related to the assurance of salvation. Bishop Jewel emphasizes that

> Christ hath ordained them that by them He might set before our eyes the mysteries of our salvation, and might more strongly confirm the faith which we have in His blood, and might seal His grace in our hearts. As princes' seals confirm and warrant their deeds and charters, so do the sacraments witness unto our conscience that God's promises are true and shall continue for ever. Thus doth God make known His secret purpose to His Church: first he declareth His mercy by His Word; then He sealeth it and assureth it by His sacraments. In the Word we have His promises: in the Sacraments we see them.[88]

Psychologically, the assurance of salvation is difficult to maintain. The doctrine of eternal security is balanced by the doctrine of total depravity. The Christian, convinced of personal sinfulness, must be continually assured of Christ's love and atonement.

> Christe, fluas semper; ne, si tua flumina cessant,
> Culpa redux ingem te neget esse Deum.
> (Herbert, "Christus in cruce," *Passio Discerpta*, 13.5–6)

> [Christ, keep welling up, for if your flooding stops,
> Revived guilt will say you're not eternal God.
> (trans. McCloskey, p. 71)]

Doubt, according to Herbert, is a function not of intellectual questioning, but of "Revived guilt." The Christian must be continually ministered to by Christ and reminded that he has been forgiven. The sacraments help one to become certain of salvation. Luther, in counseling someone who doubts his election, underscores this function of the sacraments:

> God did not come down from heaven to make you uncertain about predestination, to teach you to despise the sacraments, absolution, and the rest of the divine ordinances. Indeed, He instituted them to make you completely certain and to remove the disease of doubt from your heart, in order that you might not only believe with the heart but also see with your physical eyes and touch with your hands. Why, then, do you reject these and complain that you do not know whether you have been predestined? You have the Gospel; you have been baptized; you have absolution; you are a Christian.[89]

Herbert too relates the sacraments to the assurance of salvation. In comforting the "disaffected," Herbert's parson urges them to confess their sins, *"to do some pious charitable works, as a necessary evidence and fruit of their faith"* (the "Anglo-Calvinist" method of assurance repudiated by Calvin himself); and finally, he urges *"the participation of the Holy Sacrament, how comfortable, and sovereigne a Medicine it is to all sin-sick souls"* ("The Country Parson," 15:249–50). In "Conscience," the subjective feelings of "revived guilt" are opposed to the objective fact of forgiveness communicated in the sacrament:

> And the receit shall be
> My Saviours bloud: when ever at his board
> I do but taste it, straight it cleanseth me,
>   And leaves thee not a word;
>   No, not a tooth or nail to scratch,
>   And at my actions carp, or catch.
>   (13–18)

Thus Herbert's sacramental imagery almost always has reference to the Gospel, the free forgiveness of sins through the sacrificial death of Christ.

The Eucharist is a manifestation for Herbert, not so much of the Incarnation as of the Atonement. The waters of baptism, the bread as Christ's body, the wine of His blood communicate God's saving Word. Jesus Christ, the Holy Scriptures, the proclamation of the Gospel, and the sacraments are thus unified. As "visible words"—the Word of God expressed through the senses—the sacraments are uniquely applicable to poetry, which consists of images as well as words. Whenever Herbert employs sacramental imagery, it has reference to the Reformation Gospel:

> Love is that liquour sweet and most divine,
> Which my God feels as bloud; but I, as wine.
>
> ("The Agonie," 17–18)

The speaker receives all of the "sweet," unmerited benefits of Christ, who Himself suffered the grisly punishment of "Sinne." In "The Bunch of Grapes," Herbert celebrates God

> Who of the Laws sowre juice sweet wine did make,
> Ev'n God himself being pressed for my sake.
>
> (27–28)

The Eucharistic imagery of "The Collar," and "Love (3)," and Herbert's Baptism poems with his use of water symbolism similarly function as signs and explorations of grace.

This "logo-centric" view of the Sacraments was generally accepted by the Protestants of the day. What was at issue was the mode of Christ's presence in Holy Communion. The Roman Catholic view of transubstantiation was universally rejected. It seemed to lack any scriptural support and thus to be simply the creation of the scholastic theologians. The view that the "substance" of the bread changes into the Body of Christ, leaving only the "accidents" of the bread as perceived by the senses was objectionable for other reasons as well. To Luther, for example, it seemed insufficiently incarnational. The Incarnate Christ does not have the "substance" of God, with only the "accidents" of a human being. Rather, according to the Creeds, the two natures are present at once in His Person, so that He is "substantially" both God and man at the same time. Incarnation involves not a change in matter, as transubstantiation implies, but precisely an indwelling in and with matter.[90] As in the quotation from Cranmer above, the focus is thus often on the material elements, the sensual aspects of the sacrament—their smell, feel, manufacture, and taste, which are not illusions as in Roman Catholicism but are at the essence of the sacramental mystery, an emphasis that is everywhere in Herbert (e.g., "The Banquet").

There were three basic positions in regard to the Eucharist.[91] Luther and his followers believed in "the Real Presence," that the true Body and Blood of Christ are present "in, with, and under" the bread and wine.[92] How this is possible he explained in terms of the ubiquity of Christ. Christ, as God, is omnipresent; therefore, he can be physically present in the elements in a special way without transubstantiating them. Zwingli, on the other hand, taught that Christ's words, "This is my body" (Matt. 21:26), are metaphorical. In his position Communion does not involve Christ's presence at all, but is a memorial feast that binds believers together in a common celebration of faith.[93] Calvin sought to mediate between these two positions. This he did by distinguishing between the sign and the thing signified. Receiving the bread physically is a sign of what is happening spiritually in the reception of the sacrament, as the soul is nourished by Christ. The presence of Christ is not in the elements, but in the believer, whose faithful reception of the sacrament is accompanied by spiritual blessings.[94]

The Church of England is notable for its ability to compromise, permitting in practice a wide range of beliefs. The Anglican catechism defines *sacrament* as "an outward and visible sign of an inward and spiritual grace given unto us, ordained by Christ Himself, as a means whereby we receive the same, and a pledge to assure us thereof."[95] Here is the Calvinist distinction between the "outward and visible" and the "inward and spiritual" realms. The sacraments are, however, a true means of grace. The definition, which also includes the requirement of scriptural authority and the sacraments' connection to the assurance of salvation, derives basically from the *via media* of Calvin. Nevertheless, "higher" views were present and could also find affirmation in the *Book of Common Prayer.* There seems to have been a genuine latitude in the Anglican church and, even within particular individuals like Herbert, a belief that knowing intellectually the precise mode of Christ's presence is not important. As Herbert says, Christ knows what happens in Holy Communion, and that is all that is important:

> Lord, thou knowest what thou didst, when thou appointedst it to be done thus; therefore doe thou fulfill what thou didst appoint; for thou art not only the feast, but the way to it. ("The Country Parson," 22:257–58)

The Christian's responsibility is simply to obey what Christ ordained in His Word:

> But he doth bid us take his bloud for wine.
>   Bid what he please; yet I am sure,
> To take and taste what he doth there designe,
>   Is all that saves, and not obscure.
>
> ("Divinitie," 21–24)

Herbert is thus able in his sacramental imagery to draw imaginatively from the whole range of theological models; in his poetry Communion is portrayed as both a communal feast, as in Zwingli, and a confrontation with the crucified Christ, as in Luther. In his poems on the subject, Herbert explores the Anglican-Calvinist distinctions between the physical and the spiritual, but he often goes farther, adopting Lutheran terminology with its belief in the Real Presence.[96]

In one very early poem, "The H. Communion," which was excluded from *The Temple*, Herbert is thinking through the various theological positions:

> O Gratious Lord, how shall I know
> Whether in these gifts thou bee so
>   As thou art evry-where;
> Or rather so, as thou alone
> Tak'st all the Lodging, leaving none
>   ffor thy poore creature there?
>
> (1–6)

Herbert here describes the presence of Christ in the Eucharist in terms of Luther's doctrine of ubiquity: Christ is "in these gifts" in the same sense "As thou art evry-where." To this Protestant formulation[97] is opposed the doctrine of transubstantiation in which, to Herbert, Christ "tak'st all the lodging," displacing completely the created substance of the bread:

> Ffirst I am sure, whether bread stay
> Or whether Bread doe fly away
>   Concerneth bread, not mee.
> But that both thou and all thy traine
> Bee there, to thy truth, & my gaine,
>   Concerneth mee & Thee.
>
> And if in coming to thy foes
> Thou dost come first to them, that showes
>   The hast of thy goodwill.
> Or if that thou two stations makest
> In bread & mee, the way thou takest
>   Is more, but for mee still.
>
> (7–18)

Herbert makes his familiar Anglican disclaimer that the mode of Christ's presence is not really important to understand,[98] but the Cambridge rhetorician does so in such a way as to support the Protestant position, moving to a Calvinist and Anglican emphasis on the spiritual state of the receiver. Herbert first sets up a logical dichotomy—either the bread stays or it flies away and is no longer present. What is important, says Herbert, is Christ's spiritual presence for the believer. One possibility—Herbert was probably thinking of the Lutheran rather than the Roman Catholic position—is that Christ comes to the believer in "two stations," first entering the bread, and then entering the communicant. In this case "the road is longer," as Hutchinson paraphrases lines 17–18, but the true Gospel is still conveyed, as opposed to the Calvinist view in which Christ enters the sinner ("thy foes") directly (in fact "first," before the sacrament can be effectually administered). The directness of grace shows the "hast of thy good will." Herbert continues the conciliatory tone, ostensibly by speaking not of controversy but only of what is certain, as his argument becomes sharper:

> Then of this also I am sure
> That thou didst all those pains endure
>   To' abolish sinn, not Wheat.
> Creatures are good, & have their place;
> Sinn only, which did all deface,
>   Thou drivest from his seat.

(19–24)

Herbert argues against transubstantiation by affirming matter. "Creatures are good," as God declared (Gen. 1:31). A created substance, therefore, would not be obliterated or displaced by Christ, who insists on His creation's integrity. Herbert thus explicitly answers his question of the first stanza. Christ does not take "all the Lodging, leaving none / ffor thy poore creature there" (5–6). The physical bread, accidents and substance, all "have their place." What is driven out is not the substance of bread but sin in the heart of human beings.

> I could beleeve an Impanation
> At the rate of an Incarnation,
>   If thou hadst dyde for Bread.
> But that which made my soule to dye,
> My flesh, & fleshly villany,
>   That allso made thee dead.

(25–30)

Herbert, no doubt in a travesty of Roman dogma, conflates transubstantiation with the theory of the Eucharist in which Christ is incarnate, that is, impanate, in the bread.[99] The very point of the Incarnation, though, according to Herbert, is that Christ became flesh, not bread. Matter, as such, is good just as it is (22). The problem is not with matter, but with "my flesh," understood here in terms of the Reformation *psychomachia*.

> That fflesh is there, mine eyes deny:
> And what shold flesh but flesh discry,
>   The noblest sence of five?

(31–33)

If Christ is present on the fleshly level, why do I not perceive it on the fleshly level?

> If glorious bodies pass the sight,
> Shall they be food & strength & might
>   Even there, where they deceive?

(34–36)

If Christ's flesh is present but beyond human fleshly perception, how is it then able to benefit the human flesh, which is so limited? Herbert, having maneuvered the reader into a more "spiritual" understanding of the sacraments, next answers the questions in terms of Calvin's dichotomy:

> Into my soule this cannot pass;
> fflesh (though exalted) keeps his grass
>   And cannot turn to soule.
> Bodyes & Minds are different Spheres,
> Nor can they change their bounds & meres,
>   But keep a constant Pole.

(37–42)

The flesh and the spirit are separate. Flesh, even of "glorious bodies," no matter how "exalted," cannot pass into the soul. What is needed in the sacrament, Herbert implies, is not Christ's fleshly presence in the bread, but Christ's spiritual presence in "my soul."

> This gift of all gifts is the best,
> Thy flesh the least that I request.

(43–44)

The "gift" is the Eucharist itself, as in line 2. Herbert here affirms in the strongest terms his devotion to the Eucharist, but observes that Christ's actual flesh in the elements is the least of his needs.

> Thou took'st that pledge from mee:
> Give me not that I had before,
> Or give mee that, so I have more;
>   My God, give mee all Thee.

(45–48)

Arguing against the Lutheran view of the omnipresence of Christ, Reformed theologians stressed that Christ's body was taken up into Heaven at the Ascension and so could not also be physically in the elements (Calvin, *Institutes* 4.17.26–27). That Christ's "flesh" was given "before," in history, and that it was then taken from us until the Second Coming seems to be what Herbert is saying, the conventional Reformed view. Yet in the last two lines of the poem Herbert lurches back to the Lutheran possibility— "Or give mee" your flesh also, although according to Reformed thought it is not necessary that it be in the elements, as an expression of "superabounding" grace. "My God, give mee all Thee," the "all" recalling the Lutheran Christology alluded to in the first stanza.[100] This final line perhaps suggests the appeal for him of the Lutheran view, even as he is rehearsing the Reformed positions that he had been studying in Cambridge.

In "The H. Communion," a later poem of the same title (included in *The Temple*), Herbert develops some of the points from his earlier poem:

> Not in rich furniture, or fine array,
>> Nor in a wedge of gold,
>> Thou who for me wast sold,
> To me dost now thy self convey:
> For so thou should'st without me still have been,
>> Leaving within me sinne.
>
>   (1–6)

As Hutchinson observes, Herbert is contrasting the elaborate accessories of the Roman ritual with the relative simplicity of the Anglican rite. Herbert seems to be quarreling with the externalization of the sacrament. If the sacrament is purely external, Christ remains, ultimately, outside ("without") the sinful believer.

> But by the way of nourishment and strength
>> Thou creep'st into my breast;
>> Making thy way my rest,
> And thy small quantities my length;
> Which spread their forces into every part,
>> Meeting sinnes force and art.
>
>   (7–12)

Herbert discusses the bread as a means of grace, exploring Cranmer's symbol of "nourishment" as "the way" Christ enters the internal spiritual combat of sanctification. In the final two stanzas Herbert returns to the characteristic distinction between the elements and grace, devoting a stanza to each:

> Yet can these not get over to my soul,
>> Leaping the wall that parts
>> Our souls and fleshy hearts;
> But as th' outworks, they may controll
> My rebel-flesh, and carrying thy name,
>> Affright both sinne and shame.
>
> Onely thy grace, which with these elements comes,
>> Knoweth the ready way,
>> And hath the privie key,
>> Op'ning the souls most subtile rooms;
> While those to spirits refin'd, at doore attend
>> Dispatches from their friend.

(13–24)

"These" of line 13 must refer to the physical elements of the preceding stanza. Herbert reiterates the firm distinction between the flesh and the soul made in the earlier poem, but he goes farther in his understanding of how the "fleshly" elements are related to the flesh of the human being. Employing the familiar battle imagery of sanctification, Herbert denies that the physical elements can "leap the wall" between the soul and the flesh. They can, however, function as "outworks," that is, fortifications outside the wall (OED), which, in their physicality, can subdue "My rebel-flesh" by frightening sin and, significantly, shame (the function of the sacrament as a means of assurance). But "Onely thy grace" has the key to the fortification. In line 19 Herbert explicitly and clearly distinguishes between the elements and the grace that comes "with" the elements. "Onely thy grace" (*sola gratia*) can minister to the soul and, in fact, make it receptive to the sacraments. After grace turns the key and opens the various doors in the soul, the elements ("Those" of 23) "attend / Dispatches from their friend." The word *attend*, according to the OED, carries the senses of listening to, or of accompanying, especially in obedience to an authoritative summons. The elements are thus subordinate to grace, accompanying grace as its servant, focused on its "dispatches," an image that aligns the sacraments, in the Reformation manner, with God's Word.

Despite these formulations with their Anglican and Calvinist distinction between the physical and the spiritual, in other poems Herbert presents a more direct confrontation with Christ in the elements, seemingly experiencing, in the Lutheran manner, the Real Presence of Christ. This is particularly true of "The Invitation" and "The Banquet," which occur together and toward the very end of "The Church," so that their position in the context of Herbert's other poems gives them a special emphasis. In "The Invitation" the speaker is proclaiming the Gospel to everyone, that Gospel being imaged and presented in the sacrament:

> Come ye hither all, whose taste
> Is your waste;
> Save your cost, and mend your fare.
> God is here prepar'd and drest,
> And the feast,
> God, in whom all dainties are.

(1–6)

In contrast to the tortuous reasonings of the "H. Communion" poems, Herbert seems clear and unambiguous: "God is here"; "God is . . . the feast."

> Come ye hither all, whom wine
> Doth define,
> Naming you not to your good:
> Weep what ye have drunk amisse,
> And drink this,
> Which before ye drink is bloud.

(7–12)

Herbert here makes reference to one of the tests of doctrine that was a matter of great controversy. The Lutherans insisted that the body and blood of Christ are objectively present in the elements and are received even by unbelievers. While even Lutherans focused on the reception of the elements as the fulfillment of the sacramental mystery, Herbert, in insisting that the blood of Christ is present "before ye drink," is taking an extremely strong position on the Real Presence of Christ in the elements. The Calvinists, on the other hand, believed that Christ is communicated only spiritually; He is not in the elements themselves, so that they do not bear Christ apart from their faithful reception. Unbelievers do not receive Christ at all, only plain bread and wine. Herbert does present this latter belief, curiously, in another poem. In "Love Unknown," Herbert writes of "holy bloud,"

> Which at a board, while many drunk bare wine,
> A friend did steal into my cup for good,
> Ev'n taken inwardly.

(42–44)

Here at the Communion table (or "board"), many are drinking "bare wine"; the reception of "bloud" is separate, "taken inwardly" as the action of special grace (cf. *Institutes* 4.14.9). The wine is not blood "before ye drink," but only as it is applied spiritually, taken by faith. Nevertheless, in "The Invitation," Herbert clearly reverses this position.

Come ye hither all, whom pain
                    Doth arraigne,
Bringing all your sinnes to sight:
Taste and fear not: God is here
                    In this cheer,
And on sinne doth cast the fright.

                                        (13–18)

In the wine, which sinners misuse in drunkenness (7–12), "God is here / In this cheer." The poem continues in the same vein, imaging the Gospel, with the first three lines of each stanza describing sin and the last three imaging the message of free forgiveness expressed and offered in the sacrament.

Lord I have invited all,
                    And I shall
Still invite, still call to thee:
For it seems but just and right
                    In my sight,
Where is All, there All should be.

                                        (31–36)

Christ, as Luther teaches, is everywhere and fills all things. Here in the sacrament "All" is present in a special and direct way, to offer Himself not so much to the worthy, as Anglicans and Calvinists sometimes implied, but to sinners. Another Lutheran doctrine suggested in the poem is the Universality of Grace. Whereas Calvinists believe in "Limited Atonement," that Christ died only for the elect, Lutherans believe that Christ died for "All" and that potentially anyone may be saved. This last stanza, with its allusion to Luther's Christology, emphasizes the doctrine of the Real Presence that is suggested throughout the poem.

This doctrine is intensified in the next poem, "The Banquet," a remarkable poem that meditates lyrically on the taste and fragrance of the Communion elements. Expressing with Cranmer that in the sacrament "we may see Christ with our eyes, smell Him at our nose, and perceive Him with all our senses," Herbert writes:

Welcome sweet and sacred cheer,
                    Welcome deare;
With me, in me, live and dwell:
For thy neatnesse passeth sight,
                    Thy delight
Passeth tongue to taste or tell.

O what sweetnesse from the bowl
                    Fills my soul

Such as is, and makes divine!
. . . .

But as Pomanders and wood
       Still are good,
Yet being bruis'd are better sented;
God, to show how farre his love
       Could improve,
Here, as broken, is presented.

When I had forgot my birth,
       And on earth
In delights of earth was drown'd;
God took bloud, and needs would be
       Spilt with me,
And so found me on the ground.

Having rais'd me to look up,
       In a cup
Sweetly he doth meet my taste.
But I still being low and short,
       Farre from court,
Wine becomes a wing at last.

For with it alone I flie
       To the skie:
Where I wipe mine eyes, and see
What I seek, for what I sue;
       Him I view,
Who hath done so much for me.

                        (1–9, 25–48)

Here in the bread and wine Herbert is confronting Christ in a direct, personal way. The "sweetnesse from the bowl . . . is and makes divine." God "Here, as broken, is presented." "In a cup . . . he doth meet my taste." In the wine, "Him I view, / Who hath done so much for me." Herbert is meditating on the taste and smell of the elements themselves, not as "accidents" but as the vehicles through which Christ expresses Himself. The meaning for him of this confrontation is the Gospel: his sin canceled by the unconditional love of Christ.

The doctrine of the Real Presence seems to have been closest to Herbert's experience, although intellectually he could discuss the sacraments in the more guarded terms of Reformed, Calvinist theology. His inconsistencies are simply those of the Church of England, allowing him a wide range of reference. Thus the poems with the "highest" view of the sacrament, "The Invitation" and "The Banquet," involve also the sense of a communal feast, which was the aspect stressed by Zwingli. A final example of Herbert's liturgical temperament, his reinterpretation of traditional forms, and his latitude will help make the point. In the Reformed churches Communion was celebrated not at an altar, which implied the Roman doctrine of the mass as a sacrifice offered up for the living and the dead, but at a table, a reenactment of the biblical "Last Supper" and a feast of spiritual nourishment.[101] On this point, Anglicans at the time agreed, but there were those who would go farther. Should not one sit rather than kneel at the Communion table? Herbert ingeniously answers such objections in favor of the old forms, while also reinterpreting them:

> The Feast indeed requires sitting, because it is a Feast; but man's unpreparednesse asks kneeling. Hee that comes to the sacrament hath the confidence of a Guest, and he that kneels, confesseth himself an unworthy one, and therefore differs from other Feasters: but hee that sits, or lies, puts up to an Apostle: contentiousnesse in a Feast of Charity is more scandall than any posture. ("The Country Parson," 22:259)

Herbert sees kneeling not as worship but as a confession of unworthiness, a confession that is central to Reformation thought. Herbert does accept, with the more radical Reformers, the principle that the Communion is a feast and employs their imagery. Holy Communion is portrayed as a feast ("Invitation," 1–6; "The Banquet") at a table or "board" ("Conscience," 4; "Love Unknown," 42; "The Collar," 1). Interestingly, in light of his own practice, the very climax of *The Temple* occurs in a poem whose sacramental imagery is of a feast in which the only proper response is to sit:

> You must sit down, sayes Love, and taste my meat:
> So I did sit and eat.
> ("Love [3]," 17–18)

"The Feast indeed requires sitting." In this poem, as in the prose passage, there is also a "guest" who "confesseth himself an unworthy one"—"A guest, I answer'd, worthy to be here" (7). In the poem, however, the confession is an obstacle, made irrelevant by the declaration of love. The point is not that the two texts contradict each other in their handling of the same images but that Herbert can employ both traditional and also more "Reformed" sacramental symbols, depending on his purpose. For Herbert, it is the fact, not the interpretation, that is important. "To take and taste what he doth there designe, / Is all that saves, and not obscure" ("Divinitie," 21–24). He does not allow the interpretations to intrude themselves between himself and the confrontation with Christ that he experiences in the sacraments. He can thus use the various interpretations with unusual flexibility in helping him contemplate and explore the fact of the sacraments. Herbert sees both baptism and the Lord's Supper as "dispatches from a friend," as visible Words from God that he must attend to, direct communications of the Gospel of Christ, "dispatches" that can be "read" and interpreted endlessly.

v. The Word in Poetry

The figure of Christ, the influence of the Bible, various rhetorical parallels to preaching, the sacramental imagery, are all important components of Herbert's poetry, but there is a larger sense in which the poetry itself is "logo-centric," exhibiting not only in its incidental images but in its form and rationale the characteristics of the Reformation doctrine of the Word.[102] The dynamics of revelation, whereby God actively and personally reveals Himself through language to recalcitrant or lost sinners, is as much a formal principle of Herbert's poetry as it is the starting point for Reformation theology. The classic example of God's "Word" breaking into and resolving the poem is "The Collar," in which God's revelation, markedly separate from the feelings, ideas, and desires of the speaker, restores order and creates a word of response:

> But as I rav'd and grew more fierce and wilde
> At every word,
> Me thoughts I heard one calling, *Child!*
> And I reply'd, *My Lord.*
>
> (33–36)

The same paradigm of revelation and resolution occurs again and again in Herbert's poetry. Herbert's poems tend to be dialogues.[103] His religious poetry is different from most in that God is presented not as a passive object of contemplation, but as an active God who speaks, although from a height that makes the merely anthropomorphic unthinkable; because He speaks, God can be portrayed as a Person and thus in active personal relationship with the poet.[104]

In individual poems, the speaker often receives "instruction from without," according to John R. Mulder, generally marked, emphasized, and set off from the speaker's voice by italics. This formal trait is so intrusive that Mulder suggests that Herbert has contrived two writers—the poet, recording his experience from moment to moment, and God, "who declares his own praise in his governance of the poet's heart, from granting grace to inducing its understanding."[105] John Freed precisely expresses the connection between the theological doctrine of the Word and the formal characteristics of Herbert's verse: "God saves man by throwing him the divine lifeline of revelation, and appropriately Herbert inserts God's words at the critical points to resolve both poetic and theological conflicts."[106]

When a word, usually marked by italics,[107] breaks into the poem, what happens is that the poet, who is addressing the lines to someone else, is himself addressed. Confrontation with God's Word is no ordinary dialogue. "Thy words do find me out" ("H. Scriptures [2]," 11). God's Word—whether under the aspect of the Scriptures, preaching, or the sacraments—is experienced as being "quick, and powerful, and sharper than any two-edged sword, piercing even to the dividing asunder of soul and spirit, and of the joints and marrow, and is a discerner of the thoughts and intents of the heart" (Heb. 4:12). This penetrating, unmasking quality of the Word is a favorite topic of Luther. There can be no better gloss on "The Collar" than Luther's: "When the word of God comes, it runs contrary to our thought and desire."[108] Ebeling's summary of Luther's teaching on the subject suggests how profoundly Herbert's poems, even the ones in which he suffers God's chastening and silence, are animated by the Reformation experience of the Word:

> The law which accuses him [is] the law of God, and the anger which terrifies him [is] the anger of God—it is in fact the word of God; but it is the word of law, the word of anger, a word in which God remains absent and concealed—that is, in which he is present as one who is absent and concealed. On the other hand, the word in which God comes as one who is present and revealed is the word of God in a different and special sense. That is, it is the word through which he creates and brings about my acceptance of him as God, my honouring of him as God, my faith in him, my readiness to receive him, my trust in him and my self-abandonment to him, so that I am set free from myself and from all the powers to which I sold myself.[109]

For Luther, according to Ebeling and, one might add, for Herbert,

> Man is ultimately a hearer, someone who is seized, claimed, and subject to judgement, and . . . for this reason his existential being depends upon which word reaches and touches his inmost being. This may be a word that imposes a burden on him which he has to carry himself, makes an unlimited claim upon him as one who acts, and who acts, therefore, on his own behalf, and then presents him with the account of everything he has not done, everything in which he has failed and everything he still owes. Or it may be the word which sets him free from this imprisonment within himself, this abandonment to his own resources, and reveals to him a hope which is not founded upon himself. Such a word lays claim to him not as an active agent who has to justify himself by his works, but as one who owes nothing to himself, who has become a gift to himself, and who, moreover, is able to understand himself as one who loves through a gift, through grace, and through forgiveness.[110]

This external word takes several forms in Herbert's poetry. It can be presented as a single literal word ("The Collar," "A true Hymne"), or it can be a more extended discourse ("Artillerie," "Dialogue," "Love Unknown"). Often the "word," in accordance with Reformation thought, is a quotation or paraphrase of Scripture ("Coloss. 3.3," "The Crosse," "Decay," "Divinitie").[111] Significantly, the resolving "word" is often a statement of the Gospel, often in narrative form, recounting the story of Christ ("Unkindness," "The Bag," "Redemption," "Peace"). This voice often interacts with the human voice ("The Odour," "Affliction [3]"), and sometimes the "word" is often not present but only desired or alluded to ("Deniall") or expressed not as a voice but in figures such as God writing His law upon the human heart ("The Sinner," "Sepulchre"). The Reformation doctrine of the Word, thoroughly permeating Herbert's spirituality and imagination, accounts not only for some of Herbert's themes and images, but also for some of the aesthetic and formal characteristics of his verse.

The two voices in Herbert's poems are often in conflict—in theological language, the human being is in rebellion against God's Word, a principle dramatized in "Love (3)" and declared in "Miserie." The first stanza in "Miserie" presents the "Word," a statement from the Bible (Isa. 40:6), followed immediately by the responding human voice:

> Man is but grasse,
> He knows it, fill the glasse.   (5–6)

Not only do human beings defy God's Word, but they know what they are doing. In "The Collar," the speaker's rebellion is similarly played against the biblical images of "board," "thorn," "bloud," "wine," "fruit," and so on. The human will conflicts with God's will, until the "effectual calling" of the final lines, whereupon the speaker, in Ebeling's terms, is set free from himself. This pattern of conflicting wills and their resolution in Herbert's poetry has been treated in chapter 2; the point here is that God intervenes neither by changing the speaker's moods, guiding him into some higher insight, nor by threatening him, but by confrontation with the Word, conceived sacramentally as a vehicle of grace.

The Word not only saves, but it implies and makes possible a relationship, as celebrated in "The Odour. 2 Cor. 2.15":

> For when *My Master,* which alone is sweet,
>   And ev'n in my unworthinesse pleasing,
>   Shall call and meet,
>   *My servant,* as thee not displeasing,
> That call is but the breathing of the sweet.
>
> This breathing would with gains by sweetning me
>   (As sweet things traffick when they meet)
>   Return to thee.
>   And so this new commerce and sweet
> Should all my life employ and busie me.
>   (21–30)

Italicizing both the human and the divine voice, Herbert sets them together as two poles, not in tension but in relationship, each calling to the other. The two voices "shall call and meet," and in this mingling of breaths,[112] the human being, in an image of sanctification, becomes sweetened by God's sweetness, becoming "a sweet savour of Christ" offered in turn back "unto God" (as in 2 Cor. 2:15, the text of the poem's title). For Herbert this dynamic interchange, "this new commerce" is the ideal, enough to "employ and busie me" for a lifetime. It is not an equal partnership, of course— the human voice is defined only in terms of its *"Master."* When it pretends to autonomy, to being its own master, as in "The Collar," the result is disharmony. Wholeness comes only when the *"child"* (*"My servant"*) recognizes *"My Lord"* (*"My Master"*).

The harmony imaged in "The Odour" in terms of a dialogue can be broken either by human rebellion or by God's silence. Herbert's poems of desolation generally involve the sense that God is not listening, or, what may be the same thing, not speaking ("Deniall" brings the two senses together in complaining of God's "silent eares" [2]). God "is present as one who is absent and concealed," in Ebeling's terms. One such complaint to God is "The Crosse," the resolution of which is an especially complicated application of God's Word. The poem, as has been shown, is not about the desire to stop serving God, as in "The Collar," but about the frustrated desire to serve him. Still, the complaint is basically the same: "things sort not to my will" (19). The poem concludes with an image of frustration, shifting to thought of Christ and to submission:

> Ah my deare Father, ease my smart!
> These contrarieties crush me: these crosse actions
> Doe winde a rope about, and cut my heart:
>   And yet since these thy contradictions
> Are properly a crosse felt by thy sonne,
> With but foure words, my words, *Thy will be done.*

(31–36)

The resolution here comes not through a symbol of a voice, but through the remembrance of the biblical narrative of Christ's passion. The "foure words" are themselves a biblical text (Matt. 6:10, 26:42). The words are those of Christ, whose focus on his Father's will rather than His own enables the speaker of the poem to do the same. Christ's words, the words of Scripture, become "my words," and Christ's submission becomes his own. "My deare Father," does illumine him as his own language ("these crosse actions") calls to mind the Scriptures, which, in turn, convey Christ. The speaker's "humility" paradoxically consists of the merging of his human voice with that of God, because the italicized "foure words" are at once God's Word and "my words."[113] The various senses of the doctrine of the Word—human proclamation, Scripture, Christ—seem to come together, working backward from the human word, in the poem's resolution.

In "The Crosse," what intrudes is not just any word but, specifically, the passion of Christ. The context of the resolving Word is nearly always, indirectly or directly, Christological. In "Redemption," the speaker's world is broken into not only by a Word, but by an event that makes the Word effective and resolving:

> I straight return'd, and knowing his great birth,
>   Sought him accordingly in great resorts;
>   In cities, theatres, gardens, parks, and courts:
> At length I heard a ragged noise and mirth
>   Of theeves and murderers: there I him espied
> Who straight, *Your suit is granted,* said, & died.
>
> (9–14)

In "Unkindness," the italicized voice is simply a direct statement of Christ's atonement:

> O write in brasse, *My God upon a tree*
>   *His bloud did spill*
>   *Onely to purchase my good-will.*
> Yet use I not my foes, as I use Thee.
>
> (21–25)

Once more God's Word, here portrayed in terms of God's writing, is played against human recalcitrance and rebellion to that Word.

"The Bag" is similarly resolved, not by a voice set apart by italics, but by an internal narrative, the "strange storie" (8) of Jesus. The problem, as elsewhere, is a struggle against despair, as stated in the first stanza: "Away despair!" (1). The next four stanzas are an extended poetic narrative ("Then let me tell thee a strange storie. . . ." [8]) of the Incarnation and Atonement of Christ, with seemingly little explicit reference to the stated problem of the poem, which is despair. In the last two stanzas, however, Christ Himself is made to speak, announcing that the wound in His side is now a means whereby human words can be conveyed to the father.

> Or if hereafter any of my friends
>   Will use me in this kinde, the doore
>   Shall still be open; what he sends
> I will present, and somewhat more,
>   Not to his hurt. Sighs will convey
> Any thing to me. Harke, Despair away.
>
> (37–42)

The final half-line returns to the voice and the theme of the first half-line ("Away despair!" [1]). The psychological theme frames the internal narrative, which, in turn, frames the voice of Christ, which resolves the outermost theme.

In "Peace," the resolving "Word" also takes the form of a biblical narrative. What is discovered at the end of the pilgrimage, the search for peace, is not a place or even a state of mind—the symbols of the cave (introspection), the rainbow (transcendence), and the garden (honor)—but a story:

> At length I met a rev'rend good old man
> Whom when for Peace
> I did demand, he thus began:
> There was a Prince of old
> At Salem dwelt, who liv'd with good increase
> Of flock and fold.
>
> He sweetly liv'd; yet sweetnesse did not save
> His life from foes.
> But after death out of his grave
> There sprang twelve stalks of wheat:
> Which many wondring at, got some of those
> To plant and set.
>
> It prosper'd strangely, and did soon disperse
> Through all the earth:
> For they that taste it do rehearse,
> That vertue lies therein,
> A secret vertue bringing peace and mirth
> By flight of sinne.
>
> Take of this grain, which in my garden grows,
> And grows for you;
> Make bread of it: and that repose
> And peace, which ev'ry where
> With so much earnestnesse you do pursue,
> Is onely there.
>
> (19–42)

The "rev'rend good old man" simply tells him the story of Jesus.[114] The old man then mentions a grain, propagated through the twelve apostles, which he grows in his garden. Finally, he offers the grain to the seeker, telling him to "make bread of it," and thus find peace. Much has been made of the Eucharistic symbols in the poem,[115] but the poem presents two stages: the grain, which must be "plant and set," propagating "through all the earth," is then later made into bread. The bread is certainly Eucharistic, but the grain is first described as a seed, the common New Testament symbol (Matthew 13). In the parable of the sower, the scattering and the growth of the seeds is a symbol of the kingdom of heaven. "Now the parable is this," according to Luke 8:11: "the seed is the Word of God." In the parable all hear the Word, but respond differently. In Herbert's poem, the Word (in the sense of both the Scriptures and especially the Gospel) issues from the apostolic witness, from whom "many" obtained seed "to plant and set," until the Gospel spread "through all the earth."[116] As in

Reformation usage, the Word, the Gospel of Christ, is then made into bread, the symbol of Christ as nourishing the believer (John 6:48, 58), offered personally in the "visible word" of the sacrament. For Herbert, the symbols of nourishment and bread are images of the Word of God. In "A Prayer after Sermon" ("Country Parson," p. 290), after a lyrical celebration of the plan of redemption and the Gospel, Herbert applies the traditional Eucharistic symbols to the sermon itself:[117]

> O Lord! thy blessings hang in clusters, they come trooping upon us! they break forth like mighty waters on every side. And now Lord, thou hast fed us with the bread of life: so man did eat Angels food: O Lord, blesse it. O Lord, make it health and strength unto us; still striving and prospering so long with us, untill our obedience reach the measure of thy love, who hast done for us as much as may be.

The search for "Peace" described in the poem culminates in a *rev'rend* (the term was then, as now, applied to members of the clergy) man's communicating to the seeker the story of Christ. The Word of God, entrusted to the church ("Take of this grain, which in my garden grows"), is offered to the seeker as the Gospel of Christ, the Bread of Life. Just as through the twelve apostles the seed of the Gospel "prosper'd strangely, and did soon disperse / Through all the earth," the "rev'rend" old man shares the Gospel with the seeker, promising him peace "by flight of sinne." The poem is thus, among other things, a model of the proclamation of the Gospel. The demand for peace is met with a story, a set of words that, with artifice and symbol, communicate Grace. The Reformation doctrine of the Word makes room for creativity, for the parabolic and poetic quality of the old man's— and the poet's—use of language to communicate God's saving Word.

Herbert's devotion to the spirituality of the Word, in all of its senses, is affirmed in "The Authour's Prayer before Sermon" ("The Country Parson," p. 289), in a way that suggests also how he might have conceived the purpose of his poetry. After a lyrical summary of the story of Christ as it is expressed in the Scriptures, Herbert celebrates the Word of God, not only in terms of his sermon, but in terms of his lute and his viol and all his powers, which include his artistic and poetic gifts:

> Neither doth thy love yet stay here! for, this word of thy rich peace, and reconciliation, thou hast committed, not to Thunder, or Angels, but to silly and sinfull man: even to me, pardoning my sins, and bidding me go feed the people of thy love.
> Blessed be the God of Heaven and Earth! who onely doth wondrous things. Awake, therefore, my Lute, and my Viol! awake all my powers to glorifie thee! . . . Lo, we stand here, beseeching thee to blesse thy word, wher-ever spoken this day throughout the universall church. O make it a word of power and peace, to convert those who are not yet thine, and to confirm those that are. . . . Lord Jesu! teach thou me, that I may teach

them: Sanctifie, and inable all my powers, that in their full strength they may deliver thy message reverently, readily, faithfully, and fruitfully. O make thy word a swift word, passing from the ear to the heart, from the heart to the life and conversation: that as the rain returns not empty, so neither may thy word, but accomplish that for which it is given. . . . For thy blessed son's sake, in whose sweet and pleasing words, we say, *Our Father,* &c.

The Church and One's Calling:
Spirituality in the World

When once thy foot enters the church, be bare.
God is more there then thou: for thou art there
Onely by his permission. Then beware,
And make thy self all reverance and fear.
    Kneeling ne're spoil'd silk stocking: quit thy state.
    All equall are within the churches gate.
                      —"The Church-porch," 403–8

Reformation spirituality focuses primarily, as has been seen, on the individual's personal relationship with God. At the same time, the Reformation brought about profound institutional changes. Luther's inner realization of justification by faith, like a pebble in a pond, sent changes through nearly every level of European culture. The Reformation view of the Church with its "priesthood of all believers" radically altered the medieval social structure, with implications for politics and economics that have deeply influenced modern secular thought and assumptions.

Herbert closes *The Temple* with "The Church Militant," a poem on the Church as an institution participating in and in tension with the victories and sins of the secular world. In keeping with Reformation doctrine, Herbert is concerned in his volume both with the invisible church—the saved individuals in communion with the indwelling Christ—and the visible Church—the Church as an external institution functioning in the world. A corollary to the Reformation view of the church is the doctrine of one's "calling," which has to do with how the individual functions in the Church and in society, and how one's secular employment can be related to the glory of God. This doctrine, which is central to the ethics and to the social impact of the Reformation, was particularly important to Herbert, who wrestled with his own calling into the ministry, explored the concept and its implications in detail in *The Country Parson*, and applied it in his own vocation as a poet.

i. The Church Militant and Invisible

The concept of the Church, for theologians of the Reformation, involved two different but related entities. The invisible Church comprised all of the elect, those who have been converted and transformed into the mystical Body of Christ. The visible Church is the external institution, which errs, contains hypocrites and unbelievers, but which administers the Sacraments and proclaims God's Word to a sinful world.[1] This distinction does not mean they can be separated. The individual sinner can be converted and nourished only through the Word and the Sacraments administered by the visible Church. The invisible Church, the Church Triumphant, is known fully only to God who, through the visible Church Militant, can bring even the hypocrites and unbelievers, who had attended the external Church out of false pretenses, to a true knowledge of Himself (Calvin, *Institutes* 4.7). There is only one Church, but it can be seen from two different perspectives—in terms of its members' relationship with Christ, and in terms of its relationship to the external world. This concept is illustrated by the structure of *The Temple*. Herbert's section "The Church" depicts the relationship with Christ and is, of course, the essential part of the volume. On either side of this section, Herbert depicts the external Church, "The Church-porch" and "The Church Militant." This structure of *The Temple* is not really architectural, but it is somewhat spatial because the outside-inside-outside model portrays the Church as a whole, a "temple" both in the sense of the individual believer's being a temple of the indwelling God and in the sense of a corporate, visible entity interacting with the world. The disparity between the lyricism of Herbert's central section and the sententiousness of "The Church-porch" and the polemics of "The Church Militant" parallels that of the Church itself, whose visible and often distasteful struggle with sin and error in the world and in itself exists around the individual Christian's personal communion with Christ.

The internalizing of religion was one of the major results of the Reformation. For Herbert, the inner reality is prior. Thus Herbert characteristically defines the physical fixtures of the church in terms of an inner spiritual quality (the altar is the heart, the church floor is patience, the windows are the life of the preacher, etc.). This emphasis is explained in "Sion," which contrasts the external worship of Solomon's temple to that of the new covenant, in which the Temple of the Holy Ghost is now the individual believer (1 Cor. 3:16):

> And now thy Architecture meets with sinne;
> For all thy frame and fabrick is within.
>
> (11–12)

This is not to say that this inner Church Herbert is writing about is solip-sistic or individualized; rather, all members of the invisible Church, the Communion of Saints, share these experiences of justification and sanctification. These poems reflect personal, but archetypal spiritual states, which, Herbert hopes, can be appropriated by his readers:

> He that will passe his land,
> As I have mine, may set his hand
> And heart unto this deed, when he hath read;
> And make the purchase spread
> To both our goods, if he to it will stand.
>
> How happie were my part,
> If some kinde man would thrust his heart
> Into these lines; till in heav'ns count of rolls
> They were by winged souls
> Entred for both, farre above their desert!
>
> ("Obedience," 36–45)[2]

Herbert's evangelical purpose and his focus on universal Christian experi-ences are meant to be taken on a personal, inward level. The visible Church, in other words, rests upon the invisible Church, upon the myste-rious workings of God, who calls individual persons into a relationship with Him.

This is not to denigrate the visible Church, which Herbert deals with as well. "The Church-porch," by its title, deals with the outside of the church, the external aspect, the point where it interfaces with the world. One of the functions of the Church as an institution in society is to promote morality (Calvin, *Institutes* 4.11). This "civil righteousness," corresponding to the *usus civilis* of the Law, is the subject of "The Church-porch" as discussed earlier, with its warnings about gambling, drunkenness, and so on. Just as the famous "Puritan" austerities and moralisms are not identical with the substance of Reformation spirituality, "The Church-porch" presents only the outside. The following poem, "Superliminare," makes this clear, chal-lenging the reader, chastened by the Law, to go "further," to enter inside in order to "taste the churches mystical repast" (4). Nevertheless, the Re-formed Church was very much concerned with reforming society as well. Rejecting the medieval church's dichotomy of secular and sacred vocations and insisting that God's reign extended to all of life, the Reformation Church promoted an active social ethic. The conventional exhortations to prudence and temperance in the poem are part of a larger texture. Thus

Herbert devotes several stanzas to thrift, but then warns against the acquisition of wealth:

> Wealth is the conjurers devil;
> Whom when he thinks he hath, the devil hath him.
> Gold thou mayst safely touch; but if it stick
> Unto thy hands, it woundeth to the quick.

(165–68)

Rather, one should give to the poor.

> Man is Gods image; but a poore man is
> Christ's stamp to boot: both images regard.

(379–80)

In doing so, one is able to "Joyn hands with God to make a man to live" (376). Interestingly, the speaker of "The Church-porch," while condemning sin, does not condemn the secular pursuits of the young man he is addressing; in fact, he wants the young man to succeed at them. His success, though, is to be measured at the final judgement, as the last stanza makes clear. The challenge given by the speaker is to be godly in the world, not apart from it, to find in every sphere of ordinary life an opportunity for the love of God. "The Church-porch" looks outward to a world of politics and business; rather than shrinking away from such things, it offers advice on how to master them without making them ultimate. The worldly-wise tone of the poem and its seemingly bourgeois attitudes to conventional success—the marks noted elsewhere in the Reformation by the "Protestant ethic" theorists—can be accounted for in terms of the doctrine of one's calling and will be discussed below. In its position in *The Temple*, "The Church Porch" exemplifies how the Reformation Church and the Reformation believer, for all of their inwardness, interact with the world.

Daniel Rubey has observed how Herbert tends to move in *The Temple* from individual, personal experience to the corporate, from the personal to larger and larger perspectives.[3] Similarly, "The Church-porch," which is highly time-bound with its references to the court, silk stockings, and the whole seventeenth-century milieu, gives way to the more universal experiences of "The Church," which is followed by another vision of the Church as it exists in time, "The Church Militant." This poem, though, takes a universal perspective, viewing human history, both religious and secular, from a dizzying height, from Noah to the Apocalypse, embracing past, present, and future.[4] Just as the life of the individual Christian is a battle between the power of sin and the power of grace, the process of sanctification, Herbert portrays human history as a battle between sin and religion. This battle that the Church Militant is engaged in is not, however, limited to the church, but it involves the life of "common-weals" (5) and empires (73ff.), the progress of "the Arts" (263ff.), and such historical events as the colonization of America (235ff.).

By interweaving the history of the visible church with his account of secular civilization, Herbert demonstrates how they are related to each other. On the one hand, "Religion" is presented as complementing and bringing to fruition the accomplishments of secular society:

> Strength levels grounds, Art makes a garden there;
> Then showres Religion, and makes all to bear.
>
> (87–88)

On the other hand, the Church has a prophetic function, denouncing the sins of the society, as in Herbert's condemnation of imperialism occasioned by the pillaging of the Americas:

> Then shall Religion to *America* flee:
> They have their times of Gospel ev'n as we.
> My God, thou dost prepare for them a way
> By carrying first their gold from them away:
> For gold and grace did never yet agree:
> Religion alwaies sides with povertie.
> We think we rob them, but we think amisse:
> Thou wilt revenge their quarrell, making grace
> To pay our debts, and leave our ancient place
> To go to them, while that which now their nation
> But lends to us, shall be our desolation.
> (247–58)

The force of Herbert's comments on America and his apparent support of the radical Protestants who were settling in New England can be gauged by the fact that they nearly prevented *The Temple* from being licensed in 1633.[5]

Sin works not only in the world, but even within the visible Church, as the poem makes clear. Charles and Katherine George observe that "an interesting aspect of English Protestantism's relative downgrading of the institutional church is the general insistence that the visible church, as it exists in the world, is fallible in its judgments, has erred in the past, and may very well continue to do likewise in the future."[6] This is a crucial difference, of course, with the Roman Catholic position. To the Protestants, while the invisible church is preserved by God, the visible church is liable to corruption and error. This distinction allowed them to profess faith in "the Holy Catholic church" of the Creeds, against which the gates of Hell cannot prevail (the invisible Church), while still condemning the Church of Rome. In their view, the visible church did teach pure doctrine in the time of the Apostles and the Church Fathers, and intermittently and locally ever since. The institution and growing power of the papacy, though, accompanied and furthered the departure of the visible church from biblical doctrine. The Protestants saw in the Pope, crowned on the seven hills of Rome and claiming divine authority, the marks of the Antichrist of Revelations, and saw the visible church as having undergone, like the Jews of the Old Testament, a "Babylonian captivity,"[7] in which the Gospel was temporarily, though not totally, obscured. Herbert employs these conventional figures in his poem.

In the context of the poem, which diagrams the advance of both sin and religion, Herbert makes his polemic against Rome the structural climax, as the two forces converge in the Church of Rome. Herbert, earlier in the poem, had written about the ancient pagan civilizations. Now he recalls each of them, finding their characteristic errors brought together and united in the Church of Rome. "From *Egypt* he took pettie deities," a reference to the cult of the saints, "From *Greece* oracular infallibilities," suggesting that the doctrine of the Pope's infallibility is simply the same as that of the Delphic oracle. "And from old *Rome* the libertie of pleasure, / By free dispensings of the Churches treasure," a reference to the alleged decadence of the papal court financed by the sale of indulgences.

> Then in memoriall of his ancient throne
> He did surname his palace *Babylon.*
> Yet that he might the better gain all nations,
> And make that name good by their transmigrations;
> From all these places, but at divers times,
> He took fine vizards to conceal his crimes:
> From *Egypt* Anchorisme and retirednesse,
> Learning from *Greece,* from old *Rome* statelinesse:
> And blending these he carri'd all mens eyes,
> While Truth sat by, counting his victories.
>
> (177–90)

This Babylon does not need "Such force as once did captivate the Jews," but, through its deceptions nevertheless seizes secular power and, like the Roman empire, seeks to rule the world (191–204).

> As new and old *Rome* did one Empire twist;
> So both together are one Antichrist.
>
> (205–6)

Having thus recapitulated and united his earlier treatments of Egypt, Greece, and Rome, Herbert brings his account of the progress of sin and religion to a paradoxical climax:

> Thus sinne triumphs in Western *Babylon;*
> Yet not as sinne, but as Religion.
>
> (211–12)

Again, Herbert sees the Babylon of the Bible as typologically foreshadowing the Church of Rome:

> Old and new *Babylon* are to hell and night,
> As is the moon and sunne to heav'n and light.
> When th'one did set, the other did take place,
> Confronting equally the law and grace.
>
> (215–18)

"Confront" meant "to face in hostility or defiance," to stand against, to oppose (OED). Herbert's invective is directed against what he, conditioned by the propaganda of his time and place, perceived as a system that opposed the experience of "law and grace," the realization of both guilt and unconditional acceptance that means eternal salvation, on which the whole of *The Temple* is a commentary. Immediately after the true issue of "law and grace" is mentioned, Herbert's emotion is unleashed, so that the invective becomes nearly scabrous:

> They are hells land-marks, Satans double crest:
> They are Sinnes nipples, feeding th' east and west.
>
> (219–20)

This outburst, a catalogue recalling perversely those of "Prayer (1)," is distasteful, but it is an index perhaps to the personal and emotional stakes for Herbert of the Reformation doctrine of "law and grace."

If Herbert's virulent anti-Catholicism shows him to be less the cryptocatholic who sought to avoid all theological controversies, it does show him, with his contemporaries, to be very much a part of the Reformation tradition. He is, however, fair minded enough to criticize also the visible church established by the Reformation:

> But as in vice the copie still exceeds
> The pattern, but not so in vertuous deeds;
> So though Sinne made his latter seat the better,
> The latter Church is to the first a debter,
> The second Temple could not reach the first:
> And the late reformation never durst
> Compare with ancient times and purer yeares;
> But in the Jews and us deserveth tears.
>
> (221–28)

He is saying that sin usually outdoes its model, growing worse, whereas virtue usually falls short of its model. Thus, while the second Babylon, imitating sin, is worse than the first (223), the Reformation church, imitating virtue, falls short of its model, the "first" church as described in the Scriptures, which the Reformers held up as the norm. Again, this is presented in terms of biblical typology, as the Temple that was rebuilt *after* the Babylonian captivity fell far short of the original Temple of Solomon. The Jews who had seen the first Temple wept, when the foundations of the second were laid, at the glory that had been lost in Israel (Ezra 3:12). Not only does the "late reformation" fall short of the New Testament Church, but it is already waning:

> Nay, it[8] shall ev'ry yeare decrease and fade;
> Till such a darknesse do the world invade
> At Christs last coming, as his first did finde.
>
> (229–31)

As so often in the poem, appearance and reality are in paradox. The fading of the Reformation, evident already by his time, is accompanied by its vindication, as the triumph of "darknesse" only brings closer the day of Christ.

Herbert's *The Temple* portrays his view of the Church as a whole: In "The Church-porch" he presents the Church as it interfaces with the secular world. In "The Church" he presents the Church as a personal, inward reality, the sequence of justification and sanctification that is the substance of the invisible Church, the individual's personal relationship with God. In "The Church Militant" Herbert presents the institution of the visible Church as it exists corporately and historically, in the context of other institutions. The poem also suggests the unity of the visible and invisible Church. Because the individual Christian, according to the doctrine of sanctification, faces a continual internal battle between sin and the indwelling Holy Spirit, with the foreordained victory of the Spirit to be concluded only at the Resurrection of the Dead, the Church as a whole faces exactly the same struggle and destiny:

> Thus also Sinne and Darknesse follow still
> The Church and Sunne with all their power and skill.
> But as the Sunne still goes both west and east;
> So also did the Church by going west
> Still eastward go; because it drew more neare
> To time and place, where judgement shall appeare.
>
> (272–77)

ii. The Sacred and Secular Vocations

The Reformation critique of the medieval church had far-ranging social implications. The idea that salvation comes from an individual's personal faith in Christ alone rather than through the formal mediation of the Church, and that Scripture speaks personally to the believer apart from the *magisterium* of Church tradition implied the doctrine of the priesthood of all believers. Since each Christian is a Temple of the Holy Ghost, everyone, of any occupation or social class, has immediate access to God. This principle, first, changed worship—the laity were no longer excluded from the sacramental wine, the liturgy was translated into the languages of the people, hymns were sung by the entire congregation, the rood screens that segregated the laity from the mysteries performed at the altar were torn down.[9] The results were more than ecclesiastical. The emphasis on personal Bible reading led not only to the vernacular translations, but to the rise of literacy among all classes. Rejection of the Church hierarchy as the locus of authority led, in practice, to greater political autonomy, with the institution of the national church, as in England, and, as in the more extreme Reformed churches of Geneva and Holland, self-governing congregations and commonwealths. The priesthood of all believers meant that all vocations were of equal spiritual value, a view that gave a new dignity to ordinary labor and secular employment, with important economic ramifications. Integral to all of these changes, and a corollary to the Reformation view of the Church, is the doctrine of the calling, a concept extremely important to Herbert, who discusses the doctrine and its implications in depth in *The Country Parson*. The doctrine of the calling implies a view of the world and of one's talents that is deeply reflected in Herbert's life and imagination, both as a pastor and as a poet.

"If one seeks a single concentrate of the English Protestant abandonment of Roman Catholic asceticism for an attitude which regards the world as a worthy place of Christian trial and sojourn, one finds it best in the doctrine of the calling."[10] Charles and Katherine George go on to illustrate this point largely by quoting Herbert. Briefly, the medieval church recognized two different kinds of vocations or life-styles. The secular vocations, involving getting married and raising a family, working in the fields or in the court, were, of course, essential and valued. It seemed obvious, though, that life on the purely natural plane entailed certain compromises with spiritual values. Although marriage was a sacrament and sexuality necessary to preserve the human race, virginity was seen as especially holy. Although wealth is necessary to the economic well-being of a society and valued by merchants and kings, the Scriptures extol poverty. The medieval church balanced the claims of both nature and grace through its doctrine of vocations. This view distinguished between the commandments of Scripture, the moral law that obligates all people, and the "evangelical counsels," the more radical edicts of the Gospels, binding only on those who sought a higher holiness. These "Counsels of Perfection," schematized into poverty, obedience, and chastity, were the province of the sacred vocations. Those who entered into the priesthood and the religious orders devoted themselves to a higher calling than the laity, who, however, could share in these "supererogatory" good works through the Church's "treasury of merit" and through the continual prayers of the monastic orders. Thus the secular and the sacred vocations made up two different but complementary lifestyles. The sacred vocations were held to be more spiritual, engaging in a life totally devoted to prayer and communion with God, interceding for the laity who, necessarily, lived on a more worldly plane. The Reformation fundamentally rejected this entire system. First, as has been seen, salvation was held to have nothing to do with "merit." The idea that totally depraved human beings could not only do good, but do more than God required—"supererogatory works"—was condemned as presumptuous in the extreme.[11] Nor does the layman require the intercession of a special spiritual caste. All are equal in the sight of God, whose Law is binding and requires and not merely counsels perfection. The function of God's Law is not to be blunted by casuistry, but to reveal sin and to drive the sinners to faith in Christ. Thus the so-called secular vocations are just as acceptable before God as those of priests and monks.[12] Service to God was seen as something to be done in the world, not as something to be done by withdrawing from it. The farmer serves God in the fields and the merchant serves God in the marketplace. Just as one might be "called" to the priesthood, one might be "called" to farming, or to sailing, or to commerce, according to the gifts providentially given to each individual and to the will of God. Finding and living according to one's calling became thus a major preoccupation for Reformation Christians, as reflected in Herbert's exhortation in *The Country Parson*:

> All are either to have a Calling, or prepare for it: He that hath or can have yet no imployment, if he truly and seriously prepare for it, he is safe and within bounds. Wherefore all are either presently to enter into a Calling, if they be fit for it, and it for them, or else to examine with care, and advice, what they are fittest for, and to prepare for that with all diligence. (32:275)

This emphasis on every Christian's being called to a particular kind of work gave ordinary occupations a new dignity and value. Charles and Katherine George document, in the popular religious literature they surveyed, a distinct shift

> from the Thomistic emphasis on the penal quality of labor, and particularly of manual labor, to a contrary emphasis on the positive, creative, and even enjoyable aspects of work. . . . Occasional references to the

older view of labor may be found in this literature, to be sure, and none of the ministers specifically or entirely deny the expiatory function of arduous toil. They speak far more often and more fully, however, of the positive, self- and God-satisfying, creative and useful character of work than of its painfulness.[13]

Herbert insists that "even in Paradise man had a calling" (*Country Parson*, 32:274). Adam and Eve were given the task of tending the Garden even before the Fall, which simply added difficulty and frustration to work, which in itself is blessed by God (a point portrayed also by Milton). In fact, avoiding labor is a sin. According to Herbert, the national sin of the land is idleness, which also leads to many other sins, so that the Parson must oppose it wherever he goes. "And because Idleness is twofold, the one in having no calling, the other in walking carelessly in our calling, he first represents to every body the necessity of a vocation" (*Country Parson*, 32:274). This Herbert does in "The Church-porch":

> Flie idlenesse, which yet thou canst not flie
> By dressing, mistressing, and complement.
> If those take up thy day, the sunne will crie
> Against thee: for his light was onely lent.[14]
>   God gave thy soul brave wings; put not those feathers
>   Into a bed, to sleep out all ill weathers.
>
> (79–84)

In the next stanza, Herbert lists a number of callings, giving the appropriate behavior for each one:

> Art thou a Magistrate? then be severe:
> If studious; copie fair, what time hath blurr'd;
> Redeem truth from his jawes: if souldier,
> Chase brave employments with a naked sword
>   Throughout the world. Fool not: for all may have,
>   If they dare try, a glorious life, or grave.
>
> (85–90)

A magistrate, a scholar, a soldier all may have glory in this life, and the next, by "walking in" their calling—a magistrate by his gravity, a scholar by redeeming truth from the destructiveness of time, a soldier by reckless courage. Each is very different, but each, by fulfilling the functions of that calling, is given "glory" by God.

The doctrine of one's calling is, of course, related to what has been called the "Protestant Work Ethic." However, Max Weber's thesis, blaming the Reformation for the worst excesses of individualistic capitalism, is generally rejected by most contemporary church historians. As has already been shown in the section on Providence and Affliction, worldly success was *not* held to be a sign of God's blessing (Calvin, *Institutes* 3.2.28). Moreover, the doctrine of one's calling involved an emphasis upon service to God and to the community, not individual gain. "The calling," according to the literature of the period, "must be appropriate to one's gifts, must actually express these gifts, and must be lawful and serviceable to society."[15] "Besides," says Herbert, alluding to the Parable of the Talents (Matt. 25:14–30), "every gift or ability is a talent to be accounted for, and to be improved to our Masters Advantage" (*Country Parson*, 32:274). Discussing Weber's thesis in detail, the Georges conclude that

> In its basic morality the Protestant vocational ethic is totally opposed to the individualistic social philosophy of emerging, and soon to be triumphant, bourgeois society. The moral incentives propounded by later liberalism, the Ben Franklins and Samuel Smileses of secularized middle class culture, the "Protestant" liberalism brilliantly set out for us in the novels of Richardson, Fielding, Dickens, and Thomas Mann—all this flood of social morality based upon the priority of the individual's ego over the need of the group was absolutely the antithesis of Reformation Protestantism.[16]

The emphasis was on social benefit and a relative economic egalitarianism. All callings, even the most humble, were equal before God.[17] In fact, the leisured classes, the nobles and the bourgeoisie, were valued less than the workers, those who performed physical, productive labor.[18] "Religion alwaies sides with povertie," according to Herbert ("The Church Militant," 252), so that the net effect was not to sanction wealth, but to give a new dignity and religious status to the working classes.

As important as the doctrine of one's calling was to the self-image of the laity and to the attitudes toward work and secular employment, it also implied a broadening of focus of the religious life. Since God's sovereignty extends to all of life and since He can be served in every occupation, then everything, no matter how small, can be charged with religious significance. Herbert is thus able to insist that

> Nothing is little in Gods service: If it once have the honour of that Name, it grows great instantly. Wherfore neither disdaineth he to enter into the poorest cottage, though he even creep into it, and though it smell never so lothsomly. For both God is there also, and those for whom God dyed. (*The Country Parson*, 14:249).

The doctrine of one's calling as a spiritual discipline and an attitude toward the world finds its definitive treatment in Herbert's poem "The Elixer":

> Teach me, my God and King,
> In all things thee to see,

And what I do in any thing,
    To do it as for thee:

Not rudely, as a beast
    To runne into an action;
But still to make thee prepossest,
    And give it his perfection.

A man that looks on glasse,
    On it may stay his eye;
Or if he pleaseth, through it passe,
    And then the heav'n espie.

All may of thee partake:
    Nothing can be so mean,
Which with his tincture (for thy sake)
    Will not grow bright and clean.

A servant with this clause
    Makes drudgerie divine:
Who sweeps a room, as for thy laws,
    Makes that and th' action fine.

This is the famous stone
    That turneth all to gold:
For that which God doth touch and own
    Cannot for lesse be told.

"No task will be so sordid and base," says Calvin, "provided you obey your calling in it, that it will not shine and be reckoned very precious in God's sight" (*Institutes* 3.10.6). Not only is the servant sweeping a room able to make "drudgerie divine" through the alchemy of grace, but the speaker realizes that since God touches and owns all things, then everything, if it could only be perceived correctly, is of infinite value, and a manifestation of God.

The doctrine of the calling, that God is to be experienced, served, and praised in every type of occupation and activity, was very important to Protestant devotion, as C. J. Stranks makes clear:

The duty of living continually in the presence of God, and of sanctifying every incident in the day's routine with prayer, had been placed firmly on the shoulders of every Christian. The bedchamber, the workshop and the common street were to be what the monasteries had been in their best days, places where the work of praise and prayer were carried on continually.[19]

In his study of Anglican devotion, Stranks discusses how Protestant meditations would often focus upon the ordinary details of everyday life. For example, a work by John Bradford gives meditations on the normal events of the day. Upon waking, the Christian prays that "as thou hast awaked my body from sleep, so thou wouldst thoroughly awake, yea deliver, my soul from the sleep of sin and darkness of this world." While dressing, "Grant therefore that as I compass this my body with this coat, so thou wouldst clothe me wholely, but specially my soul, with thine own self." Going outdoors, eating, returning home at night, going to sleep, are all occasions for a confrontation with God.[20] John Donne's sickbed meditations, *Devotions Upon Emergent Occasions,* are of course, the high point of the genre,[21] but it is also apparent that this habit of mind is present in George Herbert, who creates poetry out of these same events. Waking up ("The Dawning"), getting dressed ("Aaron"), going to sleep ("Even-song"), and similar activities all become occasions for the contemplation of God. Herbert's use of "homely imagery" to express religious ideas, as well as that of "metaphysical" poetry in general, owes much, no doubt, to the practice of Scripture, as has been mentioned, but it probably owes at least as much to the doctrine of the calling, wherein every action and detail of ordinary life was seen as a sphere of revelation and of praise.

The importance of the calling for Herbert is not just evident in his exhortations in *The Country Parson* and in the texture of his poetry; it is something he struggled with personally, both in finding his own vocation as a minister and as a poet. Walton's biography emphasizes Herbert's struggle and hesitancy before he entered the priesthood. It is common now to deprecate Walton's version of Herbert's life, but in this regard he probably reflects the feelings of the time.[22] Although no more meritorious than any other calling, the "sacred calling" was a strenuous role, never to be entered into without hesitation and introspection. "The Minister of the Word," especially called and trained, was entrusted with the souls of his flock, a duty that was not fulfilled simply *ex opere operato,* by the administering of the sacraments. Rather, the Protestant priest, in communicating God's Word, must explain the Christian doctrines so that his people understand them. He must continually exhort and counsel his flock. Moreover, the minister was to be an example of the Christian life.

In a sense, therefore, the Protestant concept of the minister thrusts upon him a greater burden of responsibility for the welfare of his flock than the Catholic priest has had to bear. The minister's is a strenuous, penetrating role; he cannot only passively offer but must also actively motivate to accept. Compared to the Roman Catholic priest, the quality and effectiveness of his work, and hence his own value as a co-worker with God, come to depend far more upon his personal ability and self-directed actions and far less upon the automatic functioning of his office. There is in consequence a renewal of the old pressure upon the minister—which had once proceeded so far as to produce the Donatist heresy—to be in every sense that perfect instrument of God and to exhibit in himself the marks of God's grace and power.[23]

This view of the clergyman is embodied, of course, in Herbert's manual, *The Country Parson,* and, judging also from a poem such as "The Windows," it must have been a continual preoccupation.

If to Herbert people's calling from God involves "what they are fittest for" and that "every gift or ability is a talent to be accounted for, and to be improved to our Masters Advantage" (*Country Parson,* 32:274–75), it also follows that for Herbert poetry was also a calling. In his many poems on poetry, Herbert struggles to turn this gift also away from sin and the self, into the service of God; thus they are permeated with the doctrine of the calling:

> Farewell sweet phrases, lovely metaphors.
> But will ye leave me thus? when ye before
> Of stews and brothels onely knew the doores,
> Then did I wash you with my tears, and more,
>   Brought you to Church well drest and clad:
> My God must have my best, ev'n all I had.
>
> Lovely enchanting language, sugar-cane,
> Hony of roses, whither wilt thou flie?
> Hath some fond lover tic'd thee to thy bane?
> And wilt thou leave the Church, and love a stie?
>   Fie, thou wilt soil thy broider'd coat,
> And hurt thy self, and him that sings the note.
>
> Let foolish lovers, if they will love dung,
> With canvas, not with arras clothe their shame:
> Let follie speak in her own native tongue,
> True beautie dwells on high: ours is a flame
>   But borrow'd thence to light us thither.
> Beautie and beauteous words should go together.
>   ("The Forerunners," 13–30)

That poetry can be used for lascivious purposes does not keep it, like all vocations, from being a means of glorifying God, the theme also of "Love (1) and (2)," and "Dulnesse." Moreover, Herbert often parodies a poem about secular love, redirecting it to a more fitting object.[24] More deeply, Herbert portrays a struggle between the self and God over the spoils of his art, as his own pride in his work comes into conflict with the ultimate claims of God ("Jordan [2]," "A true Hymne").[25] Through them all is the sense that "My God must have my best, ev'n all I had." As he expressed in "The Elixer," every calling as to be directed to God and thus performed with excellence ("What I do in any thing, / To do it as for thee. . . . And give it his perfection" [3–4, 8]). In writing about Christ, "Nothing could seem too rich to clothe the sunne" ("Jordan [2]," 11). Such perfectionism is not necessary, as the speaker often discovers, but it points directly to the feelings implicit in the Reformation attitude toward work. Herbert does not doubt that his artistic gifts are from God and that therefore they are to be offered back to God, an understanding that he portrays through the repeated metaphor of a borrowed flame:

> True beautie dwells on high: ours is a flame
> But borrow'd thence to light us thither.
> ("The Forerunners," 28–29)

> Immortall Heat, O let thy greater flame
> Attract the lesser to it: let those fires,
> Which shall consume the world, first make it tame;
> And kindle in our hearts such true desires,

> As may consume our lusts, and make thee way.
> Then shall our hearts pant thee; then shall our brain
> All her invention on thine Altar lay,
> And there in hymnes send back thy fire again.
> ("Love [2]," 1–8)

In fact, Herbert's dedicatory verse to the entire volume reflects this same understanding:

> Lord, my first fruits present themselves to thee;
> Yet not mine neither: for from thee they came,
> And must return. Accept of them and me,
> And make us strive, who shall sing best thy name.
> Turn their eyes hither, who shall make a gain:
> Theirs, who shall hurt themselves or me, refrain.
> ("The Dedication")

In dedicating *The Temple,* Herbert disassociates himself from his works, even to the point of putting them in conflict with himself ("And make us strive . . ."), but they are also his "first fruits," the first and the best, which are to be offered to God (Exod. 23:19). Here is also the focus on the good of others that was essential to a true fulfilling of one's calling, together with the awareness that one's own talents are a function not of merit, but of grace.

The concept of the Church was both interiorized by Reformation doctrine and broadened, as every calling became, in effect, a ministry and a meeting point with God. It is significant that Herbert calls his series of poems "The Church," dealing as they do certainly with the institutional church, its symbols, and its mission, but also with experience, both personal and communal, and with details of ordinary life—sweeping floors, walking through gardens, weathering storms, walking into an inn—that are also made to manifest the presence of God.

— 9 —

Conclusion: Reformation Theology and Poetry

Reformation theology is part of a spiritual tradition that is psychologically and religiously complex, yet coherent, working such wide extremes as depravity and grace, guilt and security into a system that is both intellectualized and based in religious experience. Just as the achievement of Aquinas degenerated into the aridities of later scholasticism, the achievement of Luther, Calvin, and the other early Reformers was soon to be obscured, forced underground as other theologies became dominant. For the sixteenth and seventeenth centuries, however, the religious experience and understanding of the Reformation exerted a deep influence in the lives and thought—and thus, the imagination—of Englishmen such as George Herbert.[1] Moreover, Reformation theology, so devotional in its very nature, has implications for art, as is manifested in the religious poetry of George Herbert.

Calvin is so maligned as anti-art and anti-humanist (literary historians cannot forgive "Calvinists" for closing the theaters),[2] that it is worth quoting him at length on the subject of enjoyment, in which he insists, against the asceticism of monastic theorists, that beauty is a value in its own right, and that objects are thus to be valued apart from their mere utility:

> Let this be our principle: that the use of God's gifts is not wrongly directed when it is referred to that end which the Author himself created and destined them for us, since he created them for our good, not for our ruin. Accordingly, no one will hold to a straighter path than he who diligently looks to this end. Now if we ponder to what end God created food, we shall find that he meant not only to provide for necessity but also for delight and good cheer. Thus the purpose of clothing, apart from necessity, was comeliness and decency. In grasses, trees, and fruits, apart from their various uses, there is beauty of appearance and pleasantness of odor [cf. Gen. 2:9]. For if this were not true, the prophet would not have reckoned them among the benefits of God, "that wine gladdens the heart of man, that oil makes his face shine" [Ps. 104:15].

Scripture would not have reminded us repeatedly, in commending his kindness, that he gave all such things to men. And the natural qualities themselves of things demonstrate sufficiently to what end and extent we may enjoy them. Has the Lord clothed the flowers with the great beauty that greets our eyes, the sweetness of smell that is wafted upon our nostrils, and yet will it be unlawful for our eyes to be affected by that beauty, or our sense of smell by the sweetness of that odor? What? Did he not so distinguish colors as to make some more lovely than others? What? Did he not endow gold and silver, ivory and marble, with a loveliness that renders them more precious than other metals or stones? Did he not, in short, render many things attractive to us, apart from their necessary use?

Away, then, with that inhuman philosophy which, while conceding only a necessary use of creatures, not only malignantly deprives us of the lawful fruit of God's beneficence but cannot be practiced unless it robs a man of all his senses and degrades him to a block. (*Institutes* 3.10.2–3)[3]

Natural beauty and the "delight" that creation offers are gifts of God, created "for our good." Calvin's stridency is unleashed on philosophy that is "inhuman," that is degrading to the Image of God and to God's boundless generosity.

Veneration of religious images, of course, was condemned as idolatry,[4] but Calvin, even in his iconoclasm, treated the subject of art with some delicacy (*Institutes* 1.11.12). "And yet I am not gripped by the superstition of thinking absolutely no images permissible," writes Calvin, for whom irrational fear of icons is as superstitious as irrational adoration. "But because sculpture and painting are gifts of God, I seek a pure and legitimate use of each." Art is given by God "for his glory and our good"; the problem with the icons is that they obscure God's glory by limiting the Infinite to a visible form and that they are destructive of human good by causing violation of the Second Commandment. In his discussion of religious images, Calvin, especially in Thomas Norton's influential English translation, seems to reject them partly on aesthetic grounds—"how much amiss and uncomely they were for the most part fashioned"—and offers practical guidelines for Christian artists: "Therefore it remains that only those things are to be sculptured or painted which the eyes are capable of seeing." This dictum, restricting art to the tangible and the sensory, may well lie behind the specificity and concreteness of "metaphysical" imagery.[5] Calvin also exempts art that depicts "histories and events," which "have some use in teaching or admonition," from his censure of religious images, most of which, he says, lack historicity, and can have a use of pleasure, though not teaching. Herbert's attack on allegory and "fictions" in "Jordan (1)" is in the same tradition as Calvin's dissatisfaction with art that attempts to convey abstractions rather than direct truth. Calvin's teachings on art, although perhaps destructive of certain kinds of art, may well have fostered the specificity and "realism" of the "metaphysical" poets and the Jacobean playwrights, and the careful scriptural "historicity" and precision of Milton.

Paradoxically, perhaps the most important artistic contribution of Calvin and his fellow iconoclasts is the secularization of art. Since every good and perfect gift comes from God (James 1:17), Calvin could ascribe the accomplishments of "pagan," classical civilization—rhetoric, philosophy, and mathematics—to the Spirit of God, who bestows natural gifts "indiscriminately upon pious and impious" (*Institutes* 2.2.14, 15–16). Art as a natural, secular activity with its own value, unconfounded by any pretensions to religious status, was thus encouraged by Reformation thought.[6] More directly, once the churches no longer patronized the making of religious images, the artists turned to other, mostly middle-class clientele. Even such secularization of art, however, often had a positive religious impetus. The iconoclasts of Zurich, for example, who, under Zwingli, were far more radical than Calvin, destroyed the religious art of the churches but actively encouraged portraiture. Leo Jud, one of Zwingli's colleagues, offers a distinction between artificial images of God made by human beings and the true image of God—that is, human beings—made by God himself. Portraits depict "living images made by God and not by the hands of men."[7]

Poetry, however, an art consisting of words, was relatively immune to the changes wrought by the Reformation in the pictorial arts[8] and could absorb the impact of Reformation spirituality in a fairly direct and complete way, as the earlier chapters should suggest. Reformation theology, according to Halewood, "describes and demands devotional experience, and its characteristic devotional experience conforms to the description of its theology."[9] Poetry likewise can spring from "devotional experience," and therefore Reformation theology can gloss such poetry with some precision.

The mysticism of Luther or Calvin is related to, but distinguishable from traditional mysticism,[10] and the religious poetry of George Herbert is different, in certain ways, from that of other religious poets. In conclusion, it may be helpful to briefly outline the qualities of Herbert's religious verse that characterize him as "a poet of the Reformation" *vis à vis* other poets whose religious verse is based in other theologies.

First of all, Herbert's poetry and the kind of spirituality it describes is incarnational rather than transcendent. That is, human beings do not transcend the world to achieve union with God;[11] rather, God enters the world to achieve union with human beings. The soul does not come to God; rather, God comes to the soul. The figures are of descent, rather than ascent. The spirituality of Herbert's poetry is thus rather different from traditional mysticism, especially that influenced by Neoplatonism.[12] Vaughan writes of soaring into the ring of eternity ("The World," 47);[13] Herbert, of God's breaking into the sphere of His own chaotic world ("The

Collar"). It is also different from medieval mysticism, which usually is organized into patterns of ascent (St. Bonaventure, *Journey of a Mind to God;* St. John of the Cross, *Ascent of Mt. Carmel*), depicting ordered stages of experience, so different from the randomness of the Christian life[14] presented by Herbert, wherein grace always comes as a surprise.

Related to the principle of God's descent as opposed to human ascent as a means of communion with God is the presentation of the will in religious verse. For Calvin, God's will is all-important; the human will is always sinful and must be realigned by the power of God. In Herbert's poetry, God is the active partner. The soul may be active, but it is so usually in fleeing from or rebelling against God ("The Collar"). Resolution comes when the soul surrenders its will to that of God ("The Crosse"). For a Calvinist, the will is not the means of salvation, but its obstacle. The great debates of the Calvinist tradition focus on the nature of God's choice in salvation. The Arminians, on the other hand, see salvation not so much as a matter of God's choice, but as a matter of human choice. The locus of eternity for Donne is his own will, so that Arminian religious poetry is, paradoxically, more human-centered, or more self-centered, so to speak, than that of a Calvinist such as Herbert, whose theology, and thus poetry, is radically "God-centered." Milton, the other great religious poet of the seventeenth-century, is also Arminian, as he confesses in *De Doctrina Christiana*. (Again, one must be cautious in drawing theological lines in terms of political or ecclesiastical controversies: Herbert the "Anglican" is Calvinist while Milton the "Puritan" is Arminian in their soteriology.) Milton's Arminianism helps to explain his humanism and the continual focus in his religious poetry on the human will as the arena of religious concern. Although Milton is, perhaps, not very successful in portraying God, he is a master in portraying the human will and its religious significance, from the rebellion of Satan and the fall of man, to Samson's repentance and Christ's successful victory over temptation. That Milton thinks of "Paradise Regained" in terms of Christ's temptation, rather than the Atonement, may or may not be significant. It illustrates, however, that Milton tended to imagine salvation as a battle of the will, an emphasis similar to Donne's, but very different, as has been seen, from Herbert's.[15] Milton's theology, of course, is original and complex, and he would probably satisfy an orthodox Arminian no more than an orthodox Calvinist. Still, the difference between Herbert and Milton, as well as Herbert and Donne, is a theological one, and their different understandings of the importance and nature of the human will mean that their religious poetry will be different in tone and in focus.

Emotionally, religious verse based in Reformation spirituality would tend to be marked by two balancing extremes—a deep awareness of one's sinfulness, balanced by a secure assurance of God's unconditional love. Theologically, for Luther, Law is balanced by Gospel; for Calvin, "total depravity" is balanced by "the perseverance of the saints." Psychologically, guilt is countered by "eternal security." These two poles help to define the range of Herbert's verse and the vacillations that so characterize a major section of *The Temple:*

> Philosophers have measur'd mountains,
> Fathomed the depths of seas, of states, and kings,
> Walk'd with a staffe to heav'n, and traced fountains:
>   But there are two vast, spacious things,
> The which to measure it doth more behove:
> Yet few there are that sound them; Sinne and Love.
>
> ("The Agonie," 1–6)

This poem, coming after "The Sacrifice" and the two poems of response to Christ's death, is placed significantly. The "two vast, spacious things . . . Sinne and Love," are announced at the outset as the two poles that will define the subject and the dynamic of the subsequent poems. Theologically, the tension between these two poles is resolved in the doctrine of sanctification, in which sin and grace, fear and confidence, are in conflict in the life of the Christian until the spirit's preordained victory over the flesh at death. The two poles thus not only help account for Herbert's variation of moods and tones but they also function formally—in the arrangement of the poetic sequence and also in particular poems, as expressions of "depravity" are ordered according to "Love's" overmastering purpose.

In dealing with these two seemingly opposite but related poles of religious experience, Herbert is correct when he says that "few there are that sound them." It is very difficult to keep both emotions in equilibrium. Bold assurance of one's acceptance before God may be psychologically comforting, but it can result in vapid religiosity, hypocrisy, and superficial, complacent religious verse. Emphasis on one's total depravity, on the other hand, may be psychologically crippling, although, as introspection and emotional conflict heighten, it can result in good religious poetry as in Donne and Cowper. Calvinists easily tip to either extreme, so that Calvinism is popularly associated both with smugness and with gloom. Nevertheless, as a unified spiritual system, Calvinism deals with these two opposite kinds of religious experience in such a way that both are affirmed and placed in relationship to each other in a psychologically sophisticated and coherent way.

The relationship between the doctrines of total depravity and eternal security, with their feelings of both guilt and assurance, and perhaps their resolution, is suggested by Samuel Hieron, an English cleric, in *A Help with Devotion* (1612). Hieron offers a meditation on three points, which, together, he says, are very helpful in prayer:

1. Humilitie and lowlinesse of spirit, begotten by the due consideration of Gods Maiestie. 2. Confidence and assurance to bee heard, bredde by the knowledge of Gods promises. 3. Fervencie of affection, springing from the apprehension of our own vileness.[16]

For Hieron, and seemingly for Herbert, "Humilitie and lowliness" and "confidence and assurance" do not contradict each other; together, they result in the love of God. Awareness of one's total depravity without the assurance of salvation would be horrible to consider, as would confidence in one's salvation apart from the recognition of oneself as a sinner. Together, the two points define a balanced Calvinist psychology, which, of course, would sometimes tip in one direction or the other (one thinks of Cowper, on one hand, and Cotton Mather, on the other). If one truly has "lowlinesse of spirit" and is nevertheless confident, not in oneself, but in God (by having faith in His promises), the result, according to Hieron, is "fervencie of affection," a love that comes, paradoxically, "from the apprehension of our own vileness." Love of God comes as a result of true conviction of sin. As Herbert develops in "The Agonie," only by understanding the true seriousness of sin can God's unconditional love be fully grasped.

Herbert is unusual in his ability to balance, intellectually and emotionally, the two poles of Reformation spirituality. He is thus able to write positive religious verse that expresses his confidence and security with God without being fatuous. He is also able to write, with great honesty, of his own sin and wretchedness without despairing, or, in what may be a cardinal sin for the religious poet, focusing solely upon himself rather than upon the true object of religious verse.

Herbert's kind of spirituality, which can be identified with that advocated by the early Reformation theologians, is not exclusively Protestant, but as a recurring kind of Christian experience—enshrined in St. Paul and St. Augustine—it has its own catholicity. Despite my generalizations about medieval mystics, patterns of descent are also present—as in St. Theresa—as is the theology of grace and the experience of Augustine. Francis Thompson was a Roman Catholic, but nowhere is there a more "Calvinist" poem than "The Hound of Heaven," in which the human being, far from seeking, flees from God, who actively pursues the sinner until he is overmastered by grace. By the same token, no writer seems to follow the points of Calvinism more closely than the Roman Catholic (perhaps Jansenist?) Flannery O'Connor. In *The Violent Bear It Away*, a totally depraved young man is elected and called to be a prophet. He tries to avoid this calling and to do everything he can to reject God, but God never forsakes him, until, in seeing he cannot escape God's plan, he succumbs to an irresistible grace (cf. "Miserie," 25–30).

To insist upon the relevance of the early Protestants for Herbert's poetry is thus not to challenge the universality, the catholicity of Herbert's appeal; if anything, it is to show the universality of the early Protestants, who are too often minimized by literary historians as "Puritans" or art-hating fanatics. More narrowly, to insist upon the relevance of the early Protestants for Herbert's poetry is to agree with Rosemond Tuve, that "a poem is most beautiful and most meaningful to us when it is read in terms of the tradition which gave it birth."[17] A "tradition" can, of course, be traced back through medieval and patristic models, in terms of which historical criticism of Herbert has usually focused. The Reformation, though, is part of that tradition.

Just as Calvin's theology helps to explain Herbert's poetry, Herbert's poetry helps to explain Calvin's theology. Calvinism is, as Coleridge says, a sheep in wolf's clothing; externally, it seems harsh and forbidding. Through Herbert's poetry it is possible to experience Calvinism from the inside, as it were, and thus to unveil its essential nature as a positive spiritual tradition within Christianity and within literature.

In Herbert's prayer after his sermon, the theological terms he uses are not abstractions. Not only did he know their technical meanings, but to him they were full of the kind of experience out of which poetry can be made:

> Blessed be God! and the Father of all mercy! who continueth to pour his benefits upon us. Thou hast elected us, thou hast called us, thou hast justified us, sanctified, and glorified us. ("A Prayer after Sermon," "The Country Parson," p. 290)[118]

The doctrine of election helps explain the security Herbert feels with God. The doctrines of election and calling lie behind Herbert's most famous poems ("You shall be he" ["Love (3)," 8]; "Me thought I heard one calling, *Child*" ["The Collar," 35]). Justification, sanctification, and glorification, in that order, describe the theological sequence of *The Temple*. In this prayer, on the occasion of having proclaimed God's Word, Herbert suggests the terms in which his religious life and his poetry can be interpreted.

Notes

Introduction

1. See John R. Roberts, *Essential Articles For the Study of George Herbert's Poetry* (Hamden, Conn.: Archon Books, 1979), pp. xi–xv for a helpful overview of Herbert criticism.
2. William Empson, *Seven Types of Ambiguity* (New York: New Directions, 1947), pp. 231–32.
3. Nevill Coghill, "The Approach to English," *Light on C. S. Lewis*, ed. Jocelyn Gibb (New York: Harcourt Brace Jovanovich, 1965), p. 61.
4. John Stachniewski, "Probing the Protestant Psyche," *Times Literary Supplement*, 7 March 1980, p. 272.
5. Hugh M. Richmond, Review of Barbara Lewalski's *Protestant Poetics*, *Renaissance Quarterly* 33 (1980): 298.
6. Heather A. R. Asals, *Equivocal Predication: George Herbert's Way to God* (Toronto: University of Toronto Press, 1981), pp. 4–5.
7. W. Brown Patterson, "Protestant Poetics," *Sewanee Review* 88 (1980): 654.
8. Barbara Lewalski, *Protestant Poetics and the Seventeenth-Century Religious Lyric* (Princeton, N.J.: Princeton Univ. Press, 1979), p. ix.
9. Patterson, "Protestant Poetics," p. 654.
10. J. T. Mueller, *Christian Dogmatics* (St. Louis, Mo.: Concordia Press, 1955), p. 437.

Chapter 1. Seventeenth-Century Anglicanism

1. S. T. Coleridge, "Notes on Jeremy Taylor," *Notes on English Divines*, ed. Derwent Coleridge (London: Edward Moxon, 1853), 1:253–54. Coleridge is quoted at length on the subject in the chapter on John Donne below.
2. For these terms and for a fuller discussion of them see Heinrich Bornkamm, *The Heart of Reformation Faith*, trans. John W. Doberstein (New York: Harper & Row, 1965), pp. 16ff.
3. See O. Kirn, "Grace," *The New Schaff-Herzog Encyclopedia of Religious Knowledge*, 5:42. For an authoritative discussion of the difference between the Roman Catholic concept of grace and that of the English Church see Richard Hooker, "Of Justification, Works, and How the Foundation of Faith is Overthrown," printed in *Of the Laws of Ecclesiastical Polity* (New York: Everyman's Library, 1963), 1:17–22.
4. See Williston Walker, *A History of the Christian Church*, rev. ed. (New York: Charles Scribner's Sons, 1959), pp. 444–45. It should be noted that for Reformation theology one is saved neither by works nor by faith *per se*—the conventional tension within Christianity—but by grace (cf. Eph. 2:8), with both works and faith defined as corollaries. See Wilhelm Niesel, *The Theology of Calvin*, trans. Harold Knight (Philadelphia: Westminster Press, 1956), pp. 136–37.
5. See Walker, *A History*, p. 368 and Charles H. and Katherine George, *The Protestant Mind of the English Reformation* (Princeton, N.J.: Princeton Univ. Press, 1961).

251

6. See *The Book of Concord: The Confessions of the Evangelical Lutheran Church*, trans. Theodore G. Tappert (Philadelphia: Fortress Press, 1959), passim.

7. Discussed in Harold Porter, *Reformation and Reaction in Tudor Cambridge* (Cambridge: Cambridge Univ. Press, 1958).

8. George, *Protestant Mind*, p. 371.

9. For illustrations of these points see C. S. Lewis, *English Literature in the Sixteenth Century Excluding Drama* (London: Oxford Univ. Press, 1954), p. 34.

10. See Basil Hall, "Calvin against the Calvinists," *John Calvin*, ed. C. E. Duffield, Courtenay Studies in Reformation Theology (Grand Rapids, Mich.: Wm. B. Eerdmans, 1966). For popular distortions of Calvin see J. I. Packer, "Calvin the Theologian," pp. 149–51 et passim in the same volume.

11. George, *Protestant Mind*, pp. 311, 354.

12. Basil Hall, "Puritanism: the Problem of Definition," *Studies in Church History*, ed. C. J. Cuming (London: Thomas Nelson, 1965), 2:293–94.

13. Quoted in ibid., 2:292.

14. George, *Protestant Mind*, pp. 368–69.

15. Cited in Hall, "Puritanism," 2:290.

16. *The Sermons of John Donne*, ed. Evelyn M. Simpson and George Potter (Berkeley: Univ. of California Press, 1956), 9:166.

17. George, *Protestant Mind*, pp. 70–71. See also Lewalski, *Protestant Poetics*, pp. 13–14.

18. Walker, *A History*, pp. 406–7.

19. Florence Higham, *Catholic and Reformed: A Study of the Anglican Church 1559–1662* (London: S.P.C.K., 1962), p. 20.

20. George, *Protestant Mind*, p. 66.

21. C. J. Stranks, *Anglican Devotion* (London: SCM Press, 1961), pp. 35 ff.

22. J. S. Whale, *The Protestant Tradition* (Cambridge: Cambridge Univ. Press, 1955), p. 127.

23. Lawrence Sasek, *The Literary Temper of the English Puritans* (Baton Rouge: Louisiana State Univ. Press, 1961), p. 15.

24. Ibid., pp. 92ff. The main objection was to the social consequences of playhouses, which were seen as breeding grounds of crime, disease, and immorality.

25. J. F. H. New, *Anglican and Puritan: The Basis of Their Opposition 1558–1640* (Stanford: Stanford Univ. Press, 1964), takes issue with the Georges (see pp. 104–5) and others, arguing that the traditional distinction between Anglican and Puritan is real and important, but attempting to define the terms more carefully. He concedes, though, their large theological agreement—including predestination and their understanding of the sacraments. He focuses on more subtle nuances and emphases—"Anglicans" tend to have a higher regard for human reason, to emphasize joy rather than judgment in the last days, to be moral perfectionists, etc. Still, the categories seem to break down. Stanley Fish, *Self-Consuming Artifacts* (Berkeley: Univ. of California Press, 1972), pp. 70–77, praises "Anglican" sermons for their skepticism, which he prefers to the self-confident rationalism of the "Puritan" ones. New himself illustrates "Anglican" traditionalism and reverence for the sacraments by suggesting that a useful distinguishing notion between the two parties is that of infant damnation. "Anglicans" tend to believe, with Augustine, that unbaptized infants are damned; "Puritans" on the other hand, strongly reject Augustine on this point, insisting that unbaptized infants can be saved by the grace of God—here the "Puritans," not the "Anglicans," seem to be emphasizing apocalyptic joy rather than judgment. Similarly, the "Anglican" Donne, especially in his poetry, seems to emphasize the terror rather than the joy of the last days. "Moral perfectionism," on the other hand, is probably a fair characterization of the Arminian position, but it is a quality for which the "Puritans" are generally disliked. New's treatment is learned and useful in trying to link seventeenth-century controversies to the outbreak of the Civil War, which the Georges tend to neglect, and, in redefining the terms he overturns many of the traditional misunderstandings. The main problem with his study is, as the Georges document, that any given member of the Church of England is likely to have any number of "Puritan" beliefs and any number of "Anglican" beliefs. No particular individual is likely to conform to large generalizations based on selective data. Second, New accepts the conventional "Puritan" view of John Calvin, although he classifies the great Calvinist apologists Jewel, Sandys, and Ussher as "Anglicans."

26. The text and the translations of Herbert's Latin poetry are taken from Mark McCloskey

and Paul R. Murphy, *The Latin Poetry of George Herbert: A Bilingual Edition* (Athens: Ohio Univ. Press, 1965).

27. See A. G. Dickens, *The English Reformation* (New York: Schocken Books, 1964), p. 314.

28. References to Calvin's *Institutes* are to the book, chapter, and section numbers. Quotations, except where otherwise noted, are from John Calvin, *Institutes of the Christian Religion*, ed. John T. McNeill, trans. Ford Lewis Battles, 2 vols., Library of Christian Classics, vols. 20 and 21 (Philadelphia: Westminster Press, 1960).

29. All quotations of Herbert's English works are taken from *The Works of George Herbert*, ed. F. E. Hutchinson (Oxford: Clarendon Press, 1941). References to the prose works are to the chapter and the page number in Hutchinson. C. A. Patrides, ed., *The English Poems of George Herbert* (London: Everyman's Library, 1974), has also been consulted.

30. "Donne's Sources," *Sermons*, 10:375.

31. See Richard Hooker, "A Learned and Comfortable Sermon of the Certainty and Perpetuity of Faith in the Elect," "A Learned Discourse of Justification, Works, and How the Foundation of Faith is Overthrown," and "Fragments of an Answer to the Letter of Certain English Protestants," printed in *Of the Laws of Ecclesiastical Polity*, 1:1–75; 2:490–543. For Hooker's praise of Calvin see 1:79ff.

32. Lewis, *English Literature*, p. 43.

33. Izaak Walton, "The Life of Mr. George Herbert," *Lives*, ed. Charles Hill Dick (London: Walter Scott, 1899), p. 210. The implications of the debate are discussed by Joseph H. Summers, *George Herbert: His Religion and Art* (Cambridge, Mass.: Harvard Univ. Press, 1954), pp. 57–58.

34. Cf. Richard Sibbes, *The Bruised Reede and Smoaking Flax* (1630), a Calvinist who similarly emphasizes God's mercy rather than His mystery. Cited by George, *Protestant Mind*, p. 65.

35. Whale, *Protestant Tradition*, p. 121.

36. Hutchinson, ed., *Works*, p. xliv.

37. Discussed by Summers, *George Herbert*, pp. 16–17.

38. William H. Halewood, *The Poetry of Grace* (New Haven, Conn.: Yale Univ. Press, 1970), p. 102.

39. Elsie A. Leach, "John Wesley's Use of George Herbert," *Huntington Library Quarterly* 16 (1963): 183–202.

40. For Walton's revisionism see Summers, *George Herbert*, pp. 28–29, and David Novarr and John But, *The Making of Walton's Lives* (Ithaca, N.Y.: Cornell Univ. Press, 1955), pp. 301–41.

41. Quoted in Ilona Bell, " 'Setting Foot into Divinity': George Herbert and the English Reformation," *Modern Language Quarterly* 38 (1977): 221.

42. Summers, *George Herbert*, pp. 28, 35.

43. Ibid., p. 58.

44. Rosemond Tuve, *A Reading of George Herbert* (London: Faber & Faber, 1952).

45. Louis Martz, *The Poetry of Meditation* (New Haven, Conn.: Yale Univ. Press, 1954).

46. Stranks, *Anglican Devotion*, pp. 13ff., 25–26, 35–36.

47. Halewood, *Poetry of Grace*, pp. 35–36, 40–41, 75, 79.

48. Rosemond Tuve, "George Herbert and Caritas," *Journal of the Warburg and Courtauld Institute* 22 (1959): 317.

49. Patrick Grant, *The Transformation of Sin: Studies in Donne, Herbert, Vaughan, and Traherne* (Amherst: Univ. of Massachusetts Press, 1974).

50. John R. Mulder, "George Herbert's *Temple*: Design and Methodology," *Seventeenth-Century News* 31 (1973): 37–45.

51. Harold Fisch, *Jerusalem and Albion: The Hebraic Factor in Seventeenth-Century Literature* (New York: Schocken Books, 1964), pp. 5ff, and Richard Strier, *Love Known: Theology and Experience in George Herbert's Poetry* (Chicago: Univ. of Chicago Press, 1983).

52. Stanley Stewart, "Time and *The Temple*," *Studies in English Literature 1500–1900* 6 (1966): 97–110.

53. Lewalski, *Protestant Poetics*, p. 283.

54. Stanley Fish, *Self-Consuming Artifacts: The Experience of Seventeenth-Century Literature* (Berkeley: Univ. of California Press, 1972), pp. 157–159.

55. Stanley Fish, *The Living Temple: George Herbert and Catechizing* (Berkeley: Univ. of California Press, 1978), p. 135.

56. Ibid., p. 136.

57. Sheridan D. Blau, "George Herbert's Homiletic Theory," *George Herbert Journal* 1 (Spring 1978): 26. Herbert died the year of Laud's accession, so that he could have had nothing to do with the "Laudian Church." Even if he "would have" followed Laud's political and ecclesiastical doctrines, his theological doctrines (which would include homiletic theory) would be another issue.

58. Helen Vendler, *The Poetry of George Herbert* (Cambridge, Mass.: Harvard Univ. Press, 1975), p. 136.

59. Arnold Stein, *George Herbert's Lyrics* (Baltimore, Md.: Johns Hopkins Univ. Press, 1968), p. vii.

60. Quoted in Walton, "The Life," p. 244.

Chapter 2. "Sinne and Love"

1. Thomas Norton, trans., *The Institution of Christian Religion*, by John Calvin, 6th ed. (London, 1634). The notion is repeated, with variations, by Bayly, who writes that "the knowledge of *Gods Majesty*, and Mans Misery [are] the first and chiefest grounds of the *Practice of Piety*" (p. 3).

2. See Summers, *George Herbert*, pp. 29–35.

3. E.g., Joan Bennett, *Four Metaphysical Poets* (New York: Random House, 1953), pp. 58–59.

4. See Sarah Appleton Weber, *Theology and Poetry in the Middle English Lyric* (Columbus: Ohio State Univ. Press, 1969), pp. 204–7, and Rosemary Woolf, *The English Religious Lyric in the Middle Ages* (London: Oxford Univ. Press, 1968), pp. 6ff., who uses Herbert as the example of the seventeenth-century religious poet, contrasting his poetry to medieval religious verse.

5. Edmund Bunny lists the *Institutes* and Luther's *Commentary on Galatians*, the two works I emphasize in this study. See Helen C. White, *English Devotional Literature 1600–1640*, Univ. of Wisconsin Studies in Lang. and Lit., no. 29 (Madison: Univ. of Wisconsin Press, 1931), pp. 66, 90, 93.

6. See Fish, *Living Temple*, pp. 1–25, for a discussion of this paradox in Herbert's poetry and in the critical literature, which generally stresses one pole or the other.

7. Quoted by Wilhelm Niesel, *The Theology of Calvin*, trans. Harold Knight (Philadelphia: Westminster Press, 1956), p. 80, from *Corpus Reformatorum*, 36:535.

8. Quoted by Gerhard Ebeling, *Luther: An Introduction to His Thought*, trans. R. A. Wilson (London: Collins, 1970), p. 215, from *Disputatio contra scholasticam theologiam* (1517).

9. Calvin puts a good deal of weight on the radical consequences of Adam's Fall, but he quarrels with the notion of mere inherited guilt, insisting, in Niesel's words, that "it is not innocently and without having deserved it that we have to bear the guilt of Adam's transgression" (p. 86). Calvin went as far as to say that the Divine Image itself was nearly, though not completely, obliterated in man, to be "restored" in the redemption (*Institutes* 3.3.8), an extreme notion echoed in Herbert's poem "The Sinner" (12): "Lord restore thine image."

10. Cf. Augustine, "whatever good you have is from him [God]: whatever evil, from yourself," which Calvin quotes from Augustine's *Sermons*, 176. 5–6 (*Institutes* 2.2.27).

11. Citations from the Thirty-Nine Articles are from John H. Leith, ed., *Creeds of the Churches* (Garden City, N.Y.: Anchor Books, 1963), pp. 266–81.

12. "Quodlibetal Questions." 8.9.19. Translation from *The Pocket Aquinas*, ed. Vernon J. Bourke (New York: Washington Square Press, 1960), p. 192.

13. Quoted in Niesel, *Theology of Calvin*, p. 138, from *Corpus Reformatorum*, 39:120.

14. Niesel's translation, p. 111. Compare Herbert's analogy of a man fallen into a ditch and needing a helper, in "Country Parson," 21:257.

15. See Herman Hanko et al., *The Five Points of Calvinism* (Grand Rapids, Mich.: Reformed Free Publishing Association, 1976), passim.

16. "Lectures on Galatians" (1535), ed. Jaroslav Pelikan, *Luther's Works* (St. Louis, Mo.: Concordia, 1963), 26:6. Luther returns to the figure on pp. 8 and 11. For the popularity of this work, which went through eight editions in England from 1574 to 1635, see White, *English Devotional Literature*, p. 93. Lutheranism was not a major theological influence in England in the early seventeenth century. Calvin is the theological and the intellectual authority; Luther,

however, articulates with the greatest subtlety the experiential side of Reformed spirituality. He is thus a useful guide to Herbert's poetry. Luther's "Lectures on Galatians" was especially valued as a devotional text. Bunyan, in *Grace Abounding*, prefers it to all books but the Bible "as most fit for a wounded conscience." Occasionally, as this study will point out, Herbert does seem to directly allude to or draw from Luther's writings.

17. With the allusion to Gen. 3:17, the curse of Adam, Herbert not only describes the spiritual condition, but theologically accounts for it as well.

18. Water as a symbol of grace is employed fairly consistently by Herbert. The sacramental imagery of baptism is also no doubt behind the figure. In "Whitsunday" and "The Water-course" Herbert depicts the means by which grace is conveyed by the symbolism of water pipes. In "Whitsunday" the "pipes of gold, which brought / That cordiall water to our ground" are the Twelve Apostles (seen not in terms of Apostolic succession, but in the characteristic Reformation emphasis on the Primitive church and the Apostolic testimony recorded in the Scriptures). In "The Water-course" the figure is more complex, with the corollary of the theology of grace, predestination, fully realized. Cf. Calvin's metaphor of water flowing through channels in *Institutes* 4.17.9 and the discussion of the poem in chapter 4.

19. Halewood, *Poetry of Grace*, p. 24. That God works *upon* the heart, not within it or in conjunction with it, is emphasized also in the Protestant emblem books, according to Barbara Lewalski, who contrasts Protestant emblems with those deriving from Roman Catholicism (*Protestant Poetics*, p. 195).

20. This is essentially the thesis of Halewood's book, *Poetry of Grace*, to which this chapter is indebted.

21. See Calvin, *Institutes* 3.3.10–14. Calvin's insistence that believers must still struggle with sin would be challenged by later Arminians, who would argue that moral perfection is possible in this life. See chapter 6 on sanctification.

22. Calvin quotes Augustine, speaking of God, "whom no man's free choice resists when he wills to save him" (*On Rebuke and Grace* 5.8; *Institutes* 3.23.14).

23. "Solid Declaration," Article 2, *Formula of Concord*, in *Book of Concord*, pp. 532–33.

24. "Epitome," Article 11, *Formula of Concord* in *Book of Concord*, p. 496.

25. Halewood, *Poetry of Grace*, p. 99.

26. See Sr. Thekla, *George Herbert: Idea and Image* (Normanby, England: Greek Orthodox Monastery of the Assumption, 1974), p. 104.

27. Summers, *George Herbert*, p. 136.

28. The Reformers insisted that human reason, no less than the will, was damaged by the Fall.

29. Halewood, *Poetry of Grace*, p. 98.

30. For Calvin's doctrine of effectual calling see Calvin, *Institutes* 3.24.1–2, et passim.

31. Halewood, *Poetry of Grace*, p. 98.

32. Summers, *George Herbert*, pp. 90–92.

Chapter 3. Justification by Faith

1. See, for example, John David Walker, "The Architectonics of George Herbert's *The Temple*," *ELH* 29 (1962): 289–305 and Summers, *George Herbert*, pp. 83–90. For other discussions of the unity of *The Temple* see Jerry Leath Mills, "Recent Studies in Herbert," *English Literary Renaissance* 6 (1976): 111–13. Barbara Lewalski, *Protestant Poetics*, has also noticed the sequence of Justification and Sanctification in "The Church," pp. 286–87, which this study develops in detail. See also Richard Strier, *Love Known*. Since I was reading his book as I was correcting my galleys, I was not able to make use of his insights, but he explores in provocative depth the importance of justification to Herbert's poetry.

2. E. G. Rupp, *Studies in the Making of the English Protestant Tradition* (Cambridge: Cambridge Univ. Press, 1966), pp. 170–71.

3. Quoted in ibid., p. 170, from *Disput de fide* (1537), 1:6.

4. Quoted in Philip Hughes, *Theology of the English Reformers* (London: Hodder and Stoughton, 1965), pp. 49–50, from "Homily of Salvation," *Works*, 2:129.

5. Philip Hughes, *Theology*, p. 70.

6. Luther, "Galatians," p. 7.

7. See Ebeling, *Luther,* p. 139.

8. Luther, "Galatians," 26:308.

9. See Ebeling, *Luther,* p. 138.

10. Luther, "Galatians," 26:309.

11. Fish, *The Living Temple,* p. 130.

12. Ibid., p. 131.

13. Ibid., pp. 126–27. What Herbert expresses positively in "Superliminare," Calvin expresses negatively, but the image is the same: "Those who despise the spiritual food of the soul which Christ offers to them in the church deserve to perish from terrible hunger." Quoted by Niesel, *Theology of Calvin,* pp. 185–86, from *Corpus Reformatorum,* 84:14.

14. Luther, "Galatians," 26:310. In the Lutheran tradition, one "applies" the law to someone who is complacent and self-satisfied; one "applies" the Gospel, the message of free forgiveness through Christ, to "the terrified" and guilt-ridden. This alternation of Law and Gospel is made throughout the Christian's life, just as the *usus theologicus* of the Law is stressed throughout Herbert's section "The Church." See Mueller, *Christian Dogmatics,* p. 480.

15. Hutchinson, ed., *Works,* p. 100.

16. For the importance of historicity for the early Protestants, as compared to the Roman Catholic devotions of participation, see Ilona Bell, *Modern Language Quarterly,* who provocatively discusses this poem.

17. Bayly lists similar paradoxes in his contemplation of the Passion (*Practice of Piety,* pp. 805–6): "the servant doth the *fault,* the *master* endures the *strokes;*" "I did eat the *forbidden fruit,* and thou didst hang on the *cursed tree:*" Eve laughed, Mary cried; I tasted sweet fruit, you tasted gall, etc.

18. Tuve, *A Reading of George Herbert,* pp. 74–75.

19. Halewood, *Poetry of Grace,* p. 97; see also Tuve, *A Reading,* p. 68.

20. The Reformation, unlike medieval Catholicism with its teaching of "the harrowing of Hell," stressed that the Old Testament saints were also saved by Christ, insofar as they were "God's chosen people" (elected by grace out of all nations), expressing faith in the Messiah of prophecy, and in the typological sacrifices and experiences that looked forward to Christ. See Lewalski's discussion of the point, *Protestant Poetics,* pp. 125–29.

21. For Calvin's idea of "common grace" that extends "even to a crumb of bread" (*Institutes* 3.20.44), see 2.2.17n.

22. Patrick Grant, *The Transformation of Sin,* p. 124. See Grant's entire reading of the poem, to which I am indebted. See also Bell, *Modern Language Quarterly,* p. 238, who comments that "the speaker has come too late to participate. The careful attention to details of time—'long,' 'new,' 'th'old,' 'lately,' 'Long since,' 'straight,' 'At length,' 'straight'—clearly places the speaker in a Protestant world of history and sequence rather than a medieval or Catholic world of ritual reenactment and timelessness."

23. Cf. Fish, *Self-Consuming Artifacts,* p. 170: "Christ's entry into the heart is not conditional on its disposition to receive him."

24. Fish, *Living Temple,* pp. 1–11.

25. Herbert draws the corollary that "A peasant may beleeve as much / As a great Clerk, and reach the highest stature" (29–30), a typically Protestant point directed against the Roman Catholic notion of vocational hierarchies in the religious life. The Protestant doctrine of faith implied that even a peasant could "reach the highest stature," which was not based on the supererogatory "merits" of monasticism or a religious order. See chapter 8.

26. See Calvin, *Institutes* 3.11.2, 23. The doctrine of imputation was so important to Herbert that he had the text of Col. 3:3, "Our life is hid with Christ in God," painted in Bemerton Church at his wife's pew (Hutchinson, ed., *Works,* p. 505).

27. Hutchinson, ed., *Works,* pp. 542–43, points out that "heare" was misprinted "here" in all editions from 1660–1799, which was taken by Coleridge, at least, to mean that Herbert approved of the doctrine of merit.

28. Tuve, *A Reading,* pp. 165–68, who also points to an iconographical tradition of the scales of God's justice being the Cross ("like some torturing engine" [10]). Helen Vendler, *Poetry of George Herbert,* p. 76, points out in the poem that "although God (and his attributes) cannot change, God seems to us to change. . . . while the 'God of justice' of the Old Law

seems to become the 'God of mercy' in the New Law, since God is unchanging, it is actually our 'angle of vision' that makes us see now one aspect, now another."

29. *Corpus Reformatorum*, 37:335. Niesel's translation, p. 145.

30. See Calvin, *Institutes* 3.2.17.

31. See Helen Vendler, *Poetry of George Herbert*, pp. 159–60, whose comments on the poem point to Reformation spirituality. She observes that although his sins are not seen by God, he sees them. His failures to God are "balls of winde," but to himself, they are "balls of wilde-fire." This tension between having been forgiven and the experience of guilt animates the poem. On the resolution, Vendler comments as follows:

> The undeserved tenderness of this response—that one's bubble, "balls of winde," should be dignified with the name of "work" and found "sufficient"—comes as an "unmotivated" response on God's part. What guarantees for a reader the believability of God's words? After all, he has been "crost" (the pun is no doubt deliberate). Christ's words of forgiveness on the cross acknowledged, after all, the practical wickedness of men's acts, while excusing man on the basis of ignorance. Here, God's words are even more generous, relabeling foam as "work," and not forgiving indebtedness but rather acting as though it had been sufficiently repaid. We are meant to be struck, relieved, and yet mystified by God's attitude, not yet knowing exactly whence it proceeds.

"It proceeds," of course, from grace, as defined in the dogma of Reformation theology.

32. 2 Cor. 5:, Eph. 4:22–24, Col. 3:9. Vendler, in contrast, sees the third stanza as the "least Pauline" (*Poetry of George Herbert*, p. 121). Although she reads "Aaron" as a conversion poem, her assumption that Herbert is "re-inventing" the poem—changing his mind, dismissing the first harsh judgment for the self-acceptance of the last stanza—misses the continuity of the experience as it was understood by Reformation theology.

33. The point is made by Vendler, *Poetry of George Herbert*, p. 119.

34. Vendler, *Poetry of George Herbert*, p. 119.

Chapter 4. *"Unspeakable Comfort"*

1. *Summa Theologica* 1.23. See *Institutes* 3.22.3, 9 and the editor's notes for Calvin's summary and objections. Aquinas's understanding of the terms is not, of course, that of Calvin.

2. Walton, "The Life," p. 210.

3. Summers, *George Herbert*, pp. 58ff.

4. Herbert's illustration of the sun in the course of his discussion is also used by Calvin, who discusses the example at length. See *Institutes* 1.16.2.

5. See also *Corpus Reformatorum*, 32:359, quoted and discussed in Niesel, p. 70.

6. See Stanley Stewart, "Time and *The Temple*," pp. 107–9, who traces the poem's refrain to Pss. 89:6 and 139:17, on God's providence, and who quotes from Calvin's commentary on the Psalms in connection with the poem.

7. Michael McCanles, *Dialectical Criticism and Renaissance Literature* (Berkeley: Univ. of California Press, 1975).

8. Quoted in Calvin, *Institutes* 3.23.14, from *Rebuke and Grace* 5.8.

9. See *Institutes* 1.16.3.

10. Cf. ibid., 1.16.5.

11. M. K. Sutton, "The Drama of Full Consent in Herbert and Hopkins" (unpublished paper), contrasts Herbert's view with that of Hardy and his "Satires of Circumstance." See also *Institutes* 1.17.10 for a discussion of the contingency of life and the security offered by a belief in providence.

12. Niesel, *The Theology of Calvin*, p. 75.

13. See Calvin, *Institutes* 3.23.3.

14. George, *The Protestant Mind*, p. 56.

15. It is important to understand that Calvin did not deny that human choice is involved in salvation. It is precisely the will, however, that is converted by grace (*Institutes* 2.3.6–14). Calvinist evangelists agree that "whosoever will may come" (Rev. 22:17). "The will to come," according to an apologist for Calvinism, "is only an indication that the will of the Father has been drawing us, and working in us to cause us to want to come to Him" (Hanko, back cover).

16. Quoted and discussed in Porter, *Reformation and Reaction*, p. 313.

17. See Luther's *The Bondage of the Will*, *Works*, 33:288–89 for the connection between salvation by grace and the believer's assurance of salvation.

18. Philip Hughes, *Theology*, p. 52.

19. From the first edition of Calvin, *Institutes* 3.24.6, quoted in Niesel, *Theology of Calvin*, p. 169. For a good discussion of predestination and its connection to the assurance of salvation see Horton Davies, *Worship and Theology in England* (Princeton, N.J.: Princeton Univ. Press, 1970), 1:56–59.

20. Philip Hughes, *Theology*, p. 56. See also Lewis, *English Literature*, pp. 43ff.

21. Basil Hall, "Calvin Against the Calvinists," p. 29. Other deviations, according to Hall, were the rise of pragmatism, the emphasis on predestination as determinism, and the minimizing of the Church. It is often said, for instance by Max Weber in his influential work on the rise of capitalism, that "Calvinists" believed that material prosperity was a sign of God's favor, and hence, of election. Calvin, on the other hand, teaches that "Faith does not certainly promise itself either length of years or honor or riches in this life, since the Lord willed that none of these things be appointed for us. But it is content with this certainty: that, however many things fail us that have to do with the maintenance of this life, God will never fail" (*Institutes* 3.2.28).

22. From the first edition of Calvin's *Institutes* 3.14.20, quoted by Niesel, *Theology of Calvin*, p. 179.

23. The desire to produce "fruit" is a major theme, as in "Employment (2)" and "Affliction (1)." Good works are a response to grace, and Herbert deeply desires to serve God. He is often frustrated about his barrenness, but he is not wondering if he is going to be damned.

24. Quoted and commented upon in Philip Hughes, *Theology*, p. 86, from Bradford's *Works*, 1:297ff. See also Hanko, p. 95, for worry about election as evidence for election.

25. "Of the Certainty and Perpetuity of Faith in the Elect," printed in *Ecclesiastical Polity*, 1:7. Cf. Luther, "Galatians," 26:376ff. Herbert also uses consciousness of sin as evidence of God's love in "The Country Parson," 34:283.

26. Hooker, "Of the Certainty," 1:3.

27. Ibid., 1:5–6.

28. Jane E. Wolfe, "George Herbert's 'Assurance,'" *College Language Association Journal* 5 (1962): 213–22, says that the poem is addressed to Satan. Thoughts of doubt over one's salvation were seen as stratagems of the devil. Whether the poem is addressed to Satan (see 17–18), or simply to the "spitefull bitter thought" (1), Herbert recognizes how his own introspection and ruminations contribute to his uncertainty: "When wit contrives to meet with thee, / No such rank poyson can there be" (5–6).

29. Williston Walker, *History*, pp. 389–90. Melanchthon's notion of "synergism" was rejected by the Lutheran confessions in favor of the earlier Reformation position discussed here.

30. Bacon, in *The Advancement of Learning*, was discussing medieval scholasticism. The figure was borrowed by Swift in "The Battle of the Books."

31. Hooker, "Of the Certainty," p. 8.

32. Quoted in Philip Hughes, *Theology*, pp. 71–72, from Sandys, *Works*, pp. 184ff. See also his quotation from Bishop Jewell, pp. 72–73.

33. Quoted in Niesel, *Theology of Calvin*, p. 153, from *Corpus Reformatorum*, 45:218.

34. Summers, *George Herbert*, p. 126.

35. Calvin, *Institutes* 3.3.10–15. Later Arminians, such as some followers of Wesley, would disagree, insisting that after regeneration a sinless life is possible.

36. Summers, *George Herbert*, p. 125.

37. Fish, *Living Temple*, p. 5.

38. Grant, *Transformation of Sin*, p. 123. Grant's discussion of Herbert's Augustinianism includes a discussion of the formal implications of predestination, to which this section is indebted.

39. Halewood, *Poetry of Grace*, pp. 91–95, draws parallels between "The Collar" and a passage from Calvin's *Commentary on the Gospel According to John*, which employs the symbols of labor, fruit, harvest, crown, etc., in a discussion of human slothfulness, the duties of a minister, and God's grace.

40. Grant, *Transformation of Sin*, p. 125.

41. Ibid.

42. Vendler, *Poetry of George Herbert*, p. 45.

43. See Fish's discussion of this poem in *Living Temple*, pp. 30–35. "The answer to its question is given twice (in the title and the first word) even before it begins. . . . That raised another question, not of what is going on, but of why *anything* is going on, since in the first line and one half everything seems to be already settled" (pp. 30–31).

44. Fish, *Living Temple*, p. 34.

45. Ibid., p. 169.

46. Rudolf Otto, *The Idea of the Holy*, trans. John W. Harvey (New York: Oxford Univ. Press, 1950), p. 89.

47. Niesel, *Theology of Calvin*, p. 9.

Chapter 5. Calvinist and Arminian

1. Louis Martz, "The Action of the Self: Devotional Poetry in the Seventeenth-Century," *Metaphysical Poetry*, ed. Malcolm Bradbury and David Palmer, Stratford-Upon-Avon Studies, no. 11 (New York: St. Martin's Press, 1970), p. 108. See also George Williamson, *The Donne Tradition* (Cambridge, Mass.: Harvard Univ. Press, 1930), p. 100 and Helen White, *The Metaphysical Poets* (New York: MacMillan, 1936), p. 198.

2. Margaret M. Blanchard, "The Leap into Darkness: Donne, Herbert, and God," *Renascence* 17 (1964): 38–50.

3. Ibid., p. 49. In fact, Protestants tended to denigrate intellectualized theology; justification by faith was experienced as a release from the uncertainty of a salvation based on "works"; the Reformers stressed a personal relationship with God; and "legalism" was precisely the enemy. For the Reformation doctrine of the Eucharist, see the chapter on "The Word of God" below.

4. Elsie Leach, "John Wesley's Use of George Herbert," *Huntington Library Quarterly* 16 (1953): 188–92. She also demonstrates, however, how Wesley, an Arminian, excises Calvinist references in his adaptations of Herbert's poetry in hymns. Wesley rejected "Judgement" and "Praise (1)" from his edition of Herbert's works, because they repudiate the Arminian doctrine of merit, ascribing salvation to the work of Christ alone rather than to one's virtues (p. 194).

5. Grant, *Transformation of Sin*, pp. 75–76, makes a similar point in regard to Herbert's Calvinism and Donne's Arminianism, although he searches for medieval prototypes rather than comparing the two in terms of the contemporary theological issues. Grant neglects the specific doctrine of eternal security.

6. C. F. Allison, *The Rise of Moralism: The Proclamation of the Gospel from Hooker to Baxter* (New York: Seabury Press, 1966), shows how traditional Reformation and Anglican views of justification by faith gradually gave way, through Arminianism and the consequent "holy living" divines (such as Jeremy Taylor), to moralism, to a Protestant legalism that reinstituted the notion of "salvation by works." Donne, however, is taken by Allison as representative of the older view. See especially Allison's discussion of the psychological issues raised by the two positions on pp. 209–10 and his chapter on Jeremy Taylor.

7. Porter, *Reformation and Reaction*, p. 281. Barrett was representative of a native English reaction against Calvinism that was not, strictly speaking, connected to the work of Jacobus Arminius on the Continent. Porter (p. 408) warns that the term *Arminian* is not strictly applicable to any English theologian before 1610. Still, the reactions against Calvinist soteriology assumed similar forms, which I am describing as "Arminian."

8. See E. Randolph Daniel, "Reconciliation, Covenant and Election: A Study in the Theology of John Donne," *Anglican Theological Review* 48 (1966): 14–30, which summarizes other treatments of Donne's theology and examines his thought in terms of covenant theology. Daniel does not treat Donne's apparent Arminianism, but stresses the "Puritan" elements of his thought—which, again, would not necessarily be in agreement with Calvin. Most studies of Donne's thought, rightly, are studies of his sermons. The question of eternal security is more important to his poetry than to his sermons, in which Donne, as pastor, in expounding Scripture rather than wrestling with his own personal fears, is more objective, often holding out more comfort to his flock than he would accept for himself. Barbara Lewalski reads the poems in terms of Calvinism (*Protestant Poetics*, pp. 15–20).

9. Allison, *Rise of Moralism*, p. 211.

10. See John Donne, "I. Prayer," *Devotions Upon Emergent Occasions*, ed. Anthony Raspa (Montreal: McGill-Queens Univ. Press, 1975), p. 9.

11. See *The Sermons of John Donne*, 5:53; 8:124.

12. George, *Protestant Mind*, p. 71.

13. Daniel, "Reconciliation, Covenant and Election," p. 17.

14. Quotations from Donne's poetry are from Helen Gardner, ed. *The Divine Poems of John Donne* (Oxford: Clarendon Press, 1964). Her numbering of the Holy Sonnets is given throughout, with Grierson's numbering in parentheses.

15. Donne, *Sermons*, 5:53.

16. Ibid., 10:63.

17. Ibid., 5:317.

18. See Barbara Lewalski's Calvinist reading of the poem, *Protestant Poetics*, pp. 271–72.

19. Donne, *Sermons*, 8:125.

20. Ibid., 2:264–65. Cf. 3:253, in which Donne relates the eternity of marriage to marriage of Christ and the believer. Here Donne is preaching in a Calvinist vein, but he then qualifies the analogy: "he hath given me not a presumptuous impossibility, but a modest infallibility that no sin of mine shall divorce or separate one from him."

21. Donne, *Sermons*, 7:262.

22. Ibid., 5:308.

23. Ibid., 5:300.

24. Ibid., 5:300–301.

25. Ibid., 5:266.

26. The peaceful tone of his deathbed poem, "Hymn to God my God, in my Sickness," thus acquires a greater significance.

27. See Allison, *Rise of Moralism*, pp. 63ff.

28. Cf. what is perhaps a similar unresolved opposition between repentance and grace in "At the round earth's imagin'd corners, blow" (4[7]:13–14):

> Teach mee how to repent; for that's as good
> As if thou hast seal'd my pardon, with thy blood.

Helen Gardner glosses the lines as follows: "True repentance is a guarantee that the general pardon purchased by Christ's blood is sealed to a man individually" (68). The gloss is perhaps accurate theology, but literally Donne is saying that repentance is "as good / As if" Christ "seal'd" his pardon. The terminology of salvation being "sealed" was used by Calvinists to express the inviolability of salvation. Donne is perhaps suggesting that the assurance that comes from repentance is on a par with the assurance of the doctrine of eternal security. The separating of the self and Christ, achieved not only by the comparison, but by the conditional voice ("As if . . ."), may be only another example of Donne's uncertainty.

29. Donne, *Sermons*, 10:63–64.

30. See Hanko, *Five Points of Calvinism*, pp. 57–59.

31. Herbert usually avoids this doctrine. In "Invitation" and "Whitsunday," 7–8, for instance, Herbert, like Donne and Luther, writes as if he believed everyone can be saved.

32. The poem was originally in Latin. This translation appeared with its first printing. See Gardner's Appendix, "Donne's Latin Poem to Herbert and Herbert's Reply," *Divine Poems*, pp. 138–47, for a discussion of the circumstances behind the exchange.

33. The poem was originally in Latin, but the translation is by Herbert. Gardner, ed., argues that *"In Sacram Anchoram Piscatoris,"* as printed by Hutchinson, is actually three separate poems (*Divine Poems*, pp. 145–46).

34. Gardner, ed., *Divine Poems*, p. 146.

35. Blanchard, "Leap into Darkness," pp. 40–41, shows how the largest part of "The Divine Poems" are addressed to the self. She also quotes Helen White in *The Metaphysical Poets*: "The center of interest is the devotee, not the Divinity." Herbert, on the other hand, addresses God in over a hundred of his poems. Of the seventy or so in which he does not, God himself speaks in ten (p. 42).

36. Coleridge, *Notes on English Divines*, 1:253–54. Leighton was a seventeenth-century

Calvinist Archbishop (1611–84) who, according to Hutchinson, ed., *Works*, p. xliv, often quoted Herbert's poetry.

Chapter 6. Sanctification

1. Walton, "The Life," p. 244.
2. Lewalski relates the struggles in *The Temple* to the process of sanctification, *Protestant Poetics*, p. 25.
3. Calvin, *Institutes* 3.16.1 and Niesel, *Theology of Calvin*, p. 138.
4. Calvin, *Corpus Reformatorum*, 31:317; quoted from Niesel, *Theology of Calvin*, p. 129.
5. Niesel, *Theology of Calvin*, p. 129.
6. Calvin, *Institutes* 3.3.9–15. The point was an important one for Reformation theology. Arminians, especially later, tended to hold out the possibility of moral perfection in a Christian. The Reformation position is asserted in Article 16 of the Thirty-nine Articles and by Herbert in "Notes on Valdesso," a man who seemed to leave open some moral reformation to merely human effort. Responds Herbert, "I can no more free my selfe from actuall sinnes after Baptisme, then I could of Originall before, and without Baptisme. The exemption from both, is by the Grace of God" (p. 308).
7. Lewalski has shown how Protestant translators of Catholic emblem books would purposefully break up the neat order of progression shown in their portrayal of the "stages" of the spiritual life. Lewalski sees randomness, that is, the episodic quality of the spiritual life, as a structural principle for the Protestants (*Protestant Politics*, pp. 192–96).
8. McCanles, *Dialectical Criticism*, p. 77.
9. Hooker, "Of the Certainty," 1:8.
10. Infant baptism, the idea that a child is received into forgiveness even before he can reason, is insisted upon by the Reformers. Lutherans in particular stress baptismal regeneration and that one should meditate on one's baptism for the assurance of salvation. The Anabaptist position that an individual must make a conscious choice to be baptized, was rejected as dangerously Arminian. Baptism and salvation are gifts of God, imaging His choice and action, not those of the baptized. Since God does everything for salvation, it is possible for God to regenerate children even before they are born (Luke 1:15 is Calvin's example, *Institutes* 4.16.17). Calvin's connection between election and baptism, and the kind of meditation that Herbert is recommending in the poem are suggested in *Institutes* 4.16.21:

> If those whom the Lord has deigned to elect received the sign of regeneration but depart from the present life before they grow up, he renews them by the power, incomprehensible to us, of his Spirit, in whatever way he alone foresees will be expedient. If they happen to grow to an age at which they can be taught the truth of baptism, they shall be fixed with greater zeal for renewal, from learning that they were given the token of it in their first infancy in order that they might meditate upon it throughout life.

11. St. Bernard, "Sermons on the Song of Songs," 11:2, quoted in Calvin, *Institutes* 3.3.15.
12. For a discussion of this conflict see Philip Hughes, *Theology*, p. 85.
13. Bayly, "Practice of Piety," p. 697. His italics.
14. Philip Hughes, *Theology*, p. 85.
15. As the lines seem to be taken in Wilbur Sanders, " 'Childhood is Health': The Divine Poetry of George Herbert," *Melbourne Critical Review* 5 (1962): 3–15.
16. Thus Herbert's "H. Baptisme (2)" is followed by "Nature," which explicitly takes up the *psychomachia* theme ("O tame my heart").
17. The line is parallel not only in position and theme, but perhaps also through the bell-like chiming of the strong rhyme: "mone / Let me alone."
18. Not in *The Temple*. One of the poems in the Williams MS (Hutchinson, ed., *Works*, p. 204).
19. Hutchinson, ed., *Works*, p. 505, citing Aubrey's *Brief Lives*, pp. i, 310.
20. Hooker, "On the Certainty," 1:5–6.
21. Ibid., 1:6.

22. Ibid., 1:5.

23. Sr. Thekla, *George Herbert*, pp. 45ff. Similarly, "The Glimpse," is not about the contingency of grace, as Sr. Thekla says (pp. 48–51), but about the contingency of human feelings:

> Whither away delight?
> Thou cam'st but now: wilt thou so soon depart
> And give me up to night?
> For many weeks of lingering pain and smart
> But one half houre of comfort to my heart?
>
> (1–5)

The poem, on the literal level, is addressed not to God, but to "delight." The poem is about the desire for joy, the attempt to hold on to delight with "a slender thread" (20). That the "thou" of the poem is "delight" and not God, unless very indirectly, is evident in every stanza: "Yet if the heart that wept / Must let thee go, return when it doth knock" (21–22). Clearly, weeping does not cause God to leave; in fact, for Herbert, exactly the reverse is true, in that weeping is a sign of repentance ("Country Parson," 33:279 and, e.g., "Eph. 4.30"). Rather, weeping must let delight go. The scriptural allusion—"Knock, and it shall be opened unto you" (Matt. 7:7)—does show that God is involved, but, as with other biblical allusions in the poem, they point not to God's wrath, but to comfort.

24. The term is from Max Sutton, "The Drama of Full Consent in Herbert and Hopkins," p. 1.

25. Luther, *Galatians*, p. 5.

26. See Ilona Bell, "Setting Foot into Divinity," for a valuable discussion of the poem.

27. Fish, *Self-Consuming Artifacts*, p. 170.

28. Ibid., pp. 174–75.

29. Psalter of *Book of Common Prayer*. The title's allusion to Psalm 73 is noted by Hutchinson, ed., *Works*, p. 528.

30. See Amy Charles, *A Life of Herbert* (Ithaca, N.Y.: Cornell Univ. Press, 1977), pp. 150, 161, 173.

31. Hutchinson, ed., *Works*, p. 517.

32. Ibid.

33. Ibid., p. 84.

34. Ibid.

35. Ibid.

36. Ibid., pp. 84–85.

37. Ibid.

38. Calvin's two points, denial of the self and bearing the cross, are taken from Christ's injunction in Matt. 16:24.

39. In a somewhat different vein, Herbert, perhaps falling into the dilemma of a strict Calvinism, in "Church-lock and key" blames his own lack of desire for moral reformation on the sovereign will of God:

> But as cold hands are angrie with the fire,
>   And mend it still;
> So I do lay the want of my desire,
>   Not on my sinnes, or coldnesse, but thy will. (5–8)

The poem concludes with a stanza in which Christ pleads for the speaker—even though the speaker does not particularly feel like repenting, Christ's blood "pleads for me" (10). Sins, like stones in a stream, only make "His blouds sweet current much more loud to be" (12). The poem, which, like Calvinist doctrine in general, would worry an Arminian as being dangerously antinomian, does suggest how the doctrine of God's sovereignty over all events can be comforting as well as problematic. God in Christ does assume responsibility for human sin (see "Love [3]," 10–15).

40. Walton, "The Life," p. 219.

41. Bayly, *Practice of Piety*, p. 731. The metaphor derives from Heb. 12:5–11.

42. Hutchinson, ed., *Works*, p. 510. The ark is an especially appropriate symbol for a Calvinist ecclesiology. Like Noah and his family, the elect are preserved from the cataclysmic judgment that is to fall on the rest of the world.

43. For Herbert, "storms are the triumph of his art" ("The Bag," 5), and they almost invariably symbolize a condition of the soul. In "The Storm," the figure is explicitly internalized:

> Starres have their storms, ev'n in a high degree
> As well as we.
> A throbbing conscience spurred by remorse
> Hath a strange force.
>
> (7–10)

The poem concludes by praising storms, both external and internal ones:

> Poets have wrong'd poore storms: such dayes are best;
> They purge the aire without, within the breast.
>
> (17–18)

In "Affliction (1)" Herbert speaks of being "blown through with ev'ry storm and wind" (36), and in the "Country Parson," 9:237, he writes of the need *"to be clothed with perfect patience, and Christian fortitude in the cold midnight stormes of persecution and adversity."*

44. *Works*, 1:463ff.; quoted from Philip Hughes, *Theology*, pp. 100–101.

45. Luther, "The Seven Penitential Psalms" (1517), 14:141.

46. Luther, *The Bondage of the Will*, 33:62. For a discussion of this aspect of Luther's thought see Walther Von Loewenich, *Luther's Theology of the Cross*, trans. Herbert J. A. Bouman (Minneapolis, Minn.: Augsburg, 1976), pp. 112–28. See also Ebeling, *Luther*, pp. 236–38, who observes that "the concealment of revelation under its opposite is a theme that dominates Luther's thought" (p. 238). Cf. "Justice (1)."

47. Luther, "First Psalm Lectures," 10:40.

48. See "Promises" in Wilson, *A Christian Dictionary* (1622). Cf. Calvin, *Institutes* 3.17.6. In Bunyan's *Pilgrim's Progress*, God's promises are the stepping stones set in the Slough of Despond.

49. The following poem, "The Bag," contains a response to the preceding poem of despair, as Hutchinson observes (*Works*, p. 520):

> Away despair! my gracious Lord doth heare.
> Though windes and waves assault my keel,
> He doth preserve it: he doth steer,
> Ev'n when the boat seems most to reel.
> Storms are the triumph of his art:
> Well may he close his eyes, but not his heart.
>
> (1–6)

Through the figure in Matt. 8:23–27 of Christ at first sleeping while His disciples were terrified of a storm, Herbert affirms God's never ending love, even when "His face" seems to be hidden ("Well may he close his eyes, but not his heart"), and asserts His providential control—not only of the believer's life during experiences of turmoil ("he doth steer . . ."), but also in the very design of suffering ("Storms are the triumph of his art"). Here too, Herbert explores suffering *sub specie aeternitatis*, without denying, and in fact, asserting, its dreadfulness.

50. *Institutes* 3.23.2. Calvin rejected the notion of "absolute might," that righteousness is defined as whatever God wills; rather, according to Calvin, God wills whatever is righteous. Calvin is often assumed to have held the former position (see ibid., n. 6). This does not mean that sinful human beings are qualified to judge God's righteousness or that he is accountable to them. "God will be the victor whenever he is judged by mortal man."

51. Mulder, "Design and Methodology," p. 48.

52. Luther, "Genesis," 4:359.

53. Cranmer, "Original Letters Relative to the English Reformation," 1:29; quoted from Philip Hughes, *Theology*, pp. 117–18.

54. Hutchinson, ed., *Works*, p. 505, observes that the sycamore was taken to be a species of fig tree; hence it would be associated with the shame of Adam and Eve.

55. A similar view of death in terms of the warfare between the regenerate soul and the unregenerate flesh is implicit in "Church-monuments."

> While that my soul repairs to her devotion,
> Here I intombe my flesh, that it betimes
> May take acquaintance of this heap of dust;
> To which the blast of deaths incessant motion,
> Fed with the exhalation of our crimes,
> Drives all at last. Therefore I gladly trust
> My bodie to this school, that it may learn
> To spell his elements, and finde his birth
> Written in dustie heraldrie and lines;
> Which dissolution sure doth best discern,
> Comparing dust with dust, and earth with earth.
>
> (1–11)

While the soul is focusing on God (1, 17), the flesh is made to focus on death, on its dissolution into dust, a meditation designed to curb the passions of the "wanton" flesh by showing it "How tame these ashes are, how free from lust" (23). Death is a function of sin (Rom. 6:23), being both punishment and cure. See Summers, *George Herbert*, pp. 129–35.

56. See C. A. Patrides' notes, ed., *The English Poems*, pp. 62, 190.

57. Hugh Latimer, *Works*, 1:463ff.; quoted from Philip Hughes, *Theology*, pp. 101–2.

58. Luther, "Genesis," 8:74.

59. See Fish, *Living Temple*, p. 136.

60. Fish, *Living Temple*, pp. 132–33. Fish is wrong, though, in saying that "Love (3)" merely reenacts the conflicts and "confirms their durability" (p. 136). The realization that personal worthiness is not the point, that acceptance by God is unconditional, is the very resolution of sin and grace urged by Reformation theology. Fish, who misses the "sweetness" of these ideas for Herbert, takes the feast in the poem liturgically as having to do with the continuous issue of whether one should accept the Eucharist, rather than as an apocalyptic resolution, with the soul being accepted into heaven.

61. Vendler, *Poetry of George Herbert*, p. 276, suggests that the source of the line is Luke 12:37: "Blessed are those servants, whom the Lord when he cometh shall find watching: verily I say unto you, that he shall gird himself, and make them to sit down to meat, and will come forth and serve them." The text further emphasizes the eschatological context of "Love (3)," centering on the return of Christ, at which time Christ will serve the servants.

62. See Valerie Carnes, "The Unity of George Herbert's *The Temple:* A Reconsideration," *ELH* 35 (1968): 523:

One of the predominant images of "The Church" was that of the human soul tortured "in the space / Betwixt this world and that of grace" ("Affliction [4]," 5–6), torn between the two realms of flesh and spirit, unable to move decisively in one direction or the other. "The Church Militant," however, transports the poet "beyond the anxious middle where we have our being" [Bonhoeffer] to the vantage point of Divinity where all things may be viewed *sub specie aeternitatis*, with celestial detachment and more than a touch of humor."

For the point that "The Church Militant" offers an "all-inclusive" view of the earlier issues see J. D. Walker, "The Architectonics of George Herbert's *The Temple*," p. 305. For the typological significance of the poem, and how it fits into the pattern of *The Temple*, see Lewalski, *Protestant Poetics*, pp. 288–89, 304.

63. The refrain is from Pss. 139:17, 89:6 (The Psalter of the *Book of Common Prayer*). Hutchinson, ed., *Works*, p. 544.

Chapter 7. The Word of God

1. Gerhard Ebeling, *Luther,* p. 61.

2. Andrew F. Walls, "Word," *Baker's Dictionary of Theology,* ed. Everett F. Harrison (Grand Rapids, Mich.: Baker Book House, 1960), p. 558, which also lists and discusses the different senses of the term. For an especially full theological discussion of the term see R. Seeburg, "The Word of God," *Schaff-Herzog Encyclopedia of Religious Knowledge,* 12:421–24.

3. See Wilson's entry for "Word" in *A Christian Dictionary,* and Williston Walker, *History of the Christian Church,* p. 304.

4. Theologically, the different senses of the concept were unified in a sophisticated way. Wilhelm Niesel, in *The Theology of Calvin,* shows how Calvin drew the relationship between them according to the Chalcedonian definition of the divine and human natures of Christ— "union but not fusion: distinction but not separation." "The relation between the words of scripture and the incarnate Word," according to Niesel's summary, "is analogous to that between the human nature of Christ and the Logos. The written word is not interchangeable with the one Word but neither is it separable from the latter. Exactly in the same way Calvin solves the question of the relation between the divine word and the human word in preaching and the problem which was then so much discussed: the relation between sign and thing signified in the Eucharist" (pp. 247–48). So with our relation to Christ, justification and sanctification, the Old Testament and New Testament, Law and Gospel, spiritual and secular power, the Trinity, etc. (pp. 248–49).

5. Ebeling, *Luther,* pp. 30–31.

6. Luther, *Works,* 34:336–37.

7. See Charles Garside, *Zwingli and the Arts* (New Haven, Conn.: Yale Univ. Press, 1966), passim., and the final chapter of this study.

8. Besides the Second Commandment and the warnings against idolatry throughout the Old Testament, New Testament passages such as Rom. 1:23, 25 and Acts 17:24ff. were cited by the iconoclasts. For the primacy of language, see Rom. 10:14ff.: "So faith comes from what is heard, and what is heard comes by the preaching of Christ" (10:17). Not all of the Protestants were iconoclasts, of course—Anglicans and Lutherans were much more conservative than Zwingli, with Calvin probably occupying a middle ground. The destruction caused by the iconoclasts is what brought Luther out of hiding at Wartburg Castle, such was his concern to stop them.

9. Garside, *Zwingli,* pp. 172–73.

10. Seeburg, "Word of God," p. 422.

11. For a treatment of this point see James H. Nichols, "The Intent of the Calvinist Liturgy," *The Heritage of John Calvin,* ed. John H. Bratt (Grand Rapids, Mich.: Eerdmans, 1973), pp. 87–109.

12. Philip Hughes quotes this commonplace from a number of English divines and in his discussion helps to unify the different senses of "the Word," as it was sacramentally and liturgically understood: "This word, which, audible in preaching, becomes visible in the sacrament is essentially the word of the Gospel. It is the word of Christ, or about Christ, who Himself is the Incarnate Word of God" (*Theology,* p. 192). Other doctrines were also presented in terms of the verbal metaphor. Adam's sin, according to Calvin, was unfaithfulness—Adam had faith neither in God's promises, that he could have eternal life in the garden, nor in God's threat, that in eating the fruit he would die. "Adam would have never dared oppose God's authority unless he had disbelieved in God's Word" (*Institutes* 2.1.4).

13. "If he be married," says Herbert of the Parson, "the choyce of his wife was made rather by his eare, than by his eye" ("The Country Parson," 9:238). But see "The H. Communion," 32 (excluded from *The Temple*), for the conventional classical formulation. See also Donne's Sermon on the blinding of Saul and his salvation through a voice (*Sermons,* 6:2205ff.). All of these examples are discussed by William G. Madsen, *From Shadowy Types to Truth: Studies in Milton's Symbolism* (New Haven, Conn.: Yale Univ. Press, 1968), pp. 159–62. Madsen's chapter "The Eye and the Ear" (pp. 145–80) further documents and suggestively analyzes this conceptual shift from the classical Platonic emphasis on vision to the Hebraic, biblical emphasis on hearing.

14. See Garside, *Zwingli,* p. 183. See also Paul Henry Lang, *Music in Western Civilization*

(New York: Norton, 1941), pp. 471ff. and Howard McKinney and W. R. Anderson, *Music in History: The Evolution of an Art* (New York: American Book Company, 1940), pp. 302ff.

15. Denis Donoghue, *Thieves of Fire* (London: Faber and Faber, 1973), pp. 22–23. Stanley Fish, on the other hand, and others, make much of an "Augustinian" skepticism about words as vehicles for Divine Truth, versus intuitive revelation. Barbara Lewalski, in *Protestant Poetics*, p. 6, shows how the Reformation disagreed with Augustine on this point, insisting that language could be the very embodiment of divine truth.

16. See Sheridan D. Blau, "George Herbert's Homiletic Theory," *George Herbert Journal* 1 (Spring 1978): 257.

17. The complexity of Herbert's multileveled wordplay and use of language is the subject of Mary Ellen Rickey's *Utmost Art: Complexity in the Verse of George Herbert* (Lexington: Univ. of Kentucky Press, 1966).

18. Margaret Blanchard, "Leap into Darkness," p. 38.

19. Blanchard, ibid., draws on Walter Ong, *The Barbarian Within* (New York: Macmillan, 1962), whose discussion of the aural versus the visual is of great interest in regard to "the Word." Rosemary Woolf, *The English Religious Lyric in the Middle Ages*, p. 12, observes that the imagery in medieval devotional poetry was almost always visual.

20. John Mulder, "*The Temple*: Design and Methodology," p. 37.

21. See Fish, *Living Temple*, pp. 30–35 and passim.

22. Tuve, *A Reading*, p. 126.

23. Walker, *History of the Christian Church*, p. 297. See also Luther, *Galatians*, p. 178.

24. Martz, *Poetry of Meditation*, p. 163. See also Halewood, *Poetry and Grace*, p. 31.

25. Quoted in Rupp, *The Making of the English Protestant Tradition*, p. 168, from Luther, *Commentary on Galatians*, trans. E. Middleton (1807), p. 245.

26. William R. Mueller, *John Donne, Preacher* (Princeton, N.J.: Princeton Univ. Press, 1962), p. 247. Quoted in Halewood, *Poetry and Grace*, p. 31.

27. Ilona Bell, "When Faith Did Change the Scene," p. 239. Speaking of the differences between Herbert and continental Catholic devotion, Bell makes a useful distinction: "The speaker remembers Christ's suffering, but he always yearns for Christ's spiritual presence in his life rather than his devotional presence in Christ's life" (p. 238).

28. Quoted by Niesel, *Theology of Calvin*, p. 116, from *Corpus Reformatorum* 55:226. See also Calvin, *Institutes* 1.5.9 and Luther, *Galatians*, 26:28–29.

29. See, for example, the notes in the Geneva Bible on Proverbs 8.

30. Niesel, *Theology of Calvin*, p. 35.

31. Quoted by Niesel, ibid., p. 27, from *Corpus Reformatorum* 47:125.

32. Niesel's translation, *Theology of Calvin*, p. 28.

33. See Florence Higham, *Catholic and Reformed*, p. 2. George, *Protestant Mind*, pp. 341 ff., shows how even Laud insisted upon an essentially Protestant view of Scripture, for which see Philip Hughes, *Theology*, pp. 11–44.

34. See the instructions and calendar of readings in *The Book of Common Prayer* (1559), ed. John E. Booty (Charlottesville: Univ. Press of Virginia, 1976), pp. 22–47.

35. C. J. Stranks, *Anglican Devotion*, p. 45.

36. Helen White, *English Devotional Literature*, pp. 161, 177.

37. See Donne's funeral sermon on Magdalene Herbert, *Sermons*, 8:86, 90–91.

38. Niesel, *Theology of Calvin*, pp. 22ff. It is important to note also that his followers regarded him in the same way. Scripture was the authority. "They went to Calvin for information or insight in about the same spirit as a modern Shakespearean scholar might go to Coleridge; they esteemed the text more highly than the annotation," as Perry Miller observes in *New England Mind: The Seventeenth-Century* (Cambridge, Mass.: Harvard Univ. Press, 1954), p. 93.

39. Calvinism has difficulty with various texts (e.g., Matt. 11:28, 18:14; 1 Tim. 2:4; Rev. 22:17); similarly, Arminianism can explain these texts but itself tends to minimize the biblical teachings on grace (John 10:26–29; Eph. 1:4–5). Both systems, however, are logically consistent. See Herbert Schneidau, *Sacred Discontent: The Bible and Western Tradition* (Berkeley: Univ. of California Press, 1976), for a discussion of how the Bible structurally resists and breaks down human systemizations. Modern evangelical theologians, who, like Calvin, emphasize the Bible's authority, tend to forgo the temptation to create an extrabiblical system. They tend

to accept some of the points of Calvin (such as "eternal security"), rejecting others (such as "limited atonement") for Arminius's view. Lutherans retain the paradoxes, seeing in them the differing functions of Law and Gospel. See Mueller, *Christian Dogmatics*, p. 483.

40. Harold Fisch, *Jerusalem and Albion*, pp. 3–4.

41. For a thorough discussion of Valdés and various connections to Herbert's poetry see Patrick Grant's chapter, "George Herbert and Juan de Valdés: The Franciscan Mode and Protestant Manner," in *The Transformation of Sin*, pp. 100–133. Grant seems to neglect the sense in which Herbert's notes are largely a refutation of Valdés.

42. For Reformation theologians, the Roman Catholic position that the Holy Spirit teaches through the papacy and the "enthusiast's" teaching that the Holy Spirit directly illumines the individual Christian, were both examples of the same error. According to Luther, both claim to know "by the Spirit," "without and before the Word" (Ebeling, *Luther*, p. 109). For examples and discussion of "spiritual" interpretations of the Scripture, see Madsen, *From Shadowy Types to Truth*, pp. 40ff. Milton, like other separatists, comes close to this position when he calls "spirit a more certain guide than Scripture" (*De Doctrina Christiana* 1.30).

43. Quoted in Philip Hughes, *Theology*, p. 41. See also R. C. Sproul, *Knowing Scripture* (Downers Grove, Ill.: InterVarsity Press, 1977), pp. 46–48. Thus narrative passages, such as the Gospels, were interpreted according to the theological passages, such as the Epistles.

44. "First Psalm Lecture," 10:4. See also Calvin, *Institutes* 2.5.19; ibid., n. 39; and, for an example of a Protestant attack on Catholic dogma supported by allegorical interpretation of the Scriptures, ibid., 3.4.4–5.

45. See Tuve, *A Reading*, pp. 138ff., who comments on "Anagram" and other typological representations of Mary in Herbert's poetry.

46. See the entry for "Esther" in *The Catholic Encyclopedia* (1909). A. J. Mass, in the article on *Exegesis*, ibid., mentions that the apocryphal Esther 15:13 ("Thou shalt not die: for our commandment touchest the commons, and not thee") has been used, questionably in his opinion, in support of the doctrine of the Immaculate Conception and, presumably, of the Assumption of the Blessed Virgin.

47. See Madsen's chapter, "Theories of Biblical Interpretation," *From Shadowy Types to Truth*, pp. 18ff., for a thorough discussion of Reformation hermeneutics and typology.

48. Barbara Lewalski, "Typology and Poetry," in *Illustrious Evidence: Approaches to English Literature of the Early Seventeenth Century*, ed. Earl Miner (Berkeley: Univ. of California Press, 1975), pp. 42–43. Her *Protestant Poetics* is the major study of Reformation typology and its importance for seventeenth-century poetry. For the difference between medieval exegesis and Reformation typology, see pp. 111–44. See also her discussions of why the emphasis on literal sense did not exclude the figurative meaning, pp. 77ff., and how the Reformation made typology more focused, pp. 117ff.

49. For the role and authority of the Church Fathers in Protestant thought, see the "Prefatory Address to King Francis," *Institutes* and the editors' notes. Perhaps the most distinguished and widely used of the "Commenters" on Scripture was Calvin himself. Donne, who was not a Calvinist, quotes Calvin more than any other Protestant commentator (*Sermons*, 10, appendix, p. 375) and calls him "worthy to be compared to the *Ancients*, for the exposition of Scriptures" (3:177; see also 8:314, and *Biathanatos*, p. 98).

50. See Rickey, *Utmost Art*, pp. 163 and Patrides' note to the poem, ed., *The English Poems*, p. 77.

51. I am indebted for this point to a former student, Maryl Gatts. See Philip Hughes, *Theology*, pp. 74–75, who quotes Tyndale on the two functions of Bible reading. See also Bayly, *The Practice of Piety*, pp. 245–46.

52. Cf. Schneidau, *Sacred Discontent*, who argues that there is no question of a reader's demythologizing the Bible; rather, he argues throughout his study, the Bible demythologizes the reader.

53. Rickey, *Utmost Art*, p. 46. DeWitt Starnes and Ernest Talbert, *Classical Myth and Legend in Renaissance Dictionaries* (Chapel Hill: Univ. of North Carolina Press, 1955), p. 117, observe that the term *labyrinth* does not appear in Ovid's *Metamorphoses*, the widespread source of the myth, although it does appear in various classical dictionaries.

54. See also *Institutes* 1.23.21; 3.21.1; 3.25.11. See especially 1.5.12n.36 for a summary of Calvin's use of the figure.

55. See Patrides' note on the lines, ed., *The English Poems*, p. 104, which cites various sources and readings, but not this one. See also Rickey, *Utmost Art*, p. 46, who quotes Rosemond Tuve.

56. Rickey, *Utmost Art*, p. 35.

57. Ibid.

58. See, for example, Coburn Freer, *Music for a King: George Herbert's Style and the Metrical Psalms* (Baltimore, Md.: Johns Hopkins Univ. Press, 1972), a study of the influence of the Psalms and their lyric translations on Herbert's poetry. Fisch, *Jerusalem and Albion*, pp. 56–62, cites Herbert as exemplary of what he calls "Hebraic poetry." See also Summers, *George Herbert*, passim. For a comprehensive study see Chana Bloch, "Herbert and the Bible," Ph.D. diss., Berkeley, Calif., 1975, and, of course, Barbara Lewalski.

59. For example, see Summers, *George Herbert*, pp. 140–43, in which he illustrates the point that "there is hardly a phrase in 'The Altar' which does not derive from a specific biblical passage."

60. Summers, *George Herbert*, p. 113. Herbert will still allude to classical myths as Rickey shows (*Utmost Art*, pp. 1–58). Herbert's practice is generally to allude to the myths rather than to present them concretely in his poetry. As with the iconoclasts, Herbert does not reject the idea, only the image. See Rickey's comments on the matter, ibid., pp. 57–58.

61. See Summers, *George Herbert*, pp. 113–14, who comments on the relationship between biblical imagery and Herbert's poetry, showing how, "in many of Herbert's poems, the images of the market-place and the images of divine wisdom coincide." That the Bible sometimes violated principles of classical rhetoric and style seems to have been of concern among Renaissance humanists. See *Institutes* 1.8.1–2 for Calvin's discussion of the problem and for his vindication of the Bible's "lowly" images.

62. See Rickey, *Utmost Art*, passim., for the multilevel quality of Herbert's language.

63. See Sidney Gottlieb, "How Shall We Read Herbert?: A Look at 'Prayer (1),'" *George Herbert Journal* 1 (1977): 26–37, who urges and exemplifies this approach to Herbert. For a thematic discussion of Herbert's idea of context as it applies to his poetry see Mulder, "George Herbert's *Temple*," p. 40.

64. Rosalie Colie, "*Logos* in *The Temple*: George Herbert and the Shape of Content," *Journal of the Warburg and Courtauld Institutes* 26 (1963): 330.

65. The point is made by Saad El-Gabalawy, "George Herbert's Affinities with the Homiletical Mode," *Humanities Association Bulletin* (Canada) 21 (1970): 41.

66. Quoted in Philip Hughes, *Theology*, p. 130, from Latimer, *Works*, 1:178.

67. Quoted in ibid., p. 53, from Tyndale, *Works*, 1:53ff.

68. Philip Hughes, *Theology*, p. 121. Queen Elizabeth, on the other hand, in her Protestant reforms, decreed that a sermon should be preached at least once a quarter in every parish; in the absence of a learned and licensed preacher, a sermon could be read from an authorized collection (Higham, p. 9). In time, with the return of the Genevan exiles and their impact at universities such as Cambridge, the pulpits were filled with zealous and articulate ministers.

69. Stranks, *Anglican Devotion*, p. 26.

70. Walton, "The Life," pp. 228–33.

71. Fish, *The Living Temple*.

72. See, for example, Fish, *Self-Consuming Artifacts*, pp. 70–77. Fish makes large generalizations about "Anglican" versus "Puritan" sermons, but his own footnote, p. 75n, undercuts the terminology: "One can certainly find Anglican preachers who are less metaphysical than Donne. . . . And there are, of course, Puritans whose style seems anything but plain" (pp. 75–76n). See George, *Protestant Mind*, pp. 340–41, whose survey of the printed sermons of the period reveals little difference in actual practice. See also W. Fraser Mitchell, *English Pulpit Oratory from Andrewes to Tillotson* (London: Society for Promoting Christian Knowledge, 1932). Lewalski shows that not only does the conventional Anglican/Puritan dichotomy not hold, but that the "plain style" came into its own and was most forcefully advocated by the Anglican establishment preachers after the Restoration (pp. 214–15, 223).

73. Walton, "The Life," p. 228. See also George, *Protestant Mind*, p. 338, who quotes William Perkins on the plain style in preaching.

74. El-Gabalawy, "George Herbert's Affinities," p. 38.

75. See Summers, *George Herbert*, pp. 99ff., and Arnold Stein, *George Herbert's Lyrics* (Baltimore, Md.: Johns Hopkins Univ. Press, 1968), chapter 1 and passim. "Herbert's language,"

according to El-Gabalawy ("George Herbert's Affinities," p. 41), "is nearer to that of the early Reformers, especially Hugh Latimer whose plain and colloquial style springs from his zeal to imitate the simplicity and homeliness of the Bible."

76. *The Art of Prophecying* (1631), p. 670, quoted in El-Gabalawy, "George Herbert's Affinities," p. 41, who makes the connection to Herbert.

77. The specific traces of Herbert's homiletic theory on his poetry have been treated in detail by other critics, such as Sheridan Blau, "George Herbert's Homiletic Theory," who discusses the rhetorical devices that underlie the "art of plainness," and El-Gabalawy, who relates the interjections in the poems, the dramatic methods by which the poet attains a sense of immediacy, and the proverbial, sententious quality of his verse to Herbert's advice to preachers in "The Country Parson." For a thorough discussion of Protestant sermon theory and its connection to the poetics of seventeenth-century religious verse, see Lewalski, *Protestant Poetics*, pp. 213–82.

78. There were actual stained glass windows with the design described in the poem, as Rosemond Tuve reports, *A Reading*, p. 133.

79. For suggestive readings of this poem see Mulder, "George Herbert's *Temple*," pp. 40–41, and Fish, *Living Temple*, pp. 27–29. It is common to minimize the speaker's interpretation, which is seen as a "moral reading corrected by a bystander who supplies the spirit" (Mulder, p. 41). "*Joy*," however, does not seem to be a moral category, and the "*Charitie*" of the New Testament is usually contrasted with the moral law of the Old. The second voice does not seem to be "correcting" the first speaker, but rather confirming his reading—"Sir, you have not miss'd." The question is what the Christ-symbols mean (4), not what they are. The Christ-symbols are indeed "the bodie" (6), of "*Joy* and *Charitie.*" Mulder is right, though, in showing how "JESUS CHRIST" is the key, tying together and giving life to all of the different levels.

80. Cf. "H. Baptisme (1)," 1–4, for another fine rendering of optical perception.

81. Cf. Karl Barth, *Prayer and Preaching* (Naperville, Ill.: SCM Book Club, 1964), p. 95: "The preacher, having thoroughly prepared himself, comes before his congregation, first and foremost, as a man who has been pierced by the Word of God and has been led to repentance in the face of divine judgment; but also as a man who has received with thankfulness the Gospel of forgiveness and is able to rejoice in it. Only in this progression through judgment and grace can preaching become genuinely original."

82. J. Vernon Bartlett, "Worship (Christian)," *Encyclopedia of Religion and Ethics*, 12:77. He was referring specifically to the Elizabethan Prayer Book.

83. G. H. Palmer, Herbert's first modern editor, considered himself a Puritan and, in his introduction to the edition, complains about Herbert's ceremonialism. Wesley excised not only Herbert's more "Calvinist" poems, but also those emphasizing the institutional church. Not only "high churchmen" placed him in their camp, but "low churchmen" as well. The point of Herbert's "Calvinism" is not at all that Herbert was what later Anglicans would term "low church." Rather, in the seventeenth-century, Calvin himself would seem relatively "high church" to his later followers.

84. The difference between the Anglican and the Roman liturgy, however, should not be underestimated, especially in light of the influence of Calvinist rather than Lutheran rites on the *Book of Common Prayer*, as shown in Horton Davies, *Worship and Theology in England* (Princeton, N.J.: Princeton Univ. Press, 1970), 1:208. Reformed worship, as understood by Cranmer, involved seven principles, which were embodied in the Prayer Book (Philip Hughes, *Theology*, p. 149): (1) Scripturalness. According to "The Preface" of the *B.C.P.*, "nothing [is] to be read but the very pure Word of God, the Holy Scriptures, or that which is evidently grounded upon the same." The entire Bible was to be read liturgically, a major innovation in the Roman rite. (2) Catholicity. The past is not to be rejected except for cause. This principle and the nature of the "cause," were, of course, the point of controversy and also the source of the continuity with the earlier church. Special authority was given to the "Primitive Church," especially the Church Fathers. (3) Purity. "Here are left out many things whereof some be untrue, some uncertain, some vain and superstitious" (ibid.). (4) Simplicity. Overly elaborate rites are avoided. Cf. Herbert's "The H. Communion," 1–4. (5) Intelligibility. Perhaps the major and most apparent break with the medieval liturgy was in the use of the vernacular language rather than Latin (see Philip Hughes, *Theology*, pp. 144–49). It was important to the Reformers that the congregation, even the most unlettered, could understand the liturgy. The Reformers would deny that the liturgy or the sacraments functioned in any way automatically, or "magi-

cally," apart from their being understood (*Institutes* 4.14.4). Thus Walton, "The Life," pp. 228–33, records at great length how Herbert would painstakingly explain the liturgy to his congregation (cf. "The Parson in sacraments," "The Country Parson," 22:257–59 and his emphasis on catechizing, ibid., 21:255–57, and Walton, "The Life," p. 235). (6) Commonness. Corporate worship involves the participation of the entire congregation, not only the priest ("Come people, Aaron's drest," "Aaron," 25). (7) Orderliness. "Let all things be done among you, saith Saint Paul, in a seemly and due order [1 Cor. 14:40]. . . . Without some ceremonies it is not possible to keep any order or quiet discipline in the church" ("Of Ceremonies, Why Some Be Abolished and Some Retained," *B.C.P.*).

The difference between the Roman and the Anglican rites, and their different conceptions of the priesthood, can be seen in the rites of ordination. In the Roman rite, the new priest is given bread and wine, with the words "Receive power to offer sacrifice to God and to celebrate mass both for the living and for the dead." In the Anglican rite the new priest is given a Bible, with the words, "Take thou authority to preach the Word of God and to minister the holy sacraments" (Philip Hughes, *Theology*, pp. 161–62). Thus Herbert's emphasis in "The Priesthood" on wielding the Scripture (5–6, 11–12). (The title *Priest* was retained by the Church of England on the basis of its supposed etymological connection to the New Testament *presbyter*, a term of some contention. It did not have the connotation of intercessor and, while it involved special "Authority," it did not involve any supernatural "power." (See Hooker, *Ecclesiastical Polity*, 5:78). Thus the Anglican liturgy and the priesthood were "logocentric" in their original conception.

85. Philip Hughes, *Theology*, p. 162.

86. Quoted in ibid., p. 192, from Augustine's "Tract 80," 3, on the Gospel of John.

87. Ibid., p. 199, from Cranmer's *Works*, 1:41ff.

88. Ibid., p. 197, from Jewel's *Works*, 2:1099.

89. "Genesis," 5:45–46.

90. See *The Babylonian Captivity of the Church* and "The Formula of Concord," Solid Declaration, Article 7 (*Book of Concord*, pp. 575–76). Lutherans do distinguish between the "personal union" of the two natures of Christ and the "sacramental union" of the bread and the Body of Christ. See Mueller, *Christian Dogmatics*, p. 510.

91. See Williston Walker, *A History*, p. 324 and Davies, *Worship and Theology*, 1:80ff. for discussions of the Eucharistic controversies.

92. See "The Formula of Concord," Solid Declaration, Article 7 (*Book of Concord*, p. 575).

93. Williston Walker, *A History*, p. 324; Davies, *Worship and Theology*, pp. 80–85.

94. See Williston Walker, *A History*, p. 352; Davies, *Worship and Theology*, pp. 80–85; and *Institutes* 4.14.17.

95. Quoted in Philip Hughes, *Theology*, p. 7. Davies, *Worship and Theology*, pp. 111, 183ff., has shown how the *Book of Common Prayer*, while remaining distinctive, comes closest to Calvin in the controversies over the sacraments. The Anglican understanding of the sacrament is distinctive in emphasizing the spiritual state of the receiver. According to Hooker, "The real presence of Christ's most blessed body and blood is not therefore to be sought for in the sacrament, but in the worthy receiver of the sacrament" (*Ecclesiastical Polity* 5.67.6; quoted and discussed in George, p. 348). The sacraments are effectual, not merely symbolic, but only to those who believe (Article 25). See also Philip Hughes, *Theology*, p. 194.

96. For studies of Herbert and the Eucharist see, for example, Robert Ellrodt, *Les Poètes métaphysiques anglais: John Donne et les poètes de la tradition chrétienne* (Paris, 1959), 1:324ff., who sees Herbert as close to the Roman Catholic position. William J. McGill, "George Herbert's View of the Eucharist," *Lock Haven Review* 8 (1966): 16–24, says that Herbert believes in the doctrine of the real presence. Gregory Ziegelmaier, "Liturgical Symbol and Reality in the Poetry of George Herbert," *American Benedictine Review* 18 (1967): 344–53, concurs but is a little uneasy, from a Catholic point of view, about Herbert's doctrine. Sr. Thekla, more acutely, comments upon Herbert's non-Catholic view of the Eucharist. See also Malcolm Ross, *Poetry and Dogma: The Transfiguration of Eucharistic Symbols in Seventeenth Century English Poetry* (New Brunswick, N.J.: Rutgers Univ. Press, 1954), for the general "decay" of the sacramental symbol, which he sees also in Herbert (pp. 135–57). Lewalski makes the point that what Ross decries as "decay" issued in some of the greatest religious lyrics of all time. See also Asals, *Equivocal Predication* for an especially illuminating discussion.

97. Luther's view would be somewhat unusual for a seventeenth-century Anglican. If

Herbert did subscribe to Luther's doctrine of ubiquity, it is a testimony to Herbert's independence and evidence of his affinity, as this study has suggested, to the early Reformers rather than to the later ones.

98. See Hutchinson, ed., *Works*, p. 548.

99. For this doctrine see ibid., pp. 548–49.

100. Cf. Quenstedt, a Lutheran theologian: "We say that only the *body* of Christ is united with the bread, and only the *blood* is united with the wine, and (both are) sacramentally received by the mouth of the body. But the *whole Christ* is received *spiritually*, by the mouth of faith." Quoted by Mueller, *Christian Dogmatics*, p. 520. For the Lutheran positions see "The Formula of Concord," Article 7.

101. Joseph Summers observes that "when one reads 'The Altar' it is well to remember that the word altar was not applied to the communion table in the Book of Common Prayer, and that the canons of Herbert's time directed that the table should be made of wood rather than stone. Throughout his English writings Herbert always used 'altar' and 'sacrifice' according to the 'orthodox' Protestant tradition of his time: 'altar' is never applied to the communion table nor is the Holy Communion ever called a 'sacrifice' " (*George Herbert*, p. 141). See also Philip Hughes, *Theology*, pp. 218–21. The point is of some importance in "liturgical" readings of *The Temple*. Despite the liturgical connections documented by Rosemond Tuve, *A Reading*, pp. 19ff., "The Sacrifice" is about the historical crucifixion of Jesus, not an effectual sacrifice in the mass. The "sacrifice" recognized by Herbert is not the Lord's Supper, but the death of Christ. "The Altar," as Summers observes, *George Herbert*, pp. 141–42, is a biblical type of the human heart ("A broken ALTAR, Lord, thy servant reares, / Made of a heart. . . ." [1–2]). The relationship between "The Sacrifice" of Christ and that of "The Altar" is perhaps best suggested by Cranmer, who distinguishes two kinds of sacrifices: the single death of Christ and the human response to that sacrifice. The only possible "propiatory" sacrifice, effectual for the forgiveness of sin, is the death of Christ. But "Another kind of sacrifice there is which doth not reconcile us to God, but is made of them that be reconciled by Christ, to testify our duties unto God, and to show ourselves thankful unto Him. And therefore they be called sacrifices of laud, praise, and thanksgiving. The first kind of sacrifice Christ offered to God for us; the second kind we ourselves offer to God by Christ" (quoted in Philip Hughes, *Theology*, p. 222, from *Works*, 1:346). Cf. the final lines of "The Altar": "O let thy blessed SACRIFICE be mine, / And sanctifie this ALTAR to be thine."

102. See Rosalie Colie, *"Logos in The Temple,"* and Valerie Carnes, "The Unity of George Herbert's *The Temple:* A Reconsideration," *ELH* 35 (1968): 505–26, for illuminating discussions of "the Word" in regard to Herbert's poetry. Their focus, however, is on the sense of *logos* as understood by classical philosophy rather than Reformation theology *per se*.

103. Cf. J. B. Leishman, "Donne and Seventeenth-Century Verse," *Seventeenth-Century English Poetry*, ed. William R. Keast (New York: Oxford Univ. Press, 1971), p. 96.

104. For the importance of speaking to the expression of a relationship see Blanchard and her discussion from Walter Ong, *The Barbarian Within*.

105. Mulder, "George Herbert's *Temple*," pp. 37, 41.

106. John Freed, "Salvation/Damnation: The Theology and Personae of George Herbert's *Temple*," *Dissertation Abstracts* 34 (1972): 1239A. For other suggestive comments on the concept of revelation in connection with Herbert's poetry, see Fish, *Living Temple*, pp. 43–44, 176, and Ellrodt, *L'Inspiration personelle et l'Esprit du temps chez les poètes metaphysiques anglais* (Paris: Corti, 1960), 1:295.

107. Italics do not always signify God's voice. In "The Method," for example, the speaker is addressed by his conscience, although God's voice is invoked in the final lines. In "A Dialogue-Antheme," the other speaker is death, etc.

108. Quoted in Ebeling, *Luther*, p. 239, translated from the Weimar edition of Luther's *Werke*, 56:423 (1515/16).

109. Ebeling, *Luther*, p. 121.

110. Ibid., p. 120.

111. The point made by Blanchard, "Leap into Darkness," p. 44. She discusses the various voices of God as presented in the poems. The voice may be ironic ("Artillerie"), indirect ("Method," "The Quip"), or it may come through the very nature of human language ("Jesu").

112. The imagery of breath in this poem is not only a vivid evocation of intimacy, but it also

suggests the spirit/breath equivalency of the classical languages, imaging here the human soul's communion with the Holy Spirit as Christ's breath (John 20:22).

113. A similar blending of the human word and God's word takes place in "Affliction (3)":

> My heart did heave, and there came forth, *O God!*
> By that I knew that thou wast in the grief.

(1–2)

Cf. Rom. 8:15–16.

114. There is no reason to see a strong reference to Melchisedec in the lines (Hutchinson, ed., *Works*, p. 521; Tuve, *A Reading*, pp. 161–63). Melchisedec, a type of Christ, is described as "King of Salem" (Gen. 14:18) but "Salem," as Heb. 7:2 translates, simply means "peace." The *Prince* of Salem can only mean Christ, the Prince of Peace, a biblical title (Isa. 9:6) used by Herbert in "The Sacrifice" (118). In terms of the poem, peace can only come from Christ (40–42), because Christ is the Prince of Peace.

115. See Tuve, *A Reading*, pp. 162ff. I am indebted to Elizabeth Jacobson, a former student, for pointing out the relation between Herbert's "grain" and the biblical symbol for "the word of God."

116. To the Roman Catholic position that the Scriptures issued from the Church, the Reformers insisted that, ultimately, the Word—i.e., the oral testimony of the Apostles concerning Christ and their preaching of the Gospel later put into writing—was prior to the Church. The emphasis on the oral word, predating the Scriptures, helped them around the Roman argument. The Church's ratification of the canon involved, to the Reformers, simply the scholarly task of recognizing which books were Apostolic, and thus authoritative.

117. Communion would be after the sermon, so that the reference to an immediately past time ("And now Lord, Thou hast fed us") can refer only to the preaching, which is the subject and occasion of the prayer.

Chapter 8. The Church and One's Calling

1. See *Institutes* 4.1–9. This distinction and its applicability to "The Church Militant" has been observed by other critics. See, for example, Grant, *Transformation of Sin*, p. 202.

2. That by simply stating the gospel message, even in a poem, one may engender faith in someone else, is part of the Reformation doctrine of the Word. See chapter 7, section 3.

3. Daniel Rubey, "The Poet and the Christian Community: Herbert's Affliction Poems and the Structure of *The Temple*," *Studies in English Literature 1500–1900*, 20 (1980): 105–23.

4. See Stewart, "Time and *The Temple*," pp. 108–10. See also Carnes, "The Unity," p. 523.

5. See Patrides, ed., *The English Poems*, p. 199 n and A. L. Maycock, *Nicholas Ferrar of Little Gidding* (London: S.P.C.K., 1938), p. 235. For fuller treatments of the point, see Ilona Bell, "Setting Foot into Divinity."

6. George, *Protestant Mind*, p. 318.

7. That the Pope was Antichrist was held nearly universally by the Protestants, even by later "high church" Carolinian divines. See Maycock, *Nicholas Ferrar*, pp. 180, 239. See also Luther's *The Babylonian Captivity of the Church, Works*, 36.

8. The antecedent of "it" can only be "the late reformation."

9. See Bartlett, "Worship (Christian)," 12:762–76, and Ross, *Poetry and Dogma*, pp. 52–54. For a partisan discussion of worship reforms see Francis Schaeffer, *How Shall We Then Live* (Old Tappan, N.J.: Revell, 1976), pp. 79–119. For a discussion of the rood screen and its implications see pp. 87–88.

10. George, *Protestant Mind*, p. 126.

11. See Melanchthon's "Apology of the Augsburg Confession," Article 7, pp. 204, 205. For a discussion of the "evangelical counsels" see Article 27, pp. 273ff. See also Luther's *Large Catechism*, pp. 391–92 *(Book of Concord)*.

12. See "Apology of the Augsburg Confession," Article 4, p. 133 *(Book of Concord)*.

13. George, *Protestant Mind*, p. 132, who also cites the following quotation from Herbert.

14. Besides attacking idleness, a common theme of Reformation moralists was the danger of wasting time. See George, *Protestant Mind*, p. 133.

15. George, *Protestant Mind*, p. 134.

16. Ibid., p. 169. See also p. 142 and pp. 144–73 for a detailed argument against Weber's thesis.

17. See ibid., p. 138–39, 143.

18. Ibid., pp. 170–71.

19. Stranks, *Anglican Devotion*, p. 26.

20. John Bradford, *Private Prayer and Meditations with other Exercises* (1559) quoted by Stranks, *Anglican Devotion*, p. 23. See also pp. 22–25, 45 for a discussion of this kind of meditation.

21. Donne's depictions of travel, which occur throughout his poetry, are also part of this meditative tradition.

22. The finding of one's calling is, in fact, the unifying theme of Walton's *Life of Donne*.

23. George, *Protestant Mind*, pp. 327–28.

24. See Patrides, ed., *The English Poems*, "Appendix 3: Some Secular Poems Parodied by Herbert," pp. 209–13, which gives secular analogues to "The Altar," "Heaven," "Jordan (2)," "Doomsday," and, of course, "A Parodie." See also Rosemond Tuve, "Sacred 'Parody' of Love Poetry, and Herbert," *Studies in the Renaissance* 8 (1961): 249–90.

25. See Tuve, *A Reading*, pp. 194–95.

Chapter 9. Conclusion: Reformation Theology and Poetry

1. Herbert was writing in a time when the older Protestant, Calvinist orthodoxy was just starting to become unraveled. Herbert, a conservative, tended to hold to the older Reformation theology, rejecting not only Arminianism but also the contemporary presbyterian versions of Calvinism. Barbara Lewalski also observes that "Calvinism provided a detailed chart of the spiritual life for Elizabethan and seventeenth-century English Protestants and . . . this map also afforded fundamental direction to the major religious lyric poets" (*Protestant Poetics*, p. 14).

2. See Madsen, *From Shadowy Types to Truth*, pp. 166ff., who discusses and soundly rejects the common idea that "Puritans" reject art and the sensuous. The critical confusion, he suggests, comes from the assumption "that images in worship and imagery in poetry are the same kind of thing" (p. 172).

3. The editor's note cites Augustine, *On the Good of Marriage*, 9, as an instance of the doctrine of "necessary use," which Calvin is rejecting. Cf. Herbert's attack on what was perceived as monastic asceticism in "Triumphus Mortis," ("Lucus," 32:88–94). Speaking of the invention of gunpowder, Herbert blames "a monk . . . living in a dark / Cell's unjoyous doorway full of demons."

> Who denies that monks are taken up with death;
> That they grovel in the joyless dust; that they prize
> In their hearts humiliating things like this—indeed
> Things that go beneath the earth itself?

McCloskey's translation, *The Latin Poetry*, p. 117. See also George, *The Protestant Mind*, pp. 141ff.

4. On church decorations, Herbert, like most in the Church of England, desired "to keep the middle way between superstition and Slovenlinesse" ("The Country Parson," 23:246; cf. "The British Church"). Still, in regard to religious art or images in church, iconoclasm was the general viewpoint. According to George, *Protestant Mind*, pp. 360–61, even Andrewes and Laud did not believe in having religious statues in church or in venerating icons. Herbert, as has been mentioned, urged the painting, not of pictures, but of texts of Scripture.

5. Many metaphysical poets, such as Donne, were not Calvinists, of course, but none of them could escape his influence in the Church of England, and the broader movement of Protestant iconoclasm that Calvin is articulating. See the chapter on mannerism in Wylie

Sypher's *Four Stages of Renaissance Style* (Garden City, N.Y.: Doubleday, 1955), which relates the metaphysical poets and Jacobean dramatists to Calvin.

6. See Leslie P. Spelman, "Calvin and the Arts," *Journal of Aesthetics and Art Criticism* 6 (1948): 251. Cf. Gilbert Highet, trans., in his introduction to *Paideia: The Ideals of Greek Culture* by Werner Jaeger (1935; rpt. New York: Oxford Univ. Press, 1965), pp. xxvii–xxviii, quoted in Schneidau, *Sacred Discontent*, p. 262: "It was the Christians who finally taught men to appraise poetry by a purely aesthetic standard—a standard which enabled them to reject most of the moral and religious teaching of the classical poets as false and ungodly, while accepting the formal elements in their work as instructive and aesthetically delightful."

7. Quoted and discussed in Garside, *Zwingli and the Arts*, p. 182. Zwingli, although an extreme iconoclast, did permit paintings, even of Christ, as long as they were not offered reverence or in churches. According to Zwingli, "where anyone has a portrait of His humanity, that is just as fitting to have as to have other portraits. . . . No one is forbidden from having a portrait of the humanity of Christ" (p. 171). Rembrandt, of course, comes from this tradition of Protestant portraitists, whose concern, with Jud, was to discern the image of God in human beings.

8. For the "Calvinist" attitude to poetry see Lawrence Sasek, *Literary Temper*, p. 116, who compares it to the "Puritan's" almost uncritical esteem for music:

> Paradoxically, the Puritan's high esteem for music, his usual exemption of it from the criticism and suspicions directed at the other arts, arose from its nonrepresentational nature. . . . If it did not inform the mind, it at least did not absorb one's thoughts or turn them in other directions, toward competing ideas or creeds; and it could provide rest. . . . Its appeal was purely aesthetic, and by accepting it, the Puritans accepted art as form, unmixed with theological or moral elements. Poetry, on the other hand, has much greater potentialities for both good and evil. When acceptable, it was raised above the level of recreations and became a part of the necessary preparation for one's calling. When unacceptable, it was dangerous to the welfare of one's soul. Its content was representational; and when the content was good, the art gave it more force, more efficacy in impressing its message upon the reader or hearer. When the content was bad, art made it all the more dangerous by increasing its appeal. In neither case could poetry serve as mere recreation; it was too important.

Even William Prynne, the fanatical crusader against the stage, approved of poetry—even dramatic poetry if it was not acted. Prynne, in fact, gave unqualified approval to *The Canterbury Tales* (Sasek, pp. 104ff.).

9. Halewood, *Poetry of Grace*, p. 132.

10. See the chapter on Luther, pp. 94ff., and the discussion of election and predestination, pp. 86ff., in Rudolf Otto, *The Idea of the Holy*.

11. See Niesel, *Theology of Calvin*, pp. 126, 144, 222. See *Institutes* 1.5.11 for Calvin's simultaneous admiration and censure of Plato. Symbols of transcendence are perhaps inevitable in any religious poetry. In Herbert, they are severely modified in line with the principle that one can never come to God on one's own power but that only God can bring a soul to Himself. In Herbert's poetry, whenever there are figures of transcendence, the speaker's action, as a rule, is essentially passive. In "The Starre," the star first descends from heaven into his heart (1–16). Then, the star and he, together, can "take our flight." The star must "Get me a standing there" (21) before the soul can "flie home" (29). This symbolic rescuer as the only means of transcendence, in accordance with Reformation theology, occurs also in "Sunday," a device employed in conjunction with a passive verb: "we both, *being toss'd* from earth, / Flie hand in hand to heav'n" (62–63). In "Mattens," Herbert concludes his symbol of morning light with a figure of transcendence: "Then by a sunne-beam I will climbe to thee" (20). Here, too, as in "The Pearl," 37–40, he is climbing to heaven, but by means of an object let down from heaven—in this case, a sunne (son)-beam (the cross), conflated with the biblical figure of Christ as the Light (John 1:5–9). Even in "Home," a poem that most expresses the desire for transcendence in its conventional platonic sense—"Oh loose this frame, this knot of man untie! / That my free soul may use her wing, / Which now is pinion'd with mortalitie" (61–63)—the repeated prayer is that God accomplish this transcendence for him: "take me up to thee." The refrain of the poem shows a tension between incarnation ("O show thy self to

me") and transcendence ("Or take me up to thee!"). His desire for God's presence, which he does not feel, is so great that he posits the two alternatives. The poem resolves itself, though, even against the form and the rhyme scheme, into a plea for the Lord to "come." Through Herbert's poetry, one can "mount" to God only by submission to Him, by bending the knee ("H. Scriptures [1]," 14).

12. See Vendler, *George Herbert*, pp. 152, 291 n. 4, in which she opposes the "downward" movement in Herbert's verse to mystical union. See also Madsen, *From Shadowy Types*, pp. 85ff., on Neoplatonism and classical philosophy as opposed to Reformation and biblical thought.

13. Vaughan's Neoplatonism, however, is often in tension with his Protestantism. "The World" concludes by echoing "The Collar," formally and theologically (although the exclusivist emphasis of later Calvinism is already apparent), testifying to the tenacity and strength of Reformed spirituality in the poetic imagination:

> But as I did their madness so discuss
> One whisper'd thus,
> *This Ring the Bridegroome did for none provide*
> *But for his bride.*
>
> (57–60)

Lewalski, in *Protestant Poetics*, pp. 319ff., discusses Vaughan as a Calvinist. Nevertheless, his post-Restoration Arminianism and Neoplatonism tend to align him more with traditional mysticism based on transcendence.

14. See Lewalski, *Protestant Poetics*, pp. 192–96.

15. Denis Donoghue, *Thieves of Fire* (London: Faber and Faber, 1973), pp. 20ff., contrasts Herbert to the "Promethean poets," specifically to Milton, whose imagination tends to be a function of the will, of the self. In "Promethean poets," according to Donoghue, there tends to be a tension between feeling and form. Herbert's integration of form and content is, of course, his most obvious poetic achievement. For Milton's Arminian position on each of the disputed Five Points, see *De Doctrina Christiana*, 1:3, 4, 16, 17, 25. See also "Arminianism" in *The Milton Encyclopedia*.

16. Quoted in Helen White, *English Devotional Literature*, p. 202.

17. Tuve, *A Reading*, p. 22.

18. See Lewalski's discussion of this passage, *Protestant Poetics*, pp. 15ff.

Bibliography

Adler, Jacob H. "Form and Meaning in Herbert's 'Discipline.' " *Notes and Queries*, n.p. 5 (1958): 240–43.

Allison, C. F. *The Rise of Moralism: The Proclamation of the Gospel from Hooker to Baxter.* New York: Seabury Press, 1966.

Alvarez, A. *The School of Donne.* London: Chatto and Windus, 1961.

Asals, Heather A. R. *Equivocal Predication: George Herbert's Way to God.* Toronto: University of Toronto Press, 1981.

Barth, Karl. *Church Dogmatics.* Translated by G. T. Thompson. Vol. 1. Edinburgh: T. and T. Clark, 1936.

———. *Prayer and Preaching.* Naperville, Ill.: SCM Book Club, 1964.

Bartlet, J. Vernon. "Worship (Christian)." *Encyclopedia of Religion and Ethics.*

Bayly, Lewis. *The Practice of Piety.* London, 1612.

Beachcroft, T. O. "Nicholas Ferrar and George Herbert." *Criterion* 12 (1932): 24–42.

Bell, Ilona. " 'Setting Foot into Divinity': George Herbert and the English Reformation." *Modern Language Quarterly* 38 (1977): 219–41.

———. " 'When Faith Did Change the Scene': Herbert's Renascence and the Protestant Reformation." *Dissertation Abstracts International* 37 (1977): 7136 A (Boston College).

Bennett, Joan. *Four Metaphysical Poets.* New York: Random House, 1953.

Blanchard, Margaret M. "The Leap into Darkness: Donne, Herbert, and God." *Renascence* 17 (1964): 38–50.

Blau, Sheridan D. "George Herbert's Homiletic Theory." *George Herbert Journal* 1 (1978): 17–29.

Booty, John E., ed. *The Book of Common Prayer (1559): The Elizabethan Prayer Book.* Folger Shakespeare Library. Charlottesville: Univ. Press of Virginia, 1976.

Bornkamm, Heinrich. *The Heart of Reformation Faith.* Translated by John W. Doberstein. New York: Harper and Row, 1965.

Calvin, John. *Institutes of the Christian Religion.* Edited by John T. McNeill. Translated by Lewis Battles Ford. 2 vols. The Library of Christian Classics. Philadelphia: Westminster Press, 1960.

———. *The Institution of Christian Religion.* Translated by Thomas Norton. London, 1634.

Carnes, Valerie. "The Unity of George Herbert's *The Temple:* A Reconsideration." *ELH* 35 (1968): 505–26.

Charles, Amy M. *A Life of George Herbert.* Ithaca, N.Y.: Cornell Univ. Press, 1977.

Coghill, Nevill. "The Approach to English." *Light on C. S. Lewis.* Edited by Jocelyn Gibb. New York: Harcourt Brace Jovanovich, 1965.

Coleridge, Samuel Taylor. *Notes on English Divines.* Edited by Derwent Coleridge. 2 vols. London: Edward Moxon, 1853.

Colie, Rosalie. "*Logos* in *The Temple:* George Herbert and the Shape of Content." *Journal of the Warburg and Courtauld Institute* 26 (1963): 327–42.

Daniel, E. Randolph. "Reconciliation, Covenant and Election: A Study in the Theology of John Donne." *Anglican Theological Review* 48 (1966): 14–30.

Davies, Horton. *Worship and Theology in England.* Vol. 1. Princeton, N.J.: Princeton Univ. Press, 1970.

Dessner, Lawrence J. "A Reading of George Herbert's 'Man.'" *Concerning Poetry* 5 (1972): 61–63.

Dickens, A. G. *The English Reformation.* New York: Schocken Books, 1964.

Donne, John. *Devotions Upon Emergent Occasions.* Edited by Anthony Raspa. Montreal: McGill-Queen's University Press, 1975.

———. *The Divine Poems.* Edited by Helen Gardner. Oxford: Clarendon Press, 1964.

———. *The Sermons of John Donne.* Edited by George R. Potter and Evelyn M. Simpson. 10 vols. Berkeley: Univ. of California Press, 1953–62.

Donoghue, Denis. *Thieves of fire.* London: Faber and Faber, 1973.

Duffield, G. E. *John Calvin.* Courtenay Studies in Reformation Theology. Grand Rapids, Mich.: Wm. B. Eerdmans, 1966.

Ebeling, Gerhard. *Luther: An Introduction to His Thought.* Translated by R. A. Wilson. London: Wm. Collins Sons, 1970.

El-Gabalawy, Saad. "George Herbert's Affinities with the Homiletical Mode." *Humanities Association Bulletin* (Canada) 21 (1970): 38–48.

———. "George Herbert's Christian Sensibility: A Resumé." *Cithara* 11 (1972): 16–22.

Ellrodt, Robert. "George Herbert and the Religious Lyric." In *English Poetry and Prose 1540–1674,* edited by Christopher Ricks, pp. 173–205. London: Barrie and Jenkins, 1970.

Empson, William. *Seven Types of Ambiguity.* London: Chatto and Windus, 1949.

Fisch, Harold. *Jerusalem and Albion: The Hebraic Factor in Seventeenth-Century Literature.* New York: Schocken Books, 1964.

Fish, Stanley. *The Living Temple: George Herbert and Catechizing.* Berkeley: Univ. of California Press, 1978.

———. *Self-Consuming Artifacts: The Experience of Seventeenth-Century Literature.* Berkeley: Univ. of California Press, 1972.

Freed, John Edward. "Salvation/Damnation: The Theology and Personae of George Herbert's *The Temple.*" *Dissertation Abstracts* 34A (1972): 1239 A (Penn. State).

Freer, Coburn. *Music for a King: George Herbert's Style and the Metrical Psalms.* Baltimore, Md.: Johns Hopkins Univ. Press, 1972.

Frye, Roland Mushat. *Shakespeare and Christian Doctrine.* Princeton, N.J.: Princeton Univ. Press, 1965.

Garside, Charles. *Zwingli and the Arts.* New Haven, Conn.: Yale Univ. Press, 1966.

George, Charles H. and Katherine. *The Protestant Mind of the English Reformation 1570–1640.* Princeton, N.J.: Princeton Univ. Press, 1961.

Gottlieb, Sidney. "How Shall We Read Herbert?: A Look at 'Prayer (1),' " *George Herbert Journal* 1 (1977): 26–37.

Grant, Patrick. *The Transformation of Sin: Studies in Donne, Herbert, Vaughan, and Traherne.* Amherst: Univ. of Massachusetts Press, 1974.

Halewood, William H. *The Poetry of Grace: Reformation Themes and Structures in English Seventeenth-Century Poetry.* New Haven, Conn.: Yale Univ. Press, 1970.

Hall, Basil. "Calvin against the Calvinists." In *John Calvin,* edited by G. E. Duffield. Courtenay Studies in Reformation Theology. Grand Rapids, Mich.: Wm. B. Eerdmans, 1966.

———. "Puritanism: the Problem of Definition." In *Studies in Church History,* edited by G. J. Cuming, 2:283–96. London: Thomas Nelson, 1965.

Hanko, Herman; Homer C. Hocksema; and Gise J. Van Baren. *The Five Points of Calvinism.* Grand Rapids, Mich.: Reformed Free Publishing Association, 1976.

Hanley, Sara W. "Temples in *The Temple:* George Herbert's Study of the Church." *Studies in English Literature* 8 (1968): 121–35.

Herbert, George. *The English Poems of George Herbert.* Edited by C. A. Patrides. London: Everyman's Library, 1974.

———. *The Latin Poetry of George Herbert: A Bilingual Edition.* Translated by Mark McCloskey and Paul R. Murphy. Athens: Ohio Univ. Press, 1965.

———. *The Works of George Herbert.* Edited by F. E. Hutchinson. Oxford: Clarendon Press, 1941.

Higgins, Dick. *George Herbert's Pattern Poems: In Their Tradition.* New York: Unpublished Editions, 1977.

Higham, Florence. *Catholic and Reformed: A Study of the Anglican Church, 1559–1662.* London: Society for Promoting Christian Knowledge, 1962.

Hooker, Richard. *Of the Laws of Ecclesiastical Polity.* 2 vols. New York: Everyman's Library, 1963.

Hughes, Johnson Donald. "George Herbert: His Place in English Church History." *Dissertation Abstracts,* 21 (1960): 975 (Boston Univ.).

Hughes, Philip Edgcumbe. *Theology of the English Reformers.* London: Hodder and Stoughton, 1965.

Jacobs, Henry Eyster. *The Lutheran Movement in England.* Philadelphia: General Council, 1916.

Kirn, O. "Grace." *The New Schaff-Herzog Encyclopedia of Religious Knowledge* (1908–1912).

Lang, Paul Henry. *Music in Western Civilization.* New York: Norton, 1941.

Leach, Elsie A. "John Wesley's Use of George Herbert." *Huntington Library Quarterly* 16 (1953): 183–202.

Leishman, J. B. "Donne and Seventeenth-Century Poetry." In *Seventeenth-Century English Poetry: Modern Essays in Criticism,* edited by William R. Keast, pp. 89–105. New York: Oxford Univ. Press, 1971.

Leith, John H., ed. *Creeds of the Churches.* Garden City, N.Y.: Anchor Books, 1963.

Lewalski, Barbara K. *Protestant Poetics and the Seventeenth-Century Religious Lyric.* Princeton, N.J.: Princeton Univ. Press, 1979.

——. "Typology and Poetry." In *Illustrious Evidence: Approaches to English Literature of the Early Seventeenth Century,* edited by Earl Miner, pp. 41–69. Berkeley: Univ. of California Press, 1975.

Lewis, C. S. *English Literature in the Sixteenth Century Excluding Drama.* London: Oxford Univ. Press, 1954.

Luther, Martin. *Luther's Works.* Edited by Jaroslav Pelikan and Helmut T. Lehman. 55 vols. Philadelphia: Muhlenberg Press, 1955–67.

McCanles, Michael. *Dialectical Criticism and Renaissance Literature.* Berkeley: Univ. of California Press, 1975.

McGill, William J., Jr. "George Herbert's View of the Eucharist." *Loch Haven Review* 8 (1966): 16–24.

McGuire, Philip. "Private Prayer and English Poetry in the Early Seventeenth Century." *Studies in English Literature* 14 (1974): 63–77.

McKinney, Howard, and W. R. Anderson. *Music in History: The Evolution of an Art.* New York: American Book Company, 1940.

Madsen, William G. *From Shadowy Types to Truth: Studies in Milton's Symbolism.* New Haven, Conn.: Yale Univ. Press, 1968.

Maria, Mother. "George Herbert: Aspects of His Theology." In *George Herbert: Idea and Image,* edited by Sister Thekla, pp. 279–305. Normanby, England: The Greek Orthodox Monastery of the Assumption, 1970.

Martz, Louis. "The Action of the Self: Devotional Poetry in the Seventeenth Century." In *Metaphysical Poetry,* edited by Malcolm Bradbury and David Palmer. Stratford-Upon-Avon Studies, no. 11. New York: St. Martin's Press, 1970.

——. *The Poetry of Meditation.* New Haven, Conn.: Yale Univ. Press, 1954.

Maycock, A. L. *Nicholas Ferrar of Little Gidding.* London: S.P.C.K., 1938.

Miller, Perry. *The New England Mind: The Seventeenth Century.* Boston: Beacon Press, 1961.

Mills, Jerry Leath. "Recent Studies in Herbert." *English Literary Renaissance* 6 (Winter 1976): 105–18.

Milton, John. *The Student's Milton.* Edited by Frank Allen Patterson. New York: Appleton-Century-Crofts, 1930.

Mitchell, W. Fraser. *English Pulpit Oratory from Andrewes to Tillotson.* London: Society for Promoting Christian Knowledge, 1932.

Mollenkott, Virginia R. "The Many and the One in George Herbert's 'Providence.' " *College Language Association Journal* 10 (1966): 34–41.

Mueller, J. T. *Christian Dogmatics.* St. Louis: Concordia, 1955.

Mulder, John R. "George Herbert's *Temple:* Design and Methodology." *Seventeenth-Century News* 31 (1973): 37–45.

Mullinger, James. *Cambridge Characteristics in the Seventeenth-Century.* London: Macmillan, 1867.

New, John F. H. *Anglican and Puritan: The Basis of Their Opposition, 1558–1640.* Stanford, Calif.: Stanford Univ. Press, 1964.

Nichols, James H. "The Intent of the Calvinist Liturgy." In *The Heritage of John*

Calvin, edited by John H. Bratt, pp. 87–109. Grand Rapids, Mich.: Eerdmans, 1973.

Niesel, Wilhelm. *The Theology of Calvin.* Translated by Harold Knight. Philadelphia: Westminster Press, 1956.

Novarr, David, and John But. *The Making of Walton's Lives.* Ithaca, N.Y.: Cornell Univ. Press, 1958.

Ong, Walter. *The Barbarian Within.* New York: Macmillan, 1962.

Otto, Rudolf. *The Idea of the Holy.* Translated by John W. Harvey. New York: Oxford Univ. Press, 1950.

Packer, J. I. "Calvin the Theologian." In *John Calvin,* edited by G. E. Duffield, pp. 149–75. Courtenay Studies in Reformation Theology. Grand Rapids, Mich.: Wm. B. Eerdmans, 1966.

Patterson, W. Brown. "Protestant Poetics." *Sewanee Review* 88 (1980): 651–54.

Porter, H. C. *Reformation and Reaction in Tudor Cambridge.* Cambridge: Cambridge Univ. Press, 1958.

Quinn, Dennis. "Donne's Christian Eloquence." In *Seventeenth-Century Prose,* edited by Stanley Fish. New York: Oxford Univ. Press, 1971.

Ray, Robert H. "Spatial and Aural Patterns in 'The Windows.'" *George Herbert Journal* 1 (Spring 1978): 38–43.

Richmond, Hugh M. Review of Barbara Lewalski, *Protestant Poetics. Renaissance Quarterly* 33 (1980): 298–99.

Rickey, Mary Ellen. *Utmost Art: Complexity in the Verse of George Herbert.* Lexington: Univ. of Kentucky Press, 1966.

Riggs, William C. *The Christian Poet in Paradise Lost.* Berkeley: Univ. of Calif. Press, 1972.

Roberts, John R. *Essential Articles for the Study of George Herbert's Poetry.* Hamden, Conn.: Archon Books, 1979.

———. *John Donne: An Annotated Bibliography of Modern Criticism 1912–1967.* Columbia: Univ. of Missouri Press, 1973.

Ross, Malcolm M. *Poetry and Dogma: The Transfiguration of Eucharistic Symbols in Seventeenth Century English Poetry.* New Brunswick, N.J.: Rutgers Univ. Press, 1954.

Rubey, Daniel. "The Poet and the Christian Community: Herbert's Affliction Poems and the Structure of *The Temple.*" *Studies in English Literature 1500–1900,* 20 (1980): 105–23.

Rupp, E. G. *Studies in the Making of the English Protestant Tradition.* Cambridge: Cambridge Univ. Press, 1966.

Sanders, Wilbur. " 'Childhood is Health': The Divine Poetry of George Herbert." *Melbourne Critical Review* 5 (1962): 3–15.

———. "Herbert and the Scholars." *Melbourne Critical Review* 4 (1961): 102–11.

Sasek, Lawrence. *The Literary Temper of the English Puritans.* Baton Rouge: Louisiana State Univ. Press, 1961.

Schaeffer, Francis. *How Shall We Then Live: The Rise and Decline of Western Thought And Culture.* Old Tappan, N.J.: Fleming H. Revell, 1976.

Schneidau, Herbert. *Sacred Discontent: The Bible and Western Tradition.* Berkeley: Univ. of California Press, 1976.

Seeburg, R. "The Word of God." *The New Schaff-Herzog Encyclopedia of Religious Knowledge* (1908–12).

Siebert, Frederick. *Freedom of the Press in England 1476–1776.* Urbana: Univ. of Illinois Press, 1952.

Spelman, Leslie P. "Calvin and the Arts." *Journal of Aesthetics and Art Criticism* 6 (1948): 246–52.

Sproul, R. C. *Knowing Scripture.* Downers Grove, Ill.: Inter-Varsity Press, 1977.

Stachniewski, John. "Probing the Protestant Psyche." *Times Literary Supplement,* 7 March 1980, p. 272.

Starnes, DeWitt, and Ernest Talbert. *Classical Myth and Legend in Renaissance Dictionaries.* Chapel Hill: Univ. of North Carolina Press, 1955.

Stein, Arnold. *George Herbert's Lyrics.* Baltimore, Md.: Johns Hopkins Press, 1968.

Stewart, Stanley. "Time and *The Temple.*" *Studies in English Literature 1500–1900* 6 (1966): 97–110.

Strier, Richard. *Love Known: Theology and Experience in George Herbert's Poetry.* Chicago: Univ. of Chicago Press, 1983.

Stranks, C. J. *Anglican Devotion: Studies in the Spiritual Life of the Church of England between the Reformation and the Oxford Movement.* London: SCM Press, 1961.

Summers, Joseph H. *George Herbert: His Religion and Art.* Cambridge, Mass.: Harvard Univ. Press, 1954.

———. "Stanley Fish's Reading of Seventeenth-Century Literature." *Modern Language Quarterly* 35: 403–17 (rev.).

Sutton, Max K. "The Drama of Full Consent in Hopkins and Herbert." Unpublished seminar paper. The Univ. of Kansas, Lawrence.

Sypher, Wylie. *Four Stages of Renaissance Style: Transformations in Art and Literature, 1400–1700.* Garden City, N.Y.: Doubleday, 1955.

Taylor, William Leigh. "Protestant Theology in George Herbert's *The Temple.*" *Dissertation Abstracts International* 17 (1976): 5858A (Univ. of Virginia).

Thekla, Sister. *George Herbert: Idea and Image.* Normanby, England: Greek Orthodox Monastery of the Assumption, 1974.

Thomas Aquinas. *The Pocket Aquinas: Selections from the Writings of St. Thomas.* Edited by Vernon J. Bourke. New York: Washington Square Press, 1960.

———. *The Summa Theologica.* Translated by the Fathers of the English Dominican Province. 2 vols. Great Books of the Western World. Chicago: Encyclopedia Britannica, 1952.

Tuve, Rosemond. "George Herbert and *Caritas.*" *Journal of the Warburg and Courtauld Institute* 22 (1959): 303–31.

———. *A Reading of George Herbert.* London: Faber and Faber, 1952.

———. "Sacred 'Parody' of Love Poetry, and Herbert." *Studies in the Renaissance* 8 (1961): 249–90.

Vendler, Helen. *The Poetry of George Herbert.* Cambridge, Mass.: Harvard Univ. Press, 1975.

Von Loewenich, Walther. *Luther's Theology of the Cross.* Translated by Herbert J. A. Bouman. Minneapolis, Minn.: Augsburg, 1976.

Walker, J. D. "The Architectonics of George Herbert's *The Temple.*" *ELH* 29 (1962): 289–307.

Walker, Williston. *A History of the Christian Church.* Rev. ed. New York: Charles Scribners' Sons, 1959.

Walls, Andrew F. "Word." *Baker's Dictionary of Theology* (1960).

Walton, Izaak. "The Life of Mr. George Herbert." In *Lives,* edited by Charles Hill Dick. London: Walter Scott, 1899.

Weber, Sarah Appleton. *Theology and Poetry in the Middle English Lyric: A Study of Sacred History and Aesthetic Form.* Columbus: Ohio State Univ. Press, 1969.

Wedgwood, C. V. *The Trial of Charles I.* London: Collins, 1964.

West, Michael. "Ecclestiastical Controversie in George Herbert's 'Peace.' " *Review of English Studies* 22 (1971): 445–51.

Whale, J. S. *The Protestant Tradition.* Cambridge: Cambridge Univ. Press, 1955.

White, Helen C. *English Devotional Literature 1600–1640.* Univ. of Wisc. Studies in Language and Literature, no. 29. Madison: Univ. of Wisconsin Press, 1931.

———. *The Metaphysical Poets.* New York: Macmillan, 1936.

Williamson, George. *The Donne Tradition.* Cambridge, Mass.: Harvard Univ. Press, 1930.

Wilson, Thomas. *A Christian Dictionary.* London, 1616.

Wolfe, Jane E. "George Herbert's 'Assurance.' " *College Language Association Journal* 5 (1962): 213–22.

Woodhouse, A. S. P. *The Poet and His Faith: Religion and Poetry in England From Spenser to Eliot and Auden.* Chicago: Univ. of Chicago Press, 1965.

Woolf, Rosemary. *The English Religious Lyric in the Middle Ages.* London: Oxford Univ. Press, 1968.

Ziegelmaier, Gregory. "Liturgical Symbol and Reality in the Poetry of George Herbert." *American Benedictine Review* 18 (1967): 344–53.

Index